THE PANIC OF 1907

THE PANIC OF 1907

Heralding a New Era of Finance, Capitalism, and Democracy

Second Edition

ROBERT F. BRUNER
SEAN D. CARR

WILEY

Published by John Wiley & Sons, Inc., Hoboken, New Jersey.
Published simultaneously in Canada.

The authors gratefully acknowledge Cambridge University Press, Columbia University Butler Library, Deutsche Bank Group, the Federal Reserve Bank of New York, The Morgan Library & Museum, Ned Lamont, the *Southern Economic Journal*, and the University of Chicago Press for their research assistance.

For general information on our other products and services or for technical support, please contact our Customer Care Department within the United States at (800) 762-2974, outside the United States at (317) 572-3993 or fax (317) 572-4002.

Wiley also publishes its books in a variety of electronic formats. Some content that appears in print may not be available in electronic formats. For more information about Wiley products, visit our web site at www.wiley.com.

Library of Congress Cataloging-in-Publication Data:

Names: Bruner, Robert F., 1949- author. | Carr, Sean D., 1969- author.
Title: The Panic of 1907 : heralding a new era of finance, capitalism, and democracy / Robert F. Bruner, Sean D. Carr.
Description: Second edition. | Hoboken, New Jersey : John Wiley & Sons, Inc., [2023] | Includes bibliographical references and index.
Identifiers: LCCN 2022059325 (print) | LCCN 2022059326 (ebook) | ISBN 9781394180271 (hardback) | ISBN 9781394180295 (adobe pdf) | ISBN 9781394180288 (epub)
Subjects: LCSH: Depressions—1907—United States. | Financial crises—United States—History—20th century. | Stock exchanges—United States—History—20th century.
Classification: LCC HB3717 1907 .B78 2023 (print) | LCC HB3717 1907 (ebook) | DDC 330.973/0911—dc23/eng/20221216
LC record available at https://lccn.loc.gov/2022059325
LC ebook record available at https://lccn.loc.gov/2022059326

Cover Design: Wiley
Cover Photo: © Getty Images | Fotosearch / Stringer

SKY10041254_011323

RFB:

For Bobbie

"Treasure is in knowing that you are loved and that you love because you are loved, and that knowledge of self and relationship and purpose is what treasure is all about."

—Peter J. Gomes

SDC:

For Ladi

"The salvation of this human world lies nowhere else than in the human heart, in the human power to reflect, in human meekness and human responsibility."

—Vaclav Havel

Contents

Foreword

What causes perfect storms in financial markets, whether the Panic of 1907 or the Global Financial Crisis that began in 2007? Bruner and Carr's magisterial treatment of the former episode paints a lucid picture that gets to the heart of the matter.

Start with modern "fractional reserve banking," which first saw the light of day in the early seventeenth century when East India merchants arrived in London with hauls of gold and silver and no place to safely stash them. In 1650, England was a tiny, institutionally backward nation of just 5 million souls—about half the population of Italy and a third that of France— and actually less than its own population on the eve of the arrival of the Black Death in 1348–1349. The majestic, free-trading empire that straddled the globe lay yet two centuries in the future; mid-seventeenth-century Britain was a weak, backward nation, embroiled in the process of throwing off its corrupt ancient regime; its presence on the high seas emphasized raiding as much as trading.

It had no banking system, but London was home to a large number of goldsmiths, whose livelihoods demanded the safe storage of valuables. Merchants began to deposit their loot with the goldsmiths, who in exchange issued certificates, which then began to circulate as money.

Soon enough, the goldsmiths tumbled to the happy realization that they could issue the certificates in excess of the amount of precious metal they held.

In other words, they could print money.

Since the prevailing interest rate was well over 10 percent year, the goldsmiths made a good living loaning out the certificates, a process that held up only as long as a large number of certificate holders didn't redeem them all at once. If the goldsmith's safe held £10,000 of silver, and he had issued £30,000 worth of certificates—one third issued to the specie's owners and two thirds to borrowers—and the bearers of £10,001of the certificates demanded payment in silver, the goldsmith was bankrupt. In fact, if the certificate holders even *suspected* that the goldsmith was in trouble, they could precipitate a disastrous run. As banking systems grew ever more complex and interlinked, the contagion would spread through a process that social psychologists and financial economists call *herding* (which works just as well on the way up as down).

Just why, then, do financial participants herd? Because they are human. About 50,000–100,000 years ago, modern humans "escaped" from northern Africa to inhabit all of the continents except Antarctica. Even more remarkably, tribes spread over the entire New World, from the Arctic Ocean to Tierra del Fuego, over a period of just several thousand years.

Along the way, humans had to learn how make kayaks in the arctic, hunt buffalo on the Great Plains, and make poison blowguns in the Amazon. It seems highly unlikely that human evolution occurred rapidly enough to acquire these varied skills innately in the same way that, for example, birds build nests or termites build hills.

Rather than hardwire into our genes a distinct ability for making kayaks, hunting buffalos, or fashioning poison blowguns, evolution instead encoded the general-purpose skill of imitation. Given a large enough population and enough trial and error, someone will eventually figure out how to build, for example, a serviceable kayak, and the rest can accurately imitate the process.

We imitate more than almost all other animal species; as soon as someone creates a useful innovation, others quickly adopt it. Yet our propensity to imitate also serves to amplify maladaptive behaviors, primary among which is mass delusions of all types, particularly the propensity of modern societies to participate in financial panics.

We are also the ape that tells stories. When our remote ancestors needed to communicate with each other to survive, they certainly did not do so with the kinds of mathematical tools used by the competent investor. The primary mode of that communication was, and still is, narration: "You go right, I'll go left, and we'll spear the mastodon from both sides."

We are narrative animals, and a compelling tale, no matter how misleading, will more often than not trump facts and data. Not only do people respond more to narratives than to facts and data, but preliminary studies also demonstrate that the more compelling the story, the more it erodes our critical thinking skills. (This research suggests, in addition, an inherent conflict of interest between the suppliers and consumers of opinion: the former—think your stockbroker or the talking head on CNBC—wishes to convince and will devise the most compelling narratives possible, whereas the investor should intentionally avoid those narratives and rely only on data, facts, and analytical discipline.)

Toss together an unstable fractional reserve system and an army of herding participants—thousands in 1907, and millions in 2007—and you have a recipe for a panic so well described by Bruner and Carr between these covers.

Over the past two centuries, Europeans and Americans have slowly realized the need for regulatory circuit breakers in the system to throttle the booms and inject liquidity during the busts. The problem, as the authors point out, is that as the world grows wealthier and our financial system grows ever more complex, it outgrows the regulatory apparatus, which, rather than adapting to rapidly changing circumstances, becomes ever more hidebound.

In 1907, the regulatory apparatus was the clearing house system of the so-called "national banks," a relatively informal private network that provided temporary capital, when needed, to its well-behaved members. Trouble arose when a parallel system of trust banks, unconstrained by the reserve rules of the national system, began lending to increasingly speculative ventures. In that era, "American exceptionalism" expressed itself in the nation as being alone among its developed peers in its lack of a central bank that would obey Bagehot's famous rule for such institutions: act as a lender of last resort to solvent firms against good collateral at a high "penalty rate."

In 2007–2008, a nearly identical series of events played out as another parallel banking system, this time consisting of unregulated financial services companies, blew the largest credit bubble in the history of mankind—a bubble that the nation's nearly century-old central bank contributed to in no small part. To paraphrase Harry Truman, the only thing that's new in finance is the history we haven't read. And that is why reading Robert Bruner and Sean Carr's explanations of both "07s" is a must.

Floyd Norris, chief financial correspondent for the *New York Times*, appears to have meandered upon a copy of this book's first edition. He picked it up, put it down, and then apparently picked it up again (always the sign of a good book) as the next "07" started to play out. Upon later reflection, he hailed *The Panic of 1907* as "one of the most insightful books" he had ever read. "When I read it last year," noted Norris in a *Times* blog comment on February 22, 2008, "I thought it had lessons for today, but I did not realize just how quickly those lessons would become crucial." I couldn't agree more. Robert Bruner and Sean Carr have refreshed a great book and drawn further insights about the seven critical factors that created the second "07" drama that is now still playing center stage on Wall Street and Main Street and in Washington. The parallels they see, the wisdom they share into the precise nature and causes of financial crises, and their alternative views to simple "silver bullet" explanations should be studied and reread closely by those now embroiled in the financial crises that played out in 2007–2009 in the United States and in Europe in the years that followed, and appear to be playing out in the cryptocurrency markets as I type these words. Sit back, relax, and enjoy their ideas as Bruner and Carr take you back to the future.

Acknowledgments

We gratefully acknowledge the financial support of the Trustees of the University of Virginia Darden School Foundation, the Governing Council of the University of Virginia Miller Center of Public Affairs, and the generous encouragement offered by President James Ryan of the University of Virginia, Dean Scott Beardsley of the Darden School, William Antholis, director and CEO of the Miller Center, and President Ana Mari Cauce of the University of Washington.

Sylvie Merian at the Pierpont Morgan Library was a valuable guide to the immense archival resources there. Generally, we are grateful to the directors and staff members of the archives at the Morgan Library and Museum (New York), Guildhall Library (London), Federal Reserve Bank of New York, Baker Library, Harvard Graduate School of Business Administration (Boston), Butler Library, Columbia University (New York), and the Butte-Silver Bow Public Archives (Butte).

Charles Calomiris (Columbia University), Avinash Dixit (Princeton), Robert Friedel (University of Maryland), Andrew Metrick (Yale University), John Moen (University of Mississippi), Mary Tone Rodgers (SUNY–Oswego). Richard Sylla (New York University), Jean Strouse

(New York City Public Library), and Richard Tedlow (Harvard Business School) provided valuable insights at various stages of the book's development. Our colleagues at the University of Virginia's Darden Business School, including Peter Debaere, Marc Lipson, Scott Miller, Michael Schill, Frank Warnock, and the participants in the financial economics seminar, provided especially helpful insights. And we extend thanks to several hundred students in our courses at Darden and participants in professional audiences, whose penetrating questions sharpened our thinking.

We thank Julia Grammer for the preparation of graphical figures, Shawn Ritchie for assistance in information technology, and Tom Marini for bibliographical assistance. Susan Norrisey, reference librarian, exhibited an extraordinary degree of diligence, persistence, and patience in collecting archival trading data; she was tireless in her work, and for this we are especially appreciative. Equally, we are grateful to our administrative assistants, Caitlin Boyer and Gayle Noble, for shouldering tasks that made our writing easier.

Our editors at Wiley brought understanding and perspective to the work. We are grateful for the insights provided by Bill Falloon (executive editor), Purvi Patel (managing editor), and Premkumar Narayanan (content refinement specialist).

Finally, this edition would not have come forth without the patient support of our families and the sacrifices they endured while we prepared this edition.

Any inadvertent errors or omissions that may remain are ours alone.

RFB AND SDC
Charlottesville, Virginia, and Bellevue, Washington
August 2022

Prologue

These are troublous times.

—Charles T. Barney
Knickerbocker Trust Company
October 21, 1907

Around 10 A.M. on November 14, 1907, Lily Barney and a friend were chatting in the Barneys' second-story bedroom overlooking Park Avenue when they heard the crack of a gunshot echo through the house. The women bolted toward the other bedroom across the hall. Stepping inside, they saw Lily's husband, Charles, lying on the floor near his bed in his pajamas. Beside him was a revolver containing three loaded cartridges and one empty shell. The Barneys had kept pistols on every floor of the house for protection, and this one clearly belonged to Charles.[1]

As Lily Barney came near, her husband raised himself slightly but slumped in pain to the floor. She knelt beside him, cradled his head in her lap, and attempted to ease his discomfort. Ashbel Barney, one of the Barneys' two sons, had been downstairs and had also heard the shot. Running to the bedroom and seeing his mother and her friend bending over his wounded father, he raced to telephone George Dixon, the Barneys' family physician. Then, with the help of his mother and servants the 20-year-old Ashbel lifted his father to his large, brass, canopy-covered bed. Charles T. Barney remained conscious, but silent.

Dr. Dixon reached the Barney house in Manhattan's fashionable Murray Hill neighborhood 10 minutes after receiving the call. After administering an anesthetic, he began an operation in which he discovered that a .38-caliber bullet had entered the upper left quadrant of Barney's abdomen; it had taken an upward course, torn through the intestines, traveled lengthwise through the left lung, and embedded in the left shoulder just behind the collarbone. Despite their ministrations, around 2:30 in the afternoon Charles Barney was pronounced dead from shock and severe hemorrhaging. Within hours newsboys were bellowing "extra" about the incident all along Park Avenue.

Over the coming days, rumors and innuendoes about Barney's death reverberated throughout the city. Stories appeared about previous suicide attempts (although none could be confirmed)[2] and there were indications, later denied by Lily Barney, that she and her husband had become acutely estranged in recent months and that she had initiated a divorce.[3] One leading newspaper even reported that the letters of "two women, one a Parisian, long a favorite of a French prince," had been found among Charles Barney's papers.[4] Close associates called the man's morals into question. "Mr. Barney was not a God-fearing man," said A. Foster Higgins. "He could not live happily because his life was not moral. He lived a lie to his wife and children."[5]

Whatever his personal faults, though, the death of Charles T. Barney aroused extreme public interest and suspicion for one reason only: Barney had presided over New York's famed Knickerbocker Trust Company when its dramatic failure in October 1907 became the tipping point for a financial crisis of monumental proportions.

Charles Tracy Barney was truly a man of the Gilded Age. The son of a prosperous Cleveland merchant, he had married into the prominent Whitney family when he wed Lily Whitney, the sister of the financier and former U.S. Secretary of the Navy William C. Whitney. Barney pursued a career in banking, and his Whitney connections ensured him lucrative business opportunities in New York real estate development and speculation. By 1907 Barney had become a director of at least 33 corporations, and he was among the founding investors of New York City's new subway system.

Barney's ascent to New York's financial firmament coincided with his association with the Knickerbocker Trust Company. By the 1890s, he had become its vice president, and in 1897 he was elected to the firm's top office. The handsome but high-strung Barney emerged as one of the leading figures in New York's financial community, and he had developed a reputation as "one of the most imperious of Wall Street's bankers, who ruled every undertaking that he had anything to do with."[6]

Such a man, at the height of his wealth and power, could scarcely have foreseen how swiftly and ignominiously his downfall would come. In early October 1907, two speculators, F. Augustus Heinze and Charles W. Morse, had contrived an elaborate scheme to corner the market in the stock of a copper mining company. The attempt failed miserably. Such a scheme would hardly have bothered the members of New York's financial elite, such as Charles Barney, but Heinze and Morse had convinced a New York financial institution to fund their venture.[7]

Although the Knickerbocker was not a creditor of the failed speculation, rumors spread that the Knickerbocker—and perhaps even Charles Barney himself—was embroiled in the Heinze-Morse scheme. The 18,000 depositors of the trust company panicked. Simply an association with the speculators was more than most depositors could bear. On Friday, October 17, a "run" on the Knickerbocker was under way, and dozens of depositors clamored at the trust company's doors to claim their funds.

Given the close financial relationships among all the banks and trust companies in New York City, panic gripped investors and depositors alike. In an attempt to quell this spiraling hysteria, on October 21 the directors of the Knickerbocker Trust convinced Charles Barney to tender his resignation. In a statement issued later that night, Barney said humbly, "I resigned to give my associates in the company a free hand in the management." But when he was asked about the financial condition of the Knickerbocker, Barney laughed at any suggestion that the institution might be in trouble. "Nothing could be more absurd," he said. "The company was never in a stronger position. It remains the next to the largest in the city and as sound as any. There is not the slightest question of its entire solvency."[8]

A few days after his resignation from the Knickerbocker Trust Company, Barney drafted a statement in which he boasted of his role at the bank. "I built the Knickerbocker up from a company with eleven million dollars in deposits to one with over sixty-five million dollars," he said. "I am willing to take responsibility for anything pertaining to the condition of the company." Nonetheless, he steadfastly refused to accept that he should be culpable for the trust company's failure. "So far as the suspension is concerned," he said, "if there is any institution in New York that could without aid have withstood the run that the Knickerbocker experienced last Tuesday [October 22], I do not know it."[9] Less than a month later, Charles Barney would be dead.

Many surmised that Charles Barney's death was caused by his fears of personal financial failure, but reports indicate he was nowhere near insolvency. In October 1907, Barney's assets exceeded his liabilities by more than $2.5 million, mostly represented by equities in real estate.[10] Moreover, most of Barney's creditors were bank and trust companies, including the Knickerbocker itself. Just a week before his death, Barney's attorneys had worked out an arrangement that would have enabled him to stay afloat. "There was every reason why Mr. Barney should have been feeling encouraged," Barney's physician, Dr. Dixon, said. "Daylight had begun to break ahead financially. He had begun to see his way clear. If he was [sic] going to commit suicide, two weeks ago would have been the most likely time. But now, when things had begun to look up, was a time when he should have been feeling in better spirits than for two weeks."[11]

Friends of Charles T. Barney believed that neither financial crisis nor a professional reversal was his downfall. It was the loss of confidence that hurt him most. "Mr. Barney's heart was broken by the cruel treatment of his associates; that is the cause of his death," said Charles Morse, the man whose association most likely led to Barney's undoing. "It is absurd to talk of financial ruin as a cause of his act, for though he had lost money, he was by no means ruined. Mr. Barney was always an honorable man of business, and it was grief at being abused in the newspapers and suspected by his business associates that caused his death."[12] Another family friend said, "Had there been a little leniency on the part of those who were forcing him to the wall, Charles T. Barney would be alive today and in a position to revive his business standing."[13]

The failure of the Knickerbocker Trust Company was a turning point in a panic that would engulf a turbulent and rapidly growing nation as it entered the twentieth century. The run on other banks and trust companies, some of which were associated with the Heinze-and-Morse scheme, continued unabated even after the Knickerbocker closed its doors. Lines in front of banks in New York and elsewhere extended for blocks, and Wall Street was gripped by a paroxysm of fear. In the coming days, money would become scarce, banks would fail, the stock market would plummet, and the city of New York itself would reach the precipice of bankruptcy. Only a small cadre of astute and cool-headed financiers and government officials could steer a course through the oncoming gale. Like Charles Barney, the nation had lost its confidence. It would take leadership and courage to bring it back.

Introduction

The past is never dead. It's not even past.

—William Faulkner[1]

The Panic of 1907 stands out among history's financial and economic disturbances. Over a century later, this crisis seems so small—its epicenter was short and intense—but it rippled nationally and internationally for years. The economic damage of the Panic was "extremely severe," according to economists Milton Friedman and Anna Schwartz.[2] It strained the fabric of societies, producing distress, dislocation, and even revolution. Its political impact was *massive,* triggering and accelerating the final push to establish the U.S. Federal Reserve System, after years of ineffectual debate. It fundamentally changed public attitudes about government intervention into markets and economic affairs. It highlighted the role of human agency in the turn of events. The wrangling of powerful personalities such as J. Pierpont Morgan, Elbert Gary, Henry Frick, Theodore Roosevelt, Woodrow Wilson, and William Jennings Bryan exposed the diversity of ideologies and motivations that would roil the U.S. political economy throughout the twentieth century. Ranked among pivotal events of the age, the Panic of 1907 ushered out an old guard and its orthodoxy, to be replaced by a new generation of leaders who held new notions.

However, memories are short. Eclipsed by two world wars, the Great Depression, the halting emergence of a new global economic order, and a string of crises in the early twenty-first century, the events of 1907–1913 have faded from mind. Also, each rising generation tends to believe that its own crises are without precedent and that harnessing lessons from further past is pointless.

The aim of this book is to counterargue: forgetting the past is dangerous; it contains valuable lessons for the present and future. While a deep dive into one important crisis will not foretell the future, it will expose insights into crisis dynamics that can forearm the reader. To study past crises is to learn the paths that adversaries of human welfare—panic and market breakdown—might take.

The onset of the Panic of 1907 and the efforts to quell it form a valuable lens through which to examine the fragility of economic and financial systems, the contagion of fear, the challenges of mobilizing collective action, and the relevance of human agency in the context of powerful forces. Modern theories—and public policies—about financial crises must start from some concept of what a crisis is. The Panic of 1907 is an excellent point of reference.

The Progression of Financial Crisis

A financial crisis is a breakdown of normal financial market activities to such an extent that capital flees, resources are misallocated, institutions are destabilized, and disorder spills into the real economy, causing job loss, bankruptcies, recession, and social distress and political ferment.

Scholars have tended to view crises narrowly. For instance, economists Hyman Minsky and Charles Kindleberger viewed a crisis as the *moment* when market euphoria turns to revulsion. Unfortunately, this narrow view tends to disregard important events and forces that stage and summon the crisis, as well as the shocks and spillovers that ensue. We argue that to understand financial crises, one must follow the entire *progression of crisis,* from early benign conditions that sowed the crisis, through to the ultimate recovery in the economy, polity, and society that frames a new orthodoxy in thinking. The word "progression" implies that each new phase acts upon the preceding one and sets the stage for the next one for instance, boom → shock → climax → collapse → reaction → recovery. Thus, the idea of progression requires you to take a longer view.

In the account of the Panic of 1907 that follows, the narrative spans 1897 to 1913. The progression of crisis occurred in four acts. First, an economic recovery of the U.S. economy gathered momentum into one of the largest growth spurts in the country's history: business optimism rose, as did leverage and strains on the financial system. The good times peaked in early 1906, when it seemed that nothing could go wrong.

Second, shocks battered the system. As in Greek tragedies, nemesis follows hubris. To destabilize a financial system, a shock must be real (not cosmetic), large and costly, unambiguous, and surprising—the San Francisco earthquake of April 1906 surely qualifies. To that event we add discussion of some other surprises that shocked the system.

Third, trouble broke out among the less prepared and more vulnerable financial institutions, what in modern parlance would be the "shadow financial system." A system is only as strong as its most vulnerable link. Financial institutions on the periphery (out of sight and out of mind to the rest of the industry) have tended to be the vulnerable links. Then trouble traveled to other parts of the system through relations among institutions and markets. The initial responses to the crisis were halting because financial systems are complex and opaque, and it was difficult for people to know what was going on. This bred fear. Contagion spread, at first locally, then nationally, and was reflected in declining security prices and the hoarding of financial assets. Then the crisis, initially confined to the financial sector of the economy, reverberated through the real economy, causing widespread distress and dislocation.

Fourth, the crisis began to ebb as confidence recovered—but the ripple effects of the crisis set the stage for the establishment of a "new order" of public sentiment, political power, and regulation. The institutional changes that ensued from the Panic of 1907 were as much a part of the entire progression of crisis as the shocks, instability, and spillovers.

Causes and Dynamics

As the following chapters show, the speed and fury of day-to-day events left little time for reflection and understanding. Yet any plan of action must proceed from some theory about the origin and progress of crises. With what theory could J.P. Morgan or anyone else have seen the Panic coming?

One line of thought attributes crises to a hodgepodge of period-specific factors. For instance, the contemporary Wall Street observer Henry Clews cited nine causes for the panic of 1907.[3] Charles Kindleberger ascribed 13 origins to the Panic of 1873.[4] With enough detail (and imagination) an analyst could summon a long list of possible causes for financial crises. The problem with that approach is its idiosyncrasy: If there is a different explanation for each crisis, then what can we say about crises in general?

Other approaches rest on one big idea: a sole cause large enough to cover a multitude of sins. A favorite big idea among some economists, for example, is that financial crises are caused by a lack of liquidity in the financial system. The economist Milton Friedman blamed the government's failure to manage well the money supply as a leading contributor to such events. Likewise, Roger Lowenstein, writing about the stock market bubble and collapse of 1997 to 2001, blamed the credo of shareholder value.[5] A related "silver bullet" explanation is greed. Radical and progressive critics blamed financial crises on the wealthy, the profit motive, and class exploitation. Unfortunately, the silver bullet explanation produces generic remedies that poorly treat the disease. One wants a Goldilocks explanation for crises that is neither too much nor too little, neither too idiosyncratic nor too simplistic.

By drawing on a detailed history of the Panic of 1907 and on research about financial crises in general, we offer an alternative view: crises are cascades of shocks and information problems to which bank runs, market crashes, rumors, hoarding, fear, and panic are predictable responses. Scholars such as Charles Calomiris, Gary Gorton, and others have documented the informational aspects of crises. To our knowledge, this is the first book-length study of a single financial crisis to apply this view. And we extend this view to consider *institutional changes* that ensue.

Information problems are central to an understanding of financial crises. Over time, innovation in financial institutions, markets, instruments, and processes breed growing complexity in the financial system. Complexity makes it difficult for decision makers to know what is going on. The resulting information asymmetries spawn problematic behavior, arising from adverse selection* and moral hazard.† Information problems contribute to the overoptimism associated with buoyant business expansion and the tendency of debtors to overlever and of lenders to ignore prudent credit standards.

The architecture of a financial system links institutions to one another in a way that enables contagion of the crisis to spread. Trouble can travel. Safety buffers (such as cash reserves and capital) may prove inadequate to meet the coming crisis. Then, one or more shocks hit the economy and financial system, causing a sudden reversal in the outlook of investors and depositors. Confusion reigns. Public sentiment changes from optimism to pessimism that creates a self-reinforcing downward spiral. In the vicious cycle, bad news prompts behavior that generates more bad news. Collective action proves extraordinarily difficult to muster until the severity of the crisis and the insight and information held by a few actors prompts mutual response.

Information matters, as our narrative of the Panic of 1907 shows. Key figures relied on information networks to assess conditions, identify trouble spots, set priorities, allocate rescue funds, and make other changes to restore the confidence of depositors and investors. The intense round of meetings, dinners, breakfasts, telegrams, and phone calls essentially aimed to resolve information asymmetries in order to make better decisions.

* Adverse selection arises if a better-informed party in a transaction can exploit information to the disadvantage of the less well-informed party. Think of buying a used car (the seller knows more about the condition of the car, possibly a "lemon") or selling health insurance (the buyer knows more about his or her health outlook). Concern about adverse selection may drive parties out of the market, thus diminishing liquidity and the ability of the market to clear. Also, adverse selection might drive quality goods out of the market because sellers of high-quality goods cannot obtain the prices they deserve. In finance, "Gresham's Law" (i.e., bad money drives out good money) is an example of adverse selection.

† In the case of moral hazard, a party to an agreement fails to act in good faith and shifts risk onto counterparties. For instance, debtors who believe that the government will always bail them out in a crisis may simply borrow more, ultimately shifting risk onto taxpayers.

A Question of Leadership

Do times make the leaders? Or do leaders make the times? Modern historians have dismissed Thomas Carlyle's "great person theory" in which brilliant and talented individuals bend the arc of history. Instead, a modern vogue inclines some historians toward determinist theories in which the clash of large forces changes history and incidentally renders some individuals rich, powerful, and famous and others out of luck. The events surrounding the Panic of 1907 afford an interesting debate between the two theories.

Technological change (the *Second* Industrial Revolution), demographic change (waves of immigration), social change (urbanization), political change (progressivism, populism, socialism), and economic change (industrialization, growth and growing inequality) loomed over the first decade of the twentieth century. Against such powerful tides, it is easy to view the strivings of individuals as incidental to larger events.

Yet it is also true that the central figures of the episode brought to bear unusual attributes of character, intelligence, and talent. Theodore Roosevelt arguably changed politics and the presidency more than they changed him. And by virtue of his reputation, intelligence, resources, and social network, J. Pierpont Morgan mobilized a fractious financial community into collective action. One of Morgan's strengths was an ability to size up people and their problems quickly—maybe hastily. These and other big personalities brought unique attributes to the Panic as it brewed, erupted, and subsided. Perhaps their good (or bad) luck figured in their role in the unfolding events. Certainly, the choices they made reveal underlying attributes of character that also affected the course of events. Thus, this narrative commences with a sketch of the times and the financial leaders who shaped it.

What's New Here?

More breadth and depth. The first edition of this book was published in 2007, on the verge of the most serious financial crisis since the Great Depression. The Global Financial Crisis of 2007-2009 and the global financial and economic crisis associated with the COVID-19 pandemic tested conventional theories and policies. These eruptions arrested the attention of policy-makers and researchers; and they sparked new interest in their ancestor of a century earlier. Researchers in the academy, government, and business turned to the Panic of 1907 as a laboratory in which to test ideas. This version of the book adds the findings from more than four dozen relevant research papers and books published since the original edition in addition to other older sources that came to our attention. Throughout this edition, we provide more graphs and visual figures to help the reader grasp the significance of economic developments.

This new edition extends coverage of the crisis to communities across the United States and addresses international spillovers. And it illuminates the buoyant economic expansion over the decade before the crisis, along with the growth of debt financing in the economy.

Furthermore, this edition treats the civic reaction of 1908–1913 in more detail to illuminate the deep institutional changes that occurred. We examined contemporary analyses, newspaper accounts, and government archives about the civic reaction. The hearings of the Stanley Committee (1911–1912) and Pujo Committee (1912–1913), reports of Treasury Secretary Cortelyou as well as memoirs of Paul Warburg, Carter Glass, and Robert Owen yield insights into the motives of individuals who sought to shape the new regime of state intervention into financial markets and institutions.

Finally, in selected chapters we have added original findings that enrich or challenge the interpretations of researchers. In Chapter 2 we test the statistical significance of the plunge in the Bank of England's gold reserves to explain the motive behind the BoE's sharply restrictive monetary policy in October 1907. Our analysis of call loan interest rates in Chapter 14 affirms that the spike in volatility vastly exceeded the historical "noise level" and persisted much longer than implied in other accounts. In Chapter 16, we depict the declines in trust company deposits by firm size that shows the asymmetry in experience among firms. Chapter 19 gives evidence of hysteresis, a lingering slowdown in economic growth following the Panic. In Chapter 21, we analyze the panel of witnesses called to testify at the Pujo Committee hearings to illustrate the focus of the investigation. Our statistical analysis of the runs on trust companies in the technical appendix (after Chapter 24) illuminates the diversity among those firms, associated with variations in business model and the extent of affiliation with notorious figures. And various chapters show that the extensive impact of the Panic lasted well beyond the October–November 1907 period that figure in conventional discussions.

Plan of the Book

The next five chapters set the stage, with a profile of the buoyant lead-up to the Panic of 1907. Chapters 6 through 18 describe the epicenter of the Panic from mid-October to early November. What began as a failed attempt to corner the market in a stock traded "on the curb" led to runs on local trust companies, and then financial institutions throughout the nation. The New York Stock Exchange nearly closed for want of liquidity. At the center of this phase of the narrative is a close look at the difficulties of mobilizing collective action among key players in the financial community, and the success of J.P. Morgan in doing so. Chapter 19 recounts the contagion of crisis to other regions of country and world, and spillovers into the real economy.

Chapters 20–22 recount the political and civic reactions over the years 1908 to 1913, culminating in the founding of the Fed. This segment surveys the competitive jockeying for dominance of a preferred model for state intervention into the U.S. financial system. Chapter 23 affords an epilogue for the political movement and lives that figured so largely in the Panic of 1907. And the final chapter, 24, offers summary reflections on the entire narrative.

As a useful reference to the sequence of events, we offer Exhibit I.1, which lists key dates and notes their significance.

Motivating One's Attention to History

As William Faulkner argued, the past is not dead; it is always with us. Just as victims of crime and veterans of combat must endure the indelible imprint of their experience, so societies must deal with the lingering effects of financial crises. To learn from the experience of a financial crisis requires one to process events and their causes, assess consequences, acknowledge agency, and derive meaning. There are no shortcuts to insights: begin at the beginning and trace events to the end. In this volume, we offer the long view. It is insufficient to study only the climax of a panic; one must also study the precursors and the long consequences to frame a deep understanding of these events. Therefore, our narrative begins in the buoyant decade, 1897 to 1906.

Exhibit I.1 Key Dates Related to the Panic of 1907 and the Civic Reaction

Wednesday, April 18, 1906	San Francisco Earthquake. Fires resulting from the earthquake burned out of control for three more days.
Friday, October 19, 1906	Bank of England tightened monetary policy, banned American finance bills.
March 9–25, 1907	Stock market slump. Called "silent crash" or "rich man's panic."
May 1907	Economic recession began in the United States.
Friday, June 28, 1907	New York City failed to place a public bond offering. Failed again in late August. In September, the city government turned to J.P. Morgan to place the bonds privately.
	⋆ ⋆ ⋆
Tuesday, October 15, 1907	Failure of attempted "corner" on United Copper Company stock.
Wednesday, October 16, 1907	Gross & Kleeberg failed.
Thursday, October 17, 1907	Otto Heinze & Co. failed. State Savings Bank of Butte, Montana, failed. A run began on the Mercantile National Bank, of which Augustus Heinze was president. He appealed to the New York Clearing House (NYCH) for assistance. NYCH agreed to extend assistance on condition that Heinze resign as president of the Mercantile.
Sunday, October 20, 1907	J.P. Morgan returned to New York City and convened meetings with leaders in the financial community. The New York Clearing House (NYCH) agreed to aid other banks in the Heinze-Morse orbit: the Mercantile, New Amsterdam, and North America National Banks, and ordered Augustus Heinze and Charles W. Morse to be eliminated from all banking interests in New York City.
Monday, October 21, 1907	Announcements that the NYCH declined to aid the Knickerbocker and that National Bank of Commerce refused to clear payments for the Knickerbocker Trust Company. Runs began on the Knickerbocker Trust Company. Charles Barney resigned as president of the Knickerbocker.

(Continued)

Exhibit I.1 (*Continued*)

Tuesday, October 22, 1907	Runs on the Knickerbocker surged. The Knickerbocker suspended withdrawals. Credit grew scarce. Call loan interest rates rose sharply. Runs increased on Trust Company of America (TCA) and Lincoln Trust.
Wednesday, October 23, 1907	Benjamin Strong affirmed the solvency of TCA. J.P. Morgan organized a private rescue pool among some banks for TCA. Later that day, he organized a supplementary rescue pool for TCA among CEOs of other trust companies.
Thursday, October 24, 1907	The CEOs of trust companies reneged on their commitment to TCA. Therefore, Morgan organized another rescue pool for TCA with some banks. Credit crisis hit the New York Stock Exchange (NYSE): call loan interest rates peaked at 100 percent. Illiquidity threatened to cause fire-sale liquidation of stocks. J.P. Morgan organized a rescue pool for NYSE. Treasury Secretary Cortelyou committed $25 million in government funds to assist distressed financial institutions and relieve the credit crunch.
Friday, October 25, 1907	J.P. Morgan and crisis committee augmented rescue funding for NYSE, TCA, and Lincoln Trust.
Saturday, October 26, 1907	NYCH decided to issue Clearing House Loan Certificates in lieu of currency for settlement of payments among banks. President Roosevelt issued a letter commending Treasury Secretary Cortelyou and leaders in the financial sector for actions to quell the crisis.
Sunday, October 27, 1907	A New York City official visited George Perkins and warned of another financial crisis for the city.

(*Continued*)

Exhibit I.1 (*Continued*)

Monday, October 28, 1907	The mayor of New York visited J.P. Morgan and described the city's cash crisis. A loan payment was due on November 1, but the city had run out of cash and was unable to refinance the obligation.
Tuesday, October 29, 1907	J.P. Morgan organized a private placement of bonds for New York City.
Saturday, November 2, 1907	Morgan organized a proposal to rescue brokerage firm, Moore and Schley. The proposal entailed the purchase by U.S. Steel of Tennessee Coal & Iron (TC&I). The same day, Morgan learned of renewed and threatening runs at TCA and Lincoln Trust. At an overnight meeting in his library, Morgan finally mobilized the presidents of trust companies to organize a rescue pool up to $25 million for distressed trust companies, particularly Trust Company of America and Lincoln Trust.
Sunday, November 3, 1907	U.S. Steel agreed to acquire Tennessee Coal & Iron, contingent on approval by the U.S. government. Elbert Gary and Henry Frick traveled overnight to gain President Roosevelt's approval before the NYSE opened the next day.
Monday, November 4, 1907	Roosevelt agreed not to oppose U.S. Steel's acquisition of TC&I. The Bank of England raised its base interest rate from 5.5 percent to 7 percent, the highest in decades.
Wednesday, November 6, 1907	The first shipment of gold arrived from France. A total of $36 million more was expected to arrive subsequently.
Friday, November 17, 1907	The U.S. Treasury invited bids for $150 million in U.S. bonds and notes to increase the money supply. The offering was undersubscribed.

(*Continued*)

Exhibit I.1 (*Continued*)

November 25, 1907	Banks began to issue currency against new Treasury notes. Newspaper headlines suggested the money crisis had ended.[6]
December 12, 1907	The U.S. Senate adopted a resolution requesting information from Treasury Secretary Cortelyou about government deposits in national banks during the Panic. This responded to Democratic Party senators, who a week earlier had called for deeper investigation of Treasury Department policies.
January 1908	Senator Nelson Aldrich, chairman of the Senate Finance Committee, began to circulate draft legislation to create emergency currency in the event of a banking crisis.
January 29, 1908	Cortelyou delivered a 232-page report to Senate regarding Treasury actions during the Panic.
February 18, 1908	The Senate adopted a resolution to investigate New York banks for the use of Treasury Department deposits during the Panic. Cortelyou was required to present necessary data and any complaints lodged against the New York banks.
March 19, 1908	Senator La Follette alleged that the Panic was "deliberately planned" by insurance companies with the Morgan and Standard Oil groups of banks.
May 30, 1908	President Roosevelt signed the Aldrich–Vreeland Act, which empowered an expansion of the money supply in the event of a financial crisis and created the National Monetary Commission.
June 1908	Economic contraction ended. U.S. economy began its recovery.
November 3, 1908	Federal elections: William Howard Taft won the presidency, running against William Jennings Bryan.
	★ ★ ★
November 8, 1910	Mid-term federal elections. The Democratic Party won a majority in House of Representatives.

(*Continued*)

Exhibit I.1 (*Continued*)

January 16, 1911	Senator Aldrich submitted "A Suggested Plan for Monetary Legislation to the Monetary Commission."
May 16, 1911	The House of Representatives authorized the Stanley Committee Investigation into U.S. Steel. Hearings began in June.
July 1, 1911	The Commissioner of Corporations published a report that finds that U.S. Steel did not monopolize the steel industry but did display monopolistic tendencies.
July 8, 1911	Representative Charles Lindbergh, Sr., declared the existence of a "money trust" in the United States and called for an investigation.
October 26, 1911	The Department of Justice under the Taft Administration filed a lawsuit against U.S. Steel for violations of the Sherman Antitrust Act.
January 11, 1912	The National Monetary Commission published its 24-volume report that marked a major shift in thinking in favor of creating a central bank.
February 24, 1912	The House of Representatives voted to investigate the possible existence and impact of a "money trust."
May 16, 1912	Pujo Committee "money trust" hearings began. The final report was published on March 2, 1913, two days before Woodrow Wilson's inauguration as president.
August 2, 1912	The Stanley Committee published its final report of the hearings on U.S. Steel.
November 5, 1912	Federal elections. Woodrow Wilson was elected president, defeating Taft and Roosevelt. The Democratic Party won majorities in the Senate and House of Representatives.
January 15, 1913	Pujo Committee hearings ended.
December 23, 1913	Congress passed and President Woodrow Wilson signed the Federal Reserve Act, creating the Federal Reserve System "to furnish an elastic currency, to afford means of rediscounting commercial paper, to establish a more effective supervision of banking in the United States, and for other purposes."

(*Continued*)

Exhibit I.1 (*Continued*)

November 16, 1914	The Federal Reserve System commenced operations.
March 1, 1920	The U.S. Supreme Court rejected Department of Justice suit that U.S. Steel violated the Sherman Antitrust Act.

Chapter 1

A Buoyant Decade, a Fragile System, and Some Leaders at Its Apex

We still continue in a period of unbounded prosperity. This prosperity is not the creature of law, but undoubtedly the laws under which we work have been instrumental in creating the conditions . . . There will undoubtedly be periods of depression. The wave will recede; but the tide will advance. (December 2, 1902)

The Nation continues to enjoy noteworthy prosperity. (December 6, 1904)

The people of this country continue to enjoy great prosperity. (December 5, 1905)

As a nation we still continue to enjoy a literally unprecedented prosperity; and it is probable that only reckless speculation and disregard of legitimate business methods on the part of the business world can materially mar this prosperity. (December 3, 1906)

—President Theodore Roosevelt,
State of the Union Addresses

Theodore Roosevelt's State of the Union addresses emphasized themes of economic triumph and regulatory caution; and they signaled a shift in America's political economy. The first decade of the twentieth century marked the twilight of the Gilded Age and the rise of the Progressive Era. It also saw the ascendancy of American economic power on the global stage after dreadful cycles of growth and depression since the Civil War.

An economic boom from 1897 to 1906 reflected the benefits of technological change, surging exports, and a growing urban workforce. And the boom challenged longstanding orthodoxies about the economy and government's role in it. The leading agents of such challenges were not extremist outsiders to the economic and political systems, but ironically were leaders in business and government. Hence, both the boom and the leaders underpin the Panic of 1907.

The Boom

In 1906, the American economy had completed an extraordinary run of prosperity that overshadowed any previous 10-year period since 1806. Figure 1.1 shows that the 38 percent growth in GDP per capita from 1897 to 1906 simply dominated the decades before.

Preceding this boom period was the depression of the 1890s—the worst in the nineteenth century, according to economic historian Richard McCulley.[1] The depression of the 1890s ended in June 1897.[2] From 1897 to the end of 1906, the nation's industrial production then grew an average of 6.5 percent per year, almost doubling the absolute size of U.S. factory output.

Over the same period, the variability of annual growth declined over time, perhaps reflecting the growing size, maturity, and industrialization of the economy. Figure 1.2 compares the period 1897–1906 with earlier episodes of U.S. economic development. It shows that the U.S. economy in 1906 was larger, had been growing faster than ever, and yet experienced less volatility in its growth.[3]

The dramatic growth and economic development of the United States at the turn of the century drew huge capital flows, especially from Europe. In 1895 the U.S. economy added $2.5 billion to its fixed plant

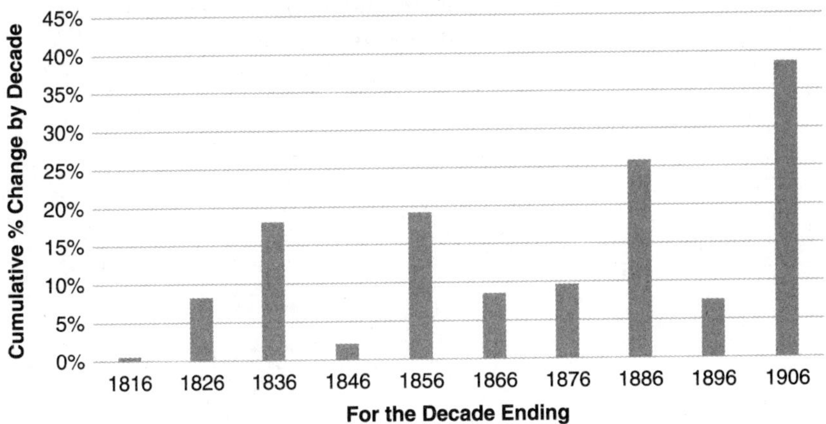

Figure 1.1 10-Year Periods of Growth in GDP per Capita
SOURCE: Authors' figure, based on data in Maddison Project Database, version 2020. Jutta Bolt and Jan Luiten van Zanden, "Maddison style estimates of the evolution of the world economy. A new 2020 update" (2020), https://www.rug.nl/ggdc/historicaldevelopment/maddison/releases/maddison-project-database-2020?lang=en.

and inventories, and by 1906 the annual rate of capital formation was running at nearly $5 billion, a blistering pace (see Figure 1.3). Much of this was financed by the country's exports, which appeared as a bulging current account surplus after 1896. But even exports were insufficient to finance the very large growth rate in the formation of capital in 1905 (12.7 percent) and 1906 (21.8 percent).

An attribute of long and large booms is buoyant optimism that leads to speculation and rapid growth in asset prices. Theodore Roosevelt's State of the Union addresses during this decade acknowledged prosperity repeatedly. From 1897 to 1906, the number of newspaper articles mentioning "optimism" more than doubled.[4] And in 1906, headlines reported "The Chicago Market: Optimism Is General,"[5] "Canadian Outlook Bright: Optimism General in Industrial and Financial Circles,"[6] "Chicago Building Boom: One Hundred Million in 1906 for New Building and Construction Work,"[7] "Land Boom in Southwest,"[8] "Building Boom in Atlanta: Nearly 100 Per Cent Increase Over Last October, and Bids Fair to Continue,"[9] "Conditions in Chicago: All Industries There Working Under High Pressure. Railroad Traffic Continues to Break All Records. . .,"[10] and

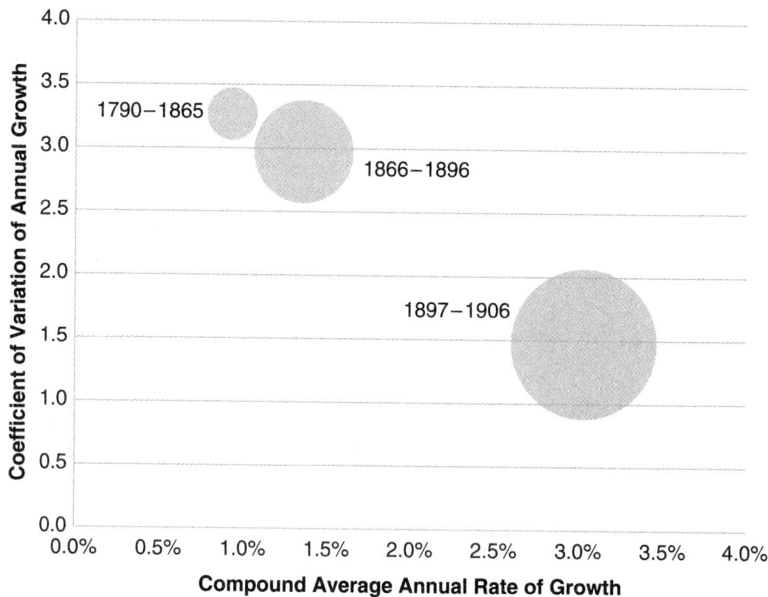

Figure 1.2 Comparison of U.S. Economic Performance Over Three Episodes
NOTE: The size of the circles indicates the relative size of the U.S. gross domestic product per capita at 1865, 1896, and 1906, respectively. The growth rate is the compound annual average over each period. The coefficient of variation is a measure of relative volatility of growth (calculated as the standard deviation of growth rates divided by the compound average rate of growth for the period).
SOURCE: Authors' figure, based on data from Maddison Project Database, version 2020. Jutta Bolt and Jan Luiten van Zanden, "Maddison style estimates of the evolution of the world economy. A new 2020 update" (2020), https://www.rug.nl/ggdc/historicaldevelopment/maddison/releases/maddison-project-database-2020?lang=en.

"Iron and Steel Notes: No Summer Let up for Steel Workers, Owing to Great Boom."[11]

The growth in stock prices at a 16 percent compounded annual rate over this decade mirrored such optimism. Figure 1.4 shows the dramatic rise—and volatility—in share prices over the boom decade. The slump in stock prices in 1903 was variously attributed to Roosevelt's trust-busting, high interest rates, and the reversal of stock-price manipulation schemes, all of which resulted in a "rich men's panic."[12] The fears

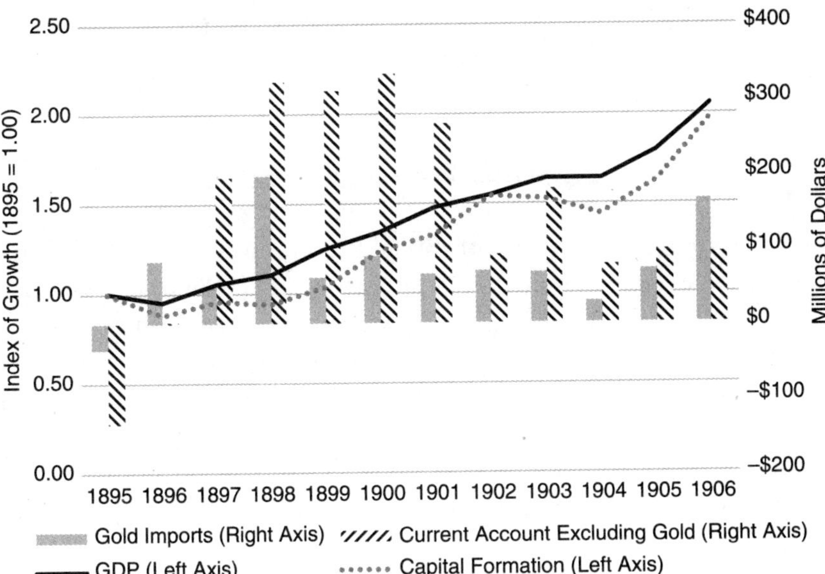

Figure 1.3 Macroeconomic Trends, 1895 to 1906
SOURCE: Authors' figure, based on data from FRED Macrohistory Database, Federal Reserve Bank of St. Louis.

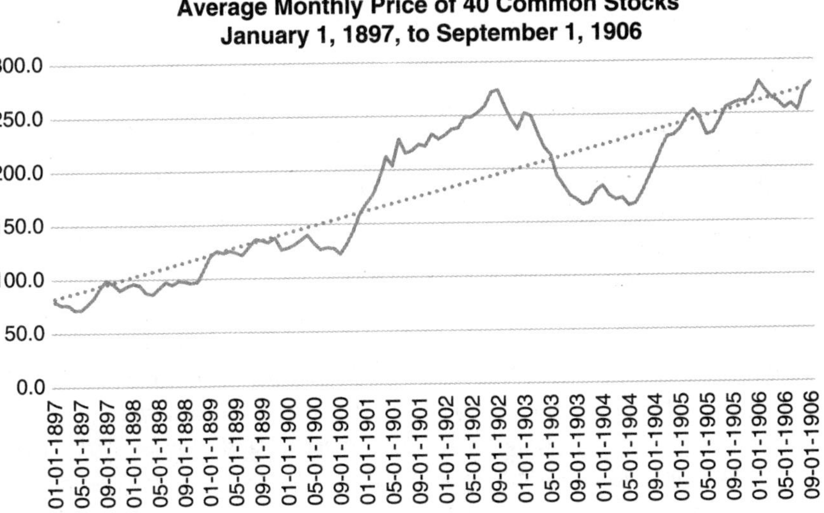

Figure 1.4 Growth in Stock Prices During the Boom Decade
SOURCE: Authors' figure, based on data from National Bureau of Economic Research, "Average Prices of 40 Common Stocks for United States," retrieved from FRED, Federal Reserve Bank of St. Louis, April 30, 2022, https://fred.stlouisfed.org/series/M11006USM315NNBR.

engendered in that slump did not materialize, prompting a large recovery in stock prices.

Wall Street Financial Leaders

Into the prodigious demand for capital moved financiers in New York and London who possessed the sophistication and credibility to raise the necessary funds for America's factories and infrastructure in the world's capital markets.[13] And over this time, the undisputed leader of the financial community in the United States was J. Pierpont Morgan. Among the major industrial combinations that he arranged were firms that remained memorable a century later: American Telephone and Telegraph, International Harvester, American Tobacco, National Biscuit (Nabisco), and others.[14] In 1901, Morgan played a central role in the formation of U.S. Steel, the largest corporation in America. Capitalized at a value of $1 billion, U.S. Steel was twice the size of the entire budget of the U.S. government in 1907.

A complex man, Morgan was a forceful personality, as all biographers agree. Historian William Harbaugh wrote of Morgan, "What a whale of a man! There seemed to radiate something that forced the complex of inferiority."[15] Morgan's nickname on Wall Street was "Jupiter," suggesting his place in the financial community. Biographer Frederick Lewis Allen described Morgan's attitude about the role of the Wall Street financial leaders: "When he put his resources behind a company, he expected to stay with it; this, he felt, was how a gentleman behaved."[16] Historian Vincent Carosso added,

> *If he had any fundamental, guiding business policy at all, it was to promote stability through responsible, competent, economical management, and to be aware of his obligations to an enterprise's owners and bondholders. There was nothing he disliked more than unrestricted competition and aggressive expansionism, which he considered wasteful and destructive. Morgan believed in orderly industrial progress, and he endorsed policies aimed at promoting cooperation. Large enterprises, he affirmed, should adhere to the principle of community of interest, not the Spencerian doctrine of survival of the fittest.*[17]

Two important figures in Morgan's circle were George F. Baker, president of First National Bank of New York, and James Stillman, president of New York's National City Bank, the largest in the United States.[18] Stillman and Baker had been both allies and competitors of Morgan in corporate financial transactions. The three men commanded great mutual respect, having worked together in business and on charitable boards.

Baker and Pierpont Morgan were close friends; they esteemed each other and shared similar views on business matters. Morgan's son once told a biographer, "Mr. Baker was closer to my father than any other man of affairs. They understood each other perfectly, worked in harmony, and there was never any need of written contracts between them."[19] Stillman, on the other hand, was somewhat of an outsider, born and raised in Brownsville, Texas. Biographer Anna Robeson Brown Burr suggested that the relationship between Stillman and Morgan was more distant, "one of respect, though they did not always see eye to eye."[20]

The success of Morgan and his circle in attracting foreign capital to America's "emerging market" was reflected in the immense importations of gold in 1906:[21] the inflow of gold to the United States spiked sharply upward to $165 million, dwarfing all annual gold flows after the Civil War, except during the year of a significant economic downturn in 1893. Fortunately, gold was plentiful in the global economy. The exploitation of gold discoveries in South Africa (beginning in 1886) and the Klondike region of Canada (beginning in 1896) contributed to a doubling of the stock of monetary gold in the United States between 1896 and 1906.[22]

America's ability to attract gold reflected its commitment to the gold standard, the backing of paper currency by a commitment to convert to gold coin on demand. This commitment became political reality with the defeat of William Jennings Bryan for president in 1896 (Jennings favored a *bimetal* standard of gold and silver) and with Congress's passage of the Gold Standard Act in 1900. From 1897 to 1906, growing gold reserves at the U.S. Treasury prompted easy credit conditions.

America's rapid industrialization during this period also hastened the emergence of business entities of unprecedented scale, complexity, and power. Between 1894 and 1904, more than 1,800 companies were consolidated into just 93 corporations.[23] Some of these large firms had grown by buying up smaller competitors during times of economic distress, while others were organized by financiers seeking to control competition and build efficiencies of scale.* Much of the volume of new debt and equity financing for these large corporations again flowed through a relatively small circle of financial institutions in New York, including J. P. Morgan & Company; Kuhn, Loeb & Company; the First National Bank; the National City Bank; Kidder, Peabody & Company; and Lee, Higginson & Company.[24]

The turbulence of this decade was reflected in at least four precedent-setting developments. First, a financial brawl in 1901 for control of the Chicago, Burlington, and Quincy Railroad (CBQ) highlighted the growing aggressions of industrialists and resulted briefly in a monopoly that would control rail traffic in the U.S. Pacific Northwest. J.P. Morgan brokered a deal between two rail barons, James J. Hill and Edward H. Harriman, to form the Northern Securities Corporation. But President Theodore Roosevelt sued the company under the Sherman Antitrust Act, a law that up to then had been enforced indifferently. The suit worked its way to the Supreme Court, which in 1904 disbanded the monopoly. This was a pivotal case in antitrust law and lent momentum to government regulation in the Progressive Era.

Second, from May to October 1902, anthracite coal miners waged an industry-wide strike for better pay and safer working conditions. Mine operators and railroads refused to negotiate. Worried that the supply of coal for home heating would dwindle with the onset of winter, President Roosevelt arbitrated negotiations to settle the strike. This was the first presidential labor arbitration in U.S. history.

Third, investigative journalists, such as Ida Tarbell, highlighted anticompetitive behavior. Her book *The History of the Standard Oil Company,* published in 1904, exposed anticompetitive tactics of

* The companies these financiers organized were popularly called "trusts," which a leading economist of the day defined as "an organization managed by a board of trustees to which all the capital stock of the constituent companies is irrevocably assigned; in other words, the original shareholders accept the trustees' certificates in lieu of former evidences of ownership." [See Ripley (1916), p. xvii.] The first and most famous of these business entities was John D. Rockefeller's Standard Oil Trust, created in 1882.

John D. Rockefeller and his colleagues. It prompted public outrage and more antitrust action by President Roosevelt.*

Finally, in 1905 a scandal among the directors and management of the Equitable Life Insurance Company highlighted excesses of the Gilded Age. A young heir had used the resources of the firm for personal purposes. The scandal prompted New York State to tighten regulation of the industry.

Such examples tarnished big businesses and tycoons in the eyes of the public. They seemed to affirm capitalists' excesses reported by muckraking journalists. And they lent momentum to the reforms of the progressives.

A Fragile System

Notwithstanding the apparently buoyant economic conditions, the financial sector of the U.S. economy harbored vulnerabilities that would figure prominently in the panic. The first vulnerability emanated from the unusually large number of small banks in the nation.

Other nations such as Britain, France, Germany, and Canada hosted a banking industry consisting of a small number of large institutions that had branches across many locations. But since the days of Andrew Jackson, politicians had feared the rise of bankers who might wield too much influence. Accordingly, U.S. regulations limited the ability of banks to open branch offices and to extend their operations across state lines.

Regulations also permitted relatively easy entry by new institutions, a policy that suited the growing nation. By 1906, the number of banking institutions expanded to 21,986,[25] growing at a rate faster than the growth rate of the population or the GDP per capita, as Figure 1.5 shows. The proliferation of banks far exceeded the rate of growth that would have been consistent with the economy. Most of these institutions were small, and typically held loan portfolios concentrated in local businesses, such as agriculture. A widespread shock, such as a single bad harvest, could challenge the stability of these banks.

The second major strain on the financial system during the runup to the Panic of 1907 was the large growth in debt financing. Between 1897 to 1906, loans by national banks nearly doubled. Since the capital

* Eventually, in 1911, the U.S. Supreme Court would order the breakup of the Standard Oil Trust into some 30 separate companies.

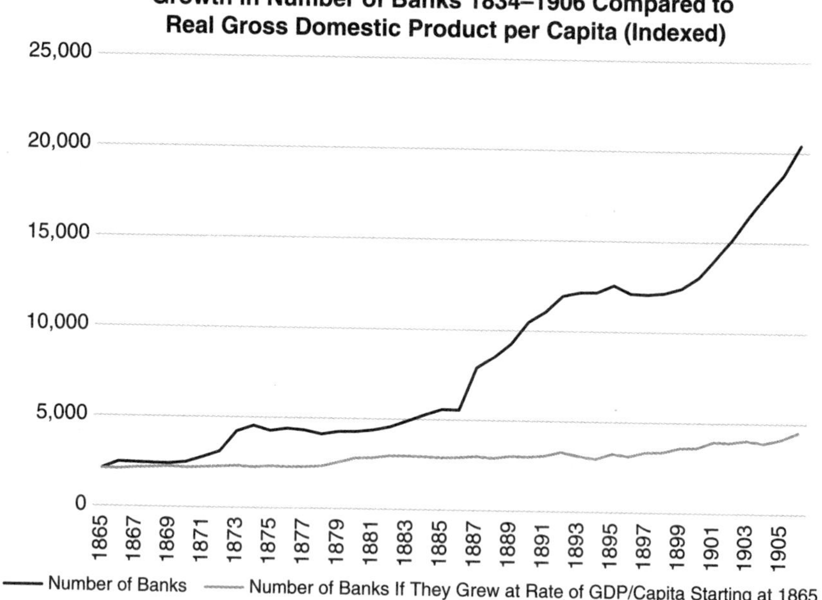

Figure 1.5 Growth of Banking Institutions
SOURCE: Authors' figure, based on data in Series X 580-587, "Financial Markets and Institutions," in *Historical Statistics of the United States: Colonial Times to 1970* (Washington, DC: U.S. Department of Commerce, Bureau of the Census).

markets were accessible only by large firms and the most creditworthy borrowers, bank lending remained the main source of financing in the country. The contemporary economist O.M.W. Sprague* noted that the economic recovery of 1897–1906 left banks awash in new deposits, which fueled the boom in bank credit.

Figure 1.6 shows that from 1897 to 1903, the growth in loans by national banks tracked the growth in industrial production and in gross national product (GNP)—but from 1904 to 1906, bank lending outgrew these benchmarks: by the end of 1906, actual loan volume exceeded the volume implied by industrial production by $630 million (13.5 percent) and GNP by $376 million (8 percent). Sprague asserted that the

* Oliver Mitchell Wentworth Sprague published in 1910 an authoritative account of U.S. financial crises under the aegis of the National Monetary Commission. At the time, he was assistant professor of banking and finance at Harvard University. Sprague's book is a starting point for commentaries on the Panic of 1907. Hereafter, for simplicity he will be cited as Professor Sprague.

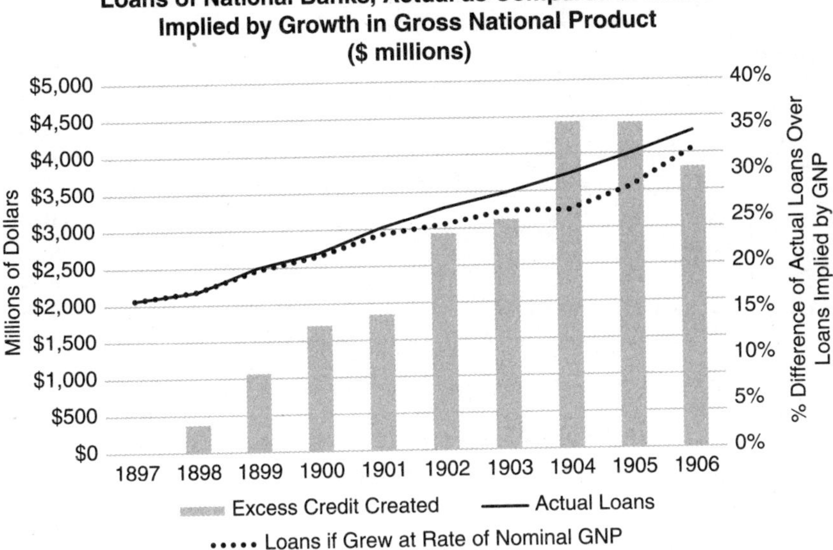

Figure 1.6 Loans of National Banks Compared to GNP
SOURCE: Authors' figure, based on data in Sprague (1910), p. 218. Data on GNP Series F1-5, "Gross National Product, Total and per Capita, in Current and 1958 Prices," in *Historical Statistics of the United States from Colonial Times to 1970*, Part 1, Chapter F (Washington DC: U.S. Bureau of the Census).

excess bank loans went to the call money market, largely fueling speculation in stocks.[26]

Third, over the 10 years from 1897 to 1906, the safety cushion of banks declined. Net deposits grew at a compound rate of 9.2 percent annually, but cash reserves did not grow quite as fast (only 6.1 percent), in part because banks loaned or invested their cash more aggressively. Figure 1.7 shows the decline in the ratio of cash reserve to net deposits for national banks by almost one-third over this period—from 17.8 percent to 13.3 percent, below the minimum reserve ratio allowed by federal regulations. It is worth noting that much of the decline in reserves occurred in the interior region of the United States—in late 1906, the reserve ratio of national banks in New York City remained at 25.5 percent, just above the required minimum for banks of their stature.

The decline in financial condition of the national banks revealed little about the condition of state-chartered banks, which vastly exceeded the number of nationally chartered banks. Generally, these were small

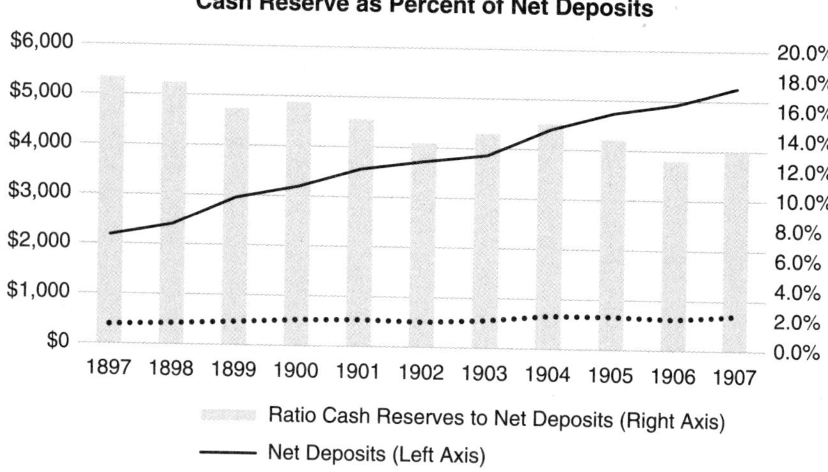

Figure 1.7 Condition of National Banks
SOURCE: Authors' figure, based on data in Sprague (1910), p. 218.

institutions and less resilient to financial shocks. To compound the worrisome decline in the bank reserve ratio, the practice of fractional reserve banking placed some part of most banks' reserves on deposit with banks in reserve cities, where the deposits could earn interest. When the banking system functioned properly, these distant reserves could be recalled on demand. But during a panic, a suspension of specie withdrawals would prevent access to those distant reserves.

Also, the advent of trust companies into the banking business—about which more will be said later—complicated any assessment of the condition of the financial system. The trust companies intruded into the banks' competition for deposits by lending money more liberally, carrying lower cash reserves to backstop depositors' claims, and enjoying lighter prudential regulation.

Fourth, this was a period that had been preceded by regular financial crises. Fragility mattered because of the memory—vivid in the recall of most people in 1906—of the frequent banking panics in nineteenth-century America. A panic featured "runs" by depositors, seeking to withdraw their funds in specie from banks. By virtue of their low ratios of reserves to deposits, banks faced the prospect of exhausting their cash.

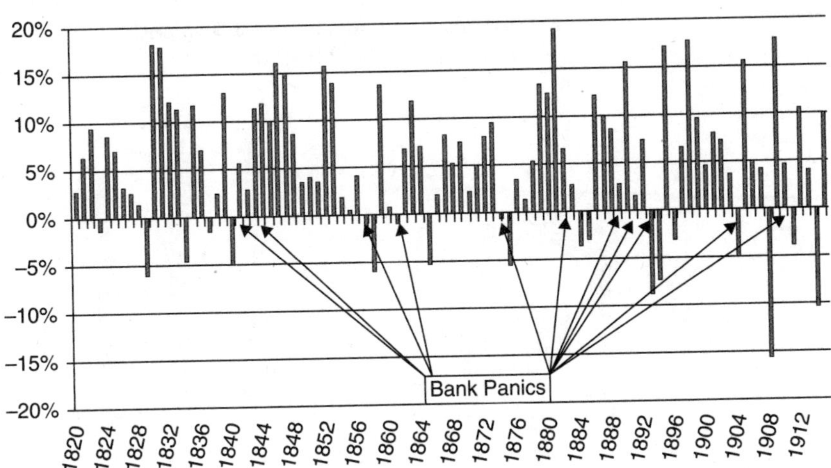

Figure 1.8 Major Bank Panic Episodes and Changes in Industrial Production
SOURCE: Authors' figure, based on data on industrial production in Davis (2004), pp. 1177–1215.

To prevent that outcome, they would suspend depositors' right to withdraw cash until the panic subsided. This left firms and individuals in the lurch, possibly unable to buy food, pay rent, or meet their own debt obligations. Bank panics led to serious spillovers into the real economy. Figure 1.8 shows that from 1820 to 1915, America endured 11 serious bank panic episodes, most associated with economic recessions.

The United States was not alone in its difficulties of finding a model for stable banking. Figure 1.9 shows that the eruptions of bank panics were the rule rather than the exception throughout the nineteenth century among 70 countries in the world. Each decade, an average of 14 countries experienced financial crises.

A Growing Movement for Stability in the United States

The instability of the financial system had been a source of concern to national leaders and the public at least since the founding of the nation. At the behest of Alexander Hamilton, in 1791 Congress enacted a charter for the Bank of the United States. Through its large size, ample reserves, and multiple branches, it functioned as a disciplinarian on banks in the fledgling republic that failed to conduct business prudentially.

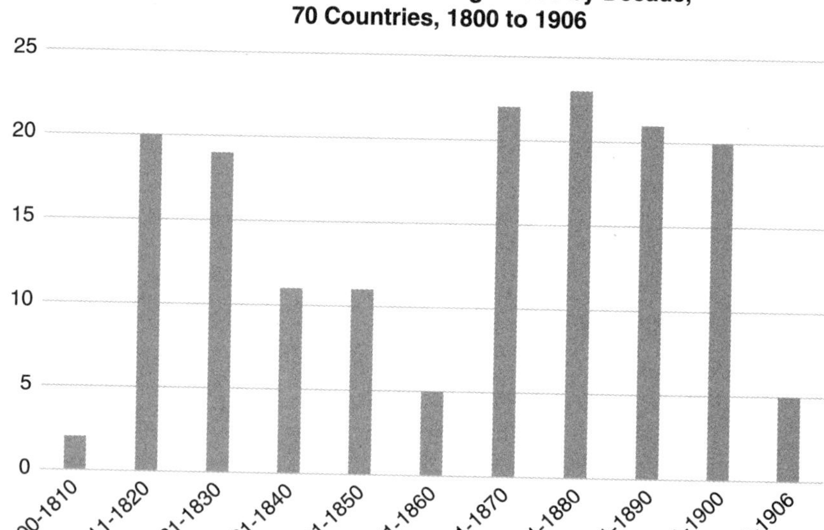

Figure 1.9 Number of Country Bank Panics per Decade
SOURCE: Authors' figure, based on data from "Global Crises Data by Country," Behavioral Finance & Financial Stability, Harvard Business School, downloaded July 28, 2021 from https://www.hbs.edu/behavioral-finance-and-financial-stability/data/Pages/global.aspx.

Unfortunately, the growing influence of the Bank of the United States worried Thomas Jefferson and James Madison, who mounted a successful campaign against renewing the bank's charter in 1811. The War of 1812 proved to be a harsh awakening to the usefulness of such a big bank. Thus, in 1816, Congress chartered the Second Bank of the United States. But again, a destabilizing banking crisis and recession in 1819 inflamed public sentiment toward banks and the Second Bank, in particular.

One important antagonist, Andrew Jackson, was elected president in 1828 on the promise of fighting the Second Bank of the United States. Although Congress passed a recharter of the Second Bank, Jackson vetoed it in 1832, ending its prudential oversight of the banking system. Then, in laws passed in 1863 and 1864, Congress permitted the national chartering of banks and the creation of the Office of the Comptroller of the Currency, which would monitor those banks. Nonetheless, serious banking crises in the 1870s, 1880s, and 1890s gradually persuaded business leaders that the unusual architecture of bank regulation was not working.

Reform proposals sprouted. These included authorization for national banks to expand their issuance of banknotes in a panic (1894),[27] to establish regional reserve banks (1896),[28] to establish a *confederation* of regional reserve banks (1901),[29] to deploy the Treasury's surplus gold to national banks at the height of the crop-moving season (1902),[30] to allow bank clearing houses to issue their own asset-backed banknotes during a panic (1904),[31] and, ultimately, to establish a central bank along the lines of major European countries (1906).[32]

The financial community's proposals to establish a central bank met with hostile opposition from progressives, populists, "Main Street" businesspeople, and country bankers. All believed that the existing powers of the U.S. Treasury to shift gold deposits as needed trumped the interests of Wall Street and best served the interests of the public. In his State of the Union message to Congress on December 3, 1906, President Roosevelt sided with the opposition: "Any plan must . . . guard the interest of Western and Southern Bankers as carefully as it guards the interests of New York or Chicago bankers and must be drawn from the standpoints of the farmer and the merchant no less than from the standpoints of the city banker and the country banker."[33]

In his annual report to Congress of December 5, 1906, Treasury Secretary Shaw argued that instead of creating a central bank, the Treasury Department should be empowered to control bank reserves and the money supply. In effect, this would designate the Treasury as the de facto central bank. Shaw feared that private interests (such as bankers) would take control of an independent central bank. Therefore, Shaw proposed that Congress should create a reserve fund of $100 million to deploy in the event of a crisis for use by the Secretary of the Treasury. He said, "in my judgment no panic as distinguished from industrial stagnation could threaten either the United States or Europe that he could not avert."[34] Events in 1907 would challenge his confident assertion.

The reforms proposed between 1894 and 1906 were notable for at least three reasons. First, they reflected the beginnings of a dramatic shift in mainstream thinking about monetary management in the United States. The old Jefferson–Jackson antipathy toward banks poorly served the needs of a nation growing rapidly. Second, the hostility they aroused displayed the new fault lines in American politics that monetary policy would encounter for decades to come. Third, they reflected components of what eventually would become the Federal Reserve System, an institution that would manage the supply of currency, pool risks, regulate banks, and fight crises as a lender of last resort.

A Portent

Those closest to the financial system saw these difficulties and their attendant risks most clearly. On January 4, 1906, with unusual clairvoyance, Jacob Schiff, senior partner of the house of Kuhn, Loeb & Company (J. P. Morgan's archrival), gave a speech to the New York Chamber of Commerce in which he declared presciently, "the money market conditions which had prevailed the previous sixty days are a disgrace to the country, and that unless our currency system was reformed a panic would sooner or later result compared with which all previous panics would seem as child's play."[35]

By 1906 J. Pierpont Morgan himself was beginning to disengage slowly from the day-to-day activities of his firm to attend to his passion for collecting art and literature, serving on boards of charitable institutions, and touring Europe. He relied heavily on his son, J. P. "Jack" Morgan Jr., to manage his firm's daily affairs, as well as his right-hand man, George W. Perkins, a partner in J. P. Morgan & Company. On April 17, 1906, the aging Morgan turned 69 years old. By this time, he was unquestionably, according to biographer Anna Burr, "the most powerful figure in the American world of business, if not the most powerful citizen of the United States. His authority was vague, but it was immense—and growing."[36]

On the morning after Morgan's birthday, an historic catastrophe devastated the city of San Francisco, California, setting in motion a chain of events that would eventually call for all the power, wisdom, strength, and influence that Old Jupiter could muster.

Chapter 2

A Shock to the System

General affairs here are about as bad as they can be.

—J. P. "Jack" Morgan Jr., August 8, 1907

The earthquake and fire that destroyed 80 percent of San Francisco, starting on April 18, 1906, was unprecedented in U.S. history.[1] The quake was massive, with an estimated magnitude of 7.9.[2] In the wake of the temblor itself, broken gas mains fueled huge fires throughout the city. Disruptions to municipal water lines prevented fire suppression, and San Francisco's mostly wood-framed architecture only fed the fires. The conflagration eventually engulfed the city, leveling over four square miles, such that most historical accounts speak of both the earthquake *and* the fire as the source of the city's destruction. San Francisco's damages were reported to range from $350 to $500 million,[3] equal to 1.2 to 1.7 percent of the U.S. gross national product in 1906.[4]

The strains from the catastrophe in California rippled quickly through the global financial system. At the time, San Francisco was the financial center of the West and home to the western branch of the U.S. Mint, so anything that disrupted business in San Francisco threatened the entire western region economically.

On the New York and London stock exchanges, news of the quake led to an immediate sell-off in stocks and a significant drop in share prices. Economists Kerry Odell and Marc Weidenmier have estimated that the disaster led directly or indirectly to about a $1 billion decline (nearly 12.5 percent) in the total market value of New York Stock Exchange securities. Prices of railway stocks fell more than 15 percent, and those of insurance companies declined between 15 and 30 percent during the two weeks after the cataclysm.[5]

Relief funds were drawn into the city from around the country and the world: England supplied $30 million; Germany, France, and the Netherlands collectively provided another $20 million. Such international effects of the earthquake were further amplified because many foreign insurers had provided San Francisco's underwriting protection. Disputes between the foreign insurers and San Franciscans arose over the fact that most people were insured against fire but not earthquakes. British insurance firms, for instance, had accounted for about half of the city's fire insurance policies; after the quake, they faced losses of close to $50 million. In fact, several insurers were overwhelmed by the claims and could not meet their insurable obligations. The Fireman's Fund Insurance Company, for example, faced liabilities of $11.5 million, exceeding its total assets by $4.5 million.[6] Consequently, some underwriters imposed lengthy delays in paying for damages, while others discounted their claims, insisting that any earthquake-related fire damage was not explicitly covered in their policies. The Hamburg-Bremen Insurance Company demanded a discount of 25 percent for all San Francisco claims. Only six companies fully honored their obligations.[7]

While some British insurers funded their payments by selling their holdings of American securities in London and New York, others liquidated assets heavily in foreign markets. The payments prompted major shipments of gold from London to the United States—$30 million in April and another $35 million in September 1906, amounting to a 14 percent decline in Britain's stock of gold—the largest outflow of gold from Britain between 1900 and 1913. Eventually, these outflows of gold created liquidity fears for the Bank of England.[8] The declining liquidity of the London capital market sparked the spread of rumors in New York that British financial houses were in trouble and required support from the Bank of England.[9]

The Gold Standard and Britain's Hegemony in Finance

At the time of the earthquake in the spring of 1906, London dominated the global market for capital. The British Empire was at its zenith, and its immense flows of capital traversed London markets. John Maynard Keynes later wrote that the Bank of England had the "power to call the tune . . . During the latter half of the nineteenth century the influence of London on credit conditions throughout the world was so predominant that the Bank of England could almost have claimed to be the conductor of the international orchestra."[10]

As a practical matter, nations wished to preserve their credit standing in global markets and the strength of their financial institutions. This desire dictated the need to ensure a stable rate at which the nation's currency could be converted into gold. Nations confronted the "impossible trilemma"[11] in which it was possible to control *only any two* of the following three levers of national financial policy:

1. Rates of currency exchange (including the rate of exchange into gold). Stable exchange rates promoted foreign trade and economic growth. Thus, national governments had an incentive to peg exchange rates at a certain target.
2. Interest rates. The cost of money influenced economic growth, and the flows of gold into and out of a country. Thus, national governments had an incentive to manage (or "fix") interest rates, rather than let them be determined by market forces.
3. Flow of capital across borders. Outflows of gold reserves (for instance, because of trade deficits) were nettlesome because they diminished the central bank's gold reserves. However, adroit management of interest rates by the central bank could reverse the outflows.

During the classic gold standard era, nations typically settled for the first two and conceded the third to the markets. They sought to stabilize currency exchange rates and to manage interest rates. Thus they had to put up with variations in the flows of capital (i.e., gold) into and out of the country as market conditions determined.*

For all practical purposes, Britain in 1906 was the financial hegemon of the world. It had the largest gold reserves; it had a massive volume of international trade (especially within the Empire); and it hosted the most significant financial markets. Thus, it could set the rules of financial behavior among nations and could enforce them—not only by virtue of its resource abundance but also, if necessary, by virtue of its powerful navy. Britain was *the* force to be reckoned with.

The Bank of England Reacts to Gold Exports to the United States

Charged with the responsibility of maintaining liquidity for the Empire, the Bank of England—the "Old Lady of Threadneedle Street"—held reserves of gold with which to meet the liquidity demands of banks and trading partners. Keeping the British mills, factories, and shops supplied with goods from the commonwealth was a fundamental aim of England's economic system.

Odell and Weidenmier estimated that the San Francisco earthquake triggered insurance payments from Britain amounting to almost £19 million, more than 2.5 times the shipments to any other country. Including payments from Britain, Germany, France, and the Netherlands, the gold exports to the United States in April and May 1906 amounted to nearly $50 million.[12] By October, the insurance payments had risen to $100 million.[13] Odell and Weidenmier reported that the drain on British gold reserves occurred in two waves: humanitarian relief payments arrived in late April and in May, and

* A balance of payments deficit would cause a decline in the central bank's gold reserve. As the gold reserve fell, the nation's money supply would decline and prompt fears about the possible suspension of convertibility of the paper currency into gold. Thus, central banks would raise interest rates to attract gold back into the country. Higher rates would depress asset prices, helping to attract foreign capital. As the nation's gold reserve recovered, the nation's money supply would expand, prompting interest rates to fall and stimulating capital investment and economic growth—also promoting consumption and speculation. Then the boom would lead to a balance of payments deficit and the cycle of automatic adjustment would repeat itself.

after insurance adjustment decisions, a second wave of gold shipments occurred in September and October 1906.

To compound matters, a booming stock market in New York led to the perception that American gold imports were fueling speculation, not investment in productive assets. A Berlin correspondent for the *New York Evening Post* reported in July that Americans "can borrow from Europe to a practically unlimited extent this season."[14] Large publicly owned corporations raised their dividends in mid-1906. The Union Pacific Railroad advanced its payout from 6 to 10 percent. And U.S. Steel resumed paying dividends (after suspending them in 1903). As Sprague wrote, these dividends "gave encouragement to the unbridled optimism which was already too much in evidence."[15] The U.S. stock market peaked in October 1906, a dramatic recovery from a low in May 1904.

To stanch the decline in Britain's gold supply, the Bank of England raised its benchmark interest rate from 3.5 to 4.0 percent on September 13, 1906. Fearing further demands for gold with the coming Egyptian cotton crop,[16] the Bank raised its rate twice again, on October 11, 1906, from 4.0 to 5.0 percent and on October 19 from 5.0 to 6.0 percent—the highest rate posted by the Bank of England since 1899.[17] Central banks in France and Germany followed suit and sharply raised their interest rates as well.[18]

Also on October 19, the Bank of England threatened other British lenders with a further rate hike to 7.0 percent if they did not stop financing gold imports to the United States—credit rationing, a rarely used policy by central banks, indicated the gravity of the Bank of England's view of conditions.

Figure 2.1 suggests why the Bank took these extreme measures. The gold reserves that stood behind its paper currency had declined materially with each wave of gold shipments to the United States. By raising Bank Rate after the first wave, the Bank's reserves had recovered. But with the second wave in August–September, the Bank's reserves had slumped from £37 million in mid-August to about £28 million in mid-October—the dashed line shows that gold reserves had fallen more than two standard deviations below the average gold reserve that had prevailed from 1901 to 1905. The loss of gold reserves to exports for the United States had grown alarming.

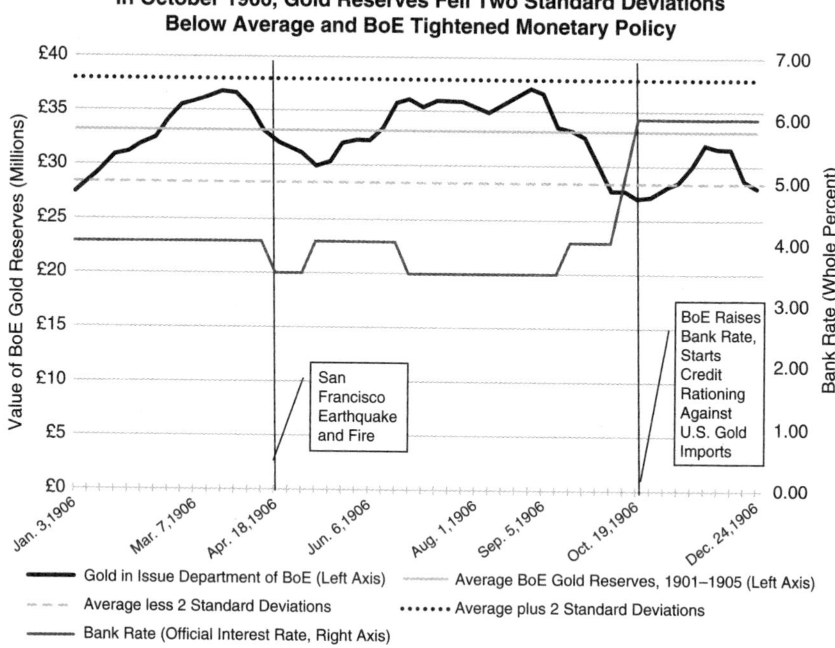

Figure 2.1 Bank Rate and Specie Reserves at Bank of England Issue Department, 1906

NOTE: The horizontal lines, depicting the average plus or minus two standard deviations, are based on weekly observations of the total coin and bullion at the Bank of England from January 1901 to December 1905. Exceeding the limits of +/– two standard deviations suggests about a 2.5 percent chance that such a movement in reserves was just due to economic "noise." In short, the BoE's slump in reserves in the fall of 1906 was a rare event that predictably tripped alarms there.

SOURCE: Authors' figure, based on data from Huaxiang Huang and Ryland Thomas, "The Weekly Balance Sheet of the Bank of England 1844–2006: Version 2," downloaded April 30, 2022 from https://www.bankofengland.co.uk/statistics/research-datasets.

After the San Francisco earthquake and fire, the mid-October policy move by the Bank of England proved to be the second major shock of 1906 to the U.S. financial system. Professor Sprague argued that the Bank of England precipitated a general credit-tightening cycle. American institutions that had issued finance bills in London for the purpose of importing gold now found that they could not "roll over" or refinance those bills. Sprague wrote, "From December 1906, the liquidation of these bills was the most potent single factor in the situation."[19]

Money Conditions Tighten

In New York City, credit was becoming scarce, too, as its gold reserves also migrated to San Francisco. The timing of these relief shipments to the West Coast was particularly unfortunate since they coincided with the ordinary demands for funds induced by the U.S. agricultural cycle: the harvesting and shipment of crops required credit until the crops reached the consumer. As a result of the credit shortage, the price of money in New York grew dear, and other sectors of the American economy started to feel the pinch. By the winter of 1906–1907, a severe credit shortage had set in.

Panic had not yet arrived, but telegrams flew across the Atlantic between the world's leading financiers, reflecting a growing anxiety within the financial community about liquidity and the likely actions of the Bank of England.[20] On December 18, 1906, Jack Morgan, who had assumed day-to-day responsibility for J.P. Morgan & Co. from his father, writing to his affiliate partners in London, offered stark language about these stringent credit conditions: "Things here are very uncomfortable owing to the tightness of money . . . we are likely to have a stiff money market for some time to come."[21] A few days later he wrote with a clarification: "There is plenty of money in the country everywhere except in New York, and the only really alarming thing about the situation appears to be a very undefined feeling that there is something wrong in New York. This feeling extending to the large centres in the West has interfered with the natural flow of money to this centre to take advantage of the high rate."[22] As the year 1907 began, there was a deep sense of foreboding among the nation's money men.

Complicating the money scarcity problem was a bull market in stocks, which had been spurred by the buoyant economic growth of the American economy. A "mammoth bull movement," in the words of one observer, was running its course on the New York Stock Exchange. Jack Morgan noted a speculative sentiment prevailing in the stock market:

For the first time in three years the public—with stocks at their present high prices—have begun to come in and buy heavily with the result that the so called market-leaders are no longer in charge, and that the stock market is running away in a fashion which I must say suggests to me possible trouble in the future although not in the immediate future.[23]

Meanwhile, enormous new issues of securities, particularly by railway and industrial companies, placed further demands on the resources of the money market. Henry Clews, a contemporary Wall Street authority, said, "Indeed, the year 1906 from beginning to end witnessed a continuation of those inordinately heavy demands for money from Wall Street and corporations, and these led to the disturbed monetary conditions."[24] French economist Pierre Paul Leroy-Beaulieu estimated that the global economy provided $2.4 billion annually in investment in new security issues, but that in 1906, issuers sought $3.25 billion in funding—a demand the financial system could not fill.[25] The railway magnate James J. Hill estimated in November 1906 that U.S. railroads would require financing of $1 billion per year for the next five years, an unheard-of ambition for investment or financing.[26]

While the equity market was attracting popular attention, the debt markets (i.e., bonds and loans) overshadowed stocks in both volume and significance. During 1906, debt market conditions diverged sharply from equities: While stock prices rose, bond prices fell (and thus, interest rates increased). The price movement in the debt markets coincided with the increasing demand for credit driven by the continued real economic growth in the United States, the agricultural cycle that drew financing to bring the bumper crop of 1906 to market, and the shock of the San Francisco earthquake. Alexander Dana Noyes, a leading observer of Wall Street, wrote in 1909, "Beginning about the middle of 1905, a strain on the whole world's capital supply and credit facilities set in, which increased at so portentous a rate during the next two years that long before October 1907, thoughtful men in many widely separated markets were discussing, with serious apprehension, what was to be the result."[27]

Chapter 3

The "Silent" Crash

The whole situation is most mysterious; undoubtedly many men who were very rich have become much poorer, but as there seems to be no one breaking, perhaps we shall get off with the fright only.[1]

—J. P. "Jack" Morgan Jr., March 14, 1907

It is a rich-man's panic and the results, however serious, will not be disastrous.[2]

—Barton Hepburn, chairman of Chase Bank, March 15, 1907

By early 1907, it seemed that the progressive tightening of money, which had been accelerated by the massive capital demands of San Francisco's earthquake, had precipitated a slow decline in equity prices—considered by some contemporaries to be a "silent" crash in the U.S. financial markets.

The Crash

Between its peak in September 1906 and the end of February 1907, the index of 40 industrial stocks fell 10.9 percent,[3] a five-month change in value unremarkable in view of the long history of the market, but pertinent as the precursor to the events of March. Indeed, on March 6, 1907, telegraph correspondence between Jack Morgan and his partner in J. P. Morgan & Company's London affiliate, Teddy Grenfell, reflected the deepening anxiety between the world's financial centers:

Grenfell: Can you give us any information and what is your opinion of the immediate future of your market?[4]

Morgan: Do not get any information showing real trouble our market although of course continued liquidation must hurt some people and may do severe damage in places. From what I can make out do not think stocks are in weak hands. Shall be surprised if immediate future brings much more liquidation, although of course impossible form opinion.[5]

In the coming days, Teddy and Jack exchanged more anxious telegrams about rumors of gold shipments. Grenfell thought that at the "first indication [of] considerable withdrawals of gold," the Bank of England would raise its interest rate. He wondered whether the U.S. Treasury would relieve the situation by releasing gold from its vaults into the financial system. On March 13 Jack wired back that he could discover no intentions to ship gold from London *this* week, although there might be attempts to buy gold next week.[6]

By mid-March the "silent" crash had become audible as equity prices turned decidedly and sharply for the worse. Declining over a series of days (March 9 to 14 and 23 to 25), the index of all listed stocks fell 9.8 percent. Especially damaged were shares in shipping (off 16.6 percent), mining (down 14.5 percent), steel and iron (down 14.8 percent), and street railways (off 13.8 percent). Railroad companies were especially hard-hit: over half of the 25 most active stocks on March 14 were rails, led by Northern Pacific, down 72.9 percent; Union Pacific, off 59.9 percent; Great Northern (preferred), off 58.2 percent; and Reading Railroad, down by 44.3 percent. One estimate placed the worst trading day of the month on March 14, with a statistically significant loss of 8.29 percent in the industrials index.[7] The *Commercial and Financial Chronicle*, the principal financial periodical at the time, observed, "The liquidation going on in Wall Street . . . is phenomenal. Stock sales . . . are among the high records in the Stock Exchange history."[8]

The proximate trigger for the slump in stocks was the apparent failure of Edward H. Harriman and National City Bank to successfully "boom"* the stocks of the Union Pacific Railroad (UP) and other railroads. Borrowing aggressively, UP had purchased shares in various railroad companies starting in June 1906. The railroad industry generally, and UP in particular, had mooted massive investments in new plant and equipment, for which equally massive security issues were in prospect—a billion dollars per year for five years, compared with the previous peak fundraising of $500 million in 1901.[9] High security prices would help the process. So would high and rising dividends: in August 1906, UP had announced an increase in the dividend from 6 percent to 10 percent of par value. Professor Sprague wrote, "Events seem to have proved conclusively the ability of these companies to earn the dividends which were then declared, but nevertheless, coming when it did, this action exercised an unfortunately general influence. It gave encouragement to the unbridled optimism which was already too much in evidence. It was preceded and followed by a speculative movement on the stock exchange which was made possible through credits granted by the banks upon the foundation of the usual summer inflow of funds from the interior."[10]

Concern about Policy Shifts

However, regime change was in prospect: years of complaints by populists and progressives about railroads' monopolistic practices had culminated in passage of the Hepburn Act on June 29, 1906. This act empowered the Interstate Commerce Commission to set railroad rates, which raised howls of complaint from business leaders. Ultimately the loans to UP and other market speculators began to mature in February and March 1907, which forced the railroad boomers to confront the worsening credit conditions that had commenced with the Bank of

* During this era, it was an open secret that investors—and even corporate executives—would manipulate the prices of corporate securities for profit (see, for instance, Edwin Lefèvre's *Reminiscences of a Stock Operator* (1919)). To "boom" a stock was to bid up and maintain high stock prices, typically around the time of a new issue. Manipulation of stock prices in public markets was rendered illegal by U.S. securities laws beginning in 1933.

England's contractionary policy in the fall of 1906. Without other sources of finance, Harriman and other speculators were forced to dump their holdings onto the market. Sprague noted, "Never before or since have such severe declines taken place on the New York Stock Exchange."[11]

J. Pierpont Morgan was absent from New York during these disturbances in the market; he had sailed for Europe at midnight on March 13, the date of the sharp market break. There, Pierpont met old friends, toured the art markets for possible acquisitions for his collection, and relaxed at various spas and villas. Meanwhile, Jack Morgan in New York grappled with the confusion and chaos in the financial system, writing in a letter to his partners in London on March 14:

> *Here we are, still alive in spite of the most unpleasant panic which we are going through. The whole trouble lies, in my mind, in the mystery of the conditions; no one seems to be in any trouble, there is money at a price for anyone who wants it, and in our loans, and in those of all the Banks I have talked to, there has been no trouble whatever of keeping the margins perfectly good, except the physical difficulty of getting the certificates round quickly enough. . . . I could not yesterday finish this letter owing to the panic and general trouble, there being so much to see to with Father and Perkins both away. Today, things seem to be so much quieter that I am in hopes that most of the trouble is over, certainly for the present. . . . The whole situation is most mysterious; undoubtedly many men who were very rich have become much poorer, but as there seems to be no one breaking, perhaps we shall get off with the fright only.*[12]

As the price declines continued during the next week, rumors of the failure of financial institutions began to circulate. The London partners of J. P. Morgan & Company cabled to Jack: "*London Daily Telegraph* today states that house of international prominence has been helped in New York. Is there any truth in this? Who is it? Do you expect much further liquidation?"[13] Jack replied, "As far as we know there is no truth in rumor international house having been helped. Newspaper reports here is that various stock exchange houses in London are in difficulties. Cable any information you can obtain. Urgent liquidation seems to be pretty well done but as many parties heavily hit look for depressed markets for some time."[14]

The Treasury Acts

Amidst these rising concerns about market conditions in New York, leaders in Washington were also taking notice. Throughout the day and late into the evening on March 13, President Theodore Roosevelt (TR) called a series of meetings with members of his cabinet, including George B. Cortelyou, who had only begun his term as Treasury Secretary on March 4.

Cortelyou had served as the Secretary of Commerce and Labor and as Postmaster General in TR's cabinet and Chair of the Republican National Committee during TR's reelection campaign in 1904. Yet his stance on financial policy was unknown. Would Cortelyou continue the policy of his predecessor, Leslie Shaw, in deploying Treasury gold to stabilize banks?

Cortelyou advised the president that the Bank of England would likely raise its discount rate, thereby temporarily restraining the importation of gold to the United States and further straining the nation's money supply. Given the urgent need for more—not less—liquidity, Cortelyou suggested that relief from the federal Treasury would urgently be necessary to quell a potential panic.

As rumors swirled that the market's sudden decline was somehow a "premeditated panic" orchestrated by "Wall Street manipulators"[15]—a conspiracy theory (oddly) predicated on the concurrent departure of J.P. Morgan from New York for a European tour, Cortelyou acted. Following late-night discussions with the president and Secretary of State Elihu Root, the Treasury announced a bold effort to calm investors and avoid a "money stringency," infusing up to $71 million into the money supply. The plan included: an immediate buyback of $25 million in federal bonds; an order to keep in circulation $16 million in notes soon scheduled for retirement; and an agreement *not* to withdraw $30 million in cash that the Treasury had placed with the banks the previous fall. Cortelyou also arranged for federal customs collectors around the country to deposit all receipts with national bank depositories, providing immediate access to funds in those cities lacking federal subtreasuries.

The quick action by Treasury was considered at the time to be among the most sweeping relief measures ever implemented by the federal government. The *New York Times* noted that Cortelyou's response was "far beyond [former Treasury Secretary] Shaw's relief."[16] And, immediately following Cortelyou's announcement, the market appeared briefly to stabilize, bringing forth accolades for Secretary Cortelyou's efforts, who had barely warmed his seat at Treasury. The administration worried that a large federal intervention risked being regarded as a precedent, potentially signaling that market disruptions would always result in federal intervention in the money supply.[17] Nevertheless, the positive response from the financial community was enthusiastic. "The prompt and clear action of Secretary Cortelyou saved the day," said the prominent New York banker Jacob Schiff. "I have strong hopes that much of good will result from the present situation."[18]

Yet the Slump Continues

This upbeat outlook was not to last. Notwithstanding initial hopes for a rapid restoration of calm, conditions remained unsettled as the unrest spread to other financial markets. On March 23, 1907, the *Commercial and Financial Chronicle* noted, "Lack of confidence [among investors] is never reflected more unerringly than in the money market; and the seriousness of the situation in that regard is shown in the inability of the railroads for over a year past to finance their new capital needs."[19] Both the municipalities of Philadelphia and St. Louis made bond offerings, and in neither case was the underwriting successful. "Money is commanding such high rates that it is impossible to float even gilt-edged securities at the low figures offered by Philadelphia and St. Louis," the *Chronicle* reported.

By now dubbed the "rich man's panic" in the popular press, equity prices continued to fall in New York, following a slump in foreign markets over the weekend. Alarmed by the situation, on March 25 Cortelyou again counseled the president, recommending that further measures should be taken by the government to prevent a further "demoralization."[20] Guided by a sense that matters could spin out of control, the secretary left Washington for New York, with a plan to confer with financiers and other business leaders to discuss how to steady the market. Thus was hatched the second major federal response to the market panic in as many weeks.

Treasury Responds Again

On the morning of March 26, with the markets already in serious decline, Secretary Cortelyou issued a statement about an unconventional and creative approach to infusing more liquidity into the financial system. National Banks had to deposit U.S. government bonds with the Treasury to be held as reserves against banknotes in circulation; if the maturing bonds were not replaced, it would force a reduction in the nation's money supply. In substitution for all U.S. 4 percent bonds maturing on July 1, Cortelyou announced that the Treasury would accept Philippine bonds and certificates, City of Manila bonds, Puerto Rican bonds, District of Columbia bonds, and Hawaiian bonds, as well as state, municipal, and high-grade railroad bonds. Altogether these moves were expected to relieve pressure on investors, thereby keeping $12 million in circulation.

As if that were not sufficient, Cortelyou also extended his order for customs collections in subtreasury cities (including New York) to be deposited in those cities' national banks. In addition, he authorized the immediate payment of interest on the federal bonds coming due in April 1907, which would be paid instantly in cash to any holders of these coupons. All told, this action added yet another $16,900,000 to the money market, providing a much-needed automatic cash infusion. It was further reported that the Treasury was prepared to release $25 million to $30 million more, while still maintaining a working balance of $75 million.[21]

Then a Rally

The net result of the Treasury's interventions was a phenomenal bull market rally on March 26, reinforced by the expectation that Cortelyou would eventually make permanent the emergency policy of depositing customs receipts with the banks rather than the subtreasury.[22] "All this serves to confirm the bold and much criticized declaration made by Secretary Shaw [Cortelyou's predecessor] in his last annual report," extolled the editors of the *Wall Street Journal*, "that if he had a balance of

$100,000,000 at his disposal, the United States treasury could at all times prevent any financial panic in any part of the world."[23]

Indeed, by the end of the week, cables between J.P. Morgan's partners suggested that the worst was past. On March 29, 1907, Jack Morgan reflected on the change in mood to his London associates:

> *The two panics within the last ten days have given people a big scare, and the losses of course are frightful. The fact that no one has failed is more of the nature of a miracle than of ordinary business, but it simply shows, as far as I can see, that practically no one was overtrading. . . . My own belief, however, is that the panic is over, and the fact that the Treasury is putting out money rather fast and that that action has really been the cause of the restoration of confidence makes me feel that it was at bottom a money panic. Not a money panic such as we have heretofore had, but an apprehension that, in view of enormous calls being made upon huge stock issues during the next few months the market might be so far drained of money that those who were obliged to pay the calls would have difficulty in arranging to get the necessary fund. The whole thing has been an interesting experience, although an extremely painful one and I shall be greatly relieved when matters finally drift—as they seem to be doing—into a state of dullness and cheaper money. . . . From all this long screed you may see that I am tired but hopeful, hopeful because of the simple fact that there is a tremendous productive capacity in this country, and that this productive capacity has not been one whit reduced by the colic we have all been having.*[24]

Almost as suddenly as it had begun, there was a sense that the mounting crisis had been stopped. The source of optimism was likely twofold: the swift and bold actions of the Treasury, thus giving much-needed liquidity to the capital markets, and the prospect of Americans buying £4 million in gold in London for shipment to New York. The *Commercial and Financial Chronicle* concluded that this "made a material change on Tuesday in the financial sentiment, the panicky tendency being arrested and a general advance in stock values taking place."[25] Within a few weeks, the disturbance in the markets seemed to have subsided.

Figure 3.1 shows that a steady decline in railroad equities from early January presaged the sharp decline in the industrial average. Railroads, the glamour stocks of the day, were off almost 15 percent before the sharp decline of the industrials began in early March.

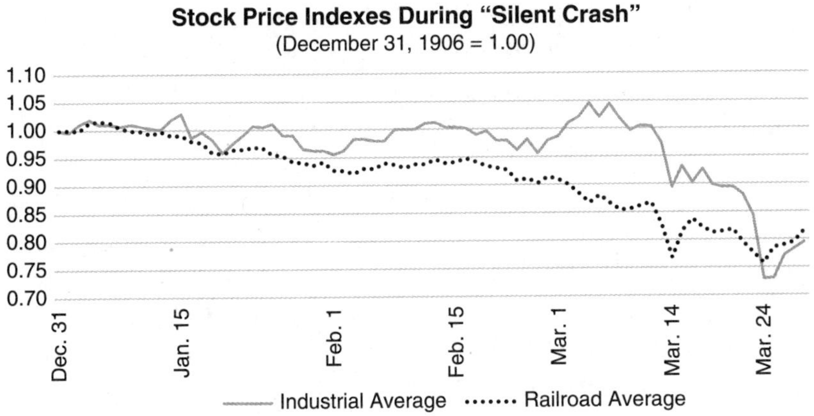

Stock Price Indexes During "Silent Crash"
(December 31, 1906 = 1.00)

1.10
1.05
1.00
0.95
0.90
0.85
0.80
0.75
0.70

Dec. 31 Jan. 15 Feb. 1 Feb. 15 Mar. 1 Mar. 14 Mar. 24

Industrial Average ······· Railroad Average

Figure 3.1 Stock Price Indexes January–March 1907
SOURCE: Authors' figure, based on hand-collected data from the *Wall Street Journal*, the *New York Times*, and the *Commercial and Financial Chronicle*.

Reflecting the financial anxieties caused by the March crash in equity prices, call money interest rates had spiked upward during this period, but they subsided when the surge of cash and gold into the New York money markets produced lower interest rates and a modest recovery in equity prices.* On April 13, the *Commercial and Financial Chronicle* observed, "The monetary situation has reversed its character for call money, from abnormally high to abnormally low rates—the relief in New York communicating a like tendency elsewhere. This change has opened the stock market here to more venturesome buying, and consequently speculative operators have again been in evidence."[26]

While an optimistic mood may have returned, robust buying behavior had not. The *Chronicle* noted an eerie slackening of trading and persistently low stock prices, which suggested an absence of investors from the exchange. During April and May, the index of all stocks fell 3 percent, with large declines in shipping (down 12 percent), household

* *Call money* consisted of loans from banks to brokers that had to be repaid upon demand and were secured by bonds or shares of stock. The interest rates on call loans were a leading barometer of money market conditions. The variability of those rates in March and July 1907 reflected tightening credit conditions and anxieties of investors.

goods (off 12 percent), machinery (off 10 percent), and copper (down 10 percent). On April 20, the *Chronicle* remained gloomy, saying, "no refuge from the old instability has been found. . . . A harsher and deeper economic irregularity is what the doctors have to deal with before real recovery will be under way."[27]

Business fundamentals also looked bleak. For the month of April, the value of claims in bankruptcy had grown 38 percent over the same month a year earlier, with the sharpest growth in the manufacturing sector.[28] On May 2, Teddy Grenfell in London queried Jack Morgan in a telegram about the stock market and when the banks in San Francisco might reopen.* Morgan replied, "Think further demand for gold is probable but impossible estimate amount. Stock market—believe decline largely speculative. Do not hear of any serious trouble any where though market vaguely apprehensive of difficulty arising largely from varied activities President USA."[29] For financiers and investors in 1907, the "varied activities President USA" were an overriding concern.

Roosevelt's Progressivism

Despite his patrician mien and pedigree, President Theodore Roosevelt was masterful at giving voice to the nation's popular will. By 1907, Americans had become increasingly disturbed by the tumultuous changes that had accompanied the country's impressive industrial growth. They were worried about the number and type of immigrants entering the country; the size, noise, and frenzy of the nation's large cities; the (in)effectiveness of their elected representatives; the consequences of old age, illness, and injury on the job; the day-to-day hazards of urban life; and even the quality of their food and water. Yet most of all they reacted with alarm to the rise of big business and

* The main reason San Francisco's banks remained closed for several weeks after the earthquake and fire was to allow time for the vaults to cool. The fire was so hot in the financial district that if banks had reopened their vaults immediately after the fire had ended, the residual heat would have caused paper inside the vaults to burst into flame. This need to wait stilted economic recovery and made the city dependent on outside cash to pay for labor needed for the city's intense rebuilding effort.

the corporate merger movement. Some Americans, calling themselves "progressives," argued vociferously for the right of a community to protect itself against those who pursued their economic self-interest without concern for the common good.[30] President Theodore Roosevelt became their most prominent advocate.

Progressives especially looked at J. P. Morgan and Wall Street with fear, some of it well founded. Since the Civil War, the history of corporate finance had been punctuated by instances of looting and self-dealing by financial promoters. It seemed that the very intimate engagement of financiers as both insiders and outside investors opened conflicts of interest against which the public could not guard. Moreover, many of the combinations these investors organized resulted in oligopolies and monopolies that sacrificed the welfare of consumers for the benefit of investors.

The sheer scale of the new corporate trusts also raised concerns about the possible abuse of economic power to achieve political ends. Standard Oil, for instance, had the market strength to extract rebates from railroads for shipping their products that were not given to its competitors, documented by Ida Tarbell in a series of magazine articles in 1902 and then a best-selling book in 1904. Other writers such as Upton Sinclair famously focused attention on unsanitary conditions in meatpacking in 1906. Ray Stannard Baker described perilous working conditions of coal miners in 1903, which was followed in 1907 by an investigation of Jim Crow living conditions for African Americans. In this context, the powerful and rather closed world of high corporation finance seemed very suspicious.

President Theodore Roosevelt personified this movement. He applied his executive power to challenge the influence of large corporations and to mediate between labor and capital. He was a pragmatist in a time of great political ferment, and he carefully navigated between opposing attitudes.

Most relevant for the events of 1907 were Roosevelt's attitudes and policies toward large corporations. On the one hand, he accepted industrialization and the large scale of firms that it brought.[31] He believed that large corporations were here to stay, and that the stance of government should not be to eradicate the large firms, but rather to identify and eliminate the types of combinations that were dangerous.* "I believe in corporations," Roosevelt said early in his presidency. "They are indispensable instruments of our modern civilization; but I believe that they should be so supervised and so regulated that they shall act for the interest of the community as a whole."[32]

To deal with the perceived ills of large corporations, Roosevelt also implemented a policy of regulation, mediation, and aggressive enforcement of the antitrust laws. In 1902, for example, Roosevelt initiated a series of important antitrust actions, beginning with a suit against the Northern Securities Company, a railroad trust organized by J. P. Morgan, James J. Hill, John D. Rockefeller, and E. H. Harriman in 1901 just five weeks after Roosevelt took office. Two years later, the Supreme Court ordered the company dissolved, yielding the first major enforcement action under the Sherman Antitrust Act of 1890. Roosevelt also filed suit against the unpopular "beef trust," an action that the Court upheld in 1905. When states began filing state antitrust suits against Standard Oil between 1904 and 1907, Roosevelt directed the Justice Department to assume leadership of the campaign against the oil monopoly.[33] By 1907, the Roosevelt administration had sued nearly 40 corporations under the Sherman Antitrust Act.

In that same spirit, Roosevelt revitalized the Interstate Commerce Commission, which had been created in 1887, by signing the Elkins Act of 1903 and the Hepburn Act of 1906, which gave the Commission the power to set maximum shipping rates for railroads. He also reenergized the presidency and asserted executive powers to protect particular social groups and supervise the economy in ways not seen since Reconstruction. In a Decoration Day speech (May 30, 1907) at Indianapolis, TR railed that the "predatory man of wealth" was the primary threat to private property in the United States:

> *One great problem that we have before us is to preserve the rights of property, and these can only be preserved if we remember that they are in less jeopardy from the*

* Just weeks after the Panic, Roosevelt said, "It is unfortunate that our present laws should forbid all combinations instead of sharply discriminating between those combinations which do good and those combinations which do evil . . . The antitrust law should not prohibit combinations that do no injustice to the public, still less those the existence of which is on the whole of benefit to the public." (Quoted from a public speech by Theodore Roosevelt, "Sherman Antitrust Law," dated December 3, 1907. Used with permission of Columbia University Rare Book and Manuscript library.)

Socialist and the Anarchist than from the predatory man of wealth. There can be no halt in the course we have deliberately elected to pursue, the policy of asserting the right of the nation, so far as it has the power, to supervise and control the business use of wealth, especially in the corporate form.[34]

Progressive activism was reflected at the state level as well; various states passed legislation sharply limiting the prices railroads could charge passengers. Business analysts believed these prices yielded revenues below the costs necessary to provide the services, thus inducing downward pressures on stock prices.[35] The *Chronicle* opined, "What is ailing the railroads and the stock market? . . . The underlying cause is the same as it was at the time of the collapse in March, the same, indeed, as it has been for about a year and a half, during all of which period a shrinkage in values has been in progress. Owing to the assaults of those high in authority and adverse legislation both by Congress and the State legislatures, confidence is almost completely gone. No one is willing to buy at what appear like ridiculously low prices because no one can tell what the future may bring forth."[36]

The judgment of some business leaders was that the break in stock prices in March 1907 had been sparked by investor fears arising from the Roosevelt administration's aggressive attitude toward railroads and industrial corporations. "For a year we have been foretelling this catastrophe, an assured result of the trials railroad property, railroad men and other large capitalists have been forced to suffer," the *Commercial and Financial Chronicle* said, commenting on a newly launched investigation of E. H. Harriman's Union Pacific railroad. "What has just taken place is not the final scene. Hereafter, if the irritant is continued, as we presume it will be, it will not be so exclusively securities and security-holders that will suffer; all sorts of industrial affairs are sure to get involved."[37] That irritant, of course, was the president of the United States.

President Roosevelt expressed surprise at the reaction of the financial community. In a letter to investment banker Jacob Schiff on March 25, Roosevelt wrote,

It is difficult for me to understand . . . why there should be this belief in Wall Street that I am a wild-eyed revolutionist. I cannot condone wrong, but I certainly do not intend to do aught save what is beneficial to the man of means who acts squarely and fairly. . . . I do not think it advantageous from any standpoint for me to ask any

> *railroad man to call upon me. I can only say to you, as I have said to Mr. Morgan when he suggested that he would like to have certain of them call upon me (a suggestion which they refused to adopt, by the way) that it would be a pleasure to me to see any of them at any time. Sooner or later, I think they will realize that in their opposition to me for the last few years they have been utterly mistaken, even from the standpoint of their own interests; and that nothing better for them could be devised than the laws I have striven and am striving to have enacted. I wish to do everything in my power to aid every honest businessman, and the dishonest businessman I wish to punish simply as I would punish the dishonest man of any type. Moreover, I am not desirous of avenging what has been done wrong in the past, especially when the punishment would be apt to fall upon innocent third parties; my prime object is to prevent injustice and work equity for the future.*[38]

Whether Roosevelt's complaints were mere posturing or accurate representations of the new industrial reality remained to be seen as the year 1907 unfolded.

Chapter 4

Credit Crunch

According to our belief, there is no other man in this country who could have done what he [J.P. Morgan] has done on this occasion.

—*Commercial and Financial Chronicle*, September 21, 1907

By mid-spring 1907, the annual financing cycle agriculture had resumed in earnest. While 1906 had yielded a bumper crop in the western United States, 1907 seemed less promising; a weak harvest would have a possible negative impact on exports from the United States and the subsequent ability of U.S. firms to find financing in Europe. Anxieties about the capital available in London soon surfaced among leading financiers. On May 2, Teddy Grenfell wrote to his partners at J. P. Morgan & Company in New York: "Can you give me any information as to further shipments of gold? We are getting short at Bank of England and may have to raise bank rate sharply. I am hoping [to] get [J. Pierpont Morgan] lunch at Bank of England tomorrow with the Governor. What is wrong with your market and is there any fear serious troubles?"[1]

What was wrong with the U.S. financial markets was the economy. A recession in output commenced in May 1907 that would not bottom out until June 1908.[2] On May 24, the *Commercial and Financial Chronicle* reported "violent declines" in selected stocks and that "security markets remain very unsettled."[3] By June, Jack Morgan was writing to his partners in London, saying, "All the world is still in the dumps here, and with it we have everything else that comes with the Summer-time, and transactions on the Stock Exchange become smaller and more nominal daily. A rest is just what is needed, however, and I think that the next change ought to be an improvement of business, since it could not be worse. But when the next change will come I cannot as yet see—nor what will start it."[4]

By the summer of 1907, the impact of the Bank of England's tight monetary policy was clear. The previous October, the BoE announced a policy of discriminating against American finance bills in the London financial markets. Finance bills were loans with which U.S. firms could buy and import gold.* The prohibition slashed the outstanding balance of finance bills in the London market from $400 million to $30 million by late in the summer of 1907. This meant that American debtors could not simply refinance their obligations in London. As a result, the flow of gold to America suddenly lurched into reverse as gold was remitted to London to settle the payment on finance bills. This further contracted U.S. gold reserves by nearly 10 percent between May and August of 1907 and contributed to a national liquidity drought.[5] Professor Sprague considered the BoE's discriminatory action "the most important financial factor in the panic of 1907."[6]

Despite relatively high U.S. interest rates, the United States *exported* $30 million in gold to London during the summer of 1907, according to economists Ellis Tallman and Jon Moen. "As a result," they wrote, "the New York money market was left with an uncharacteristically low vol-

* Economists Tallman and Moen (1990, p. 3) described finance bills as "Contracts to extend credit—essentially bonds issued to borrow overseas in hope of profit from anticipated exchange-rate fluctuations. The dollar's exchange rate varied over the year, strengthening during the harvest season when foreign demand for dollars to purchase crops was high and weakening thereafter. Finance bills were most frequently drawn in the summer, two or three months before crop movement, when the dollar price of sterling was quite high. . . . Banks and trust companies then sold sterling notes for dollars when sterling was stronger and repaid the notes when the dollar value of the sterling was lower, thus making a profit. Increased use of finance bills seems to have reduced the volatility of exchange rates and the volume of gold shipments overseas, enhancing the efficiency of the international exchange market. . . . Finance bills also provided a crude futures or forward market in foreign exchange."

ume of gold entering the fall season of cash tightness."[7] Meanwhile, the U.S. Treasury withdrew $30 million of deposits from national banks in order to redeem certain U.S. bonds maturing in July. While from a national funds-flow point of view the effect on liquidity would be nil, the reality was that the funds would have to come from the major money centers, since national banks in the agricultural regions held relatively low cash reserves owing to the need to finance crop movements during the harvest season.

Financial unrest continued to unfold. On June 28, New York City failed to place a $29 million bond offering, having received bids for only $2.1 million of the issue. Plainly, the 4 percent tax-exempt rate of interest offered on the bonds was inadequate, and a law prevented the city from offering a higher rate. By way of comparison, the *Chronicle* commented that "very good notes of railroads and other corporations can be bought at figures to net 6 and 7 percent."[8]

Worsening Credit Conditions

Jack Morgan bemoaned the worsening conditions, writing on July 19: "The money situation is now controlling everything, and there is not enough money around in this country, or in England, or on the Continent, at the moment, to finance a stock-market speculation if it arrived. As against this, people are saving money all the time and are making few new commitments, and also there seems to be a decrease in the money-hunger of the railroads, so that with care and conservatism we ought to be able to get through the Autumn stringency without any more panic."[9]

"The market keeps unstable," the *Chronicle* reported on July 27. "No sooner does the optimist settle into a half belief that things have passed the dangers that threatened the industrial situation, and a few stocks, encouraged by that belief, have begun in a half-scared, timid way to creep up on a comparison with last year's smaller earnings and fresh promises of higher dividends—no sooner are these signs of new life in evidence than something like a suggestion of a new outflow of gold to Paris sends a tremble all through the list, and the gain in values

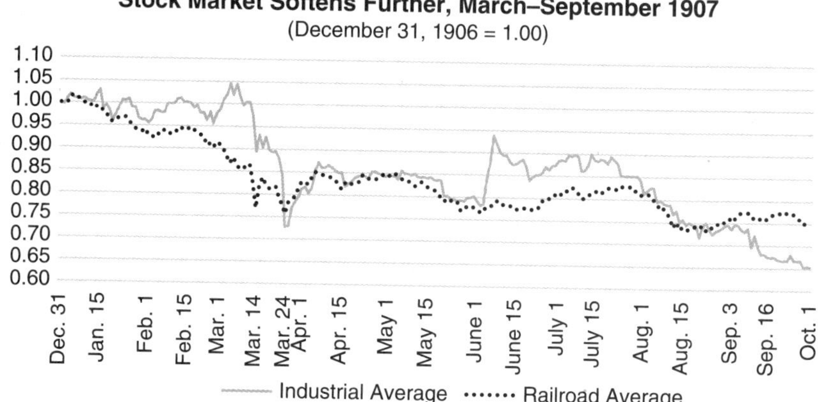

Figure 4.1 Stock Market Indexes, January–September, 1907
SOURCE: Authors' figure, based on hand-collected data from the *Wall Street Journal*, the *New York Times*, and the *Commercial and Financial Chronicle*.

and hope is gone."[10] Reflecting the deteriorating economic fundamentals, U.S. Steel Corporation reported on August 1 a 25 percent decline in its revenues compared to the same period a year earlier. This news coincided with reports of unsatisfactory conditions in the market for copper, despite recent price cuts, and a slackening demand for iron and steel.[11]

From June through September 1907, amid an atmosphere of capital stringency, the stock market's industrials index dropped another 11 percent, accumulating to a decline of 28.2 percent for the first three quarters of the year. Figure 4.1 shows that the downturn over the long summer did nearly as much investment damage as had occurred in March alone.

New Liquidity from the U.S. Treasury

As summer neared its end, the annual crop-moving period approached. This would strain the money supply even under normal conditions. Roosevelt's Treasury Secretary, George B. Cortelyou, announced a new plan to help the nation's money situation. Commencing immediately, the U.S. Treasury Secretary would make weekly deposits of government funds in national banks, "to such an amount as he deems sufficient" and "at such points in the country as he shall designate," in order to prevent an acute money stringency or even a possible panic.[12] Although the Secretary did not specify precisely *how much* funding would be forthcoming, this new approach to monetary policy was intended to provide federal relief to money markets proactively, rather than waiting until *after* a crisis was underway to intervene. It was also hoped that such small, weekly infusions during critical periods (such as harvest time) would help avoid the need for a major rescue effort. To implement this plan, the Treasury would rely on customs funds augmented by the Treasury balance. It would also be dependent on the work of a new bureau within the Treasury that would be charged with providing the secretary with up-to-date guidance on where and when monetary stringency was anticipated anywhere in the country.

Despite widespread approval of Cortelyou's plan, including an endorsement of the Treasury action by William B. Ridgely, Comptroller of the Currency, as "wise and timely," the mood of the market over these four months resembled that of the early spring.[13] The *Chronicle* reported that the stock market was "extremely variable," and that it seemed to have "very little recuperative force."[14] The French economist, Pierre Paul Leroy-Beaulieu, attributed the febrile stock market in August 1907 to America's disproportionate demand for new capital. "But," he said,

> *the world has not got it; therefore it cannot provide it. Add to this the effect of catastrophes such as the San Francisco and Valparaiso [August 17, 1906] earthquakes . . .and you will have a perfectly clear explanation of the existing crisis, rise in the interest rate and the fall of investment securities. The truth is, nations, quite as well as individuals, have reached the point where they must limit their undertakings to the possibilities of the case; that will be done, if not willingly, then by force of events.*[15]

Against this backdrop of remedial action, a sea change was nonetheless occurring in the posture of the federal government toward big business, which further heightened the sense of uncertainty. On August 3, 1907, Judge Kennesaw Mountain Landis fined Standard Oil Company of Indiana $29.24 million for violations of laws prohibiting secret rebates from railroads—the decision was remarkable not only for the relatively large size of the penalty (Standard Oil's book value of equity was only $1 million),[16] but also as a signal that the federal government would vigorously enforce new corporate regulations. Later that month, President Theodore Roosevelt charged that the wealthy caused the financial distress of the country for pursuit of their own self-interests:

> *It may well be that the determination of the Government, in which, gentlemen, it will not waver, to punish certain malefactors of great wealth, has been responsible for something of the troubles, at least to the extent of having caused these men to combine to bring about as much financial stress as they possibly can, in order to discredit the policy of the Government and thereby to secure a reversal of that policy, that they may enjoy the fruits of their own evil doing.*[17]

The editor of the *Commercial and Financial Chronicle* retorted, "It seems almost incredible that a person of superior intelligence like the President should seriously advance such an argument."[18] Ostensibly, Roosevelt was referring to the men of Standard Oil and other industrialists, but many observers assumed the president was also talking about J. Pierpont Morgan. The policy changes and escalating rhetoric seemed to many in the business community to represent a *regime shift,* a fundamental change in the stance of government against familiar commercial practices and institutions. The apparent shift created uncertainty and undermined business confidence.

In late summer 1907, President Roosevelt received a steady stream of letters and visitors warning that his rhetoric and actions were weakening the economy. In a letter to Henry Lee Higginson, a Boston banker, on August 12, 1907, Roosevelt wrote,

> *the same trouble we have now effects [sic] the bourse in Paris and Berlin and the London stock market. British consols are lower than ever before; so are British*

and Canadian railroad securities. It is very difficult for me to believe that this is due to distrust of my policies, reasonable or unreasonable. In other words, I do not believe that what I have done has had any appreciable effect in bringing about the severity of the present situation. That it has had some effect I think very possible. The most-needed surgical operation invariably means a temporary period of weakness for the patient greater than would have been the weakness during the same period if the operation had not taken place. That some trouble in Wall Street would have occurred anyhow as the result of my actions I think likely, but the present trouble is world-wide. I think it is more due to the San Francisco earthquake, to the Russo-Japanese war, to other conditions which I do not understand but which act thruout [sic] the world, than to any kind of action on my part.[19]

New York City's Renewed Difficulties

In late August 1907, New York City once again attempted to reenter the bond market. New York's municipal government was, the *Chronicle* reported, "face to face with impending disaster." Overdue debts were pressing for payment; existing contracts for municipal improvements in progress added to the debt load; and there was the concern that if the city could not secure the requisite financing, it would be forced to impose layoffs. It would have seemed that the city had nowhere to turn, given the strained conditions in the markets in the summer of 1907.

In financial circles, however, rumors circulated that this time the city had a savior, and the *Chronicle* captured the essence of the insinuations:

A person commanding large capital in Europe and America, whose name suggests success in such matters, and who has often been sought as especially capable for wisely handling threatened financial dislocation, has been named as being at the head of an important subscription for the [New York City] bonds. The rumor, however, is without authoritative confirmation, though it is quite generally believed. Yet whether true or not, the gods have clearly declared that the loan is to be a pronounced success; that Europe is to have a large share in it, and the public has full faith in that outcome.[20]

Unable to wait any longer and yet perceiving the strained conditions in the market, the city had directly approached J. Pierpont Morgan for assistance in underwriting an issue of $40 million in tax-exempt bonds priced to yield 4.5 percent.

The rumors of the deal hit Morgan's partners in London quickly; they wrote to Jack: "Is there any truth in the statement that JPM&Co. are going take $40,000,000 New York City 4½ percent bonds? If so, [we] think [we] could place [a] considerable amount here if terms [are] favorable."[21] Jack replied that bids for the issue were due on September 10 and that the company would be unable to fill orders before then. To assist the placement of the New York City bonds, the U.S. Treasury committed to placing $40 to $50 million in gold on deposit with banks. In addition, to take some of the pressure off the U.S. capital markets, Morgan proposed placing the New York City bonds in Europe.

In the final event, 960 bidders subscribed fully for the issue; the offering was a complete success. Morgan's role in the financing came to light and was reported by the *Chronicle*:

> *According to our belief, there is no other man in this country who could have done what he has done on this occasion. He did not want the bonds and only acted as an intermediary. His name, his judgment in financial centres of Europe and his knowledge of the financial markets give him an influence among the capitalists of the world unequaled, probably, by any other individual. Mayor McClellan voices the sentiment of the best circles in this country when he said: "I take this opportunity of thanking you on behalf of the city for the great public spirit you have shown." He saved the city's credit.*[22]

The concern of the financial community next turned to deteriorating conditions in the natural resources sector, particularly copper mining. The volume of transactions in raw copper had declined precipitously, as had the price: from 24 cents per pound in January to almost 15 cents per pound at the end of September.[23] The effect on stock prices of copper mining companies was significant: An index of share prices of these companies fell 41 percent over the first three quarters of 1907. Investors grew concerned that the worsening conditions threatened the ability of copper producers to continue paying dividends.[24]

New York City Street Railways Raise Alarms

Compounding the growing anxieties was the revelation of the financial distress of the "Inter-Met" street railways companies.* Financial statements revealed that on a consolidated basis, the company had been generating a cash deficit since 1903, calling into question the sustainability of its dividends.[25] Deteriorating financial conditions and operating performance triggered default on some $21 million in liabilities, forcing the firm into bankruptcy on September 24, 1907.[26] Although the firm was only local in scope, its failure coming on the heels of New York City's financing difficulties rattled investors. Professor Sprague noted that the bankruptcy of the New York street railways was the most important event that "served to weaken confidence" among investors.[27]

International Disturbances

As if conditions in the United States were not enough to animate the anxieties of American investors, worrisome situations abroad did also. Egypt suffered a credit crunch that peaked during the summer of 1907. This was related to Indian banks that borrowed gold in Alexandria and to the insufficiency of gold to finance the movement of large cotton crops. On June 22, a major local bank in Alexandria suspended convertibility of deposits into currency, having been drawn into "dangerous finance by the excitement accompanying the extraordinary prosperity of Egypt."[28] The Bank of England responded by shipping gold to Egypt in June, July, and August.[29] The situation there remained tense. In August, the Bank of England raised Bank Rate from 4 percent to 4.5 percent to stem further depletion of gold reserves. In an article titled "Severe Depression," the *Times of London* reported on August 9 that:

* From 1832, operators of numerous horse-drawn street railway companies had proliferated across Manhattan, Brooklyn, and the Bronx. Starting in the 1880s, consolidators of these smaller firms sought to create large operators through a series of mergers and acquisitions, many of which were heavily financed by debt. This process culminated in the merger of two large firms, the Interborough and Metropolitan, into the Interborough-Metropolitan Company in January 1906.

a further sharp drop in Consols jarred the already overstrained nerves of operators. With these fresh causes of depression to face, markets were left almost wholly without public support, business being reduced to the narrowest limits . . . The dealers, naturally, had no desire to become investors for the time being, and consequently there was scarcely a buyer to be found and prices tumbled rapidly in all departments, much more rapidly than the actual amount of stock offered seemed to justify.[30]

Italy felt tremors of instability as Societa Bancaria Italiana (SBI), one of the largest banks, experienced depositor runs in September 1907. During a period of rapid growth in the Italian economy, SBI had grown quickly through absorption of other banks. Some of the acquired banks were in poor financial condition. And some of the new shareholders undertook to use the bank for private benefits—this was particularly true of a group of Genoese business leaders, who had gained a controlling interest in SBI. Their loans were used to finance private business interests and speculations in the stock market. As economic conditions worsened and security prices fell over the summer of 1907, depositors questioned the credit quality of those loans and began to run. (In early October, the Bank of Italy organized a rescue financing, takeover, and housecleaning of management to avoid a contagion of runs to other banks.[31])

Japan also experienced deflationary pressures. Following its successful prosecution of the Russo-Japanese War in September 1905, Japan's economy had boomed, accompanied by a bubble of new company formations. A *Frankfurter Zeitung* correspondent in Tokyo reported:

This excessive activity in establishing new companies was accompanied by a wave of enormous speculation, all classes of the people, even down to the poorest, having been engaged in buying stocks upon margin. Instead of the hoped-for advance in prices, however, a sharp fall recently occurred, and the feeling of distrust among the people became so marked that runs on various banks occurred. Some thirteen banks were forced to suspend payment, either temporarily or permanently. . . . The depression has already been so severely felt that not less than 175 new companies went into liquidation in April and May.[32]

A Stressful Year to Date

Thus, on the threshold of the momentous month of October 1907, the year to date had been an economic shambles. The ambitious recapitalization of American railroads led by Edward Harriman had collapsed ignominiously in March. An economic recession had commenced in May. In August, strong rhetoric by the U.S. president had alarmed investors and business leaders, as had Judge Landis's verdict against Standard Oil of Indiana. New York City had refinanced its debt obligations only with great difficulty. And the city's street railways fell into receivership. Financial instability in Egypt, Italy, and Japan affirmed that credit strains were global and not merely local. By September 30, equities were worth a third less than at the start of the year.

As in years before, the crop-moving season imposed its peak demand on financial institutions. Most important, both Wall Street and Main Street felt desperate for liquidity. Interest rates had gyrated upward, reflecting the growing illiquidity of currency and gold in the financial markets. Economists Odell and Weidenmier noted that "The New York money market entered the fall of 1907 low on gold reserves and vulnerable to shocks that might otherwise have been temporary in nature."[33] The liquidity strain in the United States was felt elsewhere in the world as well. Financial institutions in Amsterdam and Hamburg were on the verge of collapse, triggering the sales of U.S. securities. All these developments sketched the state of the U.S. financial sector: shaken, weakened, and apprehensive. Optimists hoped that conditions would improve in October. However, hope is not a strategy.

Chapter 5

Copper King

There is little doubt that this week's episode in United Copper shares on the New York curb will go into Stock Exchange history as one of the most absurd pieces of speculative jugglery ever attempted.

—*Wall Street Journal*, October 19, 1907

Capital market conditions in the fall of 1907 presaged a financial storm. Volatile and falling asset prices, battered financial markets, interest rate gyrations, illiquidity, investigations, litigation, and the regulations and pronouncements of an activist U.S. president were certainly enough to strain investor confidence and vex the fortitude of owners and managers. Yet even though there had been a "silent crash" of the stock market in March, the onset of a recession in May, a credit crunch that prompted distressed financings of New York City, the bankruptcy of the New York street railways, and financial panics in Egypt, Japan, and Italy, the U.S. markets and institutions had so far in 1907 proved stable in the face of bad news.

But at the confluence of a system of thousands of small banks, weak and decentralized bank regulations, financial manipulations by bank managers and directors, and pyramid-like interdependence among banks, there appeared an individual whose actions would inadvertently expose the weaknesses of the financial system. A Brooklyn-born copper mining magnate with the audacity to challenge the most powerful financial interests in the world would provide the spark for a panic. This man's "speculative jugglery" in the fall of 1907 provided the impetus for events to come, and that story begins amid the slopes of central Montana.

Frederick Augustus Heinze

He was adventurous and sociable, stood 5 feet 10 inches tall and weighed some 200 pounds. Described as having "the torso of a Yale halfback, muscles of steel, and a face of ivory whiteness, lighted up with a pair of large blue eyes," Frederick Augustus Heinze was "a fine musician, a brilliant linguist, and, when necessary, could box like a professional."[1] Widely considered a buccaneer, who sought fortune and fame in the copper mines of Montana, Heinze earned grudging respect for his tenacity and cleverness. "Heinze was shrewd and unscrupulous," a contemporary said. "He was considered to be tough in the days when a man to be considered tough had to earn the reputation."[2]

Educated in Germany and at the Columbia School of Mines in New York City, the 20-year-old Heinze moved to Butte, Montana, in 1889 to make his fortune on the "richest hill on earth."[3] With the widespread applications for electric illumination, the copper mineral held the promise of vast riches. In Butte, Heinze lived alone in a small log cabin, and for two years worked for five dollars a day as a mining engineer for the Boston & Montana Consolidated Copper and Silver Mining Company. In 1891, Heinze conceived the idea for a custom smelting operation to treat the ores of small, independent mining concerns. Around that time, Heinze raised about $300,000 in capital in New York and established the Montana Ore Purchasing Company (MOPC).[4]

Drawing upon his formal training, Heinze successfully pioneered advanced methods of mining and smelting. Ultimately, however, he found a more clever way to make money in Butte.[5] After establishing MOPC, Heinze bought mines adjacent to rich copper properties owned by other companies. Once he discovered that their veins of ore surfaced on his property, he threatened litigation under the state's controversial "apex" law. Under this law, a mine's owner was entitled to follow any vein that surfaced ("apexed") on his property, even if it reached beneath neighboring properties. The mine owner could then seek an injunction to prevent his neighbors from continuing to mine any veins that apexed on his land, and he could sue for damages if they failed to comply. Thus, Heinze, employing as many as 37 lawyers, tied up other mining companies with injunctions and lawsuits; at one point, there were 133 suits pending between Heinze and his opponents.[6]

Heinze v. Rockefeller

Heinze's chief opponent during these years was John D. Rockefeller's Standard Oil Company, one of the largest business enterprises in the world. Henry H. Rogers and other principals of Standard Oil saw the promise of consolidating copper mining interests in the West and had formed the Amalgamated Copper Company in 1898 with a capitalization of $75 million.[7] As it happened, many of the properties Amalgamated purchased were those against which Heinze had already been litigating heavily under the apex theory. Not only did Heinze refuse to join the Amalgamated combination, but he also continued to fight against Standard Oil group in the courts.[8] Refusing to be bowed by an upstart, Amalgamated brought counterclaims against Heinze amounting to $32.5 million.[9] H. H. Rogers himself vowed to destroy Heinze, saying, "The flag has never been lowered at 26 Broadway [Standard Oil's headquarters], and I'll drive Heinze out of Montana if it takes ten millions [sic] to do it."[10] It did take millions. In February 1906, after years of litigation and nuisance, Amalgamated Copper bought Heinze out, purchasing most of his active copper interests for $12 million.[11]

Heinze Enters Banking—with the "Ice King"

Flush with cash from Amalgamated and bravado for having bested Standard Oil, the 37-year-old Heinze turned his attentions to Wall Street. Upon moving back to his native New York, Heinze's decision to enter banking was heavily influenced by his association with one of New York's most colorful and notorious Wall Street figures, Charles W. Morse, "a small, compact, portly man, of dark gray suit and neat appearance,"[12] who controlled the National Bank of North America and the New Amsterdam National Bank, and was a large stockholder in the Mercantile National as well.[13] Variously known as the "Ice King" and the "Steamship King," Morse had long been a conspicuous figure in the financial world, first through the promotion of his American Ice Company and then with his purchase and consolidation of coastal steamship lines.[14] Morse's steamship monopoly along the New England coast competed directly for freight and passenger traffic with the New York, New Haven, and Hartford Railroad, a close client of J.P. Morgan's. Because of this competition, there was no love lost between Morgan and Morse, a detail upon which later conspiracy theories about the Panic of 1907 would hang.

Morse, who once said, "Banks mean credit, and credit means power,"[15] proposed to accrue power by gaining control of a network of banks. Given the widespread prohibitions against the establishment of branches at the time, Morse pursued a strategy that was followed by many others in the industry, called "chain-banking." Morse proposed a partnership with Augustus Heinze, under which the Heinze-Morse group* would buy a controlling interest in one bank and then use shares in that bank's equity as collateral to borrow money for purchasing shares in other financial institutions. Such a technique would be repeated until Morse and his associates had created a chain of controlling positions in banks[16]—as is true of all such schemes, failure of one link in the chain tends to threaten the viability of the entire chain.

F. Augustus Heinze had had only a few, small banking interests in Montana previously, but Morse's scheme held the promise of great wealth and the opportunity for becoming a major player in New York's financial circles. Morse was familiar to Augustus's brother Arthur, with whom Morse had formed a pool in 1904 to manipulate the share price in United Copper Company stock—toward that end, Arthur had exchanged 30,000 shares in United Copper to Morse in return for shares in Morse's Knickerbocker Ice Company. The stock pool in United

* For brevity, we refer throughout this narrative to "Heinze–Morse group," which the reader might assume consisted of only two figures. As described later, Augustus Heinze was assisted by two brothers, Otto and Arthur. Also, Charles Morse drew into his financial dealings Charles Barney, president of the Knickerbocker Trust Company, and E. R. Thomas with his brother O. F. Thomas, about whom less is known. Even more affiliates may have participated in Morse's dealings.

Copper and those 30,000 shares would later play a fateful role in the Panic of 1907.

Through Morse's influence, Heinze used a portion of his buyout money from Amalgamated to purchase a controlling interest in the Mercantile National Bank in New York, becoming its president in February 1907,[17] and financed the rest with a note to the seller for $630,000. Heinze would be a front for Charles Morse, who did not want his interest in the Mercantile to be public knowledge, but who pledged to pay Heinze $500,000 for his share of the stock purchase before the end of 1907.

Thereafter, Heinze joined Morse as an interested party in other financial institutions. Heinze, who still had several properties in Nevada, California, Mexico, and elsewhere, consolidated his remaining mining interests within a holding company he had previously incorporated in 1902 for tax reasons, called United Copper Company.[18] Heinze and his two brothers, Otto and Arthur, were each major stockholders and directors of this firm.

Heinze also established a direct presence on Wall Street by purchasing a $96,000 seat on the New York Stock Exchange for his brothers, creating the brokerage house of Otto C. Heinze & Company.[19] In fact, that firm occupied offices directly across the hall from the United Copper Company at 42 Broadway—both firms used the same entrance and even split the cost of the rent.[20] During the summer and early fall of 1907, as money rates tightened and as equity prices fell broadly, the brothers became concerned about their holdings in United Copper, whose stock had been used to secure their investments in some banking concerns. To support the price of their United Copper Company shares, Augustus's brother Arthur began purchasing large quantities of the company's stock and financing them on margin with as many as 20 brokerage houses on Wall Street. A dangerous game was afoot.

The Twilight of a Resource-Based Boom

Heinze's financial ascent may be ascribed to his intelligence and cunning—but he was also lucky. Historian Mary A. O'Sullivan described the buoyant years at the start of the twentieth century as a "resource based boom . . . [due to] copper stocks . . . mining and smelting of other ores, such as lead and silver, benefiting from the worldwide commodity boom."[21]

Figure 5.1 shows that much of the increase in value in three industrial indexes occurred in the two years before 1907, consistent with discussion in earlier chapters. What is notable is the dramatic rise in share values from the trough year of 1903 to the end of 1906. The industrials index gained 74 percent over that period. In comparison, an index of copper and brass producers gained 208 percent, and the mining and smelting index gained 218 percent. Commodities are cyclical businesses, and metals are especially so.

Heinze arrived in New York from the Montana copper fields in the spring of 1906, shortly after his sale to Amalgamated in February. Figure 5.1 suggests that he left the copper industry during a market boom, near a high point in the cycle. Beginning in December 1906, stock prices began to fall.

After selling out to Amalgamated and moving to New York, Heinze may have felt that he was leaving troubles behind and starting anew. But the "Standard Oil crowd" resented Heinze's successful legal wrangling and did not forget slights. A former executive at Amalgamated, Thomas

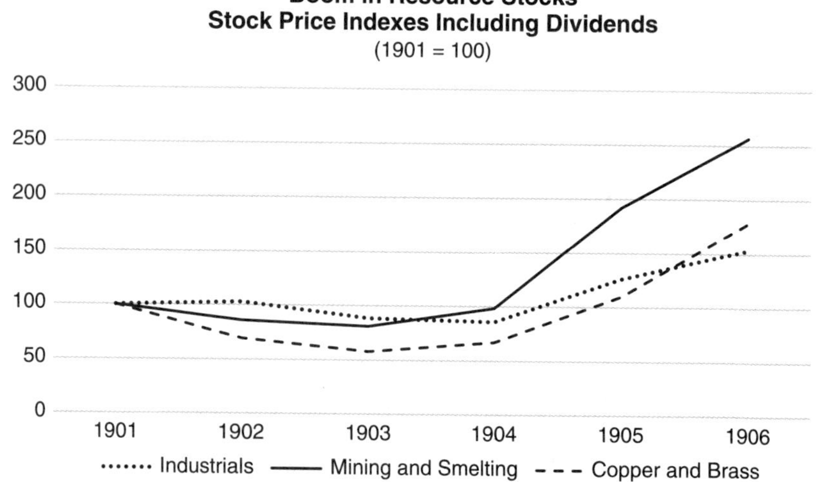

Figure 5.1 Share Price Indexes for Three Industrial Sectors
SOURCE: Authors' figure, based on data in O'Sullivan (2016), p. 192.

William Lawson, published an expose of the Amalgamated group in 1906 that characterized them in damning terms—"jugglers," "flagrant," "ruthlessly plundered," and so on—that summoned up the "crime of Amalgamated."[22] A century later the book strikes the reader as overwrought revenge literature; but even if only partly true, it still suggests dangerous enemies to have. Moreover, H. H. Rogers, Rockefeller, and others had reputations as tough—and victorious—businessmen who wanted to discourage interlopers from challenging them. Historian Robert Sobel concluded, "H. H. Rodgers and the Standard Oil crowd had not forgotten their vow to destroy Heinze."[23]

Chapter 6

The Corner and the Squeeze

Never has there been such wild scenes on the Curb, so say the oldest veterans of the outside market.

—*Wall Street Journal*, October 17, 1907

In early October 1907, Arthur Heinze, who was monitoring the activity in the Heinze-Morse stock pool, conducted a precise audit of all United Copper Company shares.[1] To his great surprise, he discovered what appeared to be an oversold position of 100,000 United Copper shares in excess of the 450,000 shares issued and outstanding.[2] In other words, it appeared that a massive short interest in United Copper of 22 percent had emerged. Otto and Arthur surmised that this was only possible if certain securities brokers were secretly loaning out their shares of United Copper to traders who wanted to speculate in the stock. Those traders, Otto believed, were then selling the borrowed shares at prevailing prices in the expectation that the prices of those shares would fall. If United Copper prices did fall, then when the traders were called upon to return the borrowed shares, they could repurchase them at lower prices and pocket the difference.*

The Squeeze

Otto Heinze believed, however, that he and his brothers owned most of the United Copper shares, many of which they had pledged as collateral for margin loans from brokers. Otto suspected that the brokers in turn had secretly loaned the shares to the short sellers. If the Heinzes "called in" those loaned shares, then the "shorts" would be squeezed. The squeeze would force the short sellers to scramble to find United Copper on the market; finding none available, the shorts would have to settle directly with the Heinzes. To execute this move, the Heinzes would need to purchase shares of United Copper for sale on the market to drive up the stock price and to blockade the short sellers from being able to cover their positions. Once the Heinzes had achieved the necessary "corner" in United Copper, they would repay their margin loans, issue the call for the delivery of all the shares they owned, and initiate the squeeze.[3]

Rising Pressure on the Heinzes

Excited by the prospect of the squeeze, Otto Heinze approached his brother, Augustus, on Thursday October 10, for help (his other brother, Arthur P. Heinze, was traveling in Europe). Augustus was aware that over the past several months, in an ongoing effort to support United Copper's price, the two brothers had been buying the company's shares through brokerage houses in New York, Philadelphia, and Boston. They had paid for most of these purchases by borrowing money from brokers, in a method called buying *on margin*. As such, the securities they purchased served as collateral for loans and the certificates remained in the brokers' possession. Otto concluded that their brokers had lent those same

* Such a trading maneuver, known as a *short sale,* appears often when a security or market is overpriced. A short interest ratio greater than 10 percent is very high.

shares to short sellers and that the company was the target of concerted short-selling.[4] By the fall of 1907, the Heinzes had become indebted to their brokers for $2 million for these margin purchases. As the market at large (and the share price of United Copper) had weakened, the brokers increasingly called for more collateral from the Heinzes.[5] If the Heinzes initiated the squeeze, the brokers from whom the Heinzes had borrowed on margin would have to be paid the full amount for the cost of these shares immediately.[6]

Otto believed that to carry out the scheme he would need to borrow at least $1.5 million (he would make up the remaining difference for his margin debts from squeezing the shorts). However, when he approached his brother on October 10, Augustus denied Otto's request, saying that he lacked the money and could not jeopardize his position as president of the Mercantile National Bank. Over the past four months, Augustus revealed, there had been a "silent run"† on his bank and depositors had quietly withdrawn $4 million. Augustus had already called in some of Mercantile's outstanding loans and would not make any substantial advances to his brother.[7]

Yet, in an apparent effort to facilitate the maneuver, Augustus arranged a meeting for himself and Otto with Charles W. Morse and Charles T. Barney. Barney was the president of the Knickerbocker Trust Company, the second-largest trust company by deposits in the city, and had been involved in various Morse schemes. They met at Barney's Fifth Avenue home on Sunday October 13, where Morse told the Heinzes that they were *wrong*. The squeeze would require far more than $1.5 million—perhaps as much as $3 million.[8] All three men rebuffed Otto. Meanwhile, as the price of United Copper shares fell, the margin calls from brokers accelerated, and Otto feared the cash reserves of his own firm would be wiped out.

The stock of United Copper Company was not listed on the New York Stock Exchange. Rather, it was traded among a crowd of brokers literally dealing "on the curb" outside the Exchange building

† Heinze's choice of words is interesting. Then and now, sophisticated and well-informed depositors monitor the condition of banks very carefully; they will be the first to withdraw funds from a bank because they gain the insight about deteriorating conditions first. The less-informed depositors will follow, perhaps having observed the actions of the well-informed depositors. The "silent" actions of the well-informed speaks volumes.

on Broad Street in Manhattan. On Saturday morning, October 12, during a short day of trading on the Curb, United Copper shares opened at $45^1/_2$. During the day's two hours of trading, it sold down to $37^3/_4$, and it appeared to the Heinzes that again the shorts were active in the stock.[9]

Executing the Squeeze

Convinced the time was right, Otto Heinze had determined to engineer the corner and the resultant squeeze by himself. On Sunday night, October 13, he called a meeting with Philip Kleeberg, a partner in the stock exchange firm of Gross & Kleeberg, and issued two instructions. First, Otto ordered the broker to purchase 6,000 shares of United Copper stock at ascending prices on Monday, to create a commanding corner. Second, he would repay the margin loans and issue a call for all the Heinze-owned United Copper shares to be delivered.

On Monday morning, October 14, the stock of United Copper opened quietly, with a few sales at $39^7/_8$, and then one at 39. Observers reported that within a few minutes of the opening a broker representing a well-known stock exchange house entered the crowd excitedly and began bidding up the stock and asking for offers on 5,000 shares. Within 15 minutes the price rose in rapid increments: 100 shares at 40, 100 at 41, 100 at $49^7/_8$, 1,000 at 51, 100 at 52, 100 at 53, 700 at 57, 1,000 at 59, 1,000 at 60.[10] By 10:50 a.m. the first advance was over, the stock having risen nearly $23 above the previous day's close. Four thousand shares had been traded in.[11]

"Traders noticed that there was very little anxiety on the part of those in the United Copper group to take real stock at the higher prices," the *New York Times* reported. "The bid and asked quotations were kept 2 or 3 points apart, and those who had stock to sell found that to get it off their hands they had to throw it out at the bid price or find the bidders dropping from the market. These circumstances, together with the fact that United Copper had been almost impossible to borrow, and therefore avoided by short sellers, were taken by curb traders as indicating deliberate bidding up of the stock rather than a squeeze of shorts."[12] After the initial flurry on Monday morning, "which occurred so rapidly that the brokers were not able to get in touch with their clients," the stock dropped almost immediately and remained between 50 and 53 for the balance of the day's session, closing at $52^{7}/_{8}$. The total shares traded for the day was 18,200, and the highest bid quoted was \$$62^{7}/_{8}$.[13]

Meanwhile, thousands of stock certificates were arriving at the offices of Otto Heinze & Company for which payment of $630,000 was due.[14] By the rules of the Exchange, the Heinzes were obliged to pay for these shares in cash by 2:15 p.m. that day.[15] Otto returned to Charles Morse, chairman of the board of Mercantile National Bank, on October 14 to plead again for a loan. This time Morse, as Otto later explained to the *New York Times*, "told me to get the money at the Mercantile Bank . . . and I took that as meaning that I was to make my note to the Mercantile and deposit the [incoming short-sold] securities there."[16]

Otto appealed once again to his brother, Augustus, for a loan to cover the cost of the incoming securities. The Heinzes calculated that since United Copper was trading around $60, to secure the loan they would need only about one-third the value of the securities, which would serve as collateral, to repay the brokers that day. This time Augustus consented, and he arranged for a loan from his Mercantile National Bank to cover any of the checks written against the Otto Heinze & Company's account.[17] Augustus had personally guaranteed the loan.

Squeeze and Delivery of Shares

On Tuesday, October 15, Otto Heinze put in motion the final phase of his plan, which the *Chicago Daily Tribune* captured, as follows:

> *Twenty stock exchange houses were carrying United Copper stock at the direction of the managers of the corner. It was decided to serve notices on these to deliver their stock at the earliest possible time, which was 2 o'clock Tuesday afternoon, and, it was said, it was undoubtedly the belief of the managers of the corner that they would find many of these houses bare of stock, and expected the brokers to default, in part, in their deliveries. In this event the Heinze brokers could buy in the stock under*

the rules and force the delinquents to pay the difference between the purchase price and the price at which the stock was carried for the Heinze brokers on the particular firms' books.[18]

United Copper opened Tuesday morning at 50, and trading in the stock remained mostly subdued during the morning session with only a few hundred shares traded in.[19] Responding to the call issued by Heinze, however, and much to his surprise, every one of the 20 brokers produced the stock that had been called.[20] There were no defaults, and United Copper stock was plentiful on the market. *Heinze had been wrong*. In fact, the brokers were producing so much stock that Heinze was eventually forced to refuse delivery.

On this news, the stock price briefly rose to 59 in heavy trading, then broke. "Thousands of shares began to appear as fast as the mails could carry them from points where news of Monday's rise had penetrated," the *New York Times* reported. "Gross & Kleeberg were unable to stem the flood and the market went to pieces."[21] The brokers, unable to transfer their shares to the Heinzes, had thrown all their shares on the market, and the corner attempt was crushed. Without any warning, the stock broke amid wild scenes. In a few minutes the price crumpled to 50, then to 45, and still to 36, which was the last sale of the day. At the market close the stock was offered at 38 with no bid, and one man rushed into the crowd to make a nominal bid of 25.[22]

The late-day slide in United Copper was stunning. "It is a long time since the Curb has seen anything of the like," the *Wall Street Journal* reported. "In fact, old-timers on the Curb say that they have never seen anything quite like it before."[23] The slide, however, was far from over. After closing at 36 on Tuesday, United Copper opened Wednesday morning with a sale at 30. Scarcely had this sale been recorded on the reporters' books when the stock was offered down to 20 within three minutes of the opening gong. On the way down, a block of 500 shares was traded in, and for a while there was a lull and the stock hovered around 25. This calm lasted about an hour when it started down again. Then came a sale at 18. During the last hour came the grand finale, "with the crowd of brokers rushing up and down the Street shouting and fighting," as the common stock of United Copper Company crashed down to $10 a share.[24] At one point, there were as many as five different simultaneous quotations. The arbitrage business in the stock was practically at a standstill. "Never has there been such wild scenes on the Curb, so say the oldest veterans of the outside market," the *Journal* reported.[25]

"Rumors of all kinds were flying round the Curb," the *New York Times* said. "Brokers demanded Stock Exchange names of their best friends and the houses had to be of the best. Traders took a hand, but after one or two had taken quick, but huge, losses they eschewed the United crowd, seeing that it was not the place for even a moderately big trader."[26] With apparently unlimited supplies of the stock at hand and no shorts in sight, the common stock price had declined 50 points in three days; the price of United Copper's preferred had also declined 50 points over two days. The last sale for the common on Wednesday was recorded at 15 (see Figure 6.1). Dealings on the day for the common amounted to 6,800 shares.[27] After the market closed, bankers held conferences across Wall Street and throughout the city trying to assess the fallout.[28]

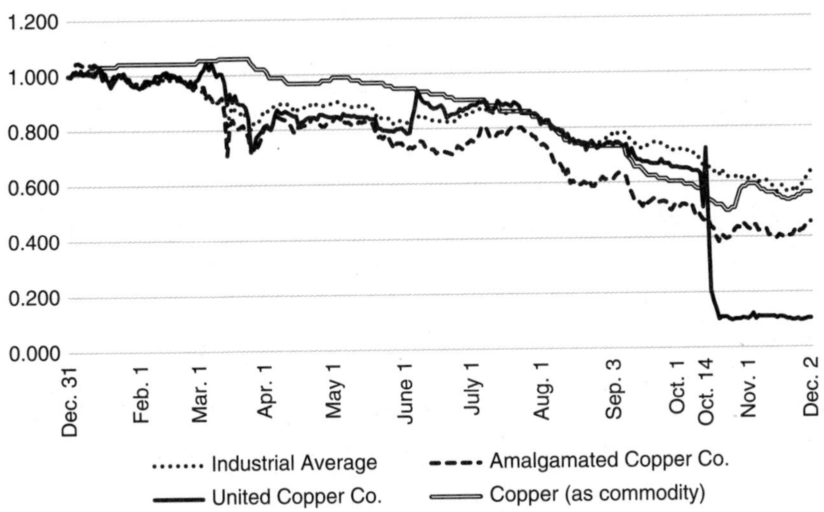

Figure 6.1 United Copper Company Share Price Trend, Compared to Copper Price, Shares of Amalgamated Copper, and an Average of Industrial Shares, Indexed to 1.00 at December 31, 1906

Source: Authors' figure, based on daily quotations in the *Wall Street Journal* and the *Commercial and Financial Chronicle,* 1907.

Why the Squeeze Failed

The slump in share price on October 14–15 is generally attributed to the inflow of shares from the market. However, Mary Tone Rodgers and James E. Payne[29] cite a source claiming that none other than Charles Morse, partner of Augustus Heinze, had dumped 30,000 shares on the market—perhaps the same 30,000 shares that Arthur Heinze had loaned Morse in 1904. If so, this was a stunning betrayal of a business partner.

However, Morse's selling alone would not have been sufficient to ruin the attempted corner on United Copper. Historian Robert Sobel argued that the corner attempt failed because of the incompetence of the brokers to coordinate their calls for delivery of shares. He also noted that some newspapers published articles "containing hints of wrongdoing" that had been planted by Heinze's enemies at Standard Oil and that Rockefeller-affiliated banks called in loans to Heinze and insisted on the sale of United Copper to meet the obligations.[30]

A final reason for failure of the attempted corner would be the inexorable pressures against copper prices, the worsening economic conditions, and the credit crunch. A recession began in May 1907.[31] The revenues of firms in the metals mining and refining sector are highly sensitive to changes in the cycle of the economy. Rodgers and Payne (2017) found that "a copper commodity price channel may have been active in transmitting the [Bank of England's restrictive monetary] policy to the New York markets."[32] If so, the Heinzes were betting against the Bank of England, with strong odds that they would lose. The Heinzes should have expected that with the onset of a recession the prices of copper companies would weaken. The evidence of a contraction was widely available and discussed in the business press of the day. In the face of worsening news about the industry, this seemed to be a poor moment to try to pump up the stock price. Investors were glad to sell when share prices suddenly rose; and they reverted to panicked selling as United Copper's share price suddenly slumped.

Figure 6.1 suggests the gravity of Otto Heinze's errors. Clearly, until June, shares in United Copper did not trade much differently from those of two benchmarks: (a) Amalgamated Copper, a close industry peer, and (b) an average of industrial stocks. The dominant insight is the downward trend in United Copper and its benchmarks from the beginning of the year onward. The slump in share prices for both firms in March was consistent with the "silent crash" described in Chapter 3.

From March to June, both United Copper and Amalgamated shares traded below the price trend of commodity copper. Amalgamated was withholding copper from the market in an effort to prop up its price, but as the figure showed, the effort failed. Meanwhile, the decline in prices and volumes for both companies took a toll.

That spring, Heinze began actively to manipulate United Copper's share price upward, financed by call loans, which were collateralized by shares in United Copper. This succeeded in the sense that United's price trend returned to that of copper prices and the industrial average. But it was unable to restore United Copper's share price to the level of January 1. From June until mid-October, United traded *above* Amalgamated. O'Sullivan notes that the difference may have motivated short sellers who believed that the small company (United) would have to fall in line with the industry leader (Amalgamated).[33] Macroeconomic pressures forced United Copper's price downward. The demands from creditors for more collateral squeezed the Heinzes and eventually prompted them to action.

In hindsight, the effort to corner United Copper shares was ill-informed and foolhardy. The comparison of United Copper's share price performance with the benchmarks makes it hard to conclude that the stock was the victim of heavy short-selling pressure. Against these findings, the Heinze brothers' assertions of mispricing and victimization by short sellers is hard to fathom. Nonetheless, the significance of the copper corner to the Panic of 1907 invites more research into the conflicting accounts and the causes of its failure.

Chapter 7

Falling Dominoes

. . . the ramifications of the failure and the possible consequences of the utter collapse of United Copper had a disastrous effect on Stock Exchange sentiment . . .

—*New York Times*, October 17, 1907

The First Domino

The first casualty of the failed corner attempt was Gross & Kleeberg, the brokerage house Otto Heinze had asked to initiate the corner. On Wednesday afternoon, October 16, Gross & Kleeberg closed its doors and suspended all trading after executing a major sell-off of all its United Copper shares. Having been instructed by Otto C. Heinze & Company to purchase 6,000 shares of United Copper, Gross & Kleeberg later found the Heinzes unwilling or unable to pay for them. The brokerage had, in fact, been the most active buyer in United Copper on the rise that began on Monday when the stock went from $39 to $60 per share. When the Heinzes refused to pay for the shares, Gross & Kleeberg was forced to sell its United Copper holdings at a large loss on Wednesday, driving the price momentarily to $10 a share.[1]

Gross & Kleeberg explained their situation in a letter to the Governors of the Stock Exchange:

> *Dear Sir: On Monday, the 14th, by direction of the firm of Otto Heinze & Co., members of the Exchange, we purchased and received for the account of said firm 3,202 shares of United Copper common and preferred, which we tendered them on Tuesday, Oct. 15, 1907, and demanded payment therefore, which payment was refused by them. Inasmuch, therefore, as they failed to comply with their contract, we were obliged to announce our suspension to the Exchange yesterday.*[2]

"While the failed firm [Gross & Kleeberg] has not been for many months active on the Stock Exchange," the *New York Times* later reported, "the ramifications of the failure and the possible consequences of the utter collapse of United Copper had a disastrous effect on Stock Exchange sentiment, which had begun the day with a hopeful attitude toward the market generally."[3]

It was estimated that the United Copper purchases had cost Gross & Kleeberg alone some $300,000. "Our principals laid down on us," said Philip Gross in explaining the failure, "that is all there is to it. Everybody knows who those principals are."[4] Another representative of the brokerage, putting it more bluntly, said that Gross & Kleeberg failed because "the firm bought United Copper for the Heinze people, who refused to receive it."[5] The brokerage house, established in December 1904, was immediately placed in the hands of an assignee, and a claim was filed against Otto Heinze & Company.[6] These actions quelled some fears in financial circles, but there was a sense of foreboding that the commitments in United Copper that had brought disaster to one house might extend elsewhere.[7]

The Second Domino

As news of the failed corner spread, attention on Wall Street turned to Otto Heinze's more famous brother, Augustus. Not only was Augustus well known and flamboyant, but he also held a controlling interest in United Copper Company and thus stood to gain personally from any attempted squeeze. Moreover, although it was not widely known at the time, Augustus had personally guaranteed the loans for Otto Heinze &

Company through the Mercantile National Bank, of which he was both president and a director. Nonetheless, Augustus Heinze and his associates publicly maintained that he had had nothing to do with the ill-fated corner in United Copper stock. They further insisted that Otto Heinze had managed the attempted corner without consultation with his brother Augustus.[8] "Augustus Heinze," the *Wall Street Journal* reported, "is in the dark regarding the affairs of his brother's firm, and in order to ascertain the exact condition he has retained special counsel and auditors."[9]

Throughout the day on Wednesday, October 16, as United Copper came crashing down, Augustus Heinze was seen going about the financial district in consultation with various banking interests. "Mr. Heinze was in conference with Mr. Morse at the latter's office in the National Bank of North America early in the afternoon. Talk of a breach between Morse and Heinze was freely heard yesterday," the *New York Times* reported. "Friends of Mr. Morse, however, made it plain yesterday, as they have in the past, that Mr. Morse had not been interested in the Heinze ventures."[10] Augustus convened a conference on Wednesday with his brother and several associates in the offices of Otto Heinze & Company that lasted until late in the day.[11]

At 1 p.m. on Thursday, October 17, the next domino fell. The Exchange announced the official suspension of Otto Heinze & Company for failure to meet its financial obligations. Until Wednesday afternoon the firm had given assurances that they would pay their debts, especially those to Gross & Kleeberg.[12] Then, Heinze offered to pay Gross & Kleeberg $100,000, representing a third of its total indebtedness, but such an offer had come too late.[13] For other creditors, the firm made a tentative offer of a 10 percent cash settlement, and the balance in three-, six-, and nine-month notes. However, when Gross & Kleeberg announced its suspension, all settlement attempts were abandoned, and several brokers sold off their Heinze accounts.[14] Announcing the news, a lawyer for the Heinze firm issued the following statement:

> *The firm of Otto C. Heinze & Co. feels itself perfectly solvent and will meet and pay all its just and legal obligations in full. It, however, refuses to pay obligations that it does not consider legal or just until a proper adjudication of the matter has been made. Rather than submit to such unjust demands it prefers to permit itself to temporarily be suspended from the privileges of the Stock Exchange.*[15]

Upon hearing news of the latest suspension, brokers literally lined up outside the firm's offices waiting impatiently for their checks. "Some of the brokers," the *Wall Street Journal* reported, "after waiting several hours shoved their accounts with certificates over the transom of the Heinze offices, while others kicked at the doors and sought for recognition which was not forthcoming."[16] That same day, the firm announced that Arthur P. Heinze, the youngest of the three Heinze brothers, had been dismissed from the firm because he had incurred individual liabilities of nearly $1 million.[17] Although Arthur Heinze had been in France during the wild gyrations in United Copper of the preceding days, it was reported that there were cable messages from him ordering purchases of the stock.[18]

A Third Domino

The next domino fell far from the canyons of Wall Street. On the very day the Governors of the Exchange shuttered Otto Heinze & Company, the State Savings Bank of Butte, Montana, announced its insolvency.[19] The incident would hardly have attracted notice, but Augustus Heinze owned this small savings institution, which served as a correspondent bank for the Mercantile National in New York. The bank, which had 6,000 depositors and was the largest savings bank in the state of Montana, had funds on deposit with the Mercantile and loans outstanding to Heinze interests amounting to nearly $1 million; the bank was also holding United Copper Company stock as collateral for some of its loans.[20] Most of the bank's depositors were small wage earners and, according to the bank's officers, its closure had been prompted by fears of a major run. The bank, which Augustus Heinze had purchased in 1905, issued a notice on Thursday, October 17:

> *Because of unsolid conditions and rumors that cannot be verified, that may cause unusual demands by depositors, and owing to the shortage of currency and inability to secure additional currency immediately to pay demands which may be made, the management has deemed it advisable in the interest of all depositors to suspend for the time being. The bank is insolvent.*[21]

The Fourth Domino

Apparently, the failed corner on United Copper, the suspensions of Gross & Kleeberg and Otto Heinze & Co., and the insolvency of the Butte State Savings Bank—all connected with Augustus Heinze—were too much for the directors of the Mercantile National Bank to bear. "It was generally understood that, owing to the close connections between President Heinze and the failed brokerage house," the *Times* said, "the situation would be extremely unpleasant for the Mercantile Bank."[22]

After a meeting of the bank's directors on Wednesday that lasted until after midnight, the controlling interests of the Mercantile assembled at 11 a.m. on Thursday, October 17, to announce the resignation of Augustus Heinze as president of the bank.[23] In a further attempt to allay concerns about the bank's management, an offer for the presidency of the Mercantile was extended to William Ridgely, the Comptroller of the Currency of the U.S. Treasury.[24] On Thursday afternoon, Augustus made the following statement regarding his "voluntary" resignation:

> *In view of the difficulties in which my brother's firm finds itself, I have determined that it is proper that I should give liberally of my time in assisting them to straighten out their affairs. In aid of this I have, after consulting with my fellow-Directors of the bank and my personal friends, and consulting as well my own personal interests as a large stockholder of the bank, this day resigned as its President, remaining, however, as a Director, and have joined with my fellow-Directors in a request that Mr. Ridgely accept the place made vacant by my resignation.*[25]

Friends of Heinze continued to support the Copper King, saying, "He did not pretend to have knowledge of the banking business," and he "meant rather to learn the business as president of the Mercantile than personally to direct its operations."[26] According to the bank's quarterly report in April, the bank showed gross deposits of $19,884,000; by Saturday, October 12, *prior to* the failed corner in United Copper, the bank's deposits had declined 42 percent to $11,569,000.[27] In the next few days the situation would grow much worse, and the interconnected nature of the relationships among the nation's financial institutions would only enable the contagion to spread.

Propagation of Shocks

The failure of two brokerage firms and a small bank in Butte, Montana, would hardly seem to presage a serious financial crisis. Yet the important question was how these small shocks might spread. Augustus Heinze was the nexus of relationships among some seven national banks, up to 12 state-chartered banks, seven trust companies, and up to six insurance companies.[28] His confederate, Charles Morse, had yet more relationships in the financial and business communities of New York. Might the crisis spread through these relationships?

The initial fallen dominoes highlighted two vulnerabilities in all financial systems that undermined confidence of depositors and investors in 1907, and later. The first was the complexity of the financial system. The rapid growth in financial markets and the number of firms made it difficult to apprehend the current state of things. The financial press was still in its infancy, as were bond rating agencies. There were no Generally Accepted Accounting Principles, Certified Public Accountants, or Chartered Financial Analysts. Nor was there a national regulator to mandate public disclosure of the financial condition and material events related to brokers, dealers, and issuers of public-traded securities. Weak institutions (laws, norms, and conventional practices) obscured the players and their transactions in the markets. True, some financial firms were required to make regular reports to federal or state regulators, but it took expertise to derive meaning from these complicated reports. In short, *complexity bred information asymmetries* that fueled distrust of markets and financial firms. It was hard to know what was going on, a condition that spawned rumors and conspiracy theories.

The second vulnerability was the economic linkage among financial institutions and the markets in which they dealt. Financial contracts (for instance, loan agreements, investment commitments, or deposit contracts) formed the spine of such linkage. And reputation and relationships added muscle: upon the fulfillment of a verbal commitment might hang the prospect of gaining new business from an acquaintance, loans, equity, an invitation to join an investment pool, or support for one's admission to a private club. Later, in 1912–1913, Congressional hearings would assert that the Wall Street business community was tightly linked into a money trust (more about that later). As the early falling dominoes revealed, *economic linkage meant that trouble could travel.* The contagion of the Panic of 1907 spread through the relational nerves that bound together the financial community.

Modern-day research[29] into system dynamics reveals that complexity and tight linkage make it difficult to detect and fight crises. Adversity can feed back through complex systems in unanticipated ways, reinforcing and accelerating the initial shock, stimulating problems of adverse selection, and resulting in a "doom loop."

Chapter 8

Clearing House

. . . the action of the Clearing House on Saturday and Sunday had eliminated practically all elements of danger from the banking situation.

—*Wall Street Journal*, October 22, 1907

Augustus Heinze's abrupt resignation from the presidency of the Mercantile National Bank focused the attention of a wider audience—depositors—on the condition of the bank. As depositors fled with their money, the erosion of the Mercantile's deposit base soon came to the attention of the New York Clearing House (NYCH). Founded in 1853 to simplify the settlement of payments among member banks, it had proved to be a source of systemic stability in times of panic. But how much stability it could provide depended on which of many kinds of financial institutions had joined the clearing house.

A Patchwork System

Unlike most European countries, the United States did not have a central bank or regulator to backstop its financial system in 1907. Ever since President Andrew Jackson had withdrawn the charter for the Bank of the United States in 1837, the prevailing political sentiment had reflected a distrust of the economic and political power of banking institutions and sought to promote a financial system consisting of small, widely dispersed banks. In 1907 various types of banks conducted business:

- National banks operated under charters issued by the federal government, had to conform to stricter capital and reserve requirements, submitted periodic reports of condition to the Comptroller of the Currency (CoC), and endured unannounced reviews by the CoC's bank inspectors, in return for which they were authorized to receive federal deposits and issue government-licensed currency. The 6,422 nationally chartered banks were generally more stable than the 15,564 non-nationally chartered banks in the United States.[1]
- State banks were typically smaller and localized institutions, chartered by state legislatures and subject to somewhat more lenient regulatory oversight. State-chartered banks had proliferated widely in the United States since the Civil War, and by 1906 held 50 percent of all commercial bank assets.[2] Approximately 12,000 state banks formed the bulk of non-nationally chartered banks.

National banks and state banks constituted the field of *commercial* banks, mobilizing deposits from individuals and firms for loans to businesses and individuals. In 1907, commercial banks were the main source of credit creation in the U.S. economy. On the periphery of the commercial banking industry in 1907 were a range of other institutions, which might be called "shadow banks" in the parlance of twenty-first-century finance:

- Mutual savings banks were usually smaller and localized institutions, chartered by states and owned by their depositors to serve more specific needs such as mortgage lending. At the end of the nineteenth century, savings bank assets averaged about a fifth of all commercial bank assets. In 1907 the United States tallied 625 such institutions, and total assets of $3.25 billion.[3]
- Private banks operated without a government charter because they served a private clientele rather than the public and did not issue banknotes (currency). These institutions ranged from international

houses, such as J. P. Morgan & Company and Kuhn, Loeb & Company to immigrant bankers who ran their businesses out of grocery stores and saloons. Private banks, especially immigrant banks, provided a wide range of services to their customers besides checking accounts, such as savings accounts, loans, and currency exchange. Immigrant private banks also transferred money abroad, sold steamship and train tickets, read and wrote letters for illiterate or non-English-speaking customers, and helped people find jobs. In mid-1907, the United States counted 2,784 private banks, which reported $565 million in assets.[4] As a general rule, private banks were not members of the NYCH.

- Trust companies operated under state charters and less onerous regulations than commercial banks. Trust companies first appeared in the mid-nineteenth century, grew slowly, and then surged in number after 1896. In 1906 the United States had 1,333 trust companies.[5] In contrast to banks, trust companies tended to invest in longer-term and less liquid assets, paid higher interest rates on deposits, and held lower reserves and more interest-earning assets (92 percent versus 70 percent for national banks). But the trust companies provided fewer payment-related services than banks and therefore had fewer clearings. The total value of New York City trust company assets had grown 2.5 times over the decade to $1.36 billion, close to the $1.8 billion of New York national banks.[6]

Fractional Reserves Create Tight Linkages

Federal and state regulators required banks to hold cash reserves against the likelihood of withdrawals by depositors—the amount was a fraction of all deposits, thus leading to the term "fractional reserve banking." As a means of enhancing returns, many banks regularly placed part of their reserves on deposit with other financial institutions. Small rural "country banks" would send reserves up to a regional "reserve city" such as San Francisco, St. Louis, or Chicago in order to earn a higher rate of return than idle cash. And reserve city banks would send a portion of *their* reserves up to banks in the money center of the nation, New York City. The flow of reserves observed a pecking order from small to large, from interior to reserve city to New York, and from non-national to nationally chartered institutions.

For instance, federal regulations required country banks to hold reserves equal to 15 percent of their deposits; 40 percent of these reserves had to be held in cash in the bank vault, but the balance could be placed on deposit at "reserve city" banks, where the reserves could earn interest. These reserve city banks had to hold a reserve equal to at least 25 percent of their deposits and half of those reserves in vault cash, with the other half typically placed on deposit with banks in New York.

A worrisome development was the mismatch between the rapid growth of bank deposits and the cash reserves available to meet depositors' demands. The interbank deposits of non-national banks and national banks almost quadrupled from 1896 to 1907.[7] Reserves of the New York national banks from 1897 to 1907 generally exceeded the 25 percent minimum ratio to deposits. On the other hand, the reserves of the nationally chartered country banks plummeted over the decade, from 11.6 percent in 1897 to 7.5 percent in 1907.[8]

Another concern was that many of the banks in New York and other major financial cities were heavily involved in the securities markets, particularly in railroad underwritings or lending to speculators and brokers in the "call money" market. Call loans typically extended for short periods and were collateralized by the pledge of marketable securities. Therefore, a slump in securities prices could potentially prompt anxiety among bank depositors. If that anxiety precipitated runs, an abrupt systemwide contraction could result. Interior banks were thus tightly coupled to financial institutions and securities markets in the nation's money centers, making them (and the system) vulnerable to a crisis. As the Panic of 1907 unfolded, the linkage among financial institutions created by fractional reserve banking would prove to be an important pathway for contagion. With tight linkage, trouble could travel.

Endemic Instability

Since the Depression of the 1890s, in which several hundred banks had failed, the American banking industry had regained its footing, although the failure of marginal institutions continued to haunt it. In

1903 there had been 52 bank failures or suspensions, but that number jumped to 125 failures in 1904, most of them by state or private banks. In 1905, 80 banks suspended, while in 1906 53 banks suspended, again most of them state banks.[9] When a bank failed, its depositors were out of luck; there was no state or federal deposit insurance. While there was no central bank to give liquidity to the financial system in periods of strain, the policy of recent secretaries of the Treasury had been to shift gold and currency to different regions and deposit the funds in banks that would then relend the funds to debtors. Occasionally, the Treasury would make advance payments of principal and interest on government bonds as an alternative means of injecting liquidity into the financial system.

Throughout the nineteenth century, bankers and public officials had debated the efficacy of various private arrangements to quell banking panics. The First and Second Banks of the United States had been publicly chartered but were privately owned disciplinary guardians of prudential practice. After President Jackson's veto of the Second Bank's charter in 1832, the United States embarked on other private market experiments aimed at stabilizing the financial system. The Suffolk System in Massachusetts (1824 to 1858) functioned as a way for banks to mutually guarantee the soundness of the banknotes they offered to the public.

However, the most enduring of the private sector remedies was the *clearing house*. The first one was founded in New York City in 1853 as an association among 52 firms. The New York Clearing House (NYCH) afforded convenience as a place to settle daily balances among members. To join, a bank had to commit to a high standard of capital and specie reserve requirements, and to present a weekly statement of financial condition to all other members, thus addressing the information asymmetry about banking conditions that was fertile ground for a banking panic. Any bank that failed to settle at once what it owed other members would be immediately expelled. Thus, membership in the NYCH was a signal of stability and a commitment to prudential banking.

As the nineteenth century advanced with its many financial crises, the NYCH evolved into an institution for mutual support of members. Knowing the condition of a member bank might make it easier for the other members to assist that bank in times of distress. In the Panic of

1857, members of the New York Clearing House issued "loan certificates" to be used in lieu of cash and backed by assets held by each institution. The Clearing House Loan Certificate (CHLC) was a joint liability of all member banks.[10] The pooling of risks among the members introduced the important concept of *coinsurance* as a means of forestalling crises.[11] In a bank panic, CHLCs could become "near money," plausible substitutes for cash. In a financial crisis, it might make sense for the entire membership to suspend convertibility of deposits into specie and to settle balances among the banks by means of issuing clearing house loan certificates that would be backed by the entire clearing house membership—such *collective action* by the clearing house would signal that the inability to convert notes into specie was not an individual problem but rather a systemic problem.

And finally, the NYCH created beneficial network effects through the sharing of information among members. As the membership grew, the network effects strengthened. Notwithstanding these benefits, the exclusive character of the clearing house prompted some critics to accuse the NYCH of monopolizing the reserves in the financial center of the nation and using them to discipline competitors.[12] By 1906, the clearing house model had spread to many other cities in the United States.

In contrast to other banking centers, such as Chicago and St. Louis, the NYCH membership included almost no trust companies. In 1903, the bank members of the NYCH had offered affiliate membership to trust companies on condition that the trust companies adhered to reporting requirements and a reserve minimum of 10 percent of deposits—well below the reserve requirement of the New York banks. To be an affiliate meant that a trust company would clear payments through a bank member of the clearing house. As contemporary journalist Alexander Dana Noyes noted,

> *A controversy of much warmth broke out. During the discussion, such contemptuous terms were used, in public statements as "the foolish fetich of a cash reserve." Banks were accused of trying to cripple trade competitors who had got ahead of them.*[13]

Three trust companies agreed to these rules: the Knickerbocker Trust Company, the Van Norden Trust Company, and the Manhattan

Trust Company. The other trust companies were loath to abandon the competitive advantage they held over the banks. Thus, in a fateful split in the New York financial community, trust companies turned their backs on the NYCH, creating an exclusion that would figure prominently as the Panic of 1907 unfolded.

Unfortunately, the deficiencies of the patchwork of private and public institutions were manifest. First, many contemporary critics charged that the currency of the United States was "inelastic," meaning that the volume outstanding could not adjust easily to meet variations in economic cycles, bumper crops, or shocks. Second, no single regulatory agency monitored monetary conditions or the overall stability of the financial system as a basis for promoting disciplined lending. Third, there was no uniformity to clearing house organizations and practices; in some geographic areas, no clearing houses existed at all.

Run on the Mercantile: NYCH Responds

In the context of this complicated and fragile system, then, anxieties about the solvency of the Mercantile National Bank gripped uneasy depositors and investors alike, prompting a run on the bank. With nowhere else to turn, Augustus Heinze sought the assistance of the New York Clearing House (NYCH).

The NYCH, of which the Mercantile National was a member, convened on Thursday, October 17, 1907, to discuss the events of the past few days, specifically the Mercantile's affairs and the activities related to United Copper. The NYCH announced it would stand by the Mercantile and see it through any troubles in the coming days—if the books were sound. The NYCH sent a committee directly to the Mercantile's offices in the Western Union Building to review its books. The detailed review went late into the night while practically all the Mercantile's staff remained on hand.[14] As one of the bankers present expressed it, "We went through it like a dose of salts."[15] At midnight, the NYCH committee reported that the Mercantile's capital was intact and that the bank would be open for business on Friday morning.[16] In a statement, the NYCH said, ". . . the bank was perfectly solvent and able to meet all its indebtedness. The capital of $3,000,000 is intact and with a large surplus."[17] This assessment assumed, of course, that the run would cease.

The NYCH's decision to aid the Mercantile, however, did not come without strings. A group of nine member banks each agreed to extend $200,000 to meet the Mercantile's debit obligations at the NYCH. But, as a condition for assistance, the NYCH demanded the resignation of all directors of the Mercantile. This move was intended to calm depositors and to give a new bank president a free hand in reorganizing the bank's management. The offer to Comptroller Ridgely was still outstanding after he had visited the Mercantile at midday.[18] "The clearing house committee minimized consequent fears," the *Chicago Daily Tribune* reported, "by declaring that the condition of the banks generally was satisfactory, though the qualification was made that in some instances changes in the directorates of other banks might be necessitated. It was insisted that there was nothing alarming in the local banking situation."[19] A representative of the NYCH said reassuringly, "The situation is now under control, and no untoward developments are looked for."[20]

Despite the actions and assurances of the NYCH, the intensity of the run on the Mercantile continued unabated, and fears of unforeseen runs on other banks were growing. On Saturday, October 19, the Mercantile showed another big debit balance in its account at the NYCH. The debit amounted to a stunning $1,137,000, indicating that depositors' withdrawals were straining the bank's reserves, which stood at $1,745,000, equal to only 15.4 percent of its deposits, far less than the 25 percent required by banking law and NYCH rules. More alarmingly, the Mercantile's total debit balances at the NYCH over the previous three days had been $2,400,000, 20 percent of its total deposits. It was estimated that at this rate the bank's debit balances would exhaust its deposits in 10 days. Other banks with connections to the Mercantile were showing even poorer reserve positions, between 4 and 5 percent. Notably, a few of the larger banks unaffiliated with Heinze interests showed heavy increases in their reserves, ranging between 29 and 40 percent, indicating that depositors were shifting their accounts to more well-established institutions.[21]

At the opening of the business day on Saturday, October 19, the NYCH met again to consider the banking situation and the exigencies of the Mercantile. It was again agreed to make up the balance of any debits that the Mercantile was unable to pay, although the NYCH made no commitments to address further debit balances in the future. Frankly, the NYCH's member banks did not intend to extend aid to Heinze's Mercantile indefinitely. But as the day wore on, news for the Mercantile only worsened. First, the officers of the Mercantile informed several banks for which it had previously provided clearing services that it could no longer do so.[22] Then, in the early afternoon, William Ridgely, Comptroller of the Currency, announced that he had refused the presidency of Mercantile National. Finally, the NYCH learned that the Heinzes' loans from the Mercantile had reached a very large, but undisclosed, total.[23]

Meanwhile, Augustus Heinze continued a public defense of his situation, issuing statements from his residence at the Waldorf Hotel, across the street from the offices of Otto Heinze & Company and the United Copper Company. He denied repeatedly that the clearing house was even assisting his bank, accusing its members of trying to profit from his difficulties, and he asserted his continued control of the Mercantile:

> *I have not sold a share of my stock and am still in control of the Mercantile Bank. The whole miserable situation is the result of the action of the Clearing House committee. Instead of coming out with a statement saying that the bank was entirely solvent, they made a lot of remarks about the impairment of surplus and started a run on the bank in the hope of attracting deposits to their institutions.*[24]

The NYCH, however, had by this time begun to turn its attentions to other banking institutions. It became clear that over the next two days the situation would extend beyond the Mercantile. Depositors were already beginning to withdraw funds from the banks owned by a man with close Heinze associations: Charles W. Morse.

On Saturday, October 19, the NYCH arranged for inspections of two banks controlled by Morse: the National Bank of North America and the New Amsterdam National. The National Bank of North America showed $15,011,600 in loans and $13,063,200 in deposits; its directors included such leading figures as William T. Havemeyer of the American Sugar Refining Company and Charles M. Schwab of U.S. Steel, as well as Charles W. Morse and Charles T. Barney. The New Amsterdam Bank had $4,447,400 in deposits and $4,495,600 in loans, and it was considered one of the most important of New York's uptown banks. The NYCH committee conducted the inspections all day and worked until late in the night.[25]

NYCH Defenestrates Heinze and Morse

By Sunday, October 20, the NYCH had decided to take its most drastic measure to date. It ordered the immediate elimination of Augustus Heinze and Charles W. Morse from all banking interests in New York City. The action was both swift and sweeping. Morse resigned from the National Bank of North America, of which he was a vice president and director; the New Amsterdam National Bank; the Garfield National Bank; the Fourteenth Street Bank; the New York Produce Exchange Bank; and two other financial institutions in his hometown of Bath, Maine.[26] Heinze, who had already stepped down from the Mercantile, was likewise removed from at least eight banks and two trust companies. The committee also insisted that Morse and Heinze had to repay their loans to their respective banks and further ruled that any evidence of "chain-banking" would disqualify such banks or bankers from the NYCH. Thereupon, the NYCH announced its willingness to lend aid to any banks that had been under suspicion, having found them to be solvent. It was reported, however, that the Mercantile would undergo a process of slow liquidation.[27]

On Monday, October 21, massive debit balances appeared at the NYCH for several Heinze and Morse banks. On that morning, the debits for Heinze's Mercantile National Bank and Mechanics and Traders Bank were, respectively, $1,903,000 and $430,000; debits for Morse's National Bank of North America and New Amsterdam National Bank were, respectively, $850,000 and $200,000. Altogether, the NYCH had disbursed $2.5 million in aid since the Mercantile's troubles began; the balance for the ongoing deficits had been covered by the bank's deposits or by calls on the banks' outstanding loans.[28] The National Bank of North America, for instance, started the day with $1,400,000 in cash to meet the demands of its depositors. According to one report, "Large heaps of gold were piled up on the counter in full view of any depositors who entered the bank." This bank repaid its debt at the NYCH from its own reserves and by collecting $1,750,000 from called loans.[29]

Heinze's personal troubles had, of course, only begun. Claims against his brother's brokerage house were estimated to be $2 million,[30] and lawyers for Gross & Kleeberg and other Wall Street firms had filed a petition to declare involuntary bankruptcy for Otto Heinze & Company. At noon on Monday, the Heinze firm called a meeting of its creditors and issued a statement:

> *We regret to say that we find our affairs so much more than we had anticipated at first that we have been unable, with the greatest effort, to get them into shape to present them at the meeting called this day, and we are therefore obliged to ask you to meet us at a day later in the week, of which you will be duly notified.*[31]

The *New York Times* reported, "the claims against Otto Heinze & Company alleged that the Heinzes made preferential payments to the Mercantile National Bank of $2 million to cover the personal debts of Arthur P. Heinze and F. Augustus Heinze. The filing further sought an injunction restraining the disposition of any further assets by the firm."[32]

The rapid intervention of the NYCH during the preceding days seemed to mitigate the likelihood of a full-blown banking panic. Sounding an optimistic tone on the morning of Monday, October 21, the *Wall Street Journal* said that "the action of the Clearing House on Saturday and Sunday had eliminated practically all elements of danger from the banking situation."[33] The interventions of the NYCH and the immediate consequences for Heinze and Morse should have been sufficient to restore public confidence. Now, scarcely a year after his triumph over Amalgamated Copper and Standard Oil, Augustus Heinze took substantial losses. And both he and Charles W. Morse had been ejected from positions of responsibility in the financial system.

Had Heinze and Morse been merely aggressive speculators, their personal reversals would have prompted no more than the passing interest of traders on the Curb. But investors and depositors understood the tight linkages among Heinze, Morse, and banking concerns throughout the nation's financial capital. Their individual failures had already toppled two brokerages and had infected at least three national banks—all in the span of a week. But on Monday, October 21, the public would also learn that Charles T. Barney, the respectable president of the Knickerbocker Trust Company, was an associate of Charles Morse and Augustus Heinze, and that he might have been involved in their schemes. Should the Knickerbocker fall, its failure would signal to the public that something more endemic was threatening the financial system. By day's end, widespread fear and uncertainty would spread like a brush fire.

Chapter 9

Knickerbocker

Outwardly and according to its balance sheet, the [Knickerbocker] Trust Company was flourishing.

—Herbert L. Satterlee, J. P. Morgan's son-in-law and biographer[1]

An Imposing Edifice

The Knickerbocker Trust Company once stood at the northwest corner of Fifth Avenue and 34th Street, in a transitional neighborhood between New York's downtown business district and its uptown residential grandeur.[2,3] On the opposite corner from the Knickerbocker towered the red sandstone palace of the Waldorf-Astoria, New York's most fashionable and grand hotel, placing the Knickerbocker literally in the shadow of the city's social, business, and political hub. As such, the Knickerbocker's designers hoped the building itself would be commensurate with its genteel surroundings. Covered in Vermont marble and fronted by four 17-ton Corinthian columns, the Knickerbocker presented, according to a contemporary reviewer, "a beautiful example of Grecian architecture, treated in the most refined way with every provision known to modern building construction for meeting the demands of the company and the service of its patrons. The structure must be considered a distinct addition to the architectural features of that part of the city."[4]

The Knickerbocker's architects, McKim, Mead & White, had designed an elegant and functional four-story structure that was intended to convey the institution's strength and sobriety. Inside its main gates, white Norwegian marble contrasted brilliantly with interior bronze detailing and mahogany woodwork. The central banking room reached nearly three stories high and had eight adjoining rooms for ancillary banking activities. An alternate entrance on 34th Street led to second, third, and fourth floors, each with 5,000 square feet of floor space and four executive offices. In the basement, the massive safety deposit vault contained 2,000 boxes, and its outer vault door weighed nearly nine tons—its hinges alone were 3,700 pounds. Elsewhere in the building was a 6,000-square-foot employee dining hall with a full kitchen.[5]

The Knickerbocker building thus captured the prevailing ethos of early-twentieth-century bank construction, as described in *Banker's Magazine*, a contemporary industry periodical:

> *[T]he public expects a bank or trust company to occupy well-furnished quarters, such that the cost of good equipment is more than repaid in advertising value. The lobby should be provided with all possible conveniences for customers, including writing desks supplied with good ink, clean pens and blotters, comfortable chairs, etc. The larger companies often provide separate reading and lounging rooms for customers, with current newspapers and magazines, writing desks and other conveniences, and other committee-rooms for the use of customers who wish to meet or arrange details of business. In many cases there are special quarters for women, equipped with numerous conveniences, and in charge of a matron who looks after the comfort of patrons.*[6]

The Insurgency by Trust Companies

As a trust company, the Knickerbocker represented a relatively new form of financial intermediary. Originally organized in the mid-nineteenth century to handle various financial tasks for private estates and corporations, the sphere of activity for trust companies gradually expanded to offer services little different from those of traditional banks.* As historian Vincent Carosso has explained:

> *Beginning in the 1890s, trust companies took on most of the functions of both commercial and private banks. They accepted deposits; made loans; participated extensively in reorganizing railroads and consolidating industrial corporations; acted as trustees, underwriters, and distributors of new securities; and served as the depositories of stocks, bonds, and titles. Corporations regularly appointed them as registrars or fiscal and transfer agents. Very often they also owned and managed real estate.*[7]

Despite their functional similarities to national and state banks, trust companies were generally less tightly regulated. They were permitted, for instance, to hold a wider variety of assets; unlike national banks, trust companies could own stock equity directly. Also, unique among large financial institutions, trusts were not required to hold reserves against deposits before 1906; in that year, New York State required that trust companies hold 15 percent of deposits as reserves, although only a third of the reserves had to be held in cash—in contrast to New York State regulations, national banks in the city had to meet a federal government minimum reserve of 25 percent. This meant that trust companies could earn a higher return on their assets compared to banks, and thus could pay higher interest rates. Accordingly, the higher interest rates attracted deposits, and the trust companies' deposits grew rapidly. In 1906, the assets of all trust companies in New York City, approximated the assets of all national banks in the city, and exceeded the assets of all state banks there. According to economists Jon Moen and Ellis Tallman, "In the ten years ending in 1907, trust company assets in New York State had grown 244 percent (from $396.7 million to $1.364 billion) in comparison to

* Perine (1916) describes the rise of the trust company in America from the first one founded in 1822 to the widespread institutions of 1907. Much like the "shadow banks" of twenty-first-century parlance, the position of trust companies in the financial services sector grew by innovation, mergers, and by exploiting gaps in regulatory reporting and supervision. State (not federal) supervision meant that regulations varied dramatically across the country. Perine argued that trust companies were generally prudently managed. Yet the failure of Ohio Life Insurance and Trust Company sparked the Panic of 1857 and offered a precedent for 1907, an event that some observers of the Knickerbocker would recall.

97 percent (from $915.2 million to $1.8 billion) for those of national banks, and 82 percent (from $297 million to $541 million) for state banks in New York."[8]

Trust companies were "shadow banks" that originated on the periphery of the formally regulated financial system and exploited their fringe status to gain a growing share of the financial services market. They owed their growth to a different business model, which exposed the banks to "an unprecedented amount of competition," according to Professor Sprague.[9]

First, they reached out to a growing segment of depositors, especially the middle class. In a booming economy, individuals could save more of their take-home pay. Throughout the nineteenth century, banks had generally not actively marketed their services to depositors and instead focused on serving merchants, large corporations, and correspondent banks. Indeed, some institutions, such as J.P. Morgan & Company (a *private* bank) accepted no deposits from the general public—you had to be recommended to become a depositor, as if joining a selective club. But trust companies welcomed individual depositors and promoted themselves more aggressively than banks through advertising and ethnic affiliation, by locating in convenient locations to individual depositors, and by paying interest on deposits, a practice that conservative bankers frowned upon. Unlike banks, trust companies could open branch offices in neighborhoods convenient to their clientele. The Knickerbocker, for instance, operated three branches in addition to its main office. Trust companies were exemplars of the growing democratization of finance in the sense of providing increased access to financial services for segments of the public not formerly served.

Second, in order to pay interest on deposits, trust companies held lower cash reserves against deposits and invested in real estate, stocks, and other longer-term assets that yielded higher returns. Moen and Tallman estimated that 92.2 percent of trust company assets in New York earned interest, in comparison to 70 percent at nationally and state-chartered banks.[10] New York State imposed lighter reserve regulations on trust companies. The practice of investing in longer-term assets meant that the trust companies' loan portfolio was less liquid than national banks. In short, trust companies were riskier (but probably yielded a higher return on investment) than national banks.

Third, trust companies in New York distanced themselves from the mainstream banking system. They engaged much less than banks in the payments system (i.e., moving money around in the form of cash, checks, bills of exchange, etc.). Classic trust deposits (not bankers' deposits) tended to be held on a long-term basis, in trust for beneficiaries, and were less subject to transactional inflows and outflows. Moen and Tallman estimated that the volume of transactions services at New York trust companies was only 7 percent that of national banks. Whereas trust companies accepted deposits from other banks (a practice called correspondent banking), such deposits accounted for less than a sixth of total deposits.[11]

Estrangement from the Clearing House

At the time of the Panic of 1907, only 3[12] of the 38[13] Manhattan trust companies were affiliates of the New York Clearing House. Four years earlier, facing steadfast insistence by the NYCH to increase reserves or leave, most of the trust companies decamped. Their absence from the NYCH meant that trust companies could not look to it as a lender of last resort in a panic. This split fueled later charges by Senator Robert La Follette, Representative Arsene Pujo, and investigator Samuel Untermyer that the Panic of 1907 sprang from vengeful discipline of the trust companies by the banks.[14]

Yet the trust companies themselves were hardly homogeneous. They varied considerably by history and business model. Younger firms pursued a retail-oriented strategy; older firms pursued a wholesale-oriented strategy. The oldest firms' executives were well-known to J.P. Morgan and his circle. The smaller and newer trust companies were generally outsiders to Morgan's social and business circles.

The Geography of Trust

Historian Bradley Hansen noted distinctive differences between trust companies that were located downtown (in the vicinity of Wall Street) and those that were uptown, which was the scene of more retail and

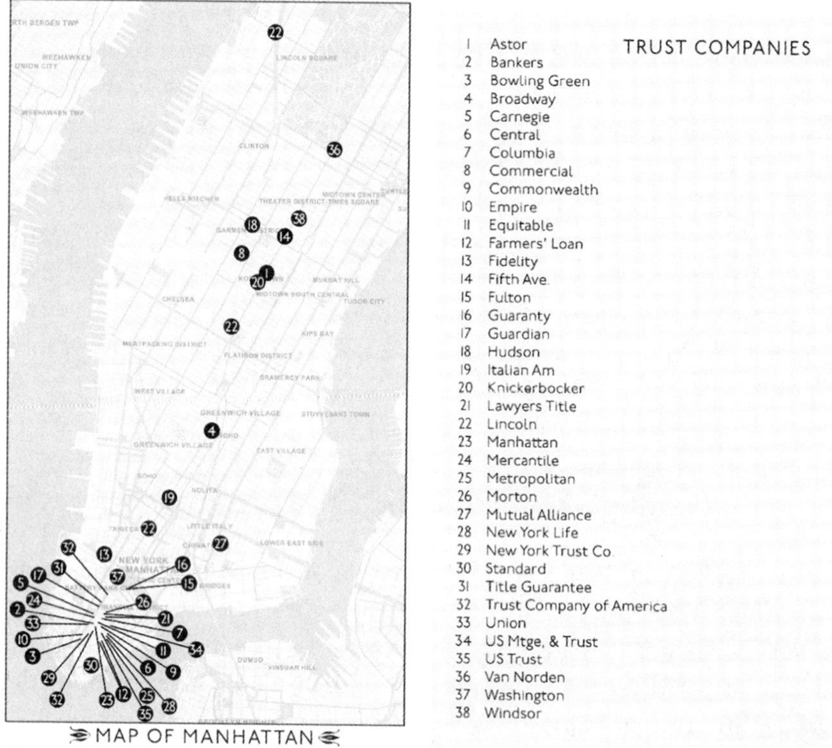

Figure 9.1 Locations of 38 Trust Companies, Manhattan, 1907
SOURCE: Authors' figure, based on a list of trust companies in Hansen (2014) and addresses in the New York State *Annual Report of the Superintendent of Banks . . . For the Year 1907* (1908).

residential activity. Figure 9.1 gives a map showing the locations of 38 Manhattan-based trust companies in 1907: what stands out is the tight cluster of 28 of them in the financial district, with the other 10 loosely dispersed north toward "uptown."

Hansen said that the uptown trusts had "large numbers of relatively small deposits. . . . Downtown firms recovered quickly [from the panic]; uptown firms did not recover."[15] Caroline Fohlin and Zikhun Liu noted that seven trust companies were closely affiliated with J.P. Morgan, Baker's First National Bank, Stillman's City National Bank, or the National Bank of Commerce. Potentially the affiliated trust companies could look to their bank affiliates for lender-of-last-resort assistance in the event of panics. Other institutions noted earlier were affiliated with the Heinze-Morse circle. As Hansen concluded, "on the eve of the Panic, New York City trust companies were far from being a homogeneous group."[16]

Our own analysis of data about the trust companies (see the Technical Appendix after Chapter 24) supports the relevance of business model differences, and associations with the Heinze-Morse circle in explaining deposit losses. And the results lend but weak support to the hypothesis that market power or links to the financial elite (Morgan and his circle, or the NYCH) resulted in better deposit results.

Whereas diversity of players in a competitive field should be no surprise, the diversity portended a fatal flaw: collective action among the trust companies to save themselves in the event of a panic would be significantly more difficult than for the bank members of the NYCH.

The Problem of Dependency

A final concern in the pre-panic period was the dependence of New York City financial institutions on correspondent bank deposits. In modern terms, these deposits might be called "hot money" owing to their tendency to be withdrawn quickly in the event of an episode of systemic instability. In addition, banks in agricultural regions of the interior tended to withdraw deposits to fund credits during the annual planting/harvest cycle. The recipients of bankers' deposits, New York banks and trust companies, tended to invest such deposits in demand loans (loans with no fixed maturity that were payable upon demand), and especially in collateralized margin loans to brokers on the stock exchange ("call loans") because of the higher interest rates and liquidity of those loans. And a *very* aggressive trust company might use bankers' deposits to fund investments in fixed term loans such as real estate mortgages.

In the event of a panicked withdrawal of bankers' deposits from trust companies, the trust companies would call in their brokers' loans, forcing market participants to sell stocks, depressing stock prices, and putting downward pressure on all speculative lending. Thus, a sudden exit by the trust companies would present the banks with the unpalatable choice of stepping in to provide liquidity to the stock market (and thus protect their own call loan business) or watching the market crash. As Sprague put it, "If, for any reason, it should become necessary for the trust companies to contract their banking operations, it would obviously be necessary for the banks to shoulder the burden in order to save the local situation."[17]

What made this panic scenario troubling was the fact that since 1897, trust companies had claimed the lion's share of growth in bankers' deposits in New York City, as shown in Figure 9.2.

Bankers' reserves at New York financial institutions grew from 1897 to 1906, at a 7.6 percent compound annual rate, well in excess of the growth of GDP per capita of 3.3 percent over the same period. Handling bankers' deposits was the growth vehicle for New York financial firms over those years.

As importantly, New York City trust companies had seized the dominant share of deposits, in comparison to national banks in New York,

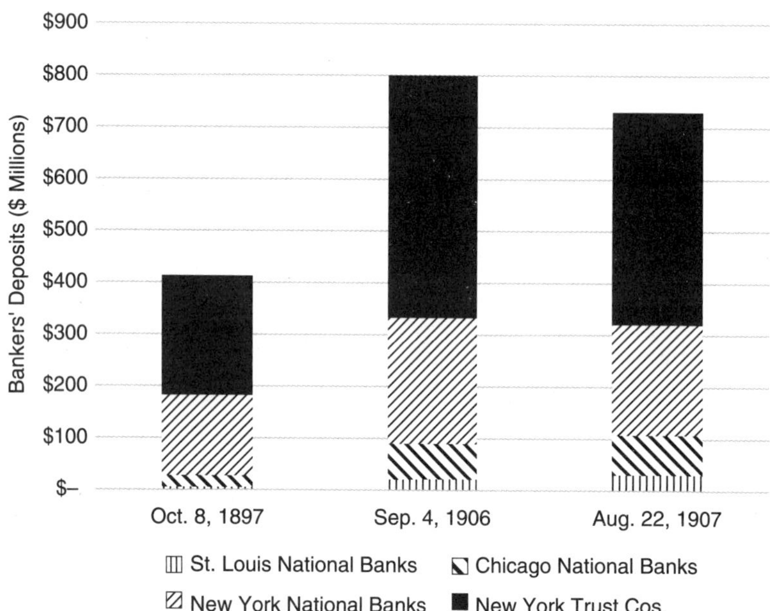

Figure 9.2 Growth of Bankers' Deposits in New York City, St. Louis, and Chicago

SOURCE: Authors' figure, based on data in Sprague (1910), pp. 223, 225. Note that the figures for trust companies include deposits from national banks and state banks, whereas the figures for New York, Chicago, and St. Louis national banks reflect bankers' deposits only from other national banks.

Chicago, and St. Louis, the principal reserve cities in the United States. Examination of the growth in trust company bankers' deposits reveals that deposits from state banks constituted a significant portion of the growth over the years 1897–1906.

A final detail warrants consideration: the largest banks and trust companies gained the dominant share of this growth in bankers' deposits, suggesting a "winner take all" dynamic in the market. The data for national banks give some indication of what was true for trust companies: of New York City's 38 national banks, six of them accounted for three quarters of such deposits.[18] The same banks accounted for more than half of individual deposits, and nearly 60 percent of national bank loans. As Sprague pointed out, the significance of this concentration was that these six banks had greater exposure to a financial crisis, and greater power for mobilizing collective action to quell it.[19]

A Pillar of the Financial Community

By 1907, the Knickerbocker Trust Company had become one of the largest and most successful trust companies in the country. Originally organized in 1884 by Fred Eldridge, who happened to be an old friend and classmate of J. Pierpont Morgan,[20] the Knickerbocker had grown its deposits in recent years by nearly 40 percent. By 1907, the Knickerbocker reported nearly $65 million in deposits, making it the second-largest trust company in New York City by deposits, with nearly 18,000 depositors. The firm acted chiefly in the traditional roles of trust companies as an executor, administrator, guardian, receiver, registrar, transfer, and financial agent for states, cities, railroads, corporations, trusts, and estates. But, like other trust companies, the firm also offered interest on time deposits and received deposits subject to demand checks.

The architecture of the Knickerbocker's new building at the corner of Fifth Avenue and 27th Street, completed in 1906, justly reflected its prominence. The company also maintained a large office downtown near Wall Street and two remote branches in the Bronx and Harlem—at this time, branches were an innovation among the trust companies.[21]

Adding to the luster of the Knickerbocker was its president, Charles T. Barney, a leading figure in New York's financial and social circles.

Born in Cleveland in 1851, Barney graduated from Williams College in 1870 and moved to New York to make a career in finance. Not nearly of the same standing as J. P. Morgan or the other heads of large national banks, Barney was still well known owing to his membership in 15 social clubs, "special membership" in an NYSE firm, and his membership on the boards of directors of 32 companies, including Trust Company of America.[22] Notably, Barney was a director in Charles Morse's American Ice Company. Also, Barney's membership on the boards of directors of the National Bank of North America and New Amsterdam National Bank were links to the chain of banks controlled by Charles Morse. Thanks to his social connections (he was the son-in-law of the financier William C. Whitney), Barney had been able to draw large accounts to the Knickerbocker from railroads, banks, and brokerage houses. During the decade of his leadership, the Knickerbocker had multiplied its deposits by 6, its surplus by 5, and its dividends by a factor of 10. "Outwardly and according to its balance sheet, the Trust Company was flourishing," wrote Herbert Satterlee, J. P. Morgan's son-in-law and biographer.[23] In short, the Knickerbocker Trust Company stood prominently in the New York and even national financial arenas.

So, as the events of October 14–15 on Wall Street unfolded, few would have suspected that the esteemed Knickerbocker Trust Company could ever be drawn into the morass. The firm's size, the apparent strength of its deposits, the social standing of its president, and even its new building in midtown gave the outward appearance of solidity and security. Of course, in hindsight, some found clues to what would unfold in the following days. "Mr. Barney had a very fine board of directors [at the Knickerbocker]," remarked Satterlee, "but they knew very little of a large part of the business of the Trust Company which Mr. Barney kept 'under his hat.' He ran his company with but few board meetings and with scant reports of his operations to his subordinates or executive committee."[24] Barney even once told a newspaper reporter that he did not "propose to waste his time answering questions asked by Directors who might try to keep in touch with the daily details of the company's business."[25] Moreover, Satterlee added, the company's "list of depositors contained a very large proportion of people of small means and those whose knowledge of banking was so slight that they would be apt to be frightened at the first sign of trouble."[26] Even so, the public at first remained ignorant of the degree of Barney's connections to the turmoil.

On Monday morning, October 21, New York City's bankers were still unsettled from the financial tremors triggered by the activities of F. Augustus Heinze and Charles W. Morse the week before. True panic had not yet set in, but the sudden collapse of the brokerage firm Gross & Kleeberg and the ensuing runs at the National Bank of North America, the New Amsterdam National Bank, and the Mercantile National Bank created an atmosphere of high tension. The quick-witted intervention by the New York Clearing House (NYCH) had nonetheless led many to believe that the problems had been contained. Professor Sprague noted that "there had been nothing in the nature of a crisis during the week the clearing house was putting its affairs in order."[27] The apparent containment of the crisis occurred because as depositors pulled their funds from institutions controlled by Morse and Heinze, they redeposited them in other New York City banks, thereby mitigating the possibility of massive runs on other national banks. Later scholars Charles Calomiris and Gary Gorton found that "the Panic of 1907 is practically a non-event from the standpoint of national bank failures."[28] The system had received a shock, but a major banking panic had not been unleashed.

At 1 a.m. on Monday, October 21, the NYCH committee concluded a meeting at which they agreed yet again to make further provisions for the payment of debit balances for the Mercantile, North America, and New Amsterdam banks. The *Wall Street Journal* reported that the NYCH had committed "to extend all necessary aid to all banks in any way involved in the unsavory transactions of United Copper, thus avoiding the possibility of a "rich men's run" on the banks."[29] Meanwhile, the new president of the Bank of North America, William F. Havemeyer, who had replaced Charles Morse, attempted to calm depositors' fears, claiming the bank's board had made headway in repaying $1.3 million in loans previously made to its own directors—$900,000 had already been repaid; the remaining $400,000 was in loans to Charles Morse. "We are busy trying to get out of debt and have little time to talk," Havemeyer said. "We are raising money and will keep on doing so. Affairs look brighter all the time."[30]

Chapter 10

A Vote of No Confidence

He said that the thing to do was to save the other trust companies and prevent general disaster.

—Herbert L. Satterlee, J. P. Morgan's son-in-law and biographer[1]

The failed corner on United Copper and the troubles of a few national banks a week earlier were but early tremors of the financial volcano that erupted on Monday afternoon, October 21. Twin shocks came in rapid succession.

First, after a meeting of the board members of the Knickerbocker Trust Company, the public learned that Charles T. Barney had been asked to tender his resignation. The week before, depositors had run on three banks affiliated with Heinze and Morse, all of which had appealed to the New York Clearing House (NYCH) for aid and received it (subject, of course, to the defenestration of Heinze, Morse, and their associates). The Knickerbocker had been one of three trust company members of the NYCH and had observed the reserve and reporting requirements. Thus, Barney appealed to the NYCH for rescue assistance like what the ailing banks received. However, the clearing house demurred, saying that "the advance of money for the protection of depositors is limited to its own members."[2] Given the practice of the NYCH of ousting management of distressed institutions, it seems likely that Barney's resignation was engineered by Knickerbocker's board in a final effort to placate the clearing house leaders.

Shortly thereafter, the National Bank of Commerce, the clearing house agent for the Knickerbocker, announced it would no longer clear for the trust company.

The End of the Clearing Relationship

The bank's announcement was a shocking development. To terminate a longstanding relationship as clearing agent for the Knickerbocker was a serious—albeit ambiguous—signal about the Bank of Commerce's confidence in the Knickerbocker's ability to fulfill its payment obligations. Was the Knickerbocker insolvent? What did the Bank of Commerce know that others did not? The termination completely severed any connection of the Knickerbocker with the Bank of Commerce and the NYCH; and it dashed any hope that the NYCH might assist the Knickerbocker in the event of trouble.

The passage of time makes the motives of the National Bank of Commerce difficult to parse. Conspiracy theorists would later assert that this was part of a coordinated action by incumbent banks to discipline the Heinze-Morse circle and/or the insurgent trust companies.

However, a recent New York law may have spurred the Bank of Commerce to act. Before 1907, banking law held that clearing agents had a priority claim on funds held on behalf of a failed institution; this had meant that the clearing agent could use those funds first to offset any obligations from the client to the agent. Then in February 1907, the New York legislature passed the Saxe Act, which amended banking law to direct the receiver in bankruptcy, not the clearing agent, to control such funds on deposit with the agent.[3] In short, the new law motivated clearing agents to be more conservative about which clients they served. Under the new law, if the Bank of Commerce had any outstanding claims against the Knickerbocker, it would now need to stand in line with all other creditors during a lengthy resolution process. Thus, the bank's decision to decamp from the Knickerbocker at the first whiff of trouble may have been an unintended consequence of the new Saxe Act.

According to a contemporary account, the action of the Bank of Commerce "came as a complete surprise."[4] The *Wall Street Journal* reported that before the National Bank of Commerce had severed its relations with the Knickerbocker Trust Company as its clearing house agent, the bank had requested a loan from the clearing house committee on behalf of the Knickerbocker, which request was denied.[5] Thereafter, the Bank of Commerce issued its notification in an unusual way. Typically, a clearing house member would send a card over to the clearing house, which would then deliver such news to all other member banks. In this case, the Bank of Commerce sent its notice directly to each bank member of the NYCH via messenger. Upon this notification, the member banks were compelled to continue clearing for the Knickerbocker only for the next 24 hours."[6] By going directly to the members of the NYCH, Bank of Commerce started the 24-hour clock immediately, reducing the exposure of the NYCH. Upon the news, the Knickerbocker's officers released a statement, saying: "Following the practice of other trust companies the Knickerbocker Trust Company has this day arranged to clear over its own counter."[7] This meant that any inadequacy of Knickerbocker's cash reserves to settle payment obligations would be a risk for Knickerbocker, not the NYCH.

The decision of the Bank of Commerce to cease clearing for Knickerbocker proved to be a significant step toward the Panic of 1907. Harry Davison, at the time a vice president of First National Bank (and who, a year later, would become a partner of J.P. Morgan & Co.) deemed the Bank of Commerce's decision "clumsy . . . ill-timed . . . a deplorable lack of cooperation."[8] On the other hand, Professor Sprague rendered a more benign judgment: "When all the circumstances are considered, however, the failure of the clearing house authorities to take any action was doubtless the most natural course, and though unfortunate in its consequences, can hardly be regarded as blameworthy."[9]

The Resignation of Charles Barney

The explicit connections between Barney and the events of the preceding week remained unknown, but the implications were made clear in another statement released by the Knickerbocker's board:

> *In view of the fact that Mr. Barney's* outside interests *had become greatly extended, and in view of his personal position in the directorate of certain institutions recently under criticism, in particular because of his connection with Mr. Morse and some of Mr. Morse's companies, he has decided that the best interests of the company would be served by his resignation, although he had no loans with the Knickerbocker Trust Company.*[10] (emphasis added)

In addition to resigning from his position as president and director, Barney also submitted his resignation from the National Bank of Commerce, the clearing house agent for the Knickerbocker. At a meeting held at the Knickerbocker's main offices at 66 Broadway, another board member, A. Foster Higgins, was elected to replace Barney immediately.[11]

Despite the evidence to the contrary, Charles Barney continued to defend both himself and the Knickerbocker. "There is not the slightest truth in any report that I was forced out of the company by the clearing house commission or by the action of the Bank of Commerce."[12] Regarding the presumed ailing condition of the Knickerbocker, Barney said, "Nothing could be more absurd. The company was never in a stronger condition. It remains next to the largest in the city and as sound as any. There is not the slightest question of its entire solvency."[13] It was reported that the accounts of the Knickerbocker had been reviewed by state banking examiners as recently as two weeks ago, and that they were then reported to be sound.[14] Moreover, the firm had announced plans in August to spend an estimated $3.5 million for the construction of a new, lavish, 22-story office building at the corner of Broadway and Exchange Place.[15] Nonetheless, the Bank of Commerce's announcement compelled the Knickerbocker not only to dismiss Barney but also to obtain emergency cash guarantees elsewhere. "The Knickerbocker has in its own vaults tonight $8,000,000 in cash," the Knickerbocker's officers declared. "If more cash is needed it will be immediately forthcoming under the guarantees."[16]

The resignation of Barney was merely an effect, of course, and not the cause of concern for the condition of the Knickerbocker. The announcement by the Bank of Commerce was far more destabilizing. According to historian Jean Strouse, the National Bank of Commerce was often referred to as J. P. Morgan's bank; Morgan had been a director of that bank since 1875, and by the time he stepped down as its vice president in 1904, the Bank of Commerce had become the second largest in the country and one of the most stable.[17] By 1907, Morgan remained a director of the bank and a member of its executive board—though as government hearings later revealed, Morgan had spread his attention so widely across boards and underwriting relationships that to attribute every corporate action to his direction implied superhuman qualities. Still, J. P. Morgan's long association with the Bank of Commerce and the bank's announcement regarding the Knickerbocker signaled apprehensions about the trust company among the highest levels of American finance that the situation was deteriorating.

Morgan Returns to New York City

As the previous week's events surrounding the failed corner in United Copper Company stock and the subsequent difficulties of the Mercantile and other banks unfolded, the 70-year-old J. Pierpont Morgan was in Richmond, Virginia, attending the Triennial Episcopal Convention. Though his visit focused on the quotidian concerns of the church, his partners in New York had kept him informed daily of market conditions and the anxiety that was brewing among the banks.

In 1907, J. Pierpont Morgan, known to his family and friends as "Pierpont," was the informal leader of the financial community in the United States. And yet, despite persistent calls for his presence, Morgan resisted any inclination to return to New York in haste, lest his departure before the end of the convention arouse suspicions that a crisis was imminent. By Thursday, October 17, however, two of Morgan's closest partners, Charles Steele and George W. Perkins, felt that the situation had become acute, and they sent a messenger to press the matter with Pierpont directly. Finally, Morgan relented and without fanfare took a private train back to New York on Saturday evening, October 19. On Sunday morning, October 20, J. P. Morgan was once again ensconced in his "library" at 36th Street and Madison Avenue, a grand repository of the art and priceless manuscripts that were his passion to collect. In the days ahead, this place would become the central headquarters for the coming rescue mission.[18]

By Sunday afternoon, the news that Morgan had returned from Richmond had already spread, and a crowd of newspaper reporters formed outside Morgan's library. Numerous bank and trust company officials came to see him throughout the day, and Morgan spent much of his time trying to get a complete picture of the situation. He assembled two teams, one that consisted of senior bankers, including himself; George Baker, president of the First National Bank; and James Stillman, president of the National City Bank; the other group included three younger, yet highly capable, men: Morgan partner George Perkins; Henry P. Davison, vice president of the First National Bank; and Benjamin Strong, vice president of the Bankers Trust Company.

Morgan carefully reviewed the financial statements of the clearing-house banks, which showed they were all in sound condition. But the status of the trust companies was less certain. Morgan finally asked his council to assess the trust companies and to determine which should be supported and which others should not.

During the day, Charles Barney, the president of the Knickerbocker, also visited the library, yet Morgan did not meet with him. Perhaps this reflected the scheduling crunch of Morgan's first day of descent into the vortex of the crisis. Or maybe Morgan had heard enough to conclude that Barney should go, and that the Knickerbocker would fail. Or perhaps Morgan resented the failure of a 1901 underwriting syndicate in Alaska salmon canning, which had been led by Charles Barney and in which Morgan sustained a large loss.[19] Later conspiracy theories about the antipathies of Morgan and his circle toward the insurgent trust companies,* the Knickerbocker, Charles Barney, and Charles W. Morse took details such as who met with whom as convincing evidence of a "money trust" bent on revenge.[20]

Around 10 a.m. on Monday, October 21, Morgan drove downtown with Charles Steele to his offices at 23 Wall Street—a building known simply as "the Corner"—where a committee of the Knickerbocker directors personally informed him of their request for Barney's resignation. As news that the Bank of Commerce would no longer clear for the Knickerbocker rattled over the ticker, Morgan advised the Knickerbocker's directors to assemble a meeting of their full board that night, review the company's books, and assess whether they could carry the company through a run. Morgan's conferences with other bankers continued throughout Monday afternoon. On Monday, Morgan privately told his son-in-law, Herbert Satterlee, that he was chiefly interested in the Knickerbocker because of its connections to his old friend Fred Eldridge, but he suspected it was already too late to save it. Satterlee later wrote, "He said that the thing to do was to save the other trust companies and prevent general disaster."[21]

The Problem of Charles W. Morse

The nagging question that afternoon was why Charles T. Barney, the president of the Knickerbocker, should have been toppled in the aftermath of the Heinzes' attempted corner of United Copper; Barney was not directly involved in the corner. However, Barney *was* long associated with Charles Morse, who *had* been associated with Augustus Heinze. Morse's two banks, the Bank of North America and the

* As satisfying as such arguments might have been to populists and progressives, Knickerbocker does not easily fit the profile of an insurgent. An examination of its board of directors before the panic reveals a number of people who, while not in the orbit of Morgan and his circle, were prominent in the business and financial community of New York. The board included Payne Whitney (wealthy businessman and son of the organizer of the American Tobacco Trust), Foster Higgins (senior officer of the Chamber of Commerce), Moses Taylor (banker, merchant, and one of the wealthiest persons of the day), and others.

New Amsterdam, had been severely compromised in the fallout from the Heinze copper corner. "[W]hen Mr. Morse was explaining his affairs to the Clearing House Committee," the *New York Times* reported, "he told them that they ought to look around in other places too if they were going to push their investigations to the end, and that set the committee thinking. Soon after, stories of the development of the situation in the Knickerbocker got afloat in the financial district."[22] These rumors regarding apparent connections between the Knickerbocker and Morse's activities gained credence on Monday with the statement from the Knickerbocker board that Barney's dismissal was caused, in part, by "his connection with Mr. [Charles W.] Morse and some of Mr. Morse's companies."

Morse had grown up in Bath, Maine, and through hard work and shrewd dealing had amassed dominant market positions in ocean transportation between New York and New England and in the delivery of natural ice to cities on the Eastern seaboard, which garnered for him the nickname "The Ice King." Morse's Consolidated Steamship Company competed directly with railroad transportation from New York to New England and specifically with the New York, New Haven, and Hartford Railroad, in which J.P. Morgan had held a longstanding financial interest. Historian Philip Wood relates that in court testimony some of Morgan's managers said that Morgan "loathed Morse."[23] According to Satterlee, Charles W. Morse "was regarded as a dangerous man in banking circles."[24]

Unfortunately, Charles Barney had been associated with the unsavory Morse both personally and professionally for many years. For example, Barney was a director in several of Morse's biggest ventures, including the National Bank of North America and the New Amsterdam National Bank; he also served on the board of the American Ice Company, sometimes called the "Ice Trust" because of its nearly absolute monopoly of the ice business in New York City.[25] Barney was also a major shareholder in the Consolidated Steamship Lines, into which Charles W. Morse had merged six coastal steamship companies, thereby dominating all freight and passenger steamship traffic along the Eastern Seaboard.[26] Furthermore, the connections between Barney and Morse extended directly to the Knickerbocker itself. By the fall of 1907, the Knickerbocker Trust Company had major holdings in numerous Morse-controlled interests, including the Bank of North America, the American Ice Company, the American Ice Securities Company, the Butterick Company, and the Clyde Steamship Company.[27]

Morse never revealed why he may have encouraged the New York Clearing House Committee to investigate Charles T. Barney, but no less than three weeks previously Morse had been denied a seat on the board of the Knickerbocker Trust Company. After acquiring a significant block of Knickerbocker stock, Morse had demanded representation on the board, but the majority of its directors threatened to resign in protest should he be elected. Whatever the motivations may have been, by Monday afternoon the implications of Barney's and the Knickerbocker's connections to Morse (and possibly Heinze) were understood to exist. Barney was out and "J. P. Morgan's bank," the National Bank of Commerce, had turned its back on the Knickerbocker Trust Company.

Knickerbocker Hopes for Assistance

At 9 p.m. on Monday, October 21, the meeting Morgan had proposed for the Knickerbocker directors was assembled at Sherry's, a popular and famous restaurant at Fifth Avenue and 44th Street. Morgan, Perkins, and Steele retired to a private room for dinner, while the directors and their friends met separately to consider the condition of the trust company. "At the meeting it became evident that the Knickerbocker situation was pretty desperate and, unless promptly in hand, would certainly cause a run on that company which might spread to others," Perkins recalled.[28] By 11 p.m., nothing had been accomplished; Perkins called for other leading bankers and trust company presidents to join them, while Morgan, who was suffering from a severe cold, returned to his library at 36th Street.

The conferences at Sherry's lasted until 1 a.m., when the Knickerbocker board decided to open the trust company the next day; if there were another run by depositors, they would keep the Knickerbocker open as long as it would take them to secure additional assistance from other financial institutions.[29] It was hoped that there would be enough time for other banks to investigate the condition of the Knickerbocker for themselves and to provide relief.

The Dilemma

The critical question was whether the Knickerbocker was merely out of cash (illiquid) or was unable to meet its liabilities even if all assets were converted to cash (insolvent). Conventional thinking at the turn of the century was that in a panic, illiquid institutions should be supported, and insolvent institutions should declare bankruptcy. The iconic expression of this was Walter Bagehot's *Lombard Street: A Description of the Money Market*, published in 1873.

In Bagehot's day, Lombard Street in London was the center of the international money market, and the location of the Bank of England. Bagehot styled the book as a kind of primer for new professionals on Lombard Street. It was an extended argument in favor of a muscular central bank, one that would serve the liberal (and mercantile) policies of Britain and that would generally create the conditions for economic stability and advancement. An important responsibility of such a bank, he argued, was to fight financial crises by being a "lender of last resort" (LOLR).*

Bagehot's advice for such lenders was that in a financial crisis, the LOLR should lend freely to solvent borrowers upon good collateral and at a penalty rate. Consider the three elements of Bagehot's instruction:

1. *Lend freely:* Illiquidity is a hallmark of financial crises. When depositors run and withdraw their savings from banks—both the healthy and distressed ones—banks call in loans. Credit, the lifeblood of commerce, stops flowing. By lending freely into the financial system, the LOLR supplies the short-term funding that banks need and

* Bagehot did not invent the phrase "lender of last resort." In 1802, Henry Thornton published *An Enquiry into the Nature and Effects of the Paper Credit of Great Britain*, in which he proposed that the Bank of England should be a backstop for the financial system. Bagehot's novel contribution was to suggest *how* the central bank should perform such a function.

thereby helps to quell runs and forestall the credit contraction that sparks a debt-deflation spiral.

2. *Solvent borrowers upon good collateral:* This is a "tough love" policy. To demand good collateral is to guard against losses by the LOLR. And it also means that the LOLR will really support only the solvent institutions and will necessarily allow insolvent institutions to fail, preventing the persistence of "zombie banks" and the misallocation of resources they entail. It has been said that capitalism without bankruptcy is like Christianity without hell.[30] A world without the risk of failure fuels moral hazard. Yet allowing some institutions to fail might worsen a crisis. Perhaps some institutions are "too big to fail." Moreover, judging the value of collateral under crisis conditions is fraught with numerous issues, not least of which is whether the market prices of securities during a crisis reflect the intrinsic value of those securities. In short, always demanding good collateral as a condition of lending freely might prolong the crisis.
3. *At a penalty rate:* Charging high rates of interest in a crisis may seem like extortion to stressed banks. But high rates may be useful. They discourage opportunists who would exploit the eagerness of the LOLR to lend freely and end the crisis. And they discourage moral hazard by penalizing lenders who were too expansive. Of course, interest rates should always be tailored to the risk of the situation, thus enticing capital to come out of hoarding. Less-than-penalty rates might distort the efficient allocation of capital in an economy and/or fuel moral hazard. But setting very high rates might work against the goal of restoring liquidity to financial markets and institutions.

Resolving the dilemma of the Knickerbocker's financial condition was thus among J.P. Morgan's chief concerns, and he assigned Henry Davison and Benjamin Strong to examine the Knickerbocker's books and report back the next day. Under Walter Bagehot's logic, if they determined that Knickerbocker was sound, Morgan would be justified to find money to keep it afloat.[31] For a bank to be "sound" meant that the value of its assets exceeded the value of its liabilities, that it passed a fundamental test of solvency.

Davison and Strong faced a nearly insuperable task. For instance, Knickerbocker's pre-panic balance sheet showed 76 investments in public securities and numerous private commercial and real estate loans—63 percent of its assets were concentrated in collateralized loans, probably call loans on the NYSE.[32] The two men faced a massive valuation exercise with only pencil and paper and none of the modern conveniences such as computers, databases, information retrieval systems, generally accepted accounting principles, certified audits, or bond ratings.

Chapter 11

A Classic Run

The worst and most dangerous feature in the view of Wall Street was the alarm among the public.

—*Wall Street Journal*, October 23, 1907

On Tuesday morning, October 22, the mid-autumn weather in New York City was fair and mild.[1] That was fortunate, since there was already an eddying crowd outside the Knickerbocker Trust Company's great bronze doors at Fifth Avenue and 34th Street by 9 a.m. Altogether about 100 people, mostly small shopkeepers, mechanics, and clerks, waited patiently on the sidewalk to reclaim their deposits. Even when the firm opened at its regular time an hour later, everything remained orderly and there were no violent scenes, tears, or frantic handwringing. Men stood in one primary line, while women stepped into a separate room to the left of the bank's main entrance. Within 15 minutes, the line extended out the doors and down the steps to the sidewalk, as company officers and policemen marshaled the growing crowd into formation.[2]

Inside the building, clerks behind the Knickerbocker's ornate bronze gratings were paying off depositors as fast as they could compute interest and stamp vouchers. "Stacks of green currency, bound into thousand dollar lots, were piled on the counters beside the tellers," the *Washington Post* reported. "One by one these stacks were broached and they dwindled rapidly. Clerks went to the vaults from time to time with arms full of notes, piled up like bundles of kindling wood."[3] As the morning wore on, many more depositors arrived carrying satchels, showing they were ready to carry off large amounts. One young man, "with his hands trembling," the *Times* reported, "stacked his trousers pockets full of one-hundred-dollar and twenty-dollar bills."[4] Meanwhile, messengers from the downtown banks were bringing in bags of money, and one of them even came laden with three big wooden boxes of silver.[5]

The line of depositors inside the green-marbled banking room turned in circles, such that every inch of the big lobby of the bank was covered. They crowded the center desk so closely that as they inched along, men and women could make out their checks without leaving the line, resting their blanks on their forearms, handbags, or bankbooks.[6] As word of the run began to spread, a line of automobiles and finely appointed carriages formed in front of the Knickerbocker, and women in silks and men in frock coats and ties took their places in the queue. "Around the stock tickers in the offices of the officials women again and again gathered and read the tape, quoting aloud the prices and showing their interest in the values of stocks and bonds as well as in their cash holdings."[7] Meanwhile, the Knickerbocker's vice president, William Trumbull, told depositors that the trust company would keep paying out until the end of official hours at 3 p.m., adding, "It will be a physical impossibility for them to count out and turn over the money they have during the time remaining."[8] For the most part, the depositors took their long wait stoically, but as the hours wore on some showed their impatience. One man complained bitterly at the slowness of those ahead of him counting their money. "Every half hour, he said, "is costing me five dollars. I have got to get cash for the Clearing House, and I am fined for each half hour's delay."[9]

At the Knickerbocker's downtown office in the Metropolitan Life Building at 66 Broadway, the scenes were largely the same. At first, the line there extended only from the banking room out to Broadway, but as the day progressed it doubled upon itself in a great "S."[10] While the morning crowd was comprised of only about 50 people, "as fast as a depositor went out of the place ten people and more came asking for their money," the *Times* reported, "and the police of the West 30th Street Station were asked to send some men to keep order."[11] Despite the apparent orderliness of the proceedings, the *Wall Street Journal* opined on the underlying dread felt by many:

> *The worst and most dangerous feature in the view of Wall Street was the alarm among the public. The frightened depositor is a proposition New York has not had to handle in recent times and assurance which would satisfy the Street and its experienced leaders might be meaningless to the sort of crowd which gathered outside 66 Broadway at the opening of business in the morning.*[12]

At 12:35 p.m., Joseph T. Brown, an officer of the Knickerbocker Trust Company, stepped onto a chair in the middle of the lines of depositors and read a statement from the state superintendent of banks, saying that the New York State banking department had examined the Knickerbocker on September 17, and had found that it had assets of $68,884,523 and liabilities of $63,701,531. When he finished, there was a weak-hearted cheer, but nobody dropped out of line and payments continued.[13] The *New York Times* described the scene that ensued:

> *About this time the crowd of depositors and messengers from brokerage houses, sent to report on the situation, filled the lobby to the doors. A small overflow on Broadway promised to draw an increasing crowd, and half a dozen policemen from the John Street Station were sent down to keep order. The sidewalks in front of the American Express offices across the street were crowded with a small mob.*[14]

The bank officer then announced that no more payments would be made. "Payments of checks will be, probably, resumed in the morning," Brown added weakly. "Louder," came the calls from a number of men in the banking room who could not hear. "The company is solvent," Brown shouted back as he sought refuge in his office. The tellers closed their windows as the remaining depositors and bank messengers within harried the other officials with questions.[15] Meanwhile, uptown, at the Knickerbocker's stately and reassuring building on Fifth Avenue, a telephone message arrived from 66 Broadway. It instructed the cessation of all payments there as well. William Trumbull, a Knickerbocker vice president, said, "Something must have happened downtown. It means that we have the assets, but that we can't realize on them just now to pay off our liabilities." Someone in the crowd shouted, "Will payment be resumed in the morning?" Trumbull said, "I can't tell."[16]

For an hour after the doors were closed most of the waiting depositors stayed in formation, while others clamored at the locked doors for more news about the situation. "Up to that time the crowd had been calm, and, in fact, somewhat sheepish," the *New York Times* reported. "The words from the doorway had been imperfectly understood, and when the banking office was shut against them those waiting in the lobby gathered in excited groups, demanding of each other what it meant."[17] Many of them simply persevered and waited outside until the close of banking hours.[18] "Idlers stood and stared at the windows in which the shades had been pulled down," Satterlee remarked, "and the police had to be summoned to clear the streets."[19]

Within two and a half hours on Tuesday, October 22, the Knickerbocker Trust Company had returned more than $8 million to depositors at its offices on Fifth Avenue, Broadway, and its two smaller branches in Harlem and the Bronx.[20] Around noon, the new president of the Knickerbocker, A. Foster Higgins, entered the building at 34th Street, where he held a series of consultations in the officers' rooms.[21] Despite the assurances of the financiers at Sherry's the day before, the officers of Knickerbocker said that no money was forthcoming when needed.[22] Of the total paid to depositors, $4 million was paid directly in cash, and another $4 million was paid through the clearing house.[23]

The proximate cause for the suspension of the Knickerbocker on Tuesday was the flood of very large checks presented for payment by other banking institutions. Just before the order to suspend, a messenger, reportedly from the Hanover National Bank, appeared at the Knickerbocker's window downtown with a check for $1.5 million, which the Knickerbocker cashed; shortly thereafter, another messenger from a different bank arrived with a check for $1 million, which was also cashed. "The paying teller handed out this money," the *Times* reported, "and immediately closed down his window. There was still some cash left in the paying teller's cage, but the officers had realized by that time that needed help was not forthcoming, and suspension was the only recourse."[24] Large numbers of messengers from brokerages and banks remained in line, holding large batches of several hundred checks, but these messengers were turned away as the tellers closed their windows.

What Prompted the Run?

The Knickerbocker's final day is emblematic of thousands of episodes before and since called bank runs. A "run," according to economist Gary Gorton, is an "unexpectedly large withdrawal of deposits" in which uninformed depositors spontaneously test whether the bank's assets have been impaired by some actual or rumored calamity.[25] A "panic" is systemic, the simultaneous occurrence of many individual runs. Gorton argues that panics are sparked by changing perceptions of deposit risk caused, for instance, by variations in the business cycle, as opposed to idiosyncratic causes such as the weather that day or what a depositor ate for breakfast.

Virtually all banks are exposed to the risk of runs because they make investments in assets that are less liquid than cash, while offering depositors the right to withdraw *upon demand*. The problem in 1907 was that depositors could not ascertain the quality of the bank's assets—this was an information asymmetry (insiders knew more than outsiders) for which depositors had few remedies other than to withdraw funds. A run, then, could be viewed as a test by which depositors essentially audited the quality of the bank's assets.[26] Gorton emphasized that a run could be a rational response to the threat of capital losses.[27]

Because depositors would be served sequentially, according to where they stood in line, they were motivated to act sooner rather than later. How soon to act would depend not based on one's own assessment of the bank, but upon what one believed others' assessment was. This led the eminent sociologist Robert K. Merton to suggest that bank runs could be generated by a "self-fulfilling prophecy," by which the mere suspicion of bank failure leads to its fulfillment.[28] As economics relentlessly emphasizes, expectations matter—whether they are well-founded or not.

Nobel Laureates in Economics Douglas Diamond and Philip Dybvig modeled bank runs as potentially triggered by a range of possible variables, even just random patterns of withdrawals.[29] A colleague once described to us a run on a small bank in China that began when a line into a coffee shop extended across the front of a bank next door and caused the public to assume that the bank was in trouble.[30] Other theorists have suggested changes in investor sentiment[31] and sunspots[32] as possible causes. The indeterminacy of causes appeals to explanations based on the idiosyncrasy of financial crises.

However, the facts surrounding the run on the Knickerbocker on October 22 seem consistent with Gorton's idea that runs start because of shocking news that raises the risk of a bank's suspension. Information problems make it impossible to know exactly what is going on. In turn, the information problems spark adverse selection: depositors run.

What the general mass of Knickerbocker depositors knew on October 22 was as follows. Business conditions turned sour starting in June 1907. Credit market conditions were tight owing to the restrictive policies of the Bank of England and other central banks; firms and municipalities found it increasingly difficult to refinance their debts. Large losses in a busted copper speculation led depositors in banks both directly and distantly affiliated with the Heinze-Morse circle to exercise their deposit contracts and withdraw their funds. Morse and Barney had had some business dealings together.* Barney restricted the release of

* Chapter 9 described Barney's service on the boards of Morse-controlled companies. Morse had been nominated to join the Knickerbocker's board—a nomination that would hardly have come forward without some acquiescence by Barney—although in the final event the board declined to elect Morse. Barney approved a loan of $200,000 by the Knickerbocker to Morse, collateralized by shares in Morse's ice business; some observers judged that the value of the shares was inadequate to backstop the loan. Morse's biographer, Philip Woods (2011, p. 28), mentions that in 1902 both Barney and Morse were ejected from the board of Knickerbocker Ice Company of Philadelphia because of stock manipulation. Woods also documents real estate investments by Morse and Barney around 1900 (2011, p. 49) and investments in banks (2011, p. 52). Mary O'Sullivan (2016, p. 205) notes that engagement between Barney and Morse included participation in pools organized to manipulate the share price of the American Ice Securities Company. Sarah McNelis (1968, p. 156) relates a comment by Otto Heinze in his unpublished manuscript that Barney "was very close to Charles Morse." Bradley Hansen (2014) reports that Morse offered Barney an opportunity to participate in the United Copper Corner, but Barney turned it down, not wanting to involve the Knickerbocker in the scheme. Barney's successor as president of the Knickerbocker told the *New York Times* that "Mr. Barney's financial embarrassment was largely due to his affiliation with Charles W. Morse . . . that Mr. Morse was his "malignant enemy." ["Barney's Successor Puts All On Morse," *New York Times,* November 16, 1907, p. 1.] Ellis Tallman and Jon Moen (2014, p. 7) acknowledge that rumors of Barney's association with the Heinze–Morse group prompted withdrawals from the Knickerbocker; they assert, however, that Barney's "involvement in any of the Heinze–Morse activities has not been proven." This is a subject worthy of further research.

information about the financial condition of the Knickerbocker, even to his own staff and directors. In short, for depositors aware of worsening macroeconomic conditions and imperfectly informed about an association between Morse and Barney, the runs at Morse-controlled banks plausibly shocked the well-informed to commence a run on the Knickerbocker.

A way to discourage bank runs is to guarantee deposits through some form of insurance. Unfortunately, in 1907 deposit guarantees were anathema to orthodox bankers on the grounds that they would foster moral hazard. The Panic of 1907 would begin a serious shift in orthodox thinking that would ultimately culminate in the creation of federal deposit insurance in 1933.

Chapter 12

Such Assistance as May Be Necessary

If we get help overnight we shall reopen in the morning. If we don't, we won't. That's all there is to it at present. We can't tell now whether we are going to get help or not.

—G. L. Boissevain, Knickerbocker Trust Company[1]

After the Bank of Commerce had announced on Monday, October 21, that it would no longer clear for the Knickerbocker Trust Company, all the other national banks also refused to cash the Knickerbocker's checks, reflecting their growing unease about the Knickerbocker's ability to honor the checks for payment. The banks would, however, accept checks for collection on behalf of the Knickerbocker's depositors, even though those depositors would not be paid until the banks received payment directly from the Knickerbocker. It was in this way that large numbers of checks started arriving at the Knickerbocker late on Tuesday morning, October 22. Throughout the day many other banks were also sending messengers to the Knickerbocker on behalf of clients or customers who had deposits with the Knickerbocker and who sought to collect through other institutions. Ultimately, such exchanges accounted for nearly $5 million of the total disbursed that day, and they quickly overwhelmed the Knickerbocker's ability to honor them.[2]

A Fateful Decision: No Rescue for the Knickerbocker

As depositors of the Knickerbocker clamored for their money, J. Pierpont Morgan's diligence team hurried to review the trust company's accounts. Later, Benjamin Strong, the leader of the review team, described the situation on Tuesday midday, October 22:

> *While sitting in the [Knickerbocker's] rear office, we could hear those forming the long line of depositors waiting to draw out their balances clamoring for information as to what was going to happen . . . Harry [Davison] came into the room some time around noon and I spent possibly fifteen or twenty minutes in hurriedly giving him a picture of the situation, although by that time we had not completed much more than an examination of one-half of the records of assets submitted to us. The question was whether, first the trust company was solvent, and second whether there were assets adequate to secure loans to see them through a serious crisis. In the short space allotted us it was absolutely impossible to give any assurances upon which any pledge of assistance could be based . . . I well remember the anxiety with which we discussed what should be said to Mr. Baker and Mr. Morgan who were awaiting our word. Most reluctantly, and with some appreciation of the possible consequences, we both agreed that honesty and fairness to everybody required us to say it was absolutely impossible in the length of time allowed us to answer those two questions or to make any reliable report.*[3]

Davison and Strong reported back to Morgan and the committee: they were unable to establish Knickerbocker's solvency in the time available. This did not mean that Knickerbocker was truly insolvent. Instead, Davison and Strong were unable to tell. Morgan and the committee faced a dilemma: Was Knickerbocker's inability to give persuasive evidence of its solvency on short notice sufficient to deny it rescue funding?

Morgan chose not to intervene, as the *New York Times* explained, because he "did not care to assume the responsibilities of previous poor management."[4] This decision would prove to be one of the pivotal events of the panic.

History has been critical of Morgan's decision: "a mistake,"[5] an "error of judgment,"[6] "Knickerbocker's closure spread havoc among New York's trust companies;"[7] and Morgan closed "the Knickerbocker because he regarded it as threat to his control of finance."[8] However, the banking orthodoxy of the day—"Bagehot's Rule"—could also explain Morgan's choice as reflecting a complex trade-off of concerns about liquidity, solvency, crisis dynamics, moral hazard, imperfect information, incentives, accountability, and effective resource allocation. Our examination of several archives yielded no evidence confirming one view over the others. Morgan's decision remains a subject worthy of future research.

When the Knickerbocker's tellers finally closed their windows, Strong, who was still inside the company's offices, remembered, "The consternation on the faces of the people on that line, many of them men whom I knew, I shall never forget."[9] One of the clearing-house bankers also confirmed that any attempts to uphold the Knickerbocker had, in fact, been abandoned early in the day:

> *The character of much of the Knickerbocker's collateral is not readily marketable, and now that it has suspended payments temporarily, it is altogether likely that its credit has been so heavily impaired that a resumption would bring about another run. That might mean that support to the amount perhaps of $25,000,000 or more would be needed to carry the institution through. Under the circumstances it is better that the trust company be liquidated than that the reserves of other institutions be so heavily depleted.*[10]

The directors of the Knickerbocker had remained in their boardroom all through the harrowing day on Tuesday. "Without exception they wore the looks of men who thought the world had used them hard," the *Wall Street Journal* reported.[11] One of the Knickerbocker's board members, G. L. Boissevain, said, "If we get help overnight we shall reopen in the morning. If we don't, we won't. That's all there is to it at present. We can't tell now whether we are going to get help or not."[12] The superintendent of the state's banking department confirmed this assessment of the situation.[13]

Reassurance to Depositors

In an attempt to reassure all depositors, the New York Clearing House (NYCH) announced that all association member banks were strong and that they would be protected; however, the NYCH refused to provide any relief for the Knickerbocker.[14] One of the chief conferees, an NYCH committee member, tried to sound a note of optimism, saying, "I think it is safe to say that no other financial institution of the least importance will have to undergo the experiences of the Knickerbocker Trust Company. I feel optimistic for the first time since these troubles began."[15] A. Barton Hepburn, president of Chase National Bank, added, "I believe the general banking conditions will continue to improve from now on. The trouble at its origin was due to peculiar methods of certain parties [i.e., Barney, Heinze, and Morse] who have now been forced out of the situation and the clearing house will continue to render such assistance as may be necessary."[16]

Despite the reassurances from the NYCH, news of the run on the Knickerbocker and its subsequent suspension was wreaking havoc on the markets. All loanable funds became hard to find as almost all the banks and trust companies hoarded their cash throughout the day. Trust companies, the largest lenders into the call money market, called in loans. At the market's opening on Tuesday, the call money rate was quoted at a nominal 10 percent, but by noon there were no offers for money at all on the floor of the exchange. During the afternoon the money rates then advanced to 60 percent, declined to 40 percent, and surged up again to 70 percent a half hour before the market closed.[17] As the call money dried up, stock prices slumped to their lowest level since December 1900. There were also reports of the failure of another prominent stock exchange house, Marcus & Mayer. And vague rumors surfaced about the condition of other institutions, "which shook Wall Street to its foundations."[18]

Back at 23 Wall Street, J. P. Morgan and his associates conferred with an oncoming flood of bankers and trust company presidents. It appeared that the runs on the trust companies were not limited to the Knickerbocker. In particular, the president of the Trust Company of America (TCA) told them he was "desperately anxious" because the withdrawals from his company on Tuesday had been exceptionally heavy.[19] TCA, also located on Wall Street, was presided over by Oakleigh Thorne, a popular member of a prominent New York family. Like Charles Barney at the Knickerbocker, Thorne had also opened several branch offices for his trust company and had grown its deposit base very rapidly;[20] TCA had about $50 million in deposits and about $100 million in assets.[21] The precise cause for the run there was unknown, but one of TCA's board members was none other than Charles T. Barney.[22]

Assistance from the U.S. Treasury

On Tuesday afternoon, J. P. Morgan decided that the Secretary of the U.S. Treasury, George B. Cortelyou, should be summoned to New York immediately for a conference. Since the cascade of financial crises in the 1890s, the U.S. Treasury Department had engaged more actively in the financial system in an effort to forestall liquidity droughts that seeded banking panics. Cortelyou's predecessor, Secretary Leslie Shaw, had pursued a policy of depositing Treasury Department gold reserves with national banks in anticipation of peak credit demands during the annual harvest cycle. Shaw had also encouraged importation of gold from Europe to boost the liquidity of the financial system.

George Cortelyou had been appointed Secretary of the Treasury on March 4, 1907, just as the U.S. equity markets were sliding into the "rich man's panic" that spring—a portent, perhaps, of the role he would play in the coming crisis.* As he now took the afternoon train from Washington, DC, to Manhattan, banks around the country were rapidly pulling their

* George Cortelyou was born in New York City in 1862, earned a law degree, and pursued a career in the public sector, beginning in the postal system. He came to the attention of President Grover Cleveland, who hired him in 1895 to be his personal secretary. In turn, Cleveland recommended Cortelyou to President-elect William McKinley, who retained him. After McKinley's assassination in 1901, Theodore Roosevelt (TR) retained Cortelyou and then appointed him to be the first U.S. Secretary of Commerce and Labor in 1903. A year later, Cortelyou agreed to chair the Republican National Committee, essentially managing TR's campaign for reelection. Critics murmured that Cortelyou engineered large gifts to the campaign that exposed the president to plutocratic influence. After TR's successful reelection, he appointed Cortelyou to be Postmaster General. Two years later, Cortelyou moved to the Treasury Department as Secretary. In short, George Cortelyou epitomized the emergence in the late nineteenth century of a new model of public servant, who over a lifetime served in a variety of senior capacities, playing an important role in shaping new policies, and yet always in the shadow of a prominent leader.

reserves out of New York, resulting in further pressures on available liquidity.[23] Upon leaving the conference at his offices at 6 p.m., Morgan, still suffering from his cold, said to a reporter, "We are doing everything we can as fast as we can, but nothing has yet crystallized."[24]

After Cortelyou arrived in New York at 9 p.m. on October 22, Morgan, Stillman (president of the National City Bank), Baker (president of the First National Bank), and Perkins (partner at J.P. Morgan & Company) went to see him at the Manhattan Hotel. At the meeting the Secretary said he was ready to deposit government money in the banks to help support the situation. The next day, Cortelyou directed $25 million in government gold to be deposited among large New York City banks, on the expectation that they would relend the funds to places of the greatest need. National City Bank received $8 million; First National Bank, led by Morgan's friend George F. Baker, received $4 million; and the National Bank of Commerce got $2.5 million. The balance of $10.5 million went to 11 other New York national banks. Notably, J.P. Morgan & Co. was not a recipient of Treasury funds, but the bulk of the funds flowed to institutions in which Morgan had influence.

Cortelyou's policy of directing rescue funds to national banks in New York City would prove controversial. Why New York? Why only large banks? His policies sharpened the divides in the country between the eastern coastal elites and the interior; between big banks and small; between banks and shadow banks; and between the circle of J.P. Morgan and everyone else.

Another problem with Cortelyou's injection of funds was that even the federal government did not have a limitless supply of cash. As the funds went into New York banks, they went out again. Country bankers clamored for more liquidity and criticized Cortelyou for dispersing Treasury cash over the past summer, in advance of the harvest season's demands. As a result of all its injections before and during the Panic, Cortelyou ran the Treasury's balance of surplus currency down to about $5 million by mid-November.[25] Cortelyou subsequently reported that about $296 million[26] vanished from the money supply of the country, through hoarding.[27] As people and companies stuffed their savings under the mattress, the credit crunch turned into a liquidity crunch.

The exhaustion of the Treasury's cash left the New York bankers with a stark choice. They could serve the demands of country bankers by (1) reducing their own reserves below the legal limit, (2) calling in loans of their own customers, which would trigger a sharp economic contraction, or (3) suspending the withdrawal of deposits, a venerable response to panics in prior years.

A Press Release on Wednesday Morning

"We adjourned at two o'clock [a.m. on Wednesday, October 23] feeling that, without much of any doubt, there would be runs on other institutions," George Perkins said.[28] Among the issues discussed that night was the situation concerning Oakleigh Thorne's Trust Company of America, and the group of bankers was considering how to aid that firm. In a statement to the *New York Times*, George Perkins said:

> *The chief sore point is the Trust Company of America. The conferees feel that the situation there is such that the company is sound. Provision has been made to supply all the cash needed this morning. The conferees feel sure the company will be able to pull through. The company has twelve million dollars cash and as much more as needed has been pledged for the purpose. It is safe to assume that J. P. Morgan & Co. will be leaders in this movement to furnish funds.*[29]

Later, in government hearings, critics would allege that the first sentence of this statement triggered runs at Trust Company of America and reflected part of a coordinated effort to bring the trust companies down.[30]

Strong's Evaluation of Trust Company of America

Around 2 a.m. on Wednesday, October 23, Benjamin Strong was contacted at his home in Greenwich, Connecticut, and was told to assemble a team at once to begin an examination of the Trust Company of America. Morgan wanted a full report on TCA in his office by noon that day.[31] Strong headed directly for Manhattan, and he and his colleagues worked through the night to ascertain the strength of the Trust Company of America.

Strong's task—like the one he executed at the Knickerbocker—was to determine whether TCA was merely illiquid, as opposed to insolvent. The straightforward test of insolvency would be to value the assets of TCA and compare that value to the liabilities outstanding. If the assets exceeded the liabilities, then TCA's problem was illiquidity, the inability to convert loans into cash fast enough to meet the demands of depositors. In that case, a bridge loan to TCA could be warranted. This must have been a challenging analysis for Benjamin Strong. According to a report submitted to the New York State Superintendent of Banks at the end of 1907, TCA's assets included $27 million in secured loans, $3.8 million in unsecured loans, and a portfolio of bonds and stocks consisting of 84 different securities.[32]

As the day began, Morgan's health had worsened, and his family could scarcely rouse him from bed. "He seemed to be in a stupor," remembered Herbert Satterlee.[33] After his personal physician was summoned, giving Pierpont sprays and gargles, the financier finally came down to breakfast, where he conferred at the library with George Perkins and reviewed the estimates of the cash that would be needed for the day's withdrawals from the banks and trusts. After a few meetings, he drove downtown to the Corner, where E. H. Harriman of the Union Pacific Railroad and Henry Clay Frick of U.S. Steel Corporation, among others, were waiting to see him about the prevailing conditions.

Morgan was acutely concerned about the situations at the trust companies. "The Knickerbocker had gone over the dam and the Trust Company of America was nearing the brink," Satterlee observed.[34] By 1 p.m. on Wednesday when he arrived at the Corner, Benjamin Strong had a reached a verdict about the Trust Company. Many of the trust company presidents were already meeting in one room, while Davison, Perkins, Baker, Stillman, and Morgan were in another. When Strong entered, Morgan remarked at once, "Have you anyone with you who can make a report to the gentlemen in the next room? They are the presidents of the trust companies, and when they came into the office they had to be introduced to each other,* and I don't think much can

* The lack of acquaintance among trust company CEOs was a symptom of the larger challenge Morgan would face in trying to organize collective action among them. For more on the absence of cohesion among the trust companies, see Chapters 9 and 24 and the technical appendix.

be expected of them. Sit down with Mr. Baker, Mr. Stillman, and me, and tell us about it."[35]

While an associate of Strong's met in the next room with the trust company presidents, Strong himself offered Morgan, Stillman, and Baker a picture of the situation at the Trust Company of America. Strong described the next few moments as follows:

> *I remember Mr. Morgan repeatedly saying, "Are they solvent?" He wanted no details, but the general facts and results, and seemed satisfied with the opinions I expressed. There were two or three large loans in the Trust Company which I had to ask Mr. Morgan, Mr. Baker, and Mr. Stillman for their own opinion, and with what I remember telling Mr. Morgan that I was satisfied that the company was solvent; that I thought their surplus had been pretty much wiped out; but that the capital was not greatly impaired, if at all, although were the company to be liquidated there were many assets which it would take some years to convert into cash.*[36]

The entire meeting with Strong lasted about 45 minutes, during which J. Pierpont Morgan spoke no more than five or six times. Morgan asked Strong if he thought the bankers would be justified in seeing the company through its troubles. Strong answered in the affirmative.

Morgan turned to Baker and Stillman: "This is the place to stop the trouble, then."[37]

Morgan's determined reply marked a pivotal moment in the panic episode. From this stage onward, Morgan (and his circle of major bankers and industrialists) assumed the role of a *lender of last resort*, implementing the advice of Walter Bagehot 34 years earlier that in a financial crisis, the rescuer should lend freely, upon good collateral, and at a penalty rate.[38]

Chapter 13

Trust Company of America

The look of relief on his face when I handed him the first earnest money I shall never forget.

—Benjamin Strong, Jr., Bankers Trust Company[1]

The Trust Company of America was in imminent peril. Morgan received the report from Strong at midday on Wednesday, October 23. And then Oakleigh Thorne, president of the Trust Company, called the Corner and told J. Pierpont Morgan that his company's meager cash supply had dwindled to $1.2 million.

The challenge to the Trust Company marked a significant new chapter in the spread of the panic. Founded in 1885 and headquartered at 27 Wall Street in the heart of the financial district of New York, the Trust Company had the trappings of stability. It was the fifth-largest trust company in Manhattan by dollar value of deposits and had the third-largest number of accounts. Yet 55 percent of the firm's assets consisted of "loans on collateral," of which a material portion probably were call loans, whose value and risk depended on the level of share prices any given day. Another 17 percent of assets were invested in stocks and bonds—however, listed at historical book value earlier in the year, by October 22, the portfolio of securities was doubtlessly worth considerably less in market value. In short, up to three-quarters of the firm's assets were linked to the securities markets, where prices had fallen sharply since the start of the year. Finally, the Trust Company's clients held relatively smaller balances in their accounts, ranking in the lower third of the field. This was a runnable client base: presumably less wealthy, less resilient to bad economic news, and more prone to withdraw.[2]

The run on the Trust Company had become formidable. Thorne was doubtful he could keep its doors open until the end of business at 3 p.m. Nearly 1,200 depositors had assembled outside the Trust Company's main offices in lower Manhattan, grouped in a line snaking east to William Street and down to Exchange Place. To stem the flow from his vaults, Thorne kept only two teller windows open all morning; he also arranged to have large piles of cash on view to reassure anxious depositors that the institution had ample reserves. But in a replay of the previous day's scenes at the Knickerbocker, worried customers, clerks, and office boys took up a desultory vigil to reclaim their (or their employer's) cash. Investors and depositors had lost faith in yet another prominent New York financial institution.

Twenty minutes later, Thorne called on Morgan again in a greater state of panic. His cash reserves were now down to $800,000, and unless he could raise $3 million, he would have to close the Trust Company instantly.

Morgan Attempts to Form a Trust Company Rescue Pool

Morgan turned to the 10 trust company presidents in the room with him, whom he had called together earlier to address the widening panic. He suggested that each of them agree to loan $300,000 to the Trust Company of America. The president of the Farmers Loan & Trust Company took up the offer right away, but the meeting fell apart and devolved into a confused debate for another 20 minutes.

At about 1:45 p.m., Thorne again pleaded for aid. Now he had only $500,000 remaining. The presidents of the other trust companies had assembled at Morgan's library—as they had done daily since J.P. Morgan had returned to New York on the 20th—and continued to argue. In their view it was not their place to intervene, and they were prepared to abandon one of their own. Morgan's efforts to mobilize collective action among the trust company presidents had failed again.

At 2:15 p.m., a committee from the Trust Company of America entered the room and reported they had only $180,000 left and they had decided to cease operations. "Well," Morgan exclaimed, "I don't see anything else to do."[3] Exasperated by the temporizing of the trust companies, he abruptly dismissed the meeting. At the suggestion of his partner and close associate, George W. Perkins, Morgan summoned the presidents of the city's two largest banks: James Stillman of the National City Bank and George F. Baker of the First National Bank of New York. After opening a direct phone line to the offices of the Trust Company of America, Morgan told Oakleigh Thorne to come see him at once, bringing with him the most valuable securities held in his company's vaults.

Within minutes, the doors of Morgan's office were thrown open and in walked a long line of men with bags and boxes filled with securities owned by the Trust Company of America. Stillman sat in an adjoining room where he maintained an open telephone line with the National City Bank. Morgan commanded a large table as Thorne and his clerks laid out the Trust Company's securities for the purpose of valuing them in exchange for a loan. Making notes on a pad as they went along, Morgan assessed the securities, and as he determined that enough collateral was available for an advance, he asked Stillman to have National City Bank send that amount in cash over to the Trust Company. Every few minutes, at Morgan's direction, money was carried in sacks directly to the Trust Company's vaults. Morgan and his men proceeded in this way until $3 million had been delivered. The doors stayed open until 3 p.m. and the Trust Company of America had been saved for a day.

At 3:15 p.m., Morgan convened the trust company presidents again, making urgent appeals for them to take action. Now they agreed to form a committee to *monitor* the situation of the trust companies over the coming days, which would have the power to call for information from any of the other trust companies. In this way, the committee would function like the banks' clearing house. The concept was that any request for assistance for the trust companies would be referred there. The new trust company committee would have five members and its chair would be Edward King, president of the Union Trust Company, the fourth-largest in Manhattan.* While the trust companies still declined to organize a common pool for assistance, their agreement for disclosure and transparency was a step in the right direction.

Once these arrangements had been made, Morgan instructed the trust company presidents to report that night at 9:00 at the uptown offices of the Union Trust on Fifth Avenue. Meanwhile, Morgan dispatched Benjamin Strong Jr., the 35-year-old secretary of the Bankers Trust Company, to proceed with another thorough examination of the Trust Company of America's books.

As these emergency measures were undertaken on behalf of the Trust Company of America, signs appeared that economic and financial conditions were deteriorating elsewhere. The Westinghouse Electric & Manufacturing Company had been placed in the hands of a receiver. The Pittsburgh Stock Exchange had suspended trading. And a run had begun at another large New York institution, the Lincoln Trust Company.

At the same time, the mayor of New York City, George B. McClellan (the son of the Civil War general), called for a conference with all his department heads when he learned that the city would be unable to pay its salaries and contractors. The *New York Times* reported that the mayor proposed cutting the city's budget to an "irreducible minimum" because the municipal government was running up against a $12 million year-end shortfall, and the flotation of another successful bond issue seemed unlikely given the stringency in the capital markets.[4]

Even as Morgan was imploring the trust company presidents to act, others were entreating *him* to solve other problems throughout the city.

* 68-year-old Edward King descended from prominent members of New York society. A graduate of Harvard, he joined his father's bank, founded his own brokerage firm, and served as president of the New York Stock Exchange. In 1873 Union Trust Company named King as its president, in which capacity he served until his death in 1908. By virtue of its large size, age (founded in 1863), and location (headquartered at 80 Broadway in the heart of the New York financial district), Union Trust was more like an incumbent than a new entrant in the New York financial community of 1907.

At one point, he received a call on Wednesday about falling prices on the New York Stock Exchange, to which he said that if any member of the Exchange sold "short" in an attempt to promote the panic and profit from falling prices, he would be "properly attended to" after the crisis was over. Morgan's admonition was widely broadcast and apparently gave pause to the bears.[5]

The Purpose of Reserves

At another time that afternoon, one of the bank presidents was greatly disturbed about the negative turn of events, and said, "Mr. Morgan, my reserve is down to 20 percent and I don't know what to do." Morgan replied sharply, "You ought to be ashamed of yourself. Your reserve *ought* to be down to 18 percent or 20 percent. What is a reserve for if not to be used in times like these?"[6]

Cash reserves acted like shock absorbers, helping an institution respond to unexpected withdrawals by depositors. By means of reserves, an institution self-insured against shocks. However, reserves were expensive: idle cash earned no return, a fact that prompted bankers to meet, but not exceed, minimum reserve ratios set by regulators.

Regulations required national banks in New York City to maintain cash reserves at least equal to 25 percent of deposits. In practice, the Comptroller of the Currency permitted temporary deficiencies from this target. On average, the New York banks did not fall below a reserve ratio of 20 percent.[7] However, the banks associated with Heinze and Morse saw their average reserve ratio fall to 11 percent, in comparison with an average of 25.5 percent for all other NYCH members.[8] The ample reserves of the healthy New York banks prompted Professor Sprague to criticize them for hoarding.

A Nod from Morgan

Exhausted by the day's events at his downtown offices, Pierpont returned to his library late in the afternoon, by which time he was suffering mightily from his cold. His voice was hoarse and his eyes were watery, but he was still alert and energetic. After taking his dinner at the library, he left by the back door and walked the one block to offices of the Union Trust Company on the northeast corner of 36th Street and Fifth Avenue. Before seeing the trust company presidents, though, Morgan met first with George W. Perkins and Henry P. Davison. The trio sat in a small coupon room in the Union Trust basement, where Benjamin Strong offered his personal assessment of the condition of the Trust Company of America. After spending a day poring through its books, Strong reported that the Trust Company had about $2 million in equity—it was still solvent—and that its ability to pay its creditors would depend on the liquidity of its assets for its continued survival. Morgan had little to say, but he nodded his head in assent vigorously from time to time.

Armed with Strong's appraisal, Morgan and his colleagues marched upstairs to a small meeting room in the Union Trust building. One after another, the trust company presidents arrived. Morgan demanded a bold and decisive move on their part that would not only stop the run but also restore the public's wavering confidence. He recounted Strong's report for the trust officials and said it was distinctly the responsibility of the trust companies to save the Trust Company of America. He also assured them that both the clearing-house member banks and the firm of J. P. Morgan & Company would do what they could to assist the trust companies in doing so. Astonishingly, the trust company presidents again demurred. "Tension was obvious on every hand, and there was general reluctance to make any commitments," Strong later recalled.[9] Finally, Morgan challenged them. He said $10 million was required and that it must be ready by the next morning.

The first to come forward was the president of Bankers Trust Company, who agreed to provide $500,000, and as much as $1 million, if necessary. Morgan reassured them that the Secretary of the Treasury, George B. Cortelyou, who had just traveled from Washington, DC, to New York, would make deposits in select New York banks so the trust companies would have access to new sources of cash. *Still*, the trust presidents balked. They shared enthusiasm neither for saving the Trust Company of America nor for weakening their own cash positions. Their aimless discussions continued.

Morgan was clearly exhausted. At first, he sat quietly smoking, until his cigar went out. Then his head dropped forward and he fell asleep in his chair. Another 30 minutes passed. Morgan then abruptly awoke, and he immediately asked Benjamin Strong for a pencil and a sheet of paper. "Well, gentlemen," Morgan continued. "The Bankers Trust Company has agreed to take its share and more of a loan. Mr. Marsten [president of the Farmers Loan & Trust Company], how much will the Farmers Loan & Trust Company subscribe?" Marsten answered that his firm would offer just as much as Bankers Trust had.[10] In just this fashion, Morgan continued around the room, one by one, until he had secured $8.25 million. He then rose from his chair and said that the First National Bank, the National City Bank, and the Hanover National Bank would temporarily be responsible for the balance of the $10 million requested, but that they would expect the trust companies to relieve them of their contribution as soon as the loan could be organized. It was nearly midnight.

During these discussions, Oakleigh Thorne was waiting outside. After the meeting Morgan asked Strong to go with Thorne to Thorne's house on Park Avenue, where the two would pull together the securities necessary to secure the next day's loan for the Trust Company of America. As chair of the trust company committee, Edward King was responsible for providing the cash on Thursday morning from the Union Trust Company's downtown office. Meanwhile, George Perkins left for the Manhattan Hotel to see the Treasury Secretary and to provide a statement to the newspaper reporters gathered there. Morgan took a cab home to 36th Street, played a game of solitaire, again spoke briefly by phone with George Perkins, and then went to bed.

Through the night and into the early hours of the next day, Benjamin Strong labored with Oakleigh Thorne to prepare a complete schedule of the collateral the Trust Company of America would need to deliver on Thursday morning.

Union Trust Reneges

After finishing their work, Strong made his way downtown to see Edward King at the Union Trust Company in the morning of Thursday, October 24. When Strong arrived at the Union Trust, however, he was astonished when King demanded further verification of the Trust Company of America's assets; in fact, King flatly refused to deliver the promised loan to Strong. Without the fresh infusion of cash, the ongoing run at the Trust Company would jeopardize everything Morgan and the others had planned the night before.

Immediately, Strong contacted Morgan and Perkins, who were by then having a breakfast meeting at Morgan's library. Having been apprised of the situation, Morgan instructed Strong to bring forth immediately all of the Trust Company's securities remaining in the vaults of J. P. Morgan & Company; Pierpont himself had valued these securities with Thorne the day before. Morgan then told Strong to exchange these securities for cash and thus secure a temporary loan from Stillman's National City Bank. With that, Strong raced frenetically to provide life support to the Trust Company of America:

> *We ran down Wall Street to the National City Bank with some millions of securities, the street being thronged with sightseers and a long line of waiting depositors also extending down William Street from the Trust Company of America office and into Exchange Place. A very hasty examination of the collateral was made at the National City Bank, and I remember giving Mr. Whitson a pencil receipt for a bundle of gold certificates—I cannot now recall whether it was $600,000 or $1,000,000—but I put them in my pocket, ran down Wall Street, and at almost exactly ten o'clock found Mr. Thorne walking up and down the gallery overlooking the banking room in the utmost anxiety lest he was to be disappointed in the loan. The minute he saw me he said that the trust companies had failed him, the money was not forthcoming, and that he expected to close the institution promptly at ten. The look of relief on his face when I handed him the first earnest money I shall never forget.*[11]

The Trust Company of America was saved a second time in as many days. Though Morgan had doused the first fire, the conflagration of panic was just beginning to take hold.

A Nagging Question

Critics would later challenge Morgan to explain why he had rescued the Trust Company of America and yet failed to assist the Knickerbocker. The two institutions were roughly similar in size and competitive position in the financial community. Both had a faint connection with Heinze and Morse. And systemic instability was already clear at the time of the Knickerbocker's distress the day before: various runs were in progress; the Heinze-Morse banks had appealed for aid from the NYCH; and people were hoarding cash.

Morgan and the crisis team acted on what they knew. Benjamin Strong had been able to affirm the adequacy of collateral at Trust Company but was unable to do so at the Knickerbocker. As Walter Bagehot had advised 34 years earlier, in a crisis the lender of last resort should lend freely *against good collateral*. Still, the decision not to aid the Knickerbocker would dog Morgan for the rest of his days.

Chapter 14

Crisis on the Exchange

Why don't you tell them what to do, Mr. Morgan?

—Belle da Costa Greene, J. P. Morgan's personal librarian

I don't know what to do myself, but sometime, someone will come in with a plan that I know will work; and then I will tell them what to do.

—J. Pierpont Morgan[1]

As Oakleigh Thorne was opening the doors to the Trust Company of America on Thursday morning, October 24, J. Pierpont Morgan boarded a Union Club brougham drawn by a white horse, which would take him to his offices at 23 Wall Street.[2] By this time people throughout the city had already seen Morgan's picture on the front pages of many newspapers, which had proclaimed him the city's savior. Herbert Satterlee, Morgan's son-in-law, was traveling in the brougham with Pierpont, and he provided a vivid description of the atmosphere surrounding the titan that morning:

All the way downtown people who got a glimpse of him in the cab called the attention of passersby. Policemen and cabbies who knew him well by sight shouted, "There goes the Old Man!" or "There goes the Big Chief!" and the people who

> *heard them understood to whom they referred and ran beside the cab to get a peep at him. Near Trinity Church a way through the crowd opened as soon as it was realized who was in the cab. The crowd moved with us. He might have been a general at the head of a column going to the relief of a beleaguered city such was the enthusiasm he created. All this time he looked straight ahead and gave no sign of noticing the excitement, but it was evident that he was pleased.*[3]

People filled the streets at the corner of Wall and Broad in lower Manhattan. As Morgan descended from the carriage and hurried up the steps of J. P. Morgan & Company, the mob first became quiet, and then they fought their way forward to peer at the man through the windows. When he arrived inside, his office was thronged with men desperate to borrow money. Morgan went directly to his private office, where he began a conference with George Baker, James Stillman, and several other bank and trust company officials.

The Federal Government Lends Assistance

While Morgan conferred with his colleagues, dozens of vehicles were parking outside the Federal Subtreasury building across Wall Street. After a late-night meeting with Morgan's partner, George Perkins, Treasury Secretary George B. Cortelyou announced his formal support for the crisis team, committing $25 million in liquidity to quell the crisis. In an official statement given to reporters at 12:30 a.m. on October 24, Cortelyou asserted,

> *Wherever there is weakness, and it has been in but a comparatively few instances, strong and able men are rendering aid; and in behalf of the Treasury Department I may say that I believe it my duty to do, and I shall do, in the largest way possible, whatever may be necessary to afford relief.*[4]

This was a precedent-setting statement, close to a "do whatever it takes"* commitment to deal with the crisis. In another comment to a

* Such a phrase is familiar in the twenty-first century as a turning point in a financial crisis. On July 26, 2012, in the depths of the Global Financial Crisis, Mario Draghi, president of the European Central Bank, said that "the ECB is ready to do whatever it takes to preserve the euro." Similarly, in his understated way Jerome Powell, chair of the U.S. Federal Reserve, expressed a similar message at the nadir of the financial crisis in March 2020.

reporter, Cortelyou said, "Not only has the stability of the business institutions impressed me deeply but also the highest courage and the splendid devotion to the public interest of many men prominent in the business life of this city."[5]

Strictly speaking, the federal government support would not go to Morgan, but to nationally chartered banks in New York[†]—and eventually elsewhere. Cortelyou expected the national banks to redirect these funds to places of greatest need. This made sense, since the national banks were closer to the condition of the financial system than were public officials in Washington, DC. The national banks were the best-monitored and generally the soundest part of the U.S. financial system. Therefore, the risk of loss to taxpayers might be lower than if the government loaned directly to distressed financial institutions. By placing the national banks in between the government and the sources of instability, the government relied on the national banks to act as shock absorbers in the event of loss. And the support to national banks would take the form of deposits or collateralized loans, not capital investments or gifts—this was an injection of liquidity, not a resolution of insolvency.

Cortelyou's announcement of federal government support on October 24 is significant: it was the first instance of a general federal intervention in a financial crisis.[6] However, Cortelyou's predecessor, Leslie Shaw, had begun a policy of liquidity management by shifting Treasury gold reserves into and out of national banks to alleviate credit needs associated with the ordinary agricultural cycle. Cortelyou's innovation was to apply Shaw's policy more aggressively during a banking panic.

Thus, from the end of September to October 31, Cortelyou had shifted about $54 million into national banks to quell the crisis. By the end of November, he would shift another 10 million into the national banks.[7] But by then, the balance of discretionary currency within the

† J.P. Morgan & Co. was a *private bank* (it did not accept deposits from the public or issue banknotes), did not hold a national bank charter, and was not a member of the clearing house. As such, the firm would not qualify as a recipient of U.S. Treasury deposits. Nonetheless, through his business connections and the respect he commanded, Pierpont had some influence with leaders of the NYCH and the large national banks. For instance, researchers Tallman and Moen (1990, p. 9) wrote, ". . . nearly all the funds contributed to aid the panic were controlled by J.P. Morgan who decided how much money to use and where." How much this influence translated into direction over distribution of the federal government deposits remains a subject for further research. Certainly, as Morgan's efforts to mobilize collective action among the trust companies reveals, even his powers were limited.

U.S. Treasury Department had fallen to $5 million, effectively sidelining Cortelyou as a crisis fighter.* Nevertheless, his active deployment of currency into national banks rendered Cortelyou a power player on par with J.P. Morgan.

Throughout the morning of Thursday, October 24, men carried bags and boxes of gold currency and greenbacks from the federal vaults at the New York Subtreasury to the various banks approved by Cortelyou. Meanwhile, John D. Rockefeller Sr. also called on Morgan to assure him of his willingness to help. Rockefeller deposited $10 million with the Union Trust Company, and promised additional deposits of $40 million, if needed.[8]

A Crisis in Call Money

The panic, however, had already spread further. Owing to the stricken trust companies that frantically demanded repayment of collateralized loans, an acute shortage of money had occurred on the New York Stock Exchange. Brokers were intensely anxious. And the credit crunch, accelerated by the events in October 1907, worsened the anxieties.

Figure 14.1 shows that the stock index had plunged 43 percent from September 1906 to November 1907. In October alone, it fell 7.3 percent. In the 132 months since 1896, only seven months had featured stock market declines of that size or greater—and four of them had occurred in 1907. Amid such declines, only short-sellers would be happy—and even they grew fearful as margin loans suddenly grew more costly and harder to find.

At 10 a.m. on October 24, the interest rate on call money at the Exchange opened at 50 percent. Yet sometime later in the morning a bid was made for 60 percent and no money was offered. By 1 p.m., call money was being loaned at the extreme rate of 100 percent.[9] "It was evident that difficulty was being caused by the calling of loans by a good many trust companies which, alarmed by the run that already had taken place on

* In late November Cortelyou would employ another strategy of issuing government bonds that banks could use as reserves upon which to issue banknotes. For more detail on Cortelyou's monetary management, see Chapter 23.

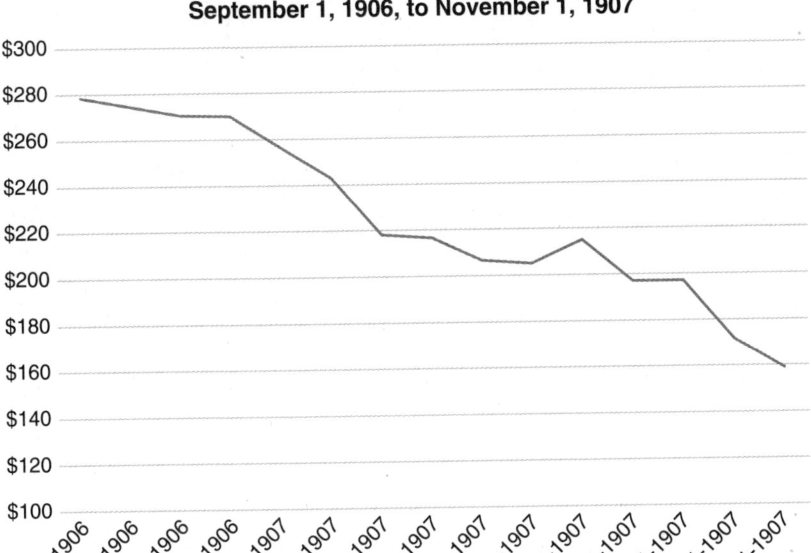

Figure 14.1 Stock Price Average, September 1906 to November 1907
SOURCE: Authors' figure, based on data from National Bureau of Economic Research, Average Prices of 40 Common Stocks for United States [M11006USM315NNBR], retrieved from FRED, Federal Reserve Bank of St. Louis; https://fred.stlouisfed.org/series/M11006USM315NNBR, April 30, 2022.

three companies [Knickerbocker Trust Company, Trust Company of America, and Lincoln Trust Company] were hurrying to strengthen their own cash position," George Perkins observed.[10] An already tight money market was now further strained by the trust companies pulling their cash out of the market. With money so scarce, prices on the Exchange were headed into a tailspin.

Call money financed the positions of stock market brokers, dealers, and speculators—all of whom helped to ensure liquidity in trading, the ability to find a counterparty whether one was buying or selling. This market was highly consequential for the banking industry: it became an attractive investment for excess liquid resources. Mary Tone Rodgers and James Payne note that "In the period leading up to the 1907 crisis, about half of all bank loans in the United States were secured by stocks in the call loan market."[11] Jon Moen and Ellis Tallman highlighted the significance of the call loan market, a business that national banks dominated and that trust companies aggressively entered after 1897, [12] in the rise of the trust companies and the dynamics of the Panic of 1907. Call loans outstanding in New York City varied from $400 million to $600 million per day.[13] Moen and Tallman wrote, "It was well known that national banks in New York invested their bankers' balances (deposits from other banks used to maintain correspondent relationships and to meet reserve requirements established under the National Banking Acts) in the call loan market at the stock exchange. But other intermediary types loaned out funds on the call loan market as well. Collateralized loans, a grouping that includes call loans, comprised over 85 percent of New York trust loans in 1907."[14] Moen and Tallman argued that trust companies free rode on an "implicit insurance contract"[15] from the NYCH banks to "alleviate the extreme liquidity demands arising from either the capital market or the payment system/money market. These actions were intended to forestall any large-scale liquidation of call loans (and potentially, of the stock collateral supporting the loans)."[16]

Interest rates on call money typically varied in the single digits since lenders saw these well-collateralized short-term loans as very liquid and low risk. However, call money interest rates periodically spiked, reflecting crises and adverse economic conditions.

Figure 14.2 presents the daily call money rates recorded during the Panic of 1907. Rates surged shortly after the failure of the corner on United Copper and did not return to single digits until the end of the year. The spike to 100 percent in call loan interest rates on October 24 suggests the extremity of capital market conditions and generally the threat to financial system stability. The figure also presents the spread between high and low call money interest rate quotations as measured by the number of standard deviations from average spreads[17]—the size of such spreads measure market dysfunction and risk. The standard deviations indicate the chance that the high–low spreads are just due to trading "noise." Of the 86 days depicted in the figure, 47 of them show standard deviations of 3.0 or more—indicating a very low probability (4 in 1,000) that these extreme high–low spreads were just random variations. Conditions in the call loan market during this period suggested great turmoil and uncertainty.

Rising interest rates on call money on October 24 reflected declining supply. Depositor runs on financial institutions (particularly trust

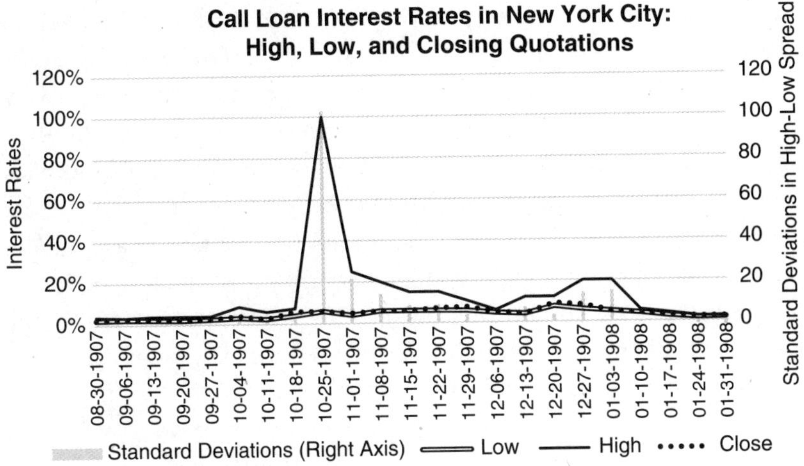

Figure 14.2 Daily Call Loan Interest Rates, August 1907 to January 1908
SOURCE: Authors' figure, based on hand-collected quotations in the *Wall Street Journal* and the *New York Times*, September 1, 1907, to January 30, 1908.

companies) triggered liquidation of loan portfolios. Demand loans ("call loans") were the easiest to liquidate. Under normal conditions, a speculator might meet a call for payment by borrowing from another institution. However, on October 24, finding the funding to "roll over" the loan suddenly proved difficult. In the absence of refinancing, the speculator would have to sell the stocks, possibly taking a loss. Falling stock prices would trigger more collateral calls and stock sales. A self-reinforcing doom loop of liquidation would begin. The impact of many investors throwing their shares on the market would have one outcome: a stock market crash.

Panic on the New York Stock Exchange

Around 1:30 p.m. on October 24, Ransom H. Thomas, the president of New York's Stock Exchange, and one of his assistants came over to the Corner in a state of great excitement. When he arrived, the offices of J. P. Morgan & Company were full of other agitated men, but Thomas rushed up to the financier and said, "Mr. Morgan, we will have to close the Stock Exchange." Morgan turned to him and asked sharply, "What?" Thomas repeated, "We will have to close the Stock Exchange." Morgan asked, "At what time do you usually close it?" Thomas answered, "Why, at three o'clock." Morgan thundered, "It must not close one minute before that hour today!" emphasizing each word by keeping time with his right hand, middle finger pointing directly at the president of the Exchange.[18] Under the circumstances, closing the exchange early would signal a breakdown in the Exchange's market-making function and would inflame fears about financial system stability, accelerating the calling-in of brokers' loans, the fire sales of assets, the failure of brokerage firms, and the downward spiral of stock prices.

Thomas then explained that unless a significant amount of money was offered on the stock exchange in a very short time, many failures would result. Morgan said he would take immediate steps to arrange a loan, and he sent Thomas back to the Exchange. The situation only seemed to get more desperate with each passing moment. "One broker after another came into our office, begging us to do something—many with tears in their eyes and others almost weak with the shock of being suddenly faced with failure," George Perkins recalled. "They had the securities on which to raise money but there was no money to be had."[19] Finally, at about 1:45, Morgan asked that the presidents of the banks (not the trust companies, this time) be called to his office immediately. The city's bankers started to arrive around 2 p.m.; the moment the brokers on the Exchange feared most would be in 20 minutes, when the Exchange customarily compared all the day's sales and adjusted brokers' accounts. This would be literally a moment of reckoning.

When the bank presidents had finally gathered at the Corner, Morgan explained the situation to them. He said simply that unless they raised $25 million within the next 10 to 12 minutes, at least 50 Stock Exchange houses would fail. James Stillman, president of the National City Bank, promptly offered $5 million; the other bankers quickly fell in line. By 2:16 p.m., Morgan had secured $23.6 million from 14 banks. He ordered that these funds should be loaned at 10 percent,[20] a rate dramatically below the interest rates currently quoted at the Exchange, to quell fears of a credit crunch. Within minutes, word of the new "money pool" buoyed the Street, as Perkins later observed:

Our outer office at this moment was filled with brokers awaiting the result of the conference. The bank presidents hurried out of our private offices into these outer offices and someone must have exclaimed that a $25 million fund had been raised because, as I hurried from the office to start the machinery of loaning in motion, I saw some man's hat sail towards the ceiling as he shouted, "We are saved, we are saved!"[21]

When the money hit the market at 2:30 p.m., men clambered over one another to get to the Exchange's "money post" seeking a loan; in the mayhem, even one of Morgan's associates had his coat and waistcoat torn off. The *New York Times* reported that money brokers scrambled wildly for the funds as fast as borrowers' names could be written down, adding that for the first time in 10 days the mood on the trading floor was cheerful. At 3:00 p.m. when the Stock Exchange closed, there was "a mighty roar of voices" that could be heard from the floor of the Exchange. The members had joined in yelling, "What's the matter with Morgan? He's all right!" followed by three cheers.[22] Of the total raised for the money pool by Morgan on Thursday afternoon, nearly $19 million was loaned out in 30 minutes at interest rates ranging from 10 to 60 percent.* After the market close, scores of men crowded in front of J. P. Morgan & Company carrying boxes of collateral to secure their share of the pool.

Around 7 p.m. Morgan and Perkins finally left their offices to head uptown. As they started to leave the building, the normally reticent Morgan approached a throng of reporters. Straightening up and squaring his shoulders, he said slowly and earnestly, "If people will keep their money in the banks, everything will be all right."[23] Then he quickly turned, went out the door, and drove uptown.

* R. Glenn Donaldson (1992) analyzed the trend of call money interest rates in comparison to a rate predicted by a model and concluded that Morgan and his circle colluded to keep interest rates exorbitantly high—consistent with the conclusions of the Pujo Committee (1912–1913) about the existence of a money trust. The facts, as reported by mainstream press, refute Donaldson's inference. Morgan directed that the offered rate on his rescue funds should be 10 percent. A possible explanation for interest rates higher than Morgan's 10 percent target would be that the higher rates were asked by lenders not belonging to Morgan's pool. Or perhaps the pool lent funds to other intermediaries, who charged the higher rates.

Distress Spreads through More Financial Institutions

J. P. Morgan's efforts had kept the Stock Exchange open on Thursday, October 24, but his victory there had not been decisive. The Twelfth Ward Bank and Empire City Savings Bank suspended in the afternoon. The Hamilton Bank of New York ceased operations, and many more institutions closed in rapid succession: First National Bank of Brooklyn, International Trust Company of New York, Williamsburg Trust Company of Brooklyn, Borough Bank of Brooklyn, and Jenkins Trust Company of Brooklyn. By Friday morning, the Union Trust Company of Providence, Rhode Island, failed to open as well. Most worrisome of all, runs continued unabated at the beleaguered Trust Company of America and the Lincoln Trust.

Early in the morning on Friday, October 25, George Perkins made successive visits to Cortelyou, Stillman, Baker, and Morgan, securing their agreement once again to save the Trust Company and the Lincoln Trust. At Morgan's library after breakfast, they finally decided to place more funds at the disposal of the two firms, and, if necessary, to consider taking up another money pool in the afternoon. In the meantime, Perkins met hurriedly with Lincoln Trust and Trust Company of America officials. He strongly urged them to open for business on time, even suggesting that they resort to paying depositors as slowly as possible, and by artifice if necessary. "It was not because we were particularly in love with these two trust companies that we wanted to keep them open," Perkins later explained. "Indeed, we hadn't any use for their management and knew that they ought to be closed, but we fought to keep them open in order not to have runs on other concerns and have another outburst of panic and alarm."[24]

Crisis Returns to the New York Stock Exchange

At 10 a.m. on Friday, October 25, trading on the stock exchange began as usual, but "with the air charged in every direction with panic."[25] Prices quickly began to collapse, and rumors abounded that one brokerage or another was in peril. "At all times during the day there were frantic men and women in our offices," Perkins recollected, "in every way giving evidence of the tremendous strain they were under."[26] Again the panic-stricken trust companies were calling in their loans, which caused an acute shortage of money. By midday, call loan interest rates reached 75 percent.[27] Morgan and his associates pleaded with the trusts to extend their loans and implored the president of the Exchange to cease all buying or selling on margin. However, their efforts could not outpace the speed with which the trust companies were pulling their cash out of the market. By 1:30 p.m., the market was in exactly the position it had been in the day before, with no money available and numerous firms on the brink of failure.

Finally, Ransom Thomas, president of the Exchange, went to see J. P. Morgan personally, asking him to call another meeting of the 14 major bank presidents. Morgan agreed, but he decided he should go in person to meet with them at the offices of the NYCH itself, where he would ask them to raise another pool of $15 million. When he did so this time, the banks were less willing to be so generous, and they agreed only to provide $9.7 million. That would have to do. Morgan insisted that these funds carry restrictions: No margin sales were allowed (only cash could be used for investments), and the full amount of the pool would not be released until the afternoon.

Following the meeting at the NYCH, J. P. Morgan, clearly at the height of his power, marched on foot to his own offices at the Corner. Herbert Satterlee, Morgan's son-in-law, provided a description of him at that very moment, which has become among the most vivid and enduring images of the man:

> *Anyone who saw Mr. Morgan going from the Clearing House back to his office that day will never forget the picture. With his coat unbuttoned and flying open, a piece of white paper clutched tightly in his right hand, he walked fast down Nassau Street. His flat-topped black derby hat was set firmly down on his head. Between his teeth he held a cigar holder in which was one of his long cigars, half smoked. His eyes were fixed straight ahead. He swung his arms as he walked and took no notice of anyone. He did not seem to see the throngs in the street, so intent was his mind on the thing that he was doing. Everyone knew him, and people made way for him, except some who were equally intent on their own affairs; and these he brushed aside. The thing that made his progress different from that of all the other people on the*

> *street was that he did not dodge, or walk in and out, or halt or slacken his pace. He simply barged along, as if he had been the only man going down the Nassau Street hill past the Subtreasury. He was the embodiment of power and purpose. Not more than two minutes after he disappeared into his office, the cheering on the floor of the Stock Exchange could be heard out in Broad Street.*[28]

The second money pool was loaned out at once on the Exchange, at rates ranging from 25 to 50 percent, and it proved sufficient to meet all demands: No brokerage failures were reported, and again the Exchange stayed open until 3 p.m. By the time of the market's close, $6 million of the new pool had been loaned out on the Exchange; the rest was offered after hours to discourage speculation. Overall trading volume was down to 637,000 shares from one million the day before. By the end of this day, however, seven more banks still had failed. To protect themselves from running out of cash, the presidents of the New York savings banks imposed a rarely invoked requirement that depositors must give a 60-day notice for any withdrawals.

Morgan's successive rescues of the NYSE engendered other criticisms, offered later. Some said that he was bailing out his cronies. Others asserted that he used taxpayer money to sustain speculative activity in the stock market. Still more said that the money would have been better applied to the needs of banks in the interior of the country. Finally, some said it was driven by greed; after all, Morgan earned interest on his loans to the NYSE.

There was a grain of truth in each of these criticisms. However, they ignored the fact that in 1907, the stability of the U.S. financial system perched precariously on the stability of the NYSE. Banks in the interior had sent their surplus reserves to trust companies in New York, to earn higher rates of interest than elsewhere. The trust companies had invested those funds in call loans to earn high interest rates during the credit crunch. Call loans fueled the stock market. A sustained absence of call money on the NYSE (as on October 24, 1907) would trigger debtor defaults and fire sales of stocks. Defaults and falling asset prices would destabilize trust companies, prompting runs, suspensions, and insolvencies. The Panic would worsen and lengthen. In short, Morgan saved the NYSE to stanch the financial panic and set the stage for recovery.

Appealing to the Public

At the library on Friday evening October 25, Morgan and his associates acknowledged that rescuing financial institutions had not achieved their chief aim of restoring public confidence and ending mass withdrawals of deposits. They turned their attention toward directly reassuring the public. They formed two committees. One was responsible for disseminating all information about the financial rescue efforts to the press; all inquiries would be directed here, and any attempts at evasion or secrecy were to be avoided. The second committee would reach out directly to the clergy, encouraging them to make reassuring statements to their congregations over the weekend. "We arranged so far as we could that sermons should be preached in the various churches on Sunday," Perkins said, "cautioning people to act calmly and not to withdraw the money and lock it up."[29] According to Satterlee, a member of this committee then visited every possible clergyman, priest, or rabbi in New York on Friday or Saturday. Having won the day's battles, Morgan finished his day with a game of solitaire in the library and then went to bed around 2 a.m.

Chapter 15

A City in Trouble

A millionaire is wicked, quite;
His doom should quick be knelled;
He should not be allowed to grow,
If grown he should be felled,
But when a city's bonds fall flat
And no one cares for them,
Who is the man who saves the day?
It's J.P.M.

When banks and trusts go crashing down
From credit's sullied name,
While speechifying Greatness adds
More fuel to the flame,
When Titan strength is needed sore,
Black ruin's tide to stem,
Who is the man who does the job?
It's J.P.M.

—McLandburgh Wilson, *New York Times*,
October 27, 1907

Criticism and Praise

During the early stage of the financial crisis, Theodore Roosevelt was on a hunting expedition in the canebrakes of Louisiana. (Upon his return, the *New York Times* quipped that "he had added several deeper shades to the bronze acquired during the Summer months at Oyster Bay."[1]) The president's first utterance about the Panic was on Tuesday, October 22, en route to Washington. He stopped in Nashville, Tennessee, where in an impromptu speech he insisted that his policies had not caused the panic. In his remarks, he made the stock speculator the focus of his ire, saying,

> *[The speculator] is doing all that he can to bring down in ruin the fabric of our institutions, and it is our business to set our faces like flint against his wrongdoing, to war to undo that wrongdoing in the interest of the people as a whole, and primarily in the interests of the honest man of means.*[2]

Within two days of making that statement, however, Secretary Cortelyou had advised Roosevelt to offer a less belligerent message to the public. On October 25, President Roosevelt wrote the following note to Cortelyou with instructions to have it published:

> *I congratulate you upon the admirable way in which you have handled the present crisis. I congratulate also those conservative and substantial businessmen who in this crisis have acted with such wisdom and public spirit. By their action they did invaluable service in checking the panic which, beginning as a matter of speculation, was threatening to destroy the confidence and credit necessary to the conduct of legitimate business. No one who considers calmly can question that the underlying conditions which make up our financial and industrial well-being are essentially sound and honest. . . . The action taken by you and by the businessmen in question has been of the utmost consequence and has secured opportunity for the calm consideration which must inevitably produce entire confidence in our business conditions.*[3]

A regularity of financial crises before and since 1907 has been the utterance of calming bromides by national leaders, regardless of how realistic or well-informed. As of October 25, the crisis was far from quelled and its impact on the real economy had even longer to run. Nevertheless, J. P. Morgan must have taken some degree of satisfaction in his apparent vindication by the president.

When the Stock Exchange opened for its regular, short day of trading on Saturday morning, October 26, the atmosphere remained tense. However, since the markets would close at noon and money could be neither called nor loaned on Saturdays, there was an incipient sense of calm. In part, the morning papers had provided the palliative that Morgan's public relations campaign had been intended to achieve. The *New York Times* quoted financier Jacob H. Schiff, head of the banking firm Kuhn, Loeb & Company, who praised the actions of both Morgan and Cortelyou. "We are doing everything we can to support the heroic efforts of Mr. J. P. Morgan to strengthen the banking situation generally," Schiff said. "The prompt, decisive, and effective course of the Secretary of the Treasury deserves unstinted praise, and all must seek in every way to aid in allaying needless alarm which has sprung up and which, I believe, is already subsiding."[4] Industrialist Andrew Carnegie also heralded Morgan's work and admonished depositors to have courage. "Above all, let no man or woman selfishly lock their hoardings in private security," Carnegie said, "but let them bring forth their surplus and add it to the public exchequer, so as to relieve the present famine in the money market."[5]

Across the Atlantic, further encouragement was heard as well. The papers printed a tribute to Morgan from Britain's Lord Rothschild, who remarked on his "admiration and respect" for the American financier.[6] A French manufacturer said, "So great is the confidence of the great French bankers in Mr. Morgan and Mr. Stillman personally, that were they to come to France tomorrow they could find $100,000,000 gold without the slightest difficulty."[7] A banker from Germany added, "We are telling our customers that it is our duty to uphold the sound American industrial situation, and heavy buying orders are resulting."[8] While the international financial community was genuinely supportive of the situation in the United States, clearly they also saw an opportunity for profiting from the severely depressed prices of American securities.

New York Stress: Meeting the Calls of Country Banks

The week ending October 25 had delivered an enormous blow to the New York financial community. Country bankers who had placed their surplus reserves with New York institutions now wanted them back. The trigger was obvious: the suspension of the Knickerbocker and runs at the Trust Company of America, Lincoln, and others fed fears that the bankers' deposits would be lost or tied up in an endless bankruptcy resolution process. This commenced a financial drain on the New York institutions that would not return to normal until January. Figure 15.1 compares the weekly cash flows from New York to the interior in 1907 to the average of the four previous years. The sharp drop in the week ending October 25 was a harbinger of financial strain on New York.

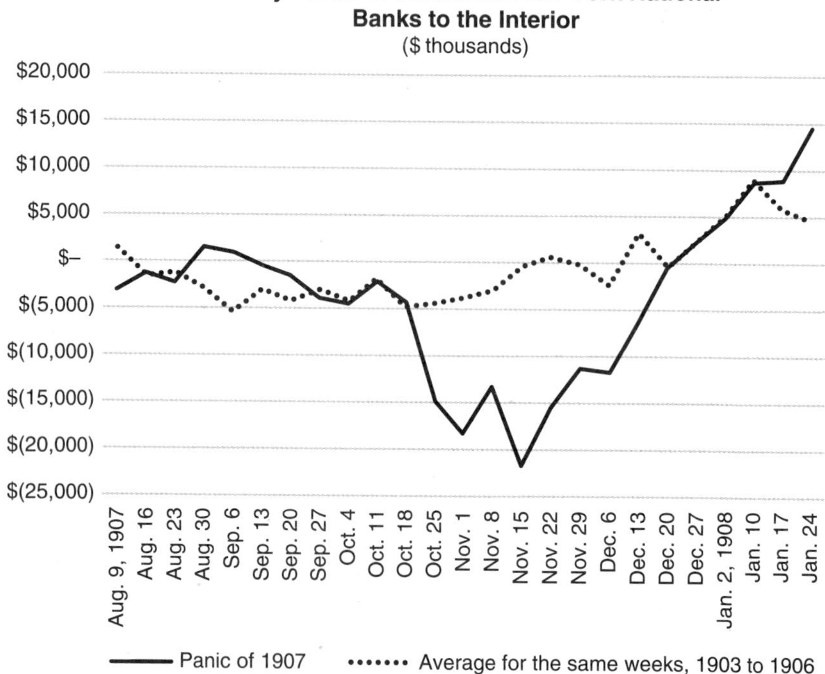

Figure 15.1 Flows of Cash from New York to the Interior

NOTE: Negative values indicate *outflows* from New York to the interior; positive values indicate inflows.

SOURCE: Authors' figure, based on data given in "Money: Sharp Decline in Cash Loss to the Interior," *New York Times*, December 16, 1907, p. 8.

Shipments of gold to the interior stressed the New York banks. Secretary Cortelyou later wrote, "more than the entire net loss in [nationwide] national-bank reserves fell upon the national banks of New York City."[9] Cortelyou employed this fact to defend his decision to bestow the early government deposits on New York national banks. As the Panic spread, he widened the geographic range of the government deposits. As of December 31, Cortelyou estimated that about $246 million in government deposits were held in U.S. national banks across the country, up from $143 million on August 22.[10]

Hoarding

A second major source of stress on the financial system was the disappearance of cash. Perkins reported that a large part of the money that Secretary Cortelyou had disbursed to the banks and which, in turn, had been handed over to depositors had since been locked up in safe deposit vaults. Perkins learned that nearly 2,000 new safe deposit boxes had been rented in New York City since Monday morning. Stories circulated about depositors locking up their cash or taking it home.

Figure 15.2 presents the time trend of rentals of new safe deposit boxes in five reserve cities. New York peaked exactly at the weekend of greatest stress, when the Stock Exchange nearly closed and when banks decided to issue loan certificates. Other cities peaked shortly thereafter. Hoarding behavior suggested that the last week of October and the first two weeks of November were the climax of the crisis.

All told, during the panic about $350 million in deposits were withdrawn from the U.S. financial system.[11] Of this amount, the bulk of it was simply socked away: stuffed under the mattress or the hearthstone. Estimates of funds hoarded ranged from $200 million to $296 million,[12] or about 17 percent[13] of all the currency in circulation in 1907. Pierpont Morgan issued a statement to the press:

> *I cannot too strongly emphasize the importance of the people realizing that the greatest injury that can be done to the present situation is the thoughtless withdrawal of funds from banks and trust companies and then hoarding the cash in safe deposit vaults or elsewhere, thus withdrawing the supply of capital always*

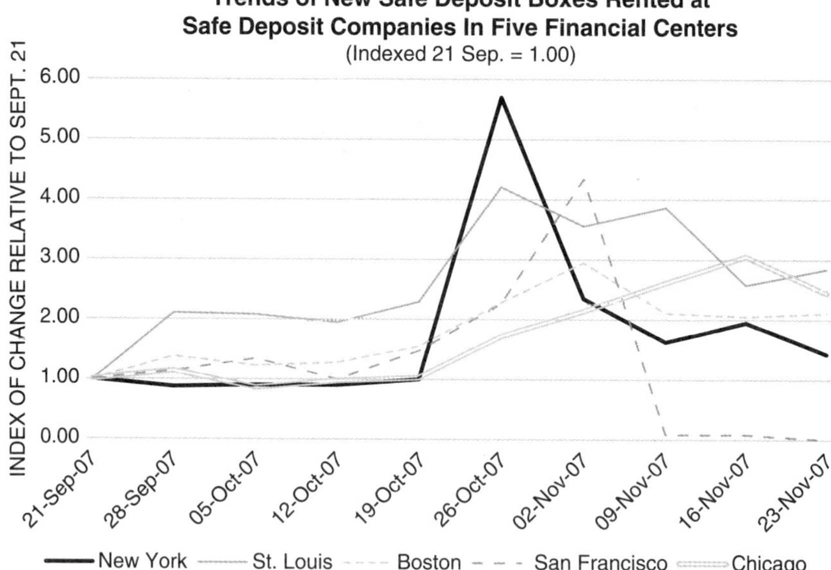

Figure 15.2 Trends in the Rentals of New Safe Deposit Boxes in Five Major U.S. Cities

SOURCE: Author's figure, based on data in Andrew (1908a), p. 294.

> *needed in such emergencies as that with which we have been confronted during the last week.*[14]

Imported Gold and More Treasury Deposits

One solution to the hoarding and shipments to the interior was to get more gold into circulation. Morgan and his associates received word by cable on Saturday morning that $3 million of gold was en route to New York from London. The news could not have come at a more propitious moment.

Also, Treasury Secretary Cortelyou directed more government money to be deposited at banks. On Saturday, October 26, another $1.8 million in gold and $185,000 in silver dollars were removed from the Subtreasury's vaults and taken to various banks in the city. Meanwhile, several tons of silver and gold and bales of paper money arrived on Saturday from

Washington, mostly of small currency, with another shipment expected by Sunday.

Unfortunately, in their weekly report on Saturday, the New York national banks reported a loss of $12.9 million in cash, which was accounted for partly by the shipments of currency to the interior and the increase in loans to other institutions needing ready money. Given the nation's dwindling currency in circulation, the news of the gold shipments and Treasury deposits, which were reported immediately by Morgan's committee to the ticker agencies, heartened both investors and depositors throughout the city. For the entire month of November, banks would import $68 million in gold,[15] facilitated in part by the efforts of J.P. Morgan's son, "Jack," who was in Paris.[16]

Figure 15.3 documents the strain that the NYCH members faced at the end of October. Between October 1 and early November, the gold reserves of the NYCH banks fell by a quarter and the surplus reserves (those in excess of the federally mandated minimum reserve) fell into a

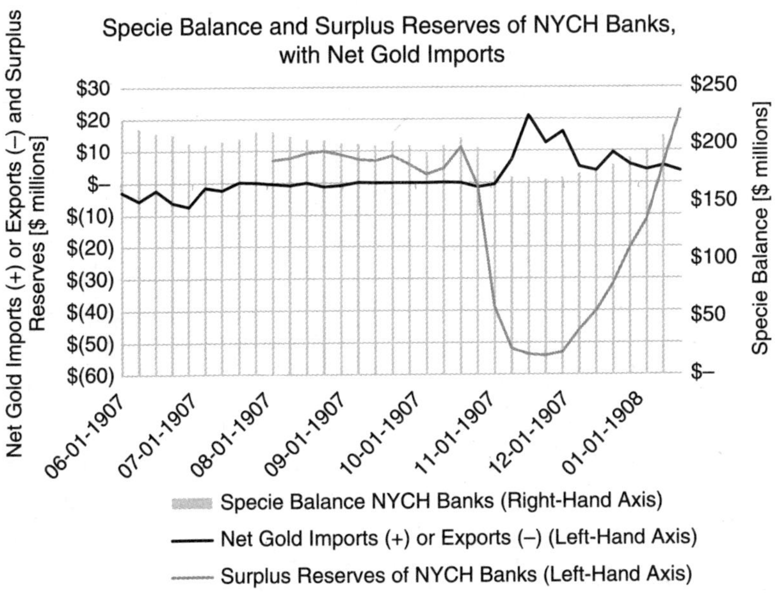

Figure 15.3 NYCH Reserves and Specie Balance Compared to Net Gold Imports
SOURCE: Authors' figure, based on data in Rodgers and Wilson (2011), pp. 169–170.

deep deficit. Gold imports helped to offset the declining balance of gold and reserves at the banks.

The figure reveals a dramatic decline in surplus reserves and specie balance among the NYCH member banks beginning in the last week of October, just after the Knickerbocker's suspension. Weekly imports of gold helped to meet the withdrawals of depositors, although the figure suggests that the gold imports—and additional deposits from the U.S. Treasury—were simply passed through the NYCH members. After mid-December, gold imports and the return of deposits from the interior and from hoarders began to restore the surplus reserves.

NYCH Issues Clearing House Loan Certificates

Another response to the financial strain on the banking system was to issue substitutes for legal tender currency, particularly clearing house loan certificates. On October 26, the New York Clearing House (NYCH) took this step, one of the pivotal events of the Panic of 1907.

During previous financial crises, such as in 1873, 1884, 1890, and 1893, the NYCH had resorted to issuing temporary, emergency loans to its member banks in the form of clearing house certificates. The banks had substituted these certificates for currency when clearing accounts with one another at the clearing house each day. Since the certificates circulated among member banks as a substitute for cash, they effectively freed up actual cash for the public, thereby artificially expanding the nation's money supply. Without a central bank to provide this function, the certificates proved to be extremely effective at restoring liquidity to the financial system during critical periods of stringency. However, the issuances of these certificates were *ad hoc*, and they often indicated a desperate, last-resort attempt to address a deepening, systemic crisis.

At various times during the preceding week, the use of clearing house certificates had been suggested in New York, especially during the conferences of the clearing house member banks. Morgan, however, had steadfastly opposed the idea of using them, convinced that their issuance would only signal deeper trouble. He was adamant about avoiding any measures that could further frighten the public. In addition, one can imagine the complex dynamic within the clearing house membership—some bankers might resist suspending convertibility on moral grounds, believing that if they have the resources, they should give depositors their cash. More darkly, delay might serve the interests of strong banks that wanted to discipline the weaker banks—as historian Elmus Wicker has argued, such behavior represented a conflict of private interest over the public interest.[17]

Having already weathered the raging storm for two weeks, the financiers were left with few other options than to issue clearing house certificates. Bank clearing houses in Chicago, Pittsburgh, and Philadelphia, in fact, had already proposed using certificates. On October 26, the 53 member banks of the NYCH decided to issue $100 million of certificates to be available on Monday, October 28, providing much-needed liquidity for the system.

At a later meeting of the NYCH banks, it was determined that each of the banks would provide securities to the clearing house as collateral for the certificates, which would be issued for up to 75 percent of the value of these securities. Interest charged on the certificates would be a standard 6 percent. As an additional means of freeing up currency, the bankers urged that the trust companies should thereafter use certified checks (i.e., checks certified by clearing house member banks) in lieu of cash to pay any depositor withdrawals. Furthermore, the clearing house also discussed the possibility of admitting the trust companies as members, with a 15 percent reserve requirement. The bankers were reported to be generally in favor of this measure, particularly if it would include a system of inspection and examination for the trusts.

The NYCH's suspension of convertibility of deposits and issuance of clearing house loan certificates immediately prompted clearing houses in other cities to suspend as well. Nevertheless, the issues of loan certificates occurred in the greatest volume in major metropolitan areas.

Figure 15.4 presents the growth of clearing house loan certificates outstanding. Two insights emerge from the figure. First, the issuance of certificates spread rapidly—almost contagion-like. Over three days, the total volume had reached $200 million, almost all of what would ultimately be issued.[18]

Second, the bulk of the certificates was issued in major metropolitan areas. Figure 15.5 presents the distribution of outstandings by city, ranked from smallest to largest.

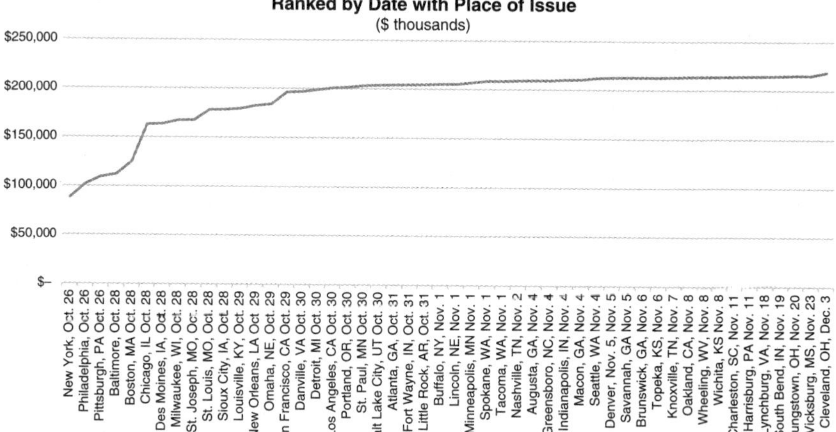

Figure 15.4 Cumulative Growth of the Adoption of Clearing House Loan Certificates and Other Currency Substitutes Across 50 American Cities

SOURCE: Authors' figure, based on data in the *Annual Report of the Comptroller of the Currency* (1908), pp. 65–66.

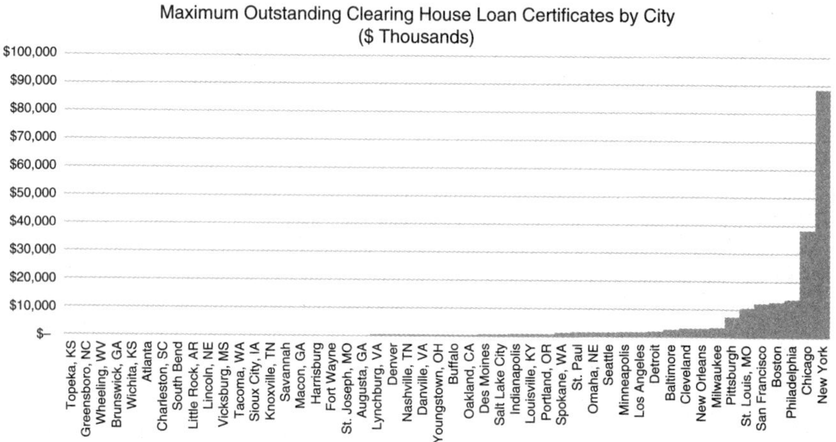

Figure 15.5 Distribution of Maximum Outstanding Clearing House Loan Certificates by City, October–November 1907

SOURCE: Authors' figure, based on data in the *Annual Report of the Comptroller of the Currency* (1908), pp. 65–66.

Six cities accounted for $175 million of the $219 million cumulative total clearing house loan certificates outstanding: New York ($88.4 million), Chicago ($38.3), Philadelphia ($13.5), Boston ($12.6), San Francisco ($12.3), and St. Louis ($10.6)—these all were "reserve cities" to where country bankers would send their surplus reserves to earn interest. Clearing houses in 13 other cities issued certificates between $1 million and $10 million. The other 31 clearing houses issued certificates in small volume. The median outstanding across the 50 cities was $544,000.

Currency Premium Widens

Currency substitutes (such as clearing house loan certificates, cashier's checks, and corporate IOUs of various kinds) began to trade at a discount to gold coin or national banknotes.

Some corporations issued "scrip," informal currency that amounted to a promise to redeem in gold coin or national banknotes at some point in the future. Streetcar companies in Omaha and St. Louis paid their employees in nickels from the fare boxes or in five-cent fare tickets.* Bank checks were useful as cash only locally, since in an environment where banks discriminated among payees, being a distant correspondent was a disadvantage. This near-money traded hands at a discount to gold coins and paper currency, reflecting fears about the solvency of banks, companies, and individuals. No region or major city was spared from the effects of the panic.[19] Economist A. Piatt Andrew estimated that by the nadir of the Panic, more than $500 million[20] in substitutes for cash had been issued nationally, which was equal to about 28 percent of all the currency in circulation before the crisis.[21]

* Steven Horwitz (1990), p. 643, wrote that the streetcar fare tickets "circulated fairly widely for several weeks, evidently because they had a redemption value as streetcar rides. . . . The essence of money is its general acceptability. Historically, stones, shells, tobacco, cigarettes and cattle have all served as money. Indeed, as Mises put it, something can become money only 'through the practice of those who take part in commercial transactions.'"

Hoarding (especially of gold coin), the effusion of money-like forms of payment, and uncertainty about whether the proto-money would be redeemable in desirable money ensured that the less desirable money medium would trade at a discount to the more valuable medium. Figure 15.6 displays the size of the gold currency premium from the date it emerged (at the start of payment in loan certificates in New York) until its extinction (largely when the loan certificates were redeemed).

The premium on currency was a barometer of anxieties about the Panic. The figure suggests the period of greatest intensity from late October until mid-November. And it also shows that the effects of the Panic in New York lasted until January, well past the salubrious utterances of business and government leaders.

To promote the atmosphere of calm engendered by the announcement of the certificates, Morgan and his colleagues encouraged Treasury Secretary Cortelyou to return to Washington. They hoped news of his departure would be perceived as an indication of his confidence in the situation in New York. Likewise, Morgan himself left the city on Saturday afternoon to spend the rest of the weekend at Cragston, his country home in Highland Falls on the Hudson River. He slept soundly on the train, not having had more than five hours of sleep on any night that week.

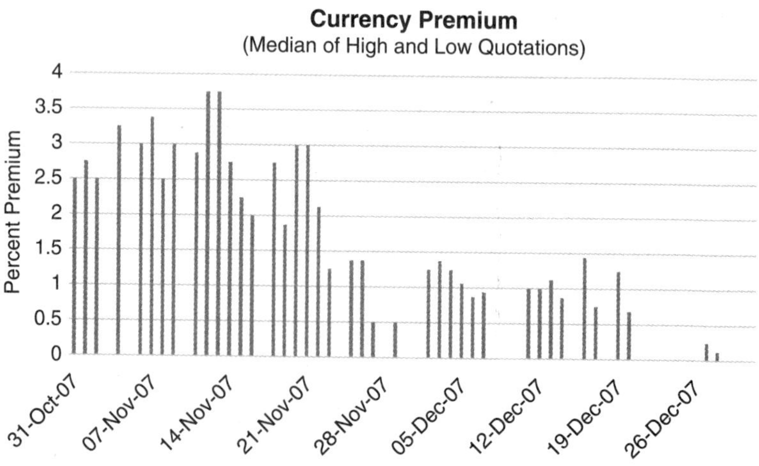

Figure 15.6 Premium on Currency from October 26, 1907, to January 4, 1908
Source: Authors' figure, based on data in Andrew (1908a), pp. 292–293.

Hope and Optimism

On Sunday morning, October 27, religious leaders urged calm, offering advice for nervous depositors and investors throughout the city. At the NYCH on Cedar Street, clerks worked busily through the day attending to the mass of details in preparation for the issuance of the certificates on Monday. Encouraged by the certificates plan, the Chase National Bank announced the importation of an additional $2 million in gold from Europe. "We have seen the worst of the 'panic' phase," the *Standard of London* opined, "and it has to be remembered that the crisis, at any rate, so far as it is connected with extraordinary trade activity, constitutes only a striking example of a complaint common in almost every financial centre, namely, a growth in the demands upon capital out of proportion to the supply."[22] Around 4 p.m., Morgan boarded a train back to New York City. Despite the rainy weather, it appeared that the skies were finally clearing.

On Monday morning, October 28, the wave of good news continued. The NYCH had authorized about $101 million in loan certificates on Saturday, of which their actual use would peak at $88 million in December. Gold shipments began to arrive from all over the world, including England, Argentina, Paris, and Australia, and the total was expected to reach $20 million. Though numerous depositors were still lined up at the Trust Company of America and the Lincoln Trust, no new runs were reported. The New York State Superintendent of Banks, Clark Williams, even announced that several banks that had closed during the past week had submitted applications to reopen.

On the Stock Exchange, call money rates reached as high as 75 percent, but the day's final loan was made at 6 percent, and all brokerages were able to obtain the money they needed. Around 11 a.m., several brokers had approached Perkins asking if more money would be available through the banking pools, but he and the others were opposed to resorting to this measure again. The bankers were convinced that sufficient liquidity was available, and money pools were all but abandoned. "The various pools which were formed last week to render assistance to the call money market have by reason of the action taken by the New York Clearing House Association been dissolved," A. B. Hepburn, president of Chase National Bank announced. "Brokers should now make their arrangements for loans with their own banks."[23] To show his confidence in the situation, J. P. Morgan remained uptown at his library all day long.

New York City Turns to J.P. Morgan . . . Again

The apparent calm, however, belied a new crisis that was brewing. "Outwardly, in the newspapers and as far as the public knew, everything was serene," Perkins said, "but four or five of us were possessed of information that made us fear that all the work we had done in the preceding week might come to naught at any moment."[24] Perkins, Morgan, and the other leading bankers had learned that the City of New York itself was on the verge of financial collapse.

On Sunday evening, an official from the City of New York came to George Perkins privately to explain that unless the municipal government could raise $20 or $30 million by November 1, the city would default on loans. It was already unable to meet its payroll obligations and could not pay its contractors. The city had tried, and failed, to float bonds over the previous summer, and succeeded in doing so in September only with Morgan's intervention. During the fall, the city had been financing its expenditures with the $40 million in short-term loans that previously had been underwritten by J. P. Morgan & Company. In September, the city felt confident of its ability to repay these debts quickly, but the intervening financial crisis and resultant market conditions now made that impossible. The city official said they had tried to access the public markets for three or four days, but they had succeeded in raising only a few million dollars. "To raise even one million dollars seemed about as possible at that moment as to move a mountain," Perkins said.[25]

Around 4 p.m. on Monday, October 28, Mayor McClellan, his deputy, the city controller, and the chamberlain came to see Morgan personally at the library. They explained that after the previous summer's financing they discovered that they needed to use the entire $40 million almost immediately, and now they needed additional funding to carry them through the rest of the year. After a few hours spent discussing the city's finances, they adjourned and agreed to meet again the next day at 3:30 p.m. Neither Morgan nor his associates believed they could place the city's short-term obligations on the market in Europe, and there would certainly be little appetite for them in America; given the current rates on money, a 6 percent return was hardly attractive. But the consequences of the city's financial failure would be severe. "We all realized the gravity of the situation," Perkins said. "How much fuel would be added to the flame if the credit of the City of New York should be questioned at such a moment?"[26]

The next day at the appointed time, Morgan and the others renewed their discussion with the mayor and his delegation. Then, without saying a word, Morgan sat at his desk in the library and took up a pen and began to write. "With scarcely a hesitation, without even stopping to select a word," Perkins recalled, "he covered three long sheets of paper and then after reading it over, he handed it to me and said, 'See what Messrs. Baker and Stillman think of that.'"[27]

With speed and clarity, Morgan had crafted a proposal that J. P. Morgan & Company would take $30 million of the city's revenue bonds, with optional terms of one, two, or three years, bearing an interest rate of 6 percent. There was an option on $20 million more, and the city was required to appoint a commission to examine its finances. Morgan planned to exchange these bonds for clearing house certificates by handing them over to the First National and National City Banks. This measure would thereby result in an additional $30 million in liquidity for the City of New York as well as provide $30 million in credit for the city through the banks.

After a discussion lasting about 20 minutes, the bankers and a lawyer concluded that Morgan's extemporaneous term sheet "was practically perfect both from the standpoint of an offer and the concise manner in which it had been put."[28] The meeting adjourned just before 7 p.m., and the representatives of the City of New York departed with a contract to receive $30 million from J. P. Morgan & Company, the First National Bank, and National City Bank the very next day. With the flourish of his pen, J. P. Morgan had quelled the financial threat to the City of New York.

The remainder of the week was very encouraging. On Wednesday, October 30, the Trust Company of America accepted over $100,000 in deposits *more* than it had paid out; it also reported seeing the fewest number of depositors than on any previous day, with fewer than 20 remaining at the close of business. By Thursday, the Trust Company had refunded $1 million that had been loaned to it over the past week.

Severe Pressure Remains

Money rates were still relatively high and stress was apparent on the Exchange, but the average interest rate on call money had declined to 20 percent, and at one point had even reached a low of 8 percent. During the week, the Bank of England raised its discount rate from 4.5 to 5.5 percent, indicating that the Bank was trying to stanch the flow of gold to the United States. By November 4, the Bank of England's rate would rise to 7 percent, the highest since 1873. Central banks in France and Germany followed suit. Secretary Cortelyou noted "severe pressure" on the money markets in those countries and observed that the grave conditions were not "localized in the United States."[29]

These global conditions reflected the fact that gold continued to arrive in the United States at a volume not seen since 1893. Still, very few firms on the Exchange were accepting margin business and the demand for cash remained strong because of numerous end-of-month payroll and debt obligations. The one alarming event during the week was the failure of a stock exchange house, Kessler & Company. That failure might have passed unremarkably, but it foreshadowed a new and unexpected turn in the crisis for which J. P. Morgan's own motivations would ultimately be called into question.

Chapter 16

Modern Medici

There wasn't going to be any mistake that night. [J. P. Morgan] intended that all should stay until the end of the party.[1]

—Recollection of Benjamin Strong Jr.,
Bankers Trust Company

On Saturday morning November 2, conditions on the Exchange in New York remained generally quiet; the market closed as usual at noon with no extraordinary activity. Earlier in the day, the State Banking Examiner had released the weekly bank statement, but the report was so bad that it was suppressed and kept from the press. The biggest troubles were occurring at the trust companies.

The situation at the Trust Company of America and the Lincoln Trust Company continued very poorly—these were the 5th- and 16th-largest trust companies in New York by total deposits at the start of 1907[2]—and there was talk that one or both would fail to open again on Monday because of continuing runs. Following the failure of the Knickerbocker on October 22, any failure would sharply set back a recovery and might return the financial community to full panic. The funds loaned to trust companies so far had not been sufficient to meet depositors' withdrawals. And depositors were still unconvinced that their money was safe. Again, the trust company crisis was coming to a head; this time, J. P. Morgan would *not* provide the solution. He decided it was time for others to come forward.

Resolving the Information Problem

For days, J. P. Morgan's partner, George W. Perkins, had been trying to get a complete statement from the trust companies regarding their financial condition, but he "had obtained nothing that was satisfactory."[3] The trusts would have a brief respite the next day because it would be Sunday, and Tuesday, November 5, would be Election Day, also a banking holiday. But Perkins felt it was critical to solve the problems with the banks and trust companies by then, or else "there was no use in making any further fight for them and that they would have to close."[4] He assigned two separate committees of examiners to ascertain the financial status of both the Trust Company of America and the Lincoln Trust.

Among the investigators he assigned to inspect the trust companies was Benjamin Strong Jr. from Bankers Trust who, along with Henry Davison, had tried to assess the health of the Knickerbocker and now faced the assessment of the other two big trust companies over a long weekend. He later described working "without sleep nor leaving the building"[5] to carry out his assignment. By 9 p.m. on Saturday, November 2, Strong reported to Morgan's library to offer his final assessment of the ailing trusts.

When he arrived at the building, about 40 or 50 men were already discussing both the brewing crisis and the troubles that lay in store for Monday. He noted that the presidents of the clearing house banks were assembled in the library's East Room, while representatives from the trust companies were gathered in the West Room. Morgan, Judge Gary, Henry Frick, Lewis Cass Ledyard, and others had retired to "neutral ground"[6] in the office of Morgan's librarian at the rear of the building.

Strong said, "I felt satisfied that something had gone wrong."[7] Henry P. "Harry" Davison, who had established Bankers Trust, told Strong that Morgan was already convinced that $25 million would be required to deal with the trust companies in addition to an estimated

$25 million to address an emerging problem at Moore & Schley, a brokerage firm. "[I]n those days $50 million* looked very large indeed in contrast with the figures to which we are accustomed now," Strong later wrote in 1924.[8] After all the earlier loans and commitments during the Panic, such a large commitment would seriously strain the capabilities of Morgan and his circle.

Morgan finally announced to his counselors in the librarian's office that he would agree to undertake the difficulties with Moore & Schley only if the trust company officials themselves would insure the needs of their weaker peers.

The Problem of Collective Action in a Diverse Group

Since 1903, when the trust companies had split from the NYCH, they had tended to go their own various ways. The years 1903–1906 had been good to the trust companies and may have inflated their confidence into overconfidence. Furthermore, as discussed in Chapter 9, the trust companies formed a heterogeneous lot, varying by age of institution, by extent of affiliation with the established financial institutions, by clientele (wholesale vs. retail), by ethnic focus, and by distance from Wall Street.

Since returning to New York on October 21, Morgan had met with many trust company presidents individually. And he had organized gatherings of trust company presidents to form an association for the pooling of risk—not unlike the NYCH. Newspapers and the Morgan archives show that Pierpont had met with some or all of the trust company presidents virtually daily. None of his meetings up to that point had successfully mobilized collective action. By November 2, the need for trust companies to rescue their own had become crucial.

Some insight into Morgan's challenge is afforded by modern research into the problems of collective action. The work of Mancur Olson,[9] Nobel laureate Elinor Ostrom,[10] and others suggest the important role of incentives to motivate individual players to commit to joint effort at some individual cost. Some benefit must override that cost, as well as any

* The purchasing power of $50 million in 1907 equaled $1.5 billion in 2022.

incentive to free-ride by some members of the collective. Benefits could accrue in the form of improved economic welfare, the avoidance of losses, reduction of injustices, and/or strengthened identity. Olson pointed out that as the group grows larger, collective action becomes more difficult. And participants tend to commit resources relative to their own capabilities; one size of contribution does not fit all contributors. Therefore, collectives tend to expect the resource-rich participants to contribute more on an absolute basis. This was the rub for Morgan and the trust company executives: some of the largest trust companies were distressed and couldn't contribute to a rescue pool—the smaller trust companies were being asked to rescue two of the larger players in the market.

Attempting to marshal a risk-pooling agreement among the trust companies must have felt to Morgan like herding cats. Estimates of the number of trust companies in New York varied from some 38[11] in Manhattan alone to 59[12] in what was then the entire city.[13] Representatives from individual trust companies came and went and varied from one day

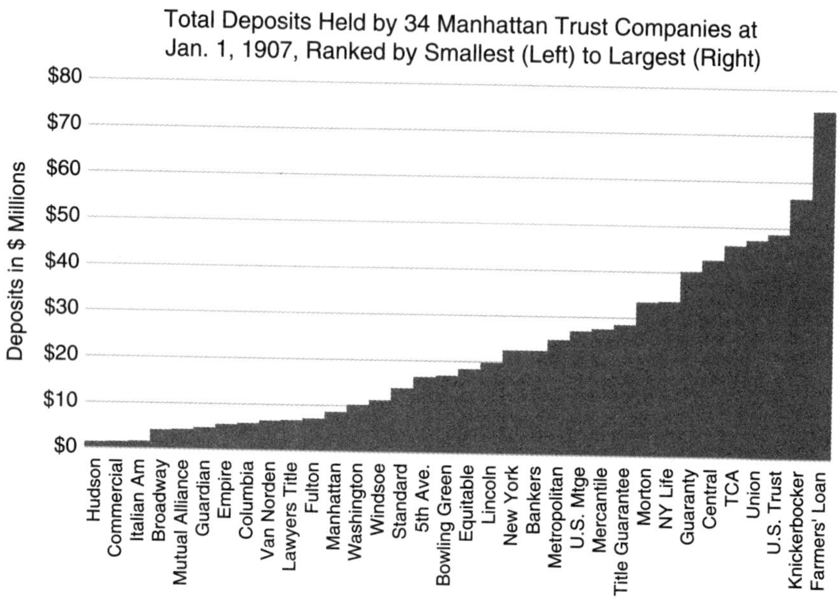

Figure 16.1 Distribution of Manhattan Trust Companies by Size of Deposits
SOURCE: Authors' figure based on calculations of data given in Hansen (2014), pp. 559–560, and *Annual Report of the Superintendent of Banks 1907* (Albany, NY: J.B. Lyon Company, March 16, 1908).

to the next. Figure 16.1 shows that the volume of deposits among the field of Manhattan trust companies was distributed asymmetrically: the five largest firms accounted for 37 percent of all deposits; the 10 largest held 61 percent.

Thus, the field of trust companies consisted of a minority of large firms and a majority of relatively small ones—and some of the larger firms (Knickerbocker, Trust Company of America, and Lincoln) were the subject of intense runs. This asymmetry may have engendered *schadenfreude* by the smaller firms toward their large and ailing peers. Competition among trust companies remained quite active, as judged from their behavior (offering interest payments on deposits and retail marketing efforts) and measures of industry concentration.[14]

Some competitors may have hungrily eyed the possibility of picking up deposits from failures of distressed peer firms. Indeed, a redistribution of deposit accounts was already underway and would benefit smaller trust

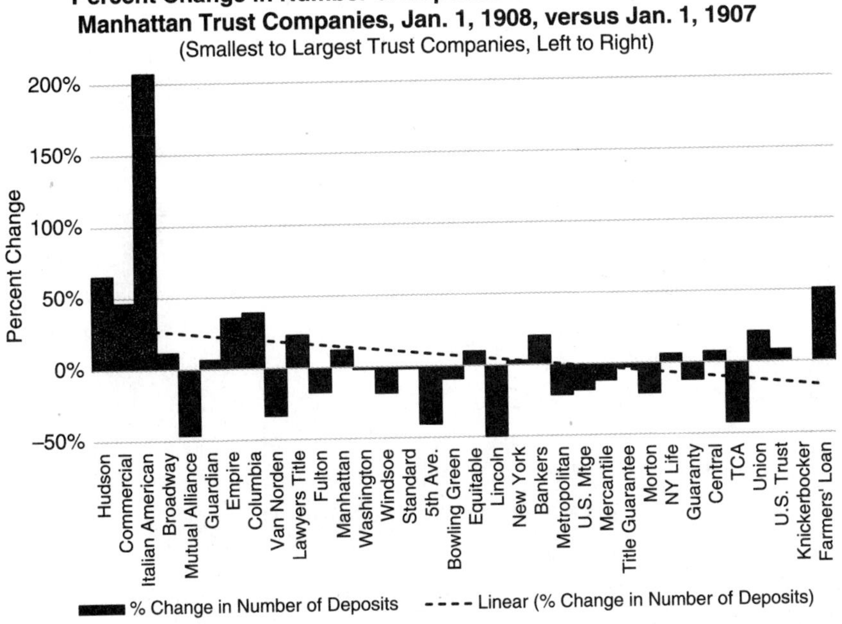

Figure 16.2 Trust Company Percent Change in Deposit Accounts During 1907

SOURCE: Authors' figure, based on calculations derived from data in Hansen (2014), pp. 559–560.

companies. Figure 16.2 shows the percent change in deposit accounts for each of the trust companies as ranked in Figure 16.1—visibly, smaller trusts tended to gain accounts, while larger ones lost. The correlation coefficient between volume of deposits and change in deposit accounts is –0.16 and is suggested by the downward-sloping trendline in Figure 16.2.

Small trust companies may have benefited from local proximity to their retail clientele and from ethnic and religious networks during the Panic. And the loss in deposits at Trust Company of America, Lincoln, and Knickerbocker* would have weighed down the results at the large end of the distribution. The distribution of gains and losses in deposits for these firms during the Panic is a worthy subject for future research.

The point is that the community of trust companies was wracked by divisions that obstructed J. P. Morgan's efforts to bring the trust company presidents toward a risk-pooling agreement. An ultimatum (a final offer backed up by a threat) is one strategy for compelling a group toward collective decision. The threat must appear to make everyone worse off. Ultimatums are plainly risky, as they are coercive and may embolden resistance. Morgan did not need to extend a threat of his own, but merely could relate the disastrous consequences of a failure to form a collective. Would an ultimatum work in the wee hours of Sunday, November 3?

A Meeting with a Locked Door

For the next several hours, Strong reported that nothing but "desultory conversation"[15] took place among the bank officials. Thomas W. Lamont, another Morgan associate, was also summoned to this plenary session of bankers, and he provided an evocative description of what he saw that night at the now-famous meeting at the library:

> *A more incongruous meeting place for anxious bankers could hardly be imagined: in one room—lofty, magnificent—tapestries hanging on the walls, rare Bibles and*

* As of November 1907, the change in Knickerbocker's deposits was not known. The firm had suspended and was in bankruptcy resolution proceedings under the New York Superintendent of Banking. However, Knickerbocker is included in Figure 16.2 for parity with Figure 16.1. Given its dramatic runs culminating on October 22, Knickerbocker likely experienced a material loss in deposits, consistent with the general trend in Figure 16.2.

illuminated manuscripts of the Middle Ages filling the cases; in another, that collection of the Early Renaissance masters—Castagno, Ghirlandaio, Perugino, to mention only a few—the huge open fire, the door just ajar to the holy of holies where the original manuscripts were safeguarded. And, as I say, an anxious throng of bankers, too uneasy to sit down or converse at ease, pacing through the long marble hall and up and down the high-ceilinged rooms, with their cinquecento background, waiting for the momentous decisions of the modern Medici.[16]

Finally, around midnight, Edwin S. Marston, the president of the Farmers Loan and Trust Company (the largest trust company), was summoned away from the trust company executives in the West Room to see J. P. Morgan. After meeting with Morgan for an hour, Marston—"looking very grave"[17] —returned to the room and explained to the trust presidents that Morgan had informed him of another serious situation, about which he was not at liberty to say more. Morgan told him that the problem would call for another $25 million, and he was working toward a solution. But Morgan was very concerned about the problems with the trusts and the risks they posed to this other situation. "Mr. Morgan was naturally unwilling to proceed with the other matter," Strong said, "with the possibility of a complete banking collapse which would render his efforts futile."[18] Clearly, this statement was an indication that Morgan was leaving the trust company problem to the trust company presidents. This time, he refused to be their rescuer, and this thrust the assembled executives into an utter state of consternation.

During the debates that ensued, Strong dozed off on a lounge chair next to James Stillman, the president of National City Bank. "I recall his asking me when I had last been in bed," Strong said, "and when I told him the previous Thursday night, he said the country wasn't going to smash if I went home to bed."[19] Finally, at 3 a.m., the assembled bank and trust company officials were ready to hear Benjamin Strong's full report on the faltering trust companies; by this time, there were approximately 120 men participating in the conference. Outside, a throng of reporters awaited news from the meeting, but secrecy was maintained through the night and into the morning.

Inside, Strong assured the trust presidents that the Trust Company of America was solvent and, with equity that amounted to $2 million, the firm had sufficient assets to pay off its depositors in time. Another committee organized by George Perkins reported that the Lincoln Trust was probably short of its ability to pay its depositors by at least $1 million. After concluding his report, Strong headed to leave the building; when he reached the door, he found that the library had been locked. "It was indeed true that Mr. Morgan, having assembled the men to deal with a perilous situation, had had the door to the library locked, and the key was in his own pocket," Strong wrote.[20] Even though Morgan was often not directly involved in the negotiations among the trust company presidents, clearly, he exerted powerful influence. "Mr. Morgan took no chances," Satterlee wrote. "He meant to have the situation cleared up before a single man left the building."[21]

By this time, Morgan himself had entered the discussion. He pointed to Edward King, the president of the Union Trust Company, who had been the unofficial leader of his fellow trust company presidents. Morgan told him that they must act now, and that they must provide a loan of $25 million to support the Trust Company of America, or else "the walls of their own edifices might come crumbling about their ears."[22] He told them again that the equity in the Trust Company would secure their loans and that the clearing house banks were looking after the situation elsewhere.

Even though Morgan had just told them that it was incumbent upon the trust presidents "to look after their own,"[23] they were still hesitant to take any action. They contended that in the absence of their boards of directors they lacked the authority to burden their institutions with such a heavy commitment. They were also convinced that it was their primary responsibility to conserve their assets to weather the financial storm swirling around them. Morgan understood their position and he sympathized with them—but he also understood that the failure of the Trust Company of America could have far-reaching implications; unless it were saved that day, they risked a complete collapse of the entire banking system. "The situation must not get further out of hand," Lamont said. "It had to be saved."[24]

Several of the lawyers present had drafted a simple subscription for a loan of $25 million. As for any possible objections from the trust companies' boards of directors, Morgan told the assembled presidents that he was confident their boards would ratify whatever decision was made there that day; Morgan clearly understood the power his personal endorsement would carry. One of the lawyers read the subscription form aloud to the bankers, and he laid it on the table. Morgan waved his hand "invitingly" toward the document.

"There you are, gentlemen," Morgan said.

He waited for a few moments, and then he put his hand on the shoulder of his friend Edward King, encouraging him to come forward.

"There's the place, King, and here's the pen," Morgan said as he placed a gold pen in the hand of the Union Trust president.

King signed, followed by every other trust company president in the room.[25]

Chapter 17

Instant and Far-Reaching Relief

They must deal with it as they see fit. I have gone with it as far as I can.[1]

—J. Pierpont Morgan, November 3, 1907

Early on Saturday morning, November 2, J. P. Morgan called an emergency conference at the library. There was a new problem on Wall Street.

Collapse threatened one of the largest brokerage houses, and its failure promised to spark another wave of panic. The brokerage firm Moore & Schley, and its senior partner Grant B. Schley, had borrowed more than $30 million from numerous banks, trust companies, and other financial institutions in New York and elsewhere. To secure the loans, the debtors had used the stock of the Tennessee Coal, Iron & Railroad Company (commonly known at the time as Tennessee Coal and Iron, or simply TC&I) as collateral. However, the strained market conditions had raised questions about the value of the TC&I shares, and on Monday many of the banks would likely call in loans to Moore & Schley, and others. If the loans were called and creditors liquidated the TC&I shares *en masse*, then the market would be flooded with TC&I stock. TC&I's price would plummet. The risk was that all this would cause Moore & Schley to fail, crash the stock market, and inflame again the financial panic.

Under ordinary circumstances, Moore & Schley's loans would not have commanded much attention from the major banks and trust companies. However, the unusually heavy demands for cash by depositors now prompted lenders to demand truly liquid securities as collateral to back their loans. TC&I's stock, it seemed, was not so liquid. In fact, the market for TC&I's shares was thin. Only a few investors, including Grant Schley, owned the majority of TC&I's shares. For months, Schley and his small pool of investors had been artificially supporting TC&I's stock price. So, even though the stock had been trading steadily at $130 per share for some time, if the banks disposed of the stock, then its price would likely fall by at least $50 or $60 before any other buyers would emerge for it. By then, both Moore & Schley and the many other institutions holding TC&I securities as collateral for Moore & Schley's loans would be in serious trouble.

J. P. Morgan was gravely concerned about this turn of events. "It is very serious," he said. "If Moore and Schley go, there is no telling what the effect on Wall Street will be and on financial institutions of New York, and how many other houses will drop with it, and how many banks might be included in the consequences."[2] Morgan quickly dispatched two reliable aides, Thomas Joyce from J. P. Morgan & Company and Richard Trimble from U.S. Steel, to examine the financial condition of Moore & Schley. He also told Grant Schley, the brother-in-law of his friend George F. Baker, president of the First National Bank, to join them.

Morgan continued the meeting at the library on November 2, discussing the general condition of TC&I and the magnitude of Moore & Schley's loans held by his friends, associates, and bankers. The simplest method for saving the brokerage house would have been to raise a loan for about $25 million, but it was unlikely such an amount could be found, particularly for an institution that was already so highly leveraged. Moreover, credit conditions were dismal. However, Lewis Cass Ledyard, a lawyer representing the syndicate controlling TC&I and a friend of Morgan's, had a bold idea. Upon hearing his daring and ultimately controversial proposal, Morgan adjourned the morning's discussion and called for an immediate meeting of the finance committee of the United States Steel Corporation. He told them to come to the library by 2:30 that afternoon.

U.S. Steel

J. P. Morgan had been intimately connected with the United States Steel Corporation (USS). In 1901 Morgan, Elbert H. Gary, and Henry Clay Frick had created the company by combining various steel producers, including the extensive operations owned by Andrew Carnegie. By 1907, USS controlled leading shares of the nation's steel markets, making it the largest steel producer in the world *and* the world's largest corporation. Despite the recent market crash and ongoing financial panic, U.S. Steel was in robust condition. The company recently reported that its quarterly earnings had surpassed $43.8 million—the second most profitable period in its history—and that it could boast cash resources of $76 million.

Elbert Gary (known by all as "Judge" Gary for having served two terms as a county judge in Illinois) was a savvy chief executive and was sensitive to the financial crisis facing investors and depositors. He recognized a positive role for the company to play during the crisis, especially at a time when "big business" was regularly under fire. Speaking to U.S. Steel's board of directors on Tuesday, October 29, at a meeting that included Morgan and Frick, Gary said:

> *There has existed during the last week a delirium of excitement. The feeling in a large measure has been without cause, and there is already a change for the better. If all of us do everything in our power to maintain a high standard for the conduct of affairs in our charge we can be of great benefit in restoring the confidence necessary to success.*[3]

In response to the crisis, on Friday, November 1, U.S. Steel announced plans to pay its employees only 20 percent in cash and the remainder by check in small denominations at various banks. "This method of payment was decided upon because of the fact that the amount of currency in the banks of the country is limited," Judge Gary said.[4] It was hoped that U.S.

Steel, which had a payroll of $3 million *per week*, could use its own cash hoard to provide much-needed liquidity to the system. The announcement showed that having plenty of cash on the balance sheet was one thing; withdrawing the cash from banks to pay workers was another.

Finance Committee Discusses TC&I

By 3 p.m. on Saturday, November 2, the members of U.S. Steel's finance committee convened at the library as Morgan had requested. Judge Gary and Henry Frick were present; the lawyers for Moore & Schley were gathered in an adjoining room. Lewis Cass Ledyard, the attorney for TC&I and Morgan's friend, had suggested to Morgan at the morning meeting that perhaps U.S. Steel could save Moore & Schley if they would consider acquiring the Tennessee Coal, Iron & Railroad Company. That was the proposal Morgan had brought them all there to discuss. Right away the lawyers from the next room brought in reports and data regarding TC&I, which the board members from U.S. Steel studied for an hour.

The Tennessee Coal, Iron & Railroad Company was an independent steel producer based in northern Alabama. The company possessed coal and steel properties that extended through Alabama, Tennessee, and Georgia. By 1907, it owned an estimated 800 million tons of iron ore and 2 billion tons of coal, plus additional reserves of limestone, dolomite, and other raw materials necessary for the manufacture of steel. Significantly, the company's ores were located within 25 miles of its furnaces—literally "sitting on its raw material"[5]—a geographic benefit many Northern steel mills did not have. Given its apparent advantages, TC&I was, by some estimates, at the forefront of a movement to consolidate the disparate Southern steel producers and was considered a potentially important competitor to U.S. Steel. As proof of its growing influence, not long before the Panic TC&I received an order for 150,000 tons of steel rails from the railroads controlled by E. H. Harriman, an order that would typically have been granted to U.S. Steel.

Tennessee Coal, Iron & Railroad had been among the original 12 companies that comprised the Dow Jones Industrial Average in 1896. Since then, its stock had become a notorious high-flier on Wall Street, and rumors of mismanagement and malfeasance appeared often in the newspapers. The muckraking journalist Ida Tarbell reported that periodically TC&I was paying dividends from borrowed funds. "As for making money," Tarbell wrote, "old-timers tell you that the only department in the concern that ever ran at a profit was the company's stores!"[6] In 1906, a syndicate, which included Grant Schley, acquired control of TC&I.[7] These new owners had begun to implement plans to rehabilitate the company's plants, but doing so had depleted the company's resources completely. By 1907, the company was left with $4 million of debt, of which $1.5 million was about to come due.

Despite TC&I's attractive assets, Henry Frick was vehemently opposed to an acquisition of TC&I by U.S. Steel. He was convinced that the firm was an inefficient producer and that its costs of production were too high to be integrated successfully with U.S. Steel. Moreover, he understood that because of the high phosphorus content of TC&I's ores, the steel it produced was generally of low quality. Morgan argued with him, saying that he felt the company's coal and iron were at least worth the company's capitalization.

Even so, Elbert Gary was skeptical, too, especially because he was already familiar with the condition of both Moore & Schley and TC&I. Just recently during the Panic, Moore & Schley had approached Gary himself for a loan, and he had exchanged $1.2 million of U.S. Steel gold bonds for $2 million of TC&I stock—now worth much less than what he had paid. Gary was, therefore, disinclined to extend himself or his company to aid either Moore & Schley or TC&I any further.

A Solution in Prospect

As the early morning sun rose above New York City on Sunday, November 3, 1907, the brass doors of Morgan's library were finally unlocked. After the trust company presidents had given J. P. Morgan sufficient assurance that they would each subscribe to the new money pool to support the weaker trust companies, they were allowed to go home. As the bankers dispersed, George F. Baker, president of the First National Bank of New York, and Lewis Cass Ledyard, the attorney for the syndicate controlling the Tennessee Coal, Iron & Railroad

Company, stopped to have a few words with Morgan. "You look tired," Morgan chirped to Ledyard; their meeting at the library had been under way at least since Saturday morning. "Go home and get a good night's rest," Morgan added, "but be back here at nine o'clock sharp!"[8] It was then 5 a.m.

Despite the promising discussions Morgan had engineered inside his library, the city's newspaper reporters outside—and the public at large—were still largely in the dark. No statements had been released, and they were told only that the financiers were considering the general financial conditions. That was clearly insufficient. "[I]t became evident from the talk about the clubs that considerable alarm existed," observed George W. Perkins, who had also attended the all-night conference. "Stocks were being offered about town at from one to two points under the closing prices of Saturday. All sorts of rumors were flying about, and by noon it became clear that the failure of Moore & Schley on Monday and the closing of the Lincoln Trust Company would bring very general trouble."[9] The papers also reported that President Roosevelt was being urged to call for a special session of Congress to enact legislation and regulation for financial institutions. Perkins, as usual, went to see Morgan after breakfast, and they planned for another conference at the library to address the still-unresolved problem of the vulnerable brokerage house Moore & Schley.

The day's major meeting convened at 4:30 p.m. "Mr. Morgan, as usual, sat in his armchair facing the blazing wood fire in the big West Room," Herbert Satterlee recalled.[10] To Morgan's right was a small table, and on the other side of this sat the city's most senior bankers and Morgan's most trusted advisers, including George Baker, James Stillman, and George Perkins. Of course, Grant Schley was also there, as well as Elbert H. Gary, Henry Clay Frick, and the finance committee of U.S. Steel Corporation. If Moore & Schley should suspend the next day, an indefinite number of brokerage houses and other financial institutions would collapse, too. Moore & Schley was *too connected to fail*. During the meeting, several bankers and financiers were intent on saving Moore & Schley, and they pressed its importance upon J. P. Morgan. Regarding the proposal for U.S. Steel to acquire TC&I, Morgan told them:

> *I have done what I can. I have never been more concerned over a situation than I am over this. I think this is the most serious thing we have had to meet in this*

panic yet, but I cannot urge upon the Steel Corporation to take this property. I hope they will do it, but I do not think I have the right to urge them or force it upon them if I could. They must deal with it as they see fit. I have gone with it as far as I can.[11]

Gary and Frick remained strongly opposed to the acquisition plan. They felt it was an unworthy investment that U.S. Steel did not need, and they feared such a combination would open their company to accusations of attempting to create a monopoly in steel production. At the time, U.S. Steel claimed from 30 to 56 percent of the market across five major product lines. By early evening, the issue remained unresolved, and the steel executives planned to convene again at the library later that night.

A Rescue Emerges

After dinner, Morgan met with Thomas Joyce and Richard Trimble, whom he had delegated the day before to perform an in-depth review of Moore & Schley's books. After working more than 24 hours straight, they presented their findings at the library privately to Morgan, Baker, and Stillman. Morgan asked Joyce how much he estimated would be needed for Moore & Schley to avoid ruin. "About seventeen or possibly eighteen millions, sir," Joyce responded.[12] With that, Morgan proclaimed that the three of them—himself, Baker, and Stillman—must raise the money at once; he announced he would take a third interest in the subscription, and he suggested that Baker and Stillman provide the remainder of the $18 million, which would be carried by their banks until U.S. Steel could arrange to take it over from them. Baker consented to Morgan's plan right away, though Stillman was unhappy.

"Why, you haven't had time to study those figures!" Stillman said.

"Well, I know my man," Morgan replied. He handed the papers back to Joyce, concluding the discussion summarily. Reluctantly, Stillman agreed.[13]

Earlier in the day, George Perkins had been conferring with Grant B. Schley of Moore & Schley and John B. Topping, the president of the Tennessee Coal, Iron & Railroad Company, to determine the exact condition of TC&I. By the time the board members of U.S. Steel reconvened at Morgan's library on Sunday evening, Perkins, Schley, and Topping had mustered significant evidence to show Gary and Frick that TC&I's condition was not as compromised as they had assumed. They demonstrated that the company had nearly completed the construction of its new rail-producing mill, which would enable TC&I to make rails more cheaply than had been previously possible. Again, the steel executives discussed their disposition toward an acquisition of the firm.

Finally, the finance committee of the United States Steel Corporation acceded to a new plan to acquire TC&I. USS would buy a majority of the company, but not by paying cash, as had been proposed earlier. U.S. Steel would instead exchange its own bonds for shares of TC&I stock at par. Specifically, USS would exchange each of its 60-year, 5 percent sinking fund gold bonds,[14] which had a par value of $11,904.76, for 100 shares of TC&I stock, which had a total par value of $10,000. Gary and Frick's agreement to this deal was contingent on three important conditions being met. First, the Roosevelt administration must interpose no objections to the acquisition; second, this arrangement must "unquestionably save Moore & Schley"[15] from failure; and third, formal arrangements must be concluded to attend to the city's struggling trust companies.

Creditors were holding TC&I stock as collateral for loans to Moore & Schley and to the members of the syndicate that controlled TC&I—and the value of that collateral was considerably diminished because of the financial crisis. Therefore, the opportunity to exchange that stock for the gold-backed bonds of U.S. Steel was enormously attractive. Few other companies could have achieved such a uniquely reassuring outcome for bankers, investors, and depositors. In addition, since the acquisition would be achieved entirely through an exchange of securities, the transaction would place no further demands on the nation's already strained cash resources. With this arrangement, Grant Schley and his syndicate partners, as well as the firm, could pledge their new U.S. Steel securities as collateral for their various debts. Moore & Schley, numerous brokerages, the banks, and trust companies would be saved, all without the need for cash. The full board of U.S. Steel was scheduled to vote on this proposed deal in the next few days, on Wednesday, November 6. Based on J. P. Morgan's leadership that weekend, it seemed that the second and third of Gary's and Frick's conditions could be met. Now, all that was required was the willingness of the Roosevelt administration to allow the deal to occur.

Would the Government Bar the Deal?

The issue was whether the acquisition would be considered a breach of the Sherman Antitrust Act. The Act declared illegal any business combination "in restraint of trade." The law had not been invoked seriously in the first decade since enactment. More recently, President Theodore Roosevelt, the Bureau of Corporations, and the attorney general of the United States had been aggressively pursuing what they felt were the anticompetitive behaviors of large corporations. Given its massive size and scope, U.S. Steel would be an obvious target of their scrutiny. Gary and Frick were particularly sensitive to this risk.

"Before we go ahead with this," Judge Gary told Morgan, "we must consult President Roosevelt."

"But what has the president to do with it?" demanded Morgan.

"If we do this without consulting the administration," persisted Gary, "a bill in equity might stop the sale, and in that case more harm than good would be done. He cannot say that we may or may not purchase, but we ought to know his attitude since he has a general direction of the law department of the United States."

Morgan considered his point briefly. "Can you go at once?"[16]

Meeting with the President

At 10 p.m. on Sunday, Judge Gary called William Loeb, President Roosevelt's private secretary, to request an interview with the president at the earliest possible time on Monday morning. Once Loeb agreed to a meeting, Gary's men called the chief dispatcher of the Pennsylvania Railroad in Newark, New Jersey, telling him to arrange a special train comprised merely of a locomotive and a Pullman sleeper car, bound for direct travel to Washington, DC; all signalmen on the route would receive instructions that the one-car special would pass through during the night. After concluding their discussions on Sunday at the library,

Judge Gary and Henry Frick left at midnight in their cab and raced to New Jersey for their private, waiting train.[17]

Early Monday morning, November 4, cables from London indicated that the prices of American securities were falling; if prices in New York followed suit, many brokers would be unable to meet their margin requirements, putting even more pressure on houses like the troubled Moore & Schley. After only a few hours of sleep, the 70-year-old Morgan arose at 8:30 a.m. to wait for the crucial call from Washington. After breakfast, he instructed George Perkins to have an employee at the Corner establish an open phone connection with the White House so they could hear Roosevelt's verdict immediately from Gary and Frick.

Gary and Frick had arrived in Washington early on Monday morning, anxious to see the president as soon as possible. For Morgan's plan to work, they sought Roosevelt's blessing for the TC&I deal *before* the stock exchange opened at 10 a.m. Upon reaching the White House at 8 o'clock, Loeb, the president's secretary, firmly refused to admit the men from U.S. Steel immediately, saying that the president would see no one before 10 o'clock. This was more than the steel men were prepared to accept.

"But this is a serious matter," pleaded Gary, "and I think that if you will tell him just what Mr. Frick and I are here for, he will see us."[18]

At that moment, James Garfield, the Secretary of the Interior, arrived. Gary and Frick confided their problem to him and explained their urgent need to see the president. At once, Garfield conveyed their message to the president, and Roosevelt hastily interrupted his breakfast to see them. Since the attorney general was away from the city, Roosevelt asked Elihu Root, his Secretary of State, to review the matter with him.

At 9:45 a.m., Loeb told the men standing by at J. P. Morgan & Company in New York that Gary and Frick had just gone in to see the president. Right away, Perkins circulated news to Wall Street that a plan to save Moore & Schley and the trust companies was under discussion with the president.

Without further news, the market opened weakly at 10 a.m. At 10:15, Judge Gary stepped out of his conference with the president to say that Roosevelt was reading the matter favorably, then he returned to the portentous meeting. Finally, at 11 a.m., Gary announced that Roosevelt was fully in favor of the proposal. "It was necessary for me to decide on the

SAN FRANCISCO DOOMED

EXTRA **Oakland Tribune.** EXTRA

VOL. LXV — OAKLAND, CALIFORNIA, WEDNESDAY EVENING APRIL 18, 1906 — NO. 49

GREAT EARTHQUAKE!

DEATH AND DESTRUCTION SWEEP THE BAY CITIES!

HUNDREDS DIE IN RUINS!

THIS MORNING AT 5:14:48 O'CLOCK AN EARTHQUAKE SHOCK WAS EXPERIENCED IN OAKLAND AND A NUMBER OF OTHER CALIFORNIA CITIES. THE TEMBLOR LASTED FOR 28 SECONDS. MANY CHIMNEYS IN PRIVATE HOUSES, MERCANTILE ESTABLISHMENTS AND MANUFACTURING INSTITUTIONS WERE KNOCKED DOWN. IN SOME CASES HOLES WERE TORN IN THE WALLS OF BUSINESS PLACES, BUT NO STRUCTURES WERE ENTIRELY DEMOLISHED. WATER FOR A TIME WAS CUT OFF FROM CONSUMERS, AND TELEGRAPH AND TELEPHONE COMMUNICATION WAS INTERRUPTED. THE LOSS WILL AGGREGATE SEVERAL HUNDRED THOUSAND DOLLARS. FIVE LIVES WERE LOST. THESE VICTIMS WERE CRUSHED TO DEATH IN A ROOMING HOUSE. IN SAN JOSE AND SAN FRANCISCO THE LOSS OF PROPERTY AND LIFE WAS EXCESSIVE, ESPECIALLY IN THE LATTER PLACE, WHERE THE EASTERN PART OF THE CITY, INCLUDING THE PALACE HOTEL, THE CALL BUILDING, THE CHRONICLE BUILDING AND THE CITY HALL AND A NUMBER OF OTHER STRUCTURES WERE REDUCED TO ASHES BY FIRE WHICH BROKE OUT IN THE DISMANTLED STRUCTURES. THE LOSS THERE WILL RUN INTO MANY MILLIONS.

TO THE PEOPLE:

Keep cool. Keep your heads. Keep your courage.

Don't exaggerate.

Don't get panic stricken.

An earthquake shock of great violence and long duration is an appalling calamity, but a panic is infinitely worse.

Reason, courage, and calmness dissolve in times of panic like snow in a spring thaw, and confusion, irresolution prevail at a time when judgment and action are the supreme necessity of the hour. Beware of crediting and circulating wild rumors, and avoid idle lamentation.

A great disaster has befallen San Francisco, Oakland and several other California cities, due to mysterious elemental disturbance. There has been widespread damage to property and considerable loss of life. Careless and imperfect construction is responsible for nine tenths of the damage and a great majority of the casualties.

It may be a thousand years before there is such another disturbance in this locality, but the consequences of this one is an admonition not to repeat the errors of the past. The damage is so far from being irreparable that it should dishearten no one. Therefore it is wise to take counsel of reason and courage, and shun the fearful infection of timid, the superstitious and weak-minded.

Now is the time for the citizen of Oakland and San

(Continued on Page 2.)

FIVE ARE KILLED

Five people were killed in the Empire Building on Twelfth Street, near Broadway.

The dead are:

OTTO WISHER, forty-five years of age.

AMELIA WISHER, thirteen years of age.

EDWARD MARNEY, about twenty-five years of age.

MRS. EDWARD MARNEY, twenty-five years old

Unknown man, about twenty-five years of age.

JOHN JUDD dropped dead of heart disease.

BUNKERS IN BAY

The sheds over the Southern Pacific Long Wharf have completely collapsed. Many of the bunkers fell into the bay carrying thousands of tons of coal.

The Long Wharf is one of the most important shipping points about the bay, and freight traffic will be interrupted considerably.

REMOVING THE DEBRIS

The Board of Police and Fire Commissioners this morning set all the street employes cleaning up debris left by the earthquake. Gangs of men with wagons, picks and shovels, have been sent to the several districts of the city and are busily at work removing, as far as possible, traces of the earthquake.

STANFORD BUILDINGS DOWN

PALO ALTO, April 18.—All the university buildings here but one are a total wreck.

KILLS HEAD OF ASYLUM

Supervisor Fred Horner, who returned from San Jose in his auto this afternoon, states that the Agnews asylum is a total wreck, that many of the inmates were killed, and that the remainder are running around loose, terrorizing the community.

The superintendent of the institution and his wife were both killed.

THE CALL IS BURNING

SAN FRANCISCO, APRIL 18.—THE SAN FRANCISCO CALL BUILDING IS ON FIRE, AND AT THIS WRITING IT SEEMS CERTAIN THAT IT WILL BE TOTALLY DESTROYED.

FLAMES ARE RAPIDLY EATING AWAY THE STRUCTURE DESPITE THE EFFORTS MADE TO SAVE THIS MAGNIFICENT BUILDING. STREAMS OF WATER ARE BEING TURNED INTO THE BLAZING PILE, BUT SO INTENSE IS THE HEAT THAT THE WATER BECOMES STEAM, AS SOON AS IT REACHES THE FIRY FURNACE.

GREAT DAMAGE HAS ALSO BEEN DONE TO THE EXAMINER AND CHRONICL BUILDING.

MINISTER IN DANGER

The Brooklyn Presbyterian church on East Fifteenth street and Twelfth avenue was scarcely damaged at all, but the residence of its pastor, Rev. Henry K. Sanborn, at [illegible] Tenth avenue, was so badly damaged that the family was compelled to move out.

SHEDS ARE DESTROYED

The coal bunkers, which for [illegible] have been doing duty on Alaska wharf, suffered destruction before the earthquake. The immense framework was thrown down and the heavy beams and rods of iron twisted and distorted.

MAYOR MOTT APPEALS TO THE PEOPLE

TO THE PEOPLE OF OAKLAND: THE EARTHQUAKE THIS MORNING VISITED UPON OUR CITY A GREAT CALAMITY, YET IT IS A SOURCE OF MUCH SATISFACTION THAT WE WERE SPARED FROM A CONFLAGRATION AND SERIOUS LOSS OF LIFE. THE OFFICIALS OF THE CITY HAVE THE SITUATION WELL IN HAND, BUT I DESIRE TO APPEAL TO THE PEOPLE TO CO-OPERATE WITH THE AUTHORITIES IN MAINTAINING PEACE AND ORDER.

AS MANY BUILDINGS ARE IN AN UNSAFE CONDITION THE PUBLIC ARE ADMONISHED TO KEEP OFF THE STREETS, AND PARTICULARLY WARNED AGAINST CONGREGATING IN GROUPS. IT IS ALSO VERY ESSENTIAL THAT PRECAUTION BE USED IN THE BUILDING OF FIRES UNTIL THE CHIMNEYS HAVE BEEN INSPECTED AND REPAIRED. THOSE WHO HAVE NOT EITHER GAS OR OIL STOVES ARE ADVISED THAT DANGER MAY BE AVOIDED BY MOVING THEIR STOVES OUT OF DOORS.

FRANK K. MOTT, MAYOR.

Front page headlines from the Oakland Tribune (Calif.) reporting the devastation in San Francisco, April 18, 1906.

Charles T. Barney, president of the Knickerbocker Trust Company.

Source: Reprinted by permission of Brown Brothers, Sterling, PA 18463.

www.brownbrothersusa.com.

F. Augustus Heinze, president of the Mercantile National Bank.

Source: Reprinted by permission of Brown Brothers, Sterling, PA 18463.

www.brownbrothersusa.com.

J. Pierpont Morgan.

Source: Reprinted by permission of Brown Brothers, Sterling, PA 18463. www.brownbrothersusa.com.

Theodore Roosevelt, President of the United States (1901–1909).
Source: Courtesy of Picture History.

George B. Cortelyou, United States Secretary of the Treasury.

Source: Courtesy of Picture History.

George F. Baker, president of the First National Bank.

Source: Reprinted by permission of Brown Brothers, Sterling, PA 18463.

www.brownbrothersusa.com.

James Stillman, president of the National City Bank.

Source: Reprinted by permission of Brown Brothers, Sterling, PA 18463.

www.brownbrothersusa.com.

George W. Perkins, partner, J.P. Morgan & Co.

Source: Reprinted by permission of Brown Brothers, Sterling, PA 18463.

www.brownbrothersusa.com.

Lines of depositors form at the midtown offices of the Knickerbocker Trust Company, October 17, 1907, 9:00 am.

Source: Reprinted by permission of Brown Brothers, Sterling, PA 18463. www.brownbrothersusa.com.

Depositors and messengers at the Lincoln Trust Company, October 1907.

Source: Reprinted by permission of Brown Brothers, Sterling, PA 18463. www.brownbrothersusa.com.

Panic erupts outside the United States Subtreasury Building in New York, October 1907.

Source: Reprinted by permission of Brown Brothers, Sterling, PA 18463. www.brownbrothersusa.com.

J.P. Morgan appearing at the Pujo Committee hearings in Washington, D.C., December 1912.

Source: Reprinted by permission of Brown Brothers, Sterling, PA 18463. www.brownbrothersusa.com.

Powerful leaders of the U.S. Senate during the late "Gilded Age," the "Senate Four:" (from left to right) Orville H. Platt (R-CT), John C. Spooner (R-WI), William B. Allison (R-IA), Nelson W. Aldrich (R-RI).

Source: Library of Congress and U.S. Senate, downloaded June 30, 2022 from https://www.senate.gov/artandhistory/history/common/image/senatefour.htm

Representative Augustus O. Stanley, Chair of the Committee that investigated U.S. Steel and its acquisition of Tennessee Coal and Iron.

Source: Library of Congress Catalog: https://lccn.loc.gov/2014686164 Image download: https://cdn.loc.gov/master/pnp/ggbain/06100/06171u.tif Original url: https://www.loc.gov/pictures/item/2014686164/

Charles A. Lindbergh Sr.

Source: Collection of the U.S. House of Representatives.

George F. Baker. Cover illustration of Harper's Weekly, November 29, 1913 by James Montgomery Flagg. OTHER PEOPLE'S MONEY by Louis D. Brandeis — Louis D. Brandeis School of Law Library (louisville .edu)

James Stillman, Cover illustration of Harper's Weekly December 13, 1913 by James Montgomery Flagg. OTHER PEOPLE'S MONEY - CHAPTER I — Louis D. Brandeis School of Law Library (louisville.edu)

Illustration from Harper's Weekly, November 13, 1913 by Walter J. Enright OTHER PEOPLE'S MONEY - CHAPTER II — Louis D. Brandeis School of Law Library (louisville.edu)

"I Like a Little Competition"—J. P. Morgan

MR. MORGAN AS THE NEW ATLAS.

Theodore Roosevelt contemplating a run for president in 1912.

Source: U.S. National Archives October 1, 1912, https://catalog.archives.gov/id/306175

Source: Federal Reserve Bank of St. Louis, "The Panic of 1907" downloaded August 19, 2022 from https://www.federalreservehistory.org/essays/panic-of-1907

Paul M. Warburg

Source: Federal Reserve Bank of St. Louis, "The Panic of 1907" downloaded August 19, 2022 from https://www.federalreservehistory.org/essays/panic-of-1907

Benjamin Strong Jr.

Source: Federal Reserve Bank of St. Louis, "The Panic of 1907" downloaded August 19, 2022 from https://www.federalreservehistory.org/essays/panic-of-1907 © Federal Reserve Bank of New York instant, before the Stock Exchange opened," Roosevelt later testified regarding this meeting, "for the situation in New York was such that any hour might be vital."[19] Gary quoted Roosevelt as replying to him, "I do not believe that anyone could justly criticize me for saying that I would not feel like objecting to the purchase under the circumstances."[20]

Roosevelt's Decision

Perhaps sensing reactions that the TC&I deal might prompt, Roosevelt drafted a note to Attorney General Charles Bonaparte on November 4 summarizing what Gary and Frick had told him and his response. The note was remarkably matter of fact and devoid of either Roosevelt's earlier rhetoric against "malefactors of great wealth" or of defensiveness of the controversy his decision would create. He wrote that:

> *[Gary and Frick] have just called upon me. They state that there is a certain business firm (the name of which I have not been told, but which is of real importance in New York business circles) which will undoubtedly fail this week if help is not given. Among its assets are a majority of the securities of the Tennessee Coal Company. Application has been urgently made to the Steel Corporation to purchase this stock as the only means of avoiding a failure. Judge Gary and Mr. Frick inform me that as a mere business transaction they do not care to purchase the stock; that under ordinary circumstances they would not consider purchasing the stock because but little benefit will come to the Steel Corporation from the purchase; that they are aware that the purchase will be used as a handle for attack upon them on the ground that they are striving to secure a monopoly of the business and prevent competition—not that this would represent what could honestly be said, but what might recklessly and untruthfully be said. They further inform me that as a matter of fact the policy of the Company has been to decline to acquire more than sixty per cent of the steel properties, and that this purpose has been persevered in for several years past, with the object of preventing these accusations, and as a matter of fact their proportion of steel properties has slightly decreased, so that it is below this sixty per cent, and the acquisition of the property in question will not raise it above sixty per cent. But they feel that it is immensely to their interest, as to the interest of every responsible businessman, to try to prevent a panic and general industrial smashup at this time, and that they are willing to go into this transaction, which they would not otherwise go into, because it seems the opinion of those best fitted to express judgment in New York that it will be an important factor in preventing*

> *a break that might be ruinous; and that bankers in New York who are now thus engaged in endeavoring to save the situation. But they asserted they did not wish to do this if I stated that it ought not to be done. I answered that while of course I could not advise them to take the action proposed, I felt it no public duty of mine to interpose any objection.*[21]

As the note revealed, Roosevelt established no new principles about anti-trust enforcement that might have justified his approval of the deal. Nor did he impose conditions on the future operation of U.S. Steel regarding pricing, labor, or investment policies that might have been used to justify the deal from the public interest standpoint. While his prompt approval amid a crisis was consistent with his identity as a Man of Action, it was also consistent with the observation of historians that Roosevelt tended to be guided more by gut feel than principled reflection.

Reaction

News of U.S. Steel's new plan to acquire TC&I brought jubilation to Wall Street, saving many brokerages, banks, and trust companies. The initial response by the mainstream press endorsed Roosevelt's decision. "The relief furnished by this transaction was instant and far-reaching," opined the *Commercial and Financial Chronicle.* "Institutions, whose solvency might at any moment have become impaired through the continued possession of Coal & Iron stock among their assets, have been reinstated through the conversion of the stock into bonds of the Steel Corporation. Accordingly, now their standing cannot be open to question or the object of suspicion."[22] On November 5, the *New York Times* headlined "Steel Trust's Action That of Trust Company Pool Effectually Relieves the Situation" and reported that:

> *[T]he President has been much exercised by the danger of a widespread financial disturbance, and he has been eager to consult with his advisers as to any measures of relief and prevention that might be taken. . . . In such situation the President is*

> *always eager to consult with men who may be able to give him suggestions, and there is no doubt that he embraced the opportunity to secure the ideas of Messrs. Gary and Frick on the subject.*[23]

"TC&I Deal Is Helpful" read a headline in a backstory of the *New York Times* on November 7.[24] The same article opined, "If anything, the entry of [U.S. Steel] into the merchant iron market may be influential toward increasing co-operation among sellers."

After the first half-hour of trading, prices on the stock exchange turned upward and stayed strong for the rest of November 4. It was the best day the exchange had seen since the troubles began.

Chapter 18

Turning the Corner

Let the people resume business the way they were doing twelve months ago, start everything with a hurrah, and we will forget all about the panic in a day or two.

—President of a local branch bank[1]

After announcements on November 4 and 5 of the trust company rescue pool and the U.S. Steel deal to acquire TC&I, the mood in the markets began to improve.[2] "A tremendous change for the better had taken place and at last we had one day when everyone was hopeful, and all talk of failure and collapse ceased,"[3] George Perkins said. The bromides issued by leaders a few days earlier finally seemed to gain traction. On October 23 Treasury Secretary Cortelyou had said, "The general situation here is well."[4] Clark Williams, the New York State Superintendent of Banking, said, "the improvement in financial circles is continuing."[5] "It is very much improved . . . the outlook is very good," said James Stillman in an article subtitled "Getting Back to Normal" on October 29.[6] Some people believed that the whole episode was simply a matter of lost confidence. Local associations, such as the "Sunshine Movement" and "Prosperity League," organized to boost economic activity and employment.[7]

Approval of TC&I Acquisition

Tuesday, November 5, was Election Day for state and local races—a banking holiday. That evening at Morgan's library, the finance committee of the U.S. Steel Corporation formally ratified the plan discussed with Roosevelt to acquire the Tennessee Coal, Iron & Railroad Company. The official announcement was released to the press around 3 a.m., and the reaction was extremely positive. J. P. Morgan & Company, which served as the transfer agent for the deal, would eventually exchange more than $35.6 million of U.S. Steel's bonds for shares of TC&I stock, thereby saving Moore & Schley. The markets responded buoyantly, showing their first gains in weeks.

A Final Plan of Support for Ailing Trust Companies

Runs at the Trust Company of America and Lincoln Trust—sites of the fiercest depositor runs—ended. Professor Sprague wrote that "confidence was not restored until on November 6 announcement was made that a majority of shares of Trust Company of North America and another trust had been placed under the control of a committee of trust company presidents."[8]

Under the terms of the trust company rescue pool that Morgan had negotiated with the trust company presidents, the Trust Company of America and the Lincoln Trust placed 66 percent of their securities in the hands of a trustee named by Morgan. To meet their daily cash needs, the firms could use these assets as collateral for loans from the syndicate of trust companies. Morgan also required that a certain percentage of the trusts' deposits could not be withdrawn for 60 to 90 days. The impact of this plan was immediate. "On Thursday both the Trust Company of America and the Lincoln Trust Company promptly met the demands of their depositors," the *Commercial and Financial Chronicle* reported, "and yesterday the runs on both institutions, it was thought, had practically ended."[9]

The Trust Company of America and the Lincoln Trust received $15 million and $5 million, respectively, through this arrangement. Reports surfaced that efforts were under way to form a depositors' committee to reopen the Knickerbocker Trust Company. In the coming months, the Knickerbocker would be resuscitated, though not before Charles T. Barney, the trust company's former president who became embroiled in the schemes of Augustus Heinze and Charles W. Morse, committed suicide in his Park Avenue home on November 14, 1907.

During the next week, President Roosevelt contributed further to these salutary measures by issuing a statement saying that the crisis had passed and announcing that no special session of Congress would be necessary to meet the needs of the present situation because the existing regulations were sufficient. "What is most needed at this time," wrote President Roosevelt, "is that people should realize how fundamentally sound business conditions in the country are and how absurd it is to permit themselves to get into a panic and create stringency by hoarding their savings instead of trusting safe banks."[10]

Liquidity Rises

The public also learned that a shipment of more than $12.4 million in gold had arrived on November 8 from Liverpool, England, aboard the *Lusitania*—"the richest cargo that ever came across the Atlantic on a single steamship."[11] J. P. Morgan's son, Jack, negotiated a $16 million gold loan from the Bank of France, which was announced on November 22.[12] These and other imports brought total gold shipments to the United States from Europe in November and December to over $94 million.[13]

Furthermore, Secretary Cortelyou embarked on another tactic aimed at boosting liquidity and confidence. On November 19, the Treasury invited subscriptions for about $50 million in U.S. gold bonds to finance ongoing construction of the Panama Canal—and $100 million in government notes.[14] By buying these bonds, the banks could use them to increase their issuance of banknotes, thus further alleviating the liquidity drought. Investor interest in the Panama Canal bonds was oversubscribed some 44 times, owing to a speculative appeal in the bonds. However, investor interest in the notes was tepid, having subscribed for merely 15 percent of the issue. Furthermore, the delays in issuing the securities meant that the impact of the tactic was not felt until December, when the recovery from panic was under way. Nonetheless, Cortelyou later argued,

> *The most potent weapon at such times in bringing a crisis to an end is often as much one of moral effect as of the definite action taken. It has been the history of many great crises in Europe, as well as in this country, that the knowledge that adequate resources existed to avoid disaster was often sufficient to obviate the necessity for employing such resources to their utmost limit.*[15]

Encomiums

The sense of turning a corner released a nimbus of praise for the efforts of Cortelyou, Morgan, and his circle. On November 1, the Boston Stock Exchange voted a resolution "to express their great and deep admiration for the timely, disinterested, courageous, and wise action of Mr. J. Pierpont Morgan and his associates during the recent crisis . . . we offer to them, as high-minded public citizens, who have preferred the good of others to the good of themselves, our heartiest thanks."[16] The *New York Times* called Morgan a "genius . . . colossus . . . [and] skillful."[17] The *Literary Digest* anointed him "The Man of the Hour."[18] A progressive-leaning newspaper, the *Seattle Star*, grumbled that Morgan quelled the crisis because it was in his own personal interest and then grudgingly conceded that "of the man himself there is much good to be written, and we write it gladly."[19]

William Jennings Bryan commended J. P. Morgan's wisdom and "splendid patriotism": "Everybody is thrilled with admiration over his magnificent contribution of $25,000,000 in the recent Wall Street stock market slump to help our country."[20] Even labor unions, following Samuel Gompers's lead, voted resolutions expressing confidence in the banks.[21] On November 22, Senator John C. Spooner lauded Morgan:

> *Who stemmed the tide of distrust and suspicion and distrust that seemed to overwhelm the business and people of this country? It was not the Federal government. It helped all it could. It was the strong, patriotic, resourceful bankers and financiers of this great city, led by the uncrowned king of them all, J.P. Morgan, who accomplished*

more in the way of correcting bad methods, of holding men to the faith involved in trusteeship, than a Congress could do in a dozen years.[22]

The next few years would challenge Spooner's hyperbole.

The Lingering Crisis

Indeed, in contrast to the calming utterances by public officials, the relief over the avoidance of another blow-up, the backslapping for Morgan and his circle, and the happy thoughts of the "Sunshine Movement," objective measures suggested that the crisis was hardly over. New rentals of safe deposit boxes declined after the first week of November, but the weekly volume of new rentals continued higher than before the Panic (see Figure 15.2)—evidently, people were still hoarding. The currency premium in Figure 15.6 did not start to decline materially until November 23. The trend of cash outflows from New York to the interior reversed on November 15 but did not return to the average of prior years until December 20 (see Figure 15.1). Clearing house loan certificates remained outstanding in New York city until the last certificate was canceled on March 28—in Macon, Georgia, loan certificates circulated until May 1.[23] Net gold imports began to subside in the week of December 7 (see Figure 15.3). The spreads between high and low quotations of call money interest rates did not subside back to the noise level until January 10, 1908 (see Figure 14.2). Thus, the quantitative measures suggested that the financial disturbance lasted well beyond public statements of leaders in business and government.

The recession that began in May 1907 would run until June 1908, sacrificing jobs, businesses, and aspirations for millions of people. The broad stock market index would not recover to the level of its previous peak in September 1906 until August 1909. And the debtors and creditors who were severely chastened by the panic would not return to the peak borrowings of August 1907 until September 1908.[24]

Yet the financial indicators tell but part of the long tail of the Panic. The wrenching experience tipped public attitudes toward government intervention in financial markets. In November, the governors of Oregon,

Nevada, and California declared legal holidays, which had the effect of closing the banks entirely. Bank holidays constrained consumers and business leaders and therefore slowed the return to normal market conditions. But they also dampened manic behavior. And an announcement on November 19 by Secretary Cortelyou of a new measure for expanding the volume of currency in circulation indicated that the scarcity of cash remained chronic.

Chapter 19

Ripple Effects

Worried over the belief that he had lost $20,000, his balance in the Knickerbocker Trust Company of New York, Valentine Hayerdahl of Mount Vernon committed suicide yesterday afternoon by shooting himself through the head at his home, 53 Rich Avenue, Chester Hill. Mr. Hayerdahl, who was formerly a salesman for the Haviland China Company of New York, resigned a short time ago to go into business for himself. All the money Mr. Hayerdahl owned was on deposit in the trust company. He told several friends that he believed that his life's earnings were gone.

—*New York Times*, November 27, 1907

The Panic of 1907 reverberated in markets, governments, and the lives of individuals throughout the United States and around the world. Some measures suggested that the instability in New York had receded by January 1908. But it lingered in the financial system of the rest of the country for several more months. And the Panic proved not to be just a financial crisis—it spilled over into the real economy, society, politics, and public policy, in which the crisis proved to have a much longer influence.

Initial Views of the Panic Beyond New York City

Initially, the impact of the panic elsewhere in the United States appeared to be mild. Just as the New York trust companies were experiencing the first shock waves of instability in late October 1907, dispatches from other cities and regional money centers showed little indication that anyone expected the contagion to spread beyond Wall Street. In fact, contemporaneous reports from Chicago and cities further west even implied that the malaise was a consequence of New York-based speculation and imprudent banking practices, hinting that it would have little effect elsewhere. "We are getting more independent of Wall Street every day, and business conditions here are not disturbed by the flurries of the market there," declared a St. Louis businessman. "St. Louis people are lending money in New York instead of borrowing it."[1] Similarly, the president of the Union Trust Company of Chicago boasted, "There has not been the slightest indication of alarm over the situation anywhere in Chicago today. It simply shows what has long been an established fact—that Chicago banks are not affected by the ups and downs of the stock market. Chicago credit is as solid as ever—there is no Wall Street in Chicago."[2]

On October 23, prominent bankers in Chicago asserted the probity of their operations and discounted the likelihood of financial unrest there. George M. Reynolds, president of the Continental National Bank and a member of the Chicago clearing house committee, said, "If you drop a pebble into a pond the ripples will extend to the farthest banks of the body of water. If you watch the ripples closely, however, you will notice that they become invisible a short distance from the spot in which the pebble fell. It is just so with the present financial situation. The pebble that has caused the New York trouble has made ripples fly, but they disappeared before they reached Chicago." Similarly, John J. Mitchell, president of Illinois Trust and Savings Bank, said, "The secret of the situation is that we have no promoting schemes here. Ours is the solid business variety of investments, and there is not occasion for worry about them."[3]

Then Troubles Spread to the Interior

Notwithstanding the evident disdain for events unfolding in New York City, within mere days the tremors of the panic were being felt far from Gotham. "The most sinister feature of today's financial news is the spreading of the strain to other cities" was already being reported by the *Manchester Guardian* on October 25. "It is no longer possible to affirm that the trouble is localized in New York."[4] By the next day, banks elsewhere in the nation were suspending operations; even the clearing house of St. Louis made a proactive decision to begin the issuance of certificates upon demand. This was quickly followed by similar actions by bank clearing houses across the country.[5] Going even further, on October 28 the governor of Oklahoma ordered the immediate closure of every bank in the Oklahoma and Indian Territory as a precautionary measure, following the decision by the banks of Kansas City and St. Louis to forward cash to the banks of the Southwest.[6] By the end of the Panic, only six states did *not* suspend or limit payments.[7]

The *national* experience of financial crisis reminded business leaders of the linkages and interdependencies across regions. President Theodore N. Vail of the American Telephone & Telegraph Co., following a trip to inspect affiliate companies in the West, admonished those who held narrower views:

> *The present crisis, whether we call it a money stringency, a business depression, or an old-fashioned panic, is teaching the West a lesson which years of unbroken prosperity had caused it nearly to forget, and that is, the essential unity of the country. In a very large sense, the states are all "members of one another." It is impossible for Wall Street to be suffering in the throes of financial stringency without the banks and industries of Missouri, Kansas and Oklahoma feeling the effect. The West seems to have forgotten this fact. It has been the fashion there to decry the "gamblers" of Wall Street and to speak of the eastern money centers as if they were isolated communities. The West is now feeling, and in the coming months is likely to feel, a severe financial stringency, with all the usual accompaniments of a money disturbance.*[8]

December 1907–January 1908: Signs of Improvement

The intensity of the Panic in late October and the precipitous decline in order volume and productivity across key industrial sectors during the months that followed was matched only by the apparent abruptness with which conditions began to improve. Barely two months after the crisis had started, notes of confidence began to appear in the popular press, with nearly buoyant optimism by the year's end. The *Washington Post* reported that:

> *[I]t is perfectly plain that the era of good times has begun and that the panic of 1907, with its resulting depression, will be confined almost entirely to 1907. . . . Business men are reassured. The world is not coming to an end. There is no lack of money in Washington. The people have currency with which to transact their business. The banks have gone on exactly as if there had been no flurry. The payments from the Treasury have been heavier than ever, and as dividends are being paid the quantity of money in circulation is larger than usual. The big holiday business being done by the shops and business houses is excellent proof of good times.*[9]

As evidence of an incipient recovery, executives from United States Steel reported that planned railroad improvements were expected to recommence, resulting in a "resumption of activity [in 1908] that would speedily erase all evidence of the recent shock."[10]

While some of the bullishness about the hoped-for turnaround may have simply been wishful thinking, there was nonetheless a deep conviction that the underlying strength of the U.S. economy, which had been booming in recent years, would buttress its resilience in the wake of the crisis. One contemporary journalist observed that, while the United States had only 5 percent of the world's population, the nation had come to produce 20 percent of the world's wheat, 25 percent of its gold, 33 percent of its coal, 35 percent of its manufactures, 38 percent of its silver, 40 percent of its iron, 42 percent of its steel, 52 percent of its petroleum, 55 percent of its copper, 75 percent of its cotton, and 80 percent of its corn.[11] It seemed unthinkable at that time that economic dislocations would be anything but short-lived. The *Washington Post* said:

> *The "panic" is having a hard time trying to live to the end of the year. Prosperity is rapidly reducing the panic to a skeleton of its former self. Many cities have resumed currency payments, the [bank] holidays have been called off in the West, and the premium on currency in New York has dropped to a trifle, with indications that it will disappear within a week. Confidence has returned to every corner of the country. The Christmas buying was heavy, everything considered, and in some places, it*

excelled that of last year. Mills and factories are preparing for an active business in the new year.[12]

And so it was; even the worst-hit firms began to show signs of life well before 1908. Westinghouse Electric and Manufacturing Company, for instance, reported a late-December order for $2 million, which resulted in an accelerated reopening of one of its major plants in Pittsburgh. At the same time, both the American Shipbuilding Company and the American Steel and Wire Company announced the rehiring of several thousand workers by January 1908. And the Sherwin-Williams Paint Company, which had sidelined all 250 salespeople in October, reported that they would be on the road again by the first week of the new year.

By early January 1908, banks in New York lifted their suspension of payments in specie.[13] And the New York Clearing House (NYCH) ended the issuance of clearing house loan certificates and resumed interbank payments in gold. The premium on currency had completely disappeared by January 17.[14] On the New York Stock Exchange (NYSE), call loan interest rates had returned to low single-digit levels by the end of December. Stock prices began to rise in February, commencing a slow "V-shaped" recovery, as Figure 19.1 depicts.

The Real Economy: Deep Immediate Impact

Beyond the banking sector, the panic hit the real economy with unanticipated intensity. Even though 1907 was, for instance, a record-breaking year for iron and steel production, the final quarter staggered the industry with a "partial but apparently progressive paralysis."[15] By year-end, more than a third of total productive capacity in the industry had been idled. The cause for this severe contraction was a major cancellation of orders by the railroads, many of which had become anxious about their own ability to secure the financing they needed to make their purchases. Consequently, the pronounced loss of confidence by the railroads in the banking and financial system hit the iron and steel producers with uncommon speed and ferocity, causing them to shutter operations

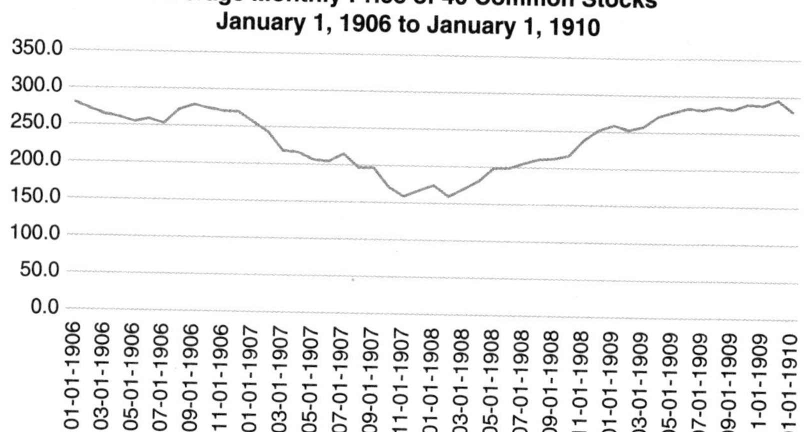

Figure 19.1 Recovery in Share Prices Began in 1908
SOURCE: Authors' figure, based on data from National Bureau of Economic Research, Average Prices of 40 Common Stocks for United States [M11006USM315NNBR], retrieved from FRED, Federal Reserve Bank of St. Louis; https://fred.stlouisfed.org/series/M11006USM315NNBR, April 30, 2022.

within just a few weeks. Thus began a cascading cycle of retrenchment, triggered not by the natural ebb and flow of supply and demand, but largely by the seizing-up of capital and credit when and where it was needed most.

Commodity prices fell 21 percent, eliminating virtually the entire increase from 1904 to 1907.[16] Industrial production dropped more than in any other U.S. panic up to 1907.[17] The dollar volume of bankruptcies declared in November spiked up by 47 percent over a year earlier—the Panic would be associated with the second-worst volume of bankruptcies up to 1907.[18] Gross earnings by railroads fell by 6 percent in December,[19] production fell 11 percent from May 1907 to June 1908, wholesale prices fell 5 percent, and imports shrank 26 percent.[20] Unemployment rose from 2.8 percent to 8 percent,[21] a dramatic increase in a short period of time. Immigration, which had reached 1.2 million people in 1907, dropped to around 750,000 by 1909; it would not reach 1 million again until 1910.

The *Commercial and Financial Chronicle* wrote, "It is probably no exaggeration to say that the industrial paralysis and the prostration was the very worst ever experienced in the country's history."[22] In characteristic understatement, Jack Morgan wrote to his partners in London, "I do not think that 1907 was a good year anywhere, from what I can make out."[23]

Hysteresis

Economic data reveal that the Panic of 1907 was associated with a subsequent malaise, a lower rate of economic performance. Economists call this "hysteresis," which means the persistence of slower growth well after the event that precipitated the slowdown. Figure 19.2 shows the actual path of real GDP per capita. And superimposed on the actual path are two hypothetical trends. One trend assumes that GDP per capita after 1906 grew at the average annual rate it achieved from 1896 to 1906 (3.9 percent); the other trend assumes the average annual growth rate from the end

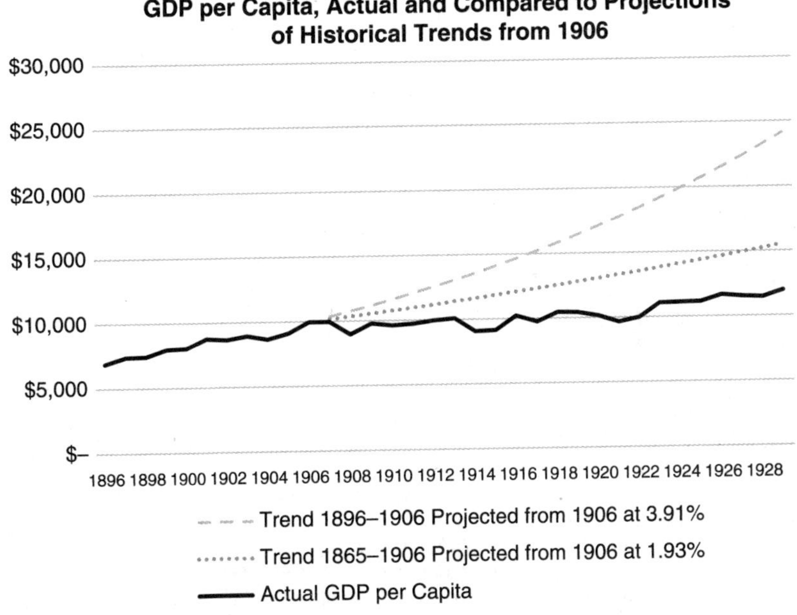

Figure 19.2 Growth in Gross Domestic Product per Capita Compared to Historical Trend Projections

SOURCE: Authors' figure, based on data in Maddison Project Database, version 2020. Jutta Bolt and Jan Luiten van Zanden, "Maddison style estimates of the evolution of the world economy. A new 2020 update"(2020), https://www.rug.nl/ggdc/historicaldevelopment/maddison/releases/maddison-project-database-2020?lang=en.

of the Civil War (1865) to 1896 (1.9 percent). In neither case does the actual GDP per capita return to the long-run trend by 1929, the onset of the Great Depression—it remains an arresting downshift, despite the fiscal stimulus of federal government spending during World War I and the consumption boom of the "Roaring '20s." The economic effects of the Panic of 1907 and its recession proved to be a major setback for the nation.

One possible cause of the setback was economic "scarring." Modern researchers have found that economic downturns can lead to long-lasting damage to workers' productivity, education, and mobility.[24]

A related cause could be the chilling effect of the crisis on innovation and entrepreneurship. We examined the time trends of three measures: (1) total factor productivity, (2) patents granted, and (3) the change in the number of concerns in business. From these measures we created an index about entrepreneurship and innovation, depicted in Figure 19.3. The figure shows a level trend from 1901 to 1907, after which the trend declines in 1908, recovers, declines again in 1910, and comes to rest at a somewhat lower level thereafter.

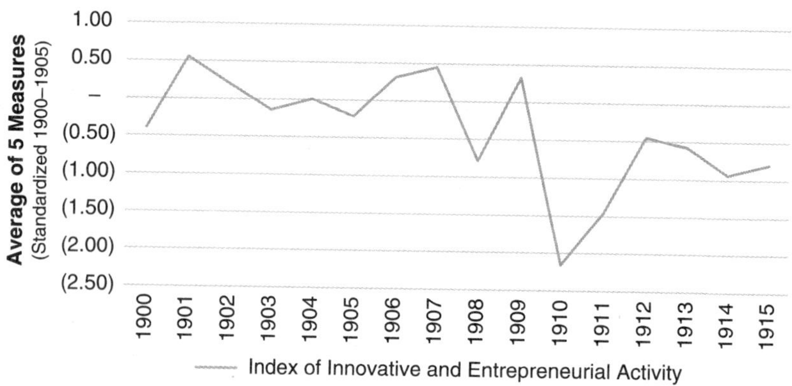

Figure 19.3 Trend of Innovative and Entrepreneurial Activity
NOTE: This figure plots an average of three measures: (1) total factor productivity, (2) patents granted, and (3) the change in the number of concerns in business. Measures 2 and 3 were converted to a per-capita quantity. All three measures were converted to standard quantities (relative to performance over the years 1900–1905) and then averaged to produce the time series in the figure.
SOURCE: Authors' figure, based on data from *Historical Statistics of the United States, Colonial Times to 1970* (U.S. Bureau of the Census, 1975), pp. 948, 957, 958, and 959. U.S. population from Maddison Project Database, version 2020. Jutta Bolt and Jan Luiten van Zanden, "Maddison style estimates of the evolution of the world economy. A new 2020 update" (2020), https://www.rug.nl/ggdc/historicaldevelopment/maddison/releases/maddison-project-database-2020.

This evidence of hysteresis in Figures 19.2 and 19.3 suggests the pivotal economic impact of the Panic of 1907. This impact was not merely local, but national and global. Nor was it merely temporary; it spanned many years.

Examples of Two Industrial Firms

Why a financial crisis can scar economic performance is illustrated by a comparison of two well-known, quasi-monopolistic enterprises of the time: the General Electric Company and the Westinghouse Electric & Manufacturing Company. At the height of the crisis in late October, Westinghouse was swiftly placed into the hands of receivers, following its failure to secure the renewal of $4 million in short-term notes from its lenders. This sudden cash stringency resulted in the company's inability to pay 11,000 members of its Pittsburgh workforce, which was then immediately followed by a massive decline in its stock price by nearly 56 percent. The spillover from the Westinghouse receivership was the closure of the Pittsburgh Stock Exchange the very same day, staying dark for nearly a week.

On the other hand, as described in an analysis by contemporary scholar Niles Carpenter Jr., General Electric fared far better during and after the most critical period of the panic in late fall 1907.[25] Despite "fundamental similarities underlying the financial operations" of the two companies, including close ties with powerful members of the nation's financial elite, such as J. P. Morgan himself, GE emerged nearly unscathed from the surrounding financial catastrophe.

According to Carpenter, GE's resilience was largely a function of its more prudent financial policies. Whereas Westinghouse relied heavily on commercial paper and short-term notes to fund operations, GE maintained "a larger margin of safety" by consistently keeping a greater proportion of working capital in reserve. GE supported this strategy by offering a lower dividend rate (than Westinghouse), implementing heavier depreciation charges, and maintaining a preference for stock issuance versus bonds to support business expansion. In fact, during the crisis itself, GE remained "effectively inactive" in the capital markets. When it did look for new financing, it only did so through convertible bonds in the later stage of the Panic as an emergency measure of relief.

Though Westinghouse survived the Panic, it remained in the hands of receivers until April 1908, whereas the crisis had "no appreciable effect" on the General Electric Company.

While GE's "cautious conservativism" had served the company far better than Westinghouse's debt-fueled fiscal policies, both companies had entered 1907 on roughly equal terms, following a period of unprecedented growth in the electrical equipment industry. In fact, by the early part of 1907, both firms had seen the largest volume of business in their respective histories. And even after the trouble commenced in March 1907, the overall economic momentum continued to sustain the electrical business. So, when the Panic erupted in October, the negative effects were not a function of any fundamental business instability or weakness in the economy. To the contrary, business growth was strong, tempered only by the sudden decline in stock prices and an inability (at least for Westinghouse) to secure financing to meet immediate needs.

Such dynamics as experienced by Westinghouse and General Electric were playing out elsewhere in the U.S. economy. As Carpenter notes, "For a large part of this time, the two corporations under consideration did not vary much from any of the dozens of other large industrials attempting to ride out the storm." Even during the late, critical days of October, executives at the nation's largest industrial companies remained confident about their firms' prospects and were generally optimistic about economic conditions, while acknowledging that a contraction was likely. "Representatives of the leading industrial companies declare that the recent financial disturbances have not affected general business to the extent one would suppose," the *Wall Street Journal* reported on October 29, "and now that the worst is over, there should be a rapid restoration in confidence."[26] As evidence, the newspaper cited the soundness of the United States Steel Corporation and the Standard Oil Company, both of which held substantial reserves of cash on hand during the crisis and could be expected to weather a period of monetary stringency.

International Impact

Responding to the gold imports by the United States, central banks in Britain, France, and Germany raised their base interest rates to attract gold back to their countries. The Bank of England raised Bank Rate to 7 percent, the highest since 1865.[27]

More broadly, 1907 was a year of global financial instability. The U.S. crisis coincided with financial crises in Egypt (January to May 1907), Japan (July and beyond), Hamburg (October), Chile (October), Amsterdam (September–November), Genoa (September), and Copenhagen (winter 1908).[28] One conduit for contagion was international ownership of American securities—when prices on the NYSE plummeted, global institutional investors took losses. In Hamburg the firm of Haller Sohler & Co. failed because of its sizeable holdings in United Copper and Amalgamated Copper, while some 15 firms in Amsterdam failed in November owing to the decline in U.S. equities.[29] Contemporary Wall Street observer Alexander Dana Noyes wrote,

> *The case simply was that the crisis affected the world at large, part of the world passing through the acute stage before our own markets did. . . . The strain on the financial world was so severe a character that it was bound to result in a break in the chain of credit, wherever the link was weakest or wherever the strain was greatest. The link was weakest, no doubt, in markets such as Egypt and Chile; the strain was incalculably greatest in New York, where credit had been so grossly abused, and where inflation of prices had prevailed on such as scale of magnitude as to render the situation, despite the country's immense resources, more vulnerable than that of any other in the long chain of connecting markets.*[30]

A case in point was the impact of the crash and Panic of 1907 on Mexico, a country heavily dependent on mineral and agricultural prices, and on flows of investment capital from the United States. Historian Kevin Cahill noted:

> *In 1906 over $57 million of foreign investment poured directly into Mexican banks, but when this influx ceased at the end of 1907, money became scarce. . . . The loss of foreign investment caused the total assets of Mexican banks to plummet from $360 million in 1907 to $305 million in 1908. . . . New bank loans also declined. . . . A large majority of borrowers were unable to repay their loans. Two consecutive years of drought curtailed agricultural production, making it impossible for the commercial farmers to repay their debts. Moreover, individuals throughout the republic had borrowed money to buy stocks on margin. The collapse of the economy caused stock prices to decline, and many of these investors faced bankruptcy. The inability of the banks to collect their debts produced profound difficulties for banks at all levels.*[31]

Cahill suggested that the financial strains in Mexico had political consequences and that the panic and subsequent depression were among the catalysts for the Mexican Revolution. "[Scholars] contend that because Mexico depended heavily on foreign markets and capital, particularly that of the United States," Cahill wrote, "the U.S. depression crippled the Mexican Economy. Generating widespread dissatisfaction with President Porfirio Díaz's government, it thus was one of the factors that provoked the Maderistas and other revolutionaries to rebellion in 1910."[32]

The experience of Mexico from 1907 illustrates the fragility of developing economies in the face of financial crises. Dependent on foreign direct investment, borrowing in foreign currencies (called "original sin"[33]), reliant on commodity exports whose prices oscillate wildly in a crisis, and governed by a regime for whom a poor populace has waning patience comprised an explosive mixture.

Social Impact of the Crisis

The Panic of 1907 lingered in other ways, less easily captured in financial and economic data. Comments in letters, telegrams, and the news media suggested immense social stress. To gauge the association of the Panic with subsequent social stress, we constructed an index based on five factors: (1) number of homicides, (2) number of suicides, (3) numbers of African Americans lynched, (4) failure rate of businesses, and (5) deaths from cardiac disease, depicted in Figure 19.4.

The index of social stress rose materially in 1907 and peaked sharply in 1908, following the Panic year—in statistical terms, the jump cannot be attributed to random variation or "noise." By the third year after the Panic, it still had not subsided to pre-panic levels.

Political Impact

Financial crises tend to be hard on elected officials. No federal government election occurred in 1907. But 1908 was a significant year:

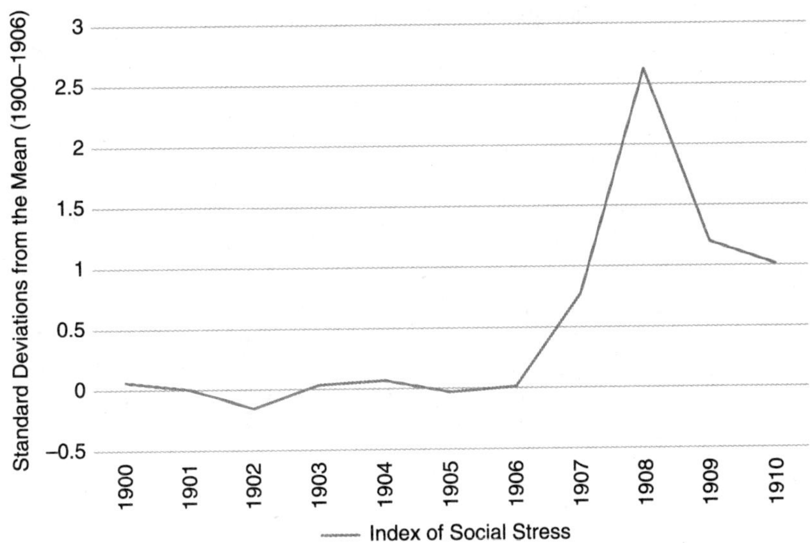

Figure 19.4 Trend in Index of Social Stress
NOTE: This figure plots an average of five measures: (1) number of homicides, (2) number of suicides, (3) numbers of African Americans lynched, (4) failure rate of businesses, and (5) deaths from cardiac disease. All five measures were converted to standard quantities relative to performance over the years 1900–1906, and then averaged to produce the time series in the figure.
SOURCE: Authors' figure(s), based on data from *Historical Statistics of the United States, Colonial Times to 1970* (U.S. Bureau of the Census, 1975), pp. 414, 422, 908, and 912.

President Roosevelt (who had declared that he would not run in 1908) engineered the Republican Party nomination of William Howard Taft for president. Taft was elected by a 52 percent popular majority. And the Party continued to hold majorities in the two houses of Congress. However, the election results began a weakening trend, as depicted in Figure 19.5.

At the next federal mid-term election in 1910, the Republican Party lost control of the House of Representatives. And in the disastrous election of 1912, the Republicans also lost the Senate and the White House. Thus, in the five years following the Panic of 1907, a massive realignment took place. Beginning in 1913, progressives stood at the levers of power.

The economic, social, and political ripple effects of the Panic of 1907 went deep into the nation, spread globally, and lasted well after the

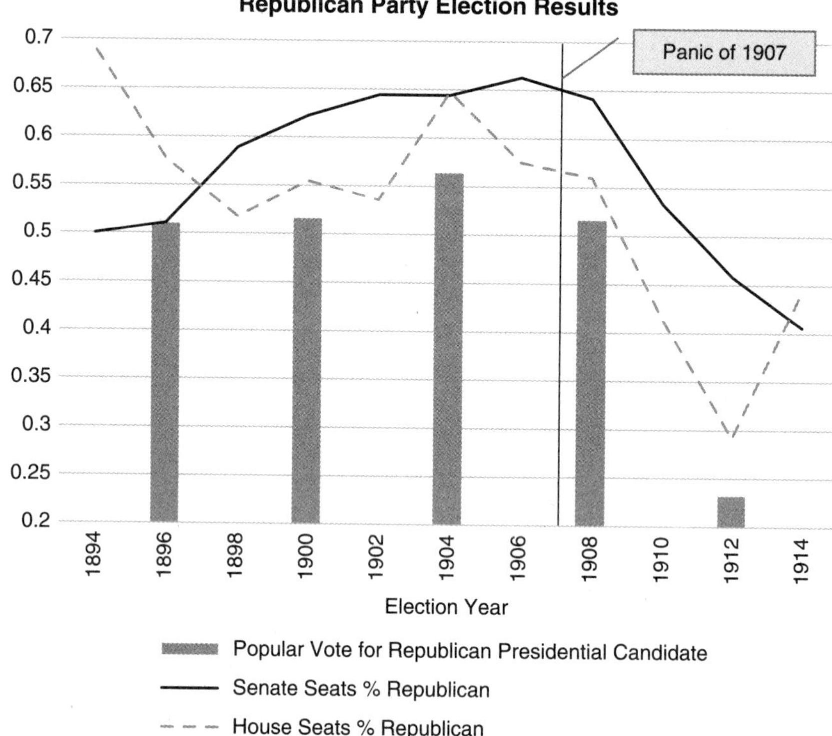

Figure 19.5 Republican Party Election Results, 1894–1914
SOURCE: Authors' figure, based on data from the following sources: American Presidency Project (Santa Barbara: University of California–Santa Barbara), downloaded May 12, 2022 from https://www.presidency.ucsb.edu/statistics/elections. Also, "Party Divisions of the House of Representatives, 1789 to Present," History, Art & Archives (United States House of Representatives), downloaded May 12, 2022 from https://history.house.gov/Institution/Party-Divisions/Party-Divisions/. And finally, "Party Division of the United States Senate" (Washington, DC: United States Senate), downloaded May 12, 2022 from https://www.senate.gov/history/partydiv.htm.

events of October–November 1907. This contrasted with conventional notions that the Panic was essentially a New York City phenomenon and restricted to a few financial institutions—indeed, the crisis may have started there, but then it radiated widely.

Chapter 20

Reckoning and a Split

But the progressive movement does not consist of a few self-constituted leaders. It consists of millions of thoughtful citizens drawn together by a common belief in certain principles. They will permit no combination of special interests and political expediency to secure control of the progressive cause, which is ultimately to redeem democracy and restore government to the people.

—Senator Robert La Follette, June 28, 1912[1]

As the economic ripples spread across the country, the mood of the public and its elected representatives dimmed. By December 1907, congratulations for crisis fighters dissolved into demands for investigations. Democratic senators wanted to scrutinize the pattern of the Treasury Department's deposits of gold in national banks and the government bond issues in November—they hinted darkly at favoritism in the distribution of government largesse. On December 12, the Senate adopted a resolution to investigate and called on Cortelyou to report. He responded in January 1908 with a 232-page document. In February, Congress resolved to investigate further, though that effort led nowhere. Yet in March, Senator La Follette charged that banks and insurance companies allied with J. P. Morgan and John D. Rockefeller had created the Panic of 1907 to serve their own interests.[2] La Follette's allegation resonated for years.

The turn of congressional dialogue played out against a larger canvas. President Roosevelt had announced that he would retire from the White House at the end of his term in March 1909—this made him a "lame duck" leader for the year following the Panic, hampered by declining influence and effectiveness. Democrats sensed political advantage in tarring the Republicans with the Panic of 1907. The jockeying among hopeful presidential successors to Roosevelt offered the Democrats an opportunity to drive a wedge through the Republican coalition of progressives and old-line conservatives. Among the hopeful successors was George Cortelyou, who had allowed an underling to tout him as presidential or vice-presidential timber. Thus, Cortelyou became a lightning rod for partisan and intraparty criticism. In every hearing from 1907 to 1913, Cortelyou remained a star witness.

However, more than political bickering, the congressional debates of early 1908 necessarily reflected the shocking impact of the Panic. What was to be done about it? What was the role of government in preventing or quelling financial crises? Anyway, what was the problem? Was it the insufficiency of currency in a time of crisis, or the instability of the financial system? More fundamentally, was the Panic of 1907 a child of Gilded Age capitalism's elites and tendency toward monopoly?

Stopgap Banking Measures

New laws to guarantee bank deposits quickly sprouted in eight states, mainly in the West and South. Populists resurrected their earlier calls for the nationalization of banks, which would ultimately put the U.S. government behind a guarantee of bank deposits. Meanwhile, William Jennings Bryan—again, a presidential hopeful—darkly called U.S. Steel's acquisition of Tennessee Coal & Iron "another link in the chain of monopoly."[3]

To forestall radical reforms, Republican conservatives Senator Nelson W. Aldrich and Representative Edward B. Vreeland led the enactment of an amendment to the national banking laws that Roosevelt signed on May 30, 1908. The Aldrich–Vreeland Act created an emergency currency scheme to permit national banks to form associations to issue emergency currency, backed by government and mortgage bonds.

The Act also established a National Monetary Commission to study the adequacy of the financial system in the United States. Political wrangling ensued.[4] The co-chairs of the commission were Aldrich and Vreeland, who were identified with the Eastern financial community. Democrats and progressive Republicans scoffed at the co-chairs and predicted that the Commission would design a system to the advantage of Wall Street. The National Monetary Commission did not report back until January 1911, by which time the political landscape had changed significantly. Nonetheless, the Commission fed the progressives' zeal for technocratic analysis and gave Nelson Aldrich time to survey the many competing interests around central banking.

A Heightened Focus on Monopolies

The aftermath of the Panic of 1907 also featured a major sea change in public policy toward tougher enforcement of antitrust laws. Theodore Roosevelt's activism in antitrust enforcement had reversed more than a decade of federal government lassitude in the face of monopolies growing on the business landscape.* However, he sought not so much to end monopolies, as to regulate them.

Roosevelt distinguished between "good" monopolies that exploited economies of scale to bring products at better quality and lower price to consumers from "bad" monopolies that simply enriched their owners at the expense of the public. He thought that the public's apprehension of trusts was "largely irrational."[5] In his 1902 State of the Union Address, Roosevelt declared that "we are not attacking the corporations but endeavoring to do away with any evil in them. We are not hostile to them; we are merely determined that they shall be so handled as to subserve the

* Prominent examples of Roosevelt's activism were his breakup of a monopoly of railroads in the Pacific Northwest (the Northern Securities case, decided in 1904), tightening the regulation of railroads' ability to set rates through the Elkins Anti-Rebate Act of 1903 and the Hepburn Act of 1906, and suits against Standard Oil (1906) and American Tobacco (1907) for violations of the Sherman Act.

public good."[6] Accordingly, he decided not to dismember U.S. Steel, which had been formed through merger six months before McKinley was assassinated. Roosevelt viewed U.S. Steel and International Harvester (another J. P. Morgan creation) as benign trusts, receptive to focused interventions by regulators. To him, antitrust enforcement through lawsuits was a blunt weapon: slow-moving, costly to the government, and uncertain in outcome.

In contrast, Roosevelt's successor, William Howard Taft, who assumed the presidency in 1909, took the view that violations of the Sherman Act should be prosecuted, not regulated. A federal judge before joining the McKinley Administration in 1901, Taft had written the majority opinion in *Addyston Pipe & Steel Co. v. United States* (1899), a pillar in the antitrust legal literature.* The opinion held that horizontal price-fixing was *per se* illegal, a view that was later adopted by the Supreme Court as the orthodox interpretation of the Sherman Act. Taft brought into his administration George W. Wickersham, an attorney general of similar attitude, who subsequently earned the soubriquet "the scourge of Wall Street."[7] The team of Taft and Wickersham would emerge as the most active administration in antitrust history. More antitrust cases would be filed in Taft's four-year term than in Roosevelt's seven years in the White House. In comparison to Roosevelt, Taft was an inflexible enforcer of the law, less prone to pragmatic resolution.

As the Taft administration got to work, Congress renewed a focus on monopolies in general and the acquisition of Tennessee Coal and Iron (TC&I) by United States Steel (USS) in particular. In January 1909, the Senate requested documents from the Bureau of Corporations regarding the deal. And in May, the House of Representatives asked the Department of Justice to inform it of any steps to annul the deal. In June 1910, the House asked the Department of Justice to opine on whether U.S. Steel had violated the Sherman Act. Then in a precedent-setting decision in May 1911, the Supreme Court found that the Standard Oil and American Tobacco Companies violated the Sherman Act and ordered their dissolution—this juiced the antitrust sentiments of Congress.

* Robert Bork called it "one of the greatest, if not the greatest antitrust opinions in the history of the law." [Robert Bork, *The Antitrust Paradox: A Policy at War with Itself*, 1978, p. 26.]

TC&I Reexamined

When the Democratic Party gained control of the House of Representatives in the federal elections of 1910, the movement to investigate U.S. Steel and its acquisition of Tennessee Coal & Iron gained traction. That May, the House empaneled a special committee chaired by Kentucky progressive Augustus O. Stanley that would hold hearings from June 1911 to April 1912 and publish its eight-volume report in August, just before the federal elections that year.

Representative Stanley was born in 1867, taught school, worked as a school principal, and began to practice law in 1894. Engaged in Democratic Party politics since 1900, he was elected to Congress in 1903 from a district in Kentucky's tobacco country. He championed the interests of farmers and small businesspeople. Stanley was a flamboyant orator, a "demagogue,"[8] whose leadership promised media attention for the hearings.

The mission of the Stanley Committee was to investigate two allegations: first, that the acquisition violated the Sherman Antitrust Act by virtue of a conspiracy in restraint of trade, and second, that the merger created a monopoly in steel production. Because the committee could not reach a consensus on findings, the Democratic majority on the committee issued a report separately from the Republican minority. The Majority Report concluded that U.S. Steel had: (1) absorbed a competitor that had challenged its share of market, (2) bolstered a monopoly position in its industry, and (3) had used the Panic to acquire a valuable asset at a discounted price.

The hearings alleged a host of errors of omission or commission by Frick and Gary in their presentation to Roosevelt on November 4, 1907.[9] For instance, testimony revealed that Moore & Schley did not actually own a controlling interest in TC&I—some individuals affiliated with the brokerage firm did. The firm was, as it turned out, not in grave difficulty and needed a loan of only $5–6 million to calm creditors—other securities on hand could have been pledged to gain such a loan. The firm of Moore & Schley was not insolvent; it was merely illiquid.

In their presentation to Roosevelt, Frick and Gary also did not disclose that TC&I was not distressed and that it held vast undeveloped reserves of coal and iron (second only to U.S. Steel) and that its recent capital investments might allow TC&I to underprice U.S. Steel. Also, it appeared that U.S. Steel had a strategic interest in acquiring TC&I, both to eliminate a price competitor and to enter the South, where U.S. Steel had no production capacity. The Stanley Committee's revelations about U.S. Steel's acquisition of TC&I mainly suggested that it was motivated by monopoly power rather than public-spirited rescue of an endangered financial firm.

However, data embedded in the Majority Report challenged its own conclusions. First, TC&I was a small fish in the sea and was unlikely to steal much business from USS. Second, TC&I and USS were players in different regions of the country: U.S. Steel in the North and Northeast, TC&I in the South. Although TC&I enjoyed a cost advantage from its use of more advanced open-hearth furnaces, the advantage would largely vanish when the cost of transporting goods to the North was considered.[10]

Third, the Majority Report did not try to prove the existence of a monopoly position. And if it had, would have confronted the questions of the size of the relevant market and what share of market would be deemed to constitute a monopoly. Gary and Frick wanted to go no higher than a 60 percent share, implying that it was a threshold into monopoly. In 1906, William Jennings Bryan had suggested a monopoly threshold of 50 percent. Furthermore, the Stanley Committee relied on figures provided by U.S. Steel and TC&I, rather than independently producing their own figures. Figure 20.1 compares the output of U.S. Steel and TC&I as percentages of the entire industry and shows that across five major product segments TC&I would not have been a significant threat to U.S. Steel nor would its absorption materially change the market shares of U.S. Steel.

To sustain its finding that U.S. Steel had exploited the Panic to acquire a valuable asset at an advantageous price, the Stanley Committee provided no original independent evidence. A year after the acquisition, the railroad bond analyst John Moody had opined that TC&I was worth much more than its acquisition price, owing to the firm's vast reserves of coal and iron ore that had yet to be developed. Moody estimated these reserves to be worth $1 billion and concluded, "the acquisition of this property for $45,000,000, added an almost unheard-of value to the equity back of the steel corporation stocks."[11] This implies that TC&I

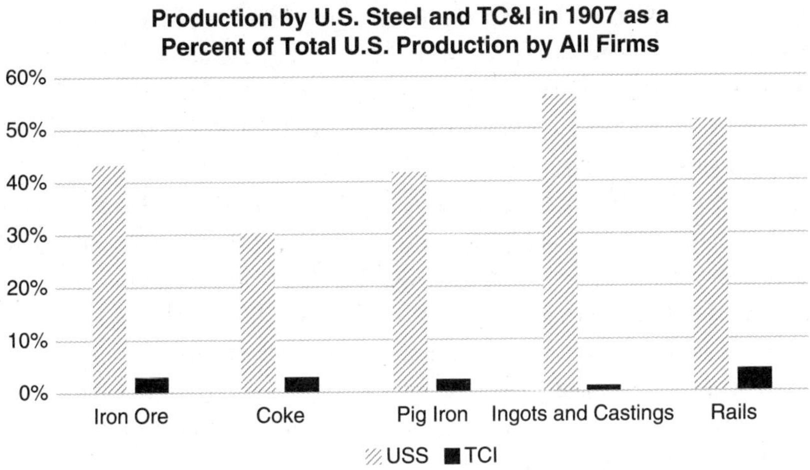

Production by U.S. Steel and TC&I in 1907 as a Percent of Total U.S. Production by All Firms

60%
50%
40%
30%
20%
10%
0%
Iron Ore
Coke
Pig Iron
Ingots and Castings
Rails
USS TCI

Figure 20.1 Shares of Market by U.S. Steel and TC&I by Output Across Five Major Product Segments
SOURCE: Authors' figure, based on estimates given in McLaughlin (1971), p. 82. McLaughlin's data derive from U.S. Department of Commerce, *Report of the Commissioner of Corporation on the Steel Industry*, July 1, 1911, Part III, Table 29, p. 238.

shares were worth much more than investors in the stock market thought. Moody also testified that the value of the TC&I ore deposits was "well known."[12]

That neither Gary nor Frick had disclosed to Roosevelt the potential value of the reserves augmented the Stanley Committee's argument of a conspiracy in restraint of trade. However, drawing on U.S. Geological Survey data, McLaughlin (1971) shows that the iron ore reserves obtained in the acquisition added only 9 percent to the already sizable reserves of USS, and that they increased its control of total U.S. iron ore reserves from 32 percent to 34 percent. McLaughlin concluded that the acquisition "did nothing to enhance the Corporation's monopoly position."[13]

Of more interest to an understanding about the Panic of 1907 are the Stanley Committee Majority Report's revelations about the origins of the U.S. Steel/TC&I deal. The committee sought to prove that the sellers were coerced and that the resistance of Gary and Frick was a sham. The accumulated testimony suggested the opposite.

TC&I was acquired in 1905 by a syndicate of investors led by John "Bet-a-Million" Gates. He had been the president of American Steel and Wire, a monopoly in the production of barbed wire that was protected by various patents. As his nickname suggested, he had the reputation as a Gilded Age buccaneer, who gambled prodigiously, sold short the shares in his own company, and exploited corporate resources for his personal use.

When J. P. Morgan organized U.S. Steel in 1901, Gates eventually decided to join. But upon consummation of the merger, Gates found that his services were no longer required. Bitter and vengeful, he eventually resolved to build a competitor to U.S. Steel through acquisition. His strategy was to cobble together marginal steel producers and railroads, with each new acquisition pledged as collateral for loans to finance more acquisitions. This was a strategy that depended on rising asset prices. TC&I was the keystone in this plan. Gates helped to organize an investor syndicate that bought the controlling interest in TC&I and manipulated its share prices to a high level to maximize its collateral value for loans. If stock prices remained buoyant, Gates's buy-borrow-buy strategy would work. But the market slump in 1907, along with banks' reduction in call loans, ruined the plan.

Grant Schley, managing partner of Moore & Schley, felt the credit crunch as his lenders called for more collateral than afforded by the value of TC&I shares. Starting in the spring of 1907, a member of the syndicate told J.P. Morgan that the syndicate was willing to sell out—but Gary and Frick declined. By the fall, the distress of the syndicate members had turned desperate. The syndicate sent a lawyer, Lewis Cass Ledyard, to Gary with another proposal to sell. Gary again demurred—instead, he offered a loan to Schley of $1.2 million on October 23, against collateral of $2 million in TC&I stock. On November 1, Ledyard approached Morgan with news that the stability of Moore & Schley was threatened. Schley later testified that "Moore & Schley never owned any stock of the Tennessee Coal & Iron Co."[14] Yet the financial distress of the syndicate members—and especially Grant Schley—had spilled over to Moore & Schley. Schley said:

> *We were oppressed by rumors, some of them untrue, but Moore & Schley were the subject of attack, serious attack, and their credit, which is the life of the business was being destroyed. It was a matter of serious import. . . . The rumors were flying*

tremendously about, and nobody can escape those, you know. They may be true or untrue, and they affect the credit of this institution or that.[15]

To compound the emergency, rumors about Schley and TC&I threatened the stability of Trust Company of America (TCA). It appeared that TCA had made call loans of about $480,000 collateralized by TC&I shares[16]—a small amount relative to TCA's assets of almost $50 million. Yet the rumors about TC&I and Moore & Schley threatened to refuel the runs on TCA. Thus commenced the intense meetings of early November, recounted in Chapter 17.

In short, TC&I was an instance of a leveraged industry roll-up strategy, whose syndicate investors nearly failed during a financial maelstrom. Schley had to find a buyer for TC&I or declare bankruptcy.[17] In contrast to assertions of the Stanley Committee, Gates and Schley were not coerced to sell by Gary and Frick.

However, the Majority Report of the Stanley Committee raised other troubling insights. First, "[n]either the solvency of the Trust Co. of America nor of any other bank in New York was in any way affected by the presence of Tennessee Coal & Iron stock. . . . the Trust Co. of America . . . [was] in no danger or trouble whatever."[18] But this contradicted Schley's own testimony that rumors fed a reluctance to extend credit to Moore & Schley—a silent run of a different sort. Second, contrary to what President Roosevelt said, TC&I was not purchased at a loss to USS.[19] Key to this were assertions about the value of TC&I ore reserves. The absence of scrutiny into the value of the reserves was a shortcoming in the Stanley Committee's Majority Report. The fact that call loan creditors had deeply discounted the collateral value of TC&I shares to 50 percent of market price[20] suggests that claims of hidden value may have been optimistic. Third, the report asserted that the "panic was over prior to the interview" between TR, Gary, and Frick.[21] Yet as demonstrated elsewhere in this narrative, by November 4 the Panic had not been quelled. Nevertheless, the committee concluded:

If the merger was in violation of the law it is equally clear that the President had no right to condone or encourage its violation, or to prevent the Attorney General from performing his duty, even though the prosperity of a dozen bankers in New York

> *had depended upon it, much less the fate of a single stock broker, whose reckless transactions had involved him in financial disaster.*[22]

The Stanley Committee report raises a final reflection: Did J. P. Morgan truthfully communicate the emergency to the trust company presidents in the early morning of November 3? Morgan asserted that the instability of another firm threatened to refuel the panic, and that he would be unable to stump up another rescue fund for the trust companies because his resources were demanded for the other urgent rescue. Yet the facts as summarized here yield a different situation. First, Morgan knew by then that the deal in development would require the resources of U.S. Steel, not J.P. Morgan & Co. Second, owing to his connections, he probably knew that the *individual,* Grant B. Schley, was in financial distress, not the firm—however, he also could appreciate that continuation of the silent run by creditors (presaging similar runs a century later) would eventually kill the firm. Third, as organizer, investor, and director in U.S. Steel, he probably had intimate knowledge of the industry and TC&I's financial condition. It seems likely that he saw a healthy bargain rather than a messy cleanup. Perhaps future archival research will clarify the extent to which Morgan was bluffing with the trust company presidents on November 3. Either way, his communication to them succeeded in compelling their collective action.

Attention Turns to Roosevelt

A highlight of the Stanley Committee's investigation was Theodore Roosevelt's testimony on August 5, 1911. He was adamant in asserting the correctness of his action, his belief that approving the USS/TC&I deal would help to quell the Panic, and his certainty that he had the facts necessary to justify the approval. Yet in the several thousand pages of testimony and financial data the Stanley Committee argues the opposite. The deal had uncertain impact on rescuing Moore & Schley and the Trust Company of America or on sustaining Tennessee Coal & Iron. Frick and Gary failed to tell TR several material facts. And alternative courses of action could have achieved the same outcome on the Panic.

Before the conclusion of the Stanley Committee hearings, Taft's Justice Department sued U.S. Steel on October 26 for violation of the Sherman Antitrust Act when it acquired Tennessee Coal & Iron. The petition contained information that appeared to question Roosevelt's diligence and judgment. Consistent with evidence that surfaced in the Stanley hearings, the suit alleged that Gary and Frick had not disclosed several important pieces of information that would have invalidated both the urgency and rationale for permitting the deal. In this move, Taft appeared to rebuke Roosevelt for his earlier approval.

In response to the news, Democratic-leaning publications convulsed with opprobrium and mockery: "Mr. Roosevelt Fooled" ran a headline in the *Fergus County Democrat* of Lewistown, Montana.[23] The *Urbana Courier-Herald* declared that Roosevelt was an "unwitting tool" of financiers and U.S. Steel executives.[24]

Roosevelt went ballistic. Unable to admit an error, he dug himself in more deeply despite contrary factual evidence and testimony during the Stanley investigation:

> *I was not misled. The representatives of the Steel Corporation told me the truth as to what the effect of the action at that time would be, and any statement that I was misled or that the representatives of the Steel Corporation did not thus tell me the truth as to the facts of the case is itself not in accordance with the truth . . . I reaffirm everything . . . not only as to what occurred, but also as to my belief in the wisdom and propriety of my action—indeed, the action not merely was wise and proper, but it would have been a calamity from every standpoint had I failed to take it.*[25]

Bitterly, TR also denounced his former protégé:

> *Taft was a member of my cabinet when I took that action. We went over it in full and in detail, not only at once but at two or three meetings. He was enthusiastic in his praise of what was done. It ill becomes him either by himself or through another afterwards to act as he is now acting. I am sorry to say that . . . both he and Wickersham are playing small, mean and foolish politics in the matter.*[26]

In an article in the Republican-leaning magazine *The Outlook*, Roosevelt argued that it was not necessary for him "to search the hidden domain of motive.. . . My concern was that the action should be taken and the situation saved in the interests of the people of the United States." Roosevelt's narrative placed him at the crux of the effort to stop the panic. "I dealt with facts as they were, not with facts as they might or might not afterwards become."[27]

Roosevelt Breaks with Taft

The antitrust lawsuit against U.S. Steel was the turning point for Roosevelt, who thereafter opposed Taft for the Republican renomination for president in the 1912 election. Failing to win the party's nod, Roosevelt broke with the Republicans to form a third party. This split the Republican coalition of conservatives and progressives and helped to deliver the White House to the Democratic Party. The irony is that all three presidential candidates in November 1912 regarded themselves as progressives. The intensity of that campaign reflected a bitter contest to define the true faith of progressivism.

Unfortunately, the politically timed revelations about the TC&I acquisition damaged Roosevelt's reputation. Yet he refused to relent. A year later, Roosevelt published his *Autobiography,* garnished with the same defenses about the TC&I acquisition that he had offered earlier—and this time, wrapped in a higher calling:

> *I would have been derelict in my duty, I would have shown myself a timid and unworthy public servant, if in that extraordinary crisis I had not acted precisely as I did act. In every such crisis the temptation to indecision, to nonaction, is great, for excuses can always be found for non-action, and action means risk and the certainty of blame to the man who acts. But if the man is worth his salt he will do his duty, he will give the people the benefits of the doubt, and act in any way which their interests demand and which is not affirmatively prohibited by law, unheeding the likelihood that he himself, when the crisis is over and the danger past, will be assailed for what he had done.*[28]

Chapter 21

Money Trust

In 1873, . . . [t]he Money Trust began forming soon after the [Civil War] to control the volume and issue of money, the same as Industrial Trusts have since sought to control the products in which they deal. . . . This organization is the principal ally of the political party that champions the interests of the privileged classes. . . . What is the outcome if class legislation and Trusts continue unchecked? . . . The Financial Trust will own all the other Trusts.

—William H. "Coin" Harvey, 1899[1]

Conspiracy theories of a moneyed elite taking over American society had sprouted episodically since the founding of the Republic. In the 1890s, the populist reaction to growing industrial concentration and financial crises spawned the notion of a "money trust." Books and articles by William Harvey (under the pen name "Coin") promoted the idea. But it circulated mainly among activists until the Panic of 1907, after which it entered the political mainstream.

On March 17, 1908, Senator Robert La Follette resurrected the money trust idea to claim that the Aldrich–Vreeland Act was a sop to some 100 financial leaders, a "comparatively small clique, which has succeeded in dominating the finances of the country." Furthermore, La

Follette argued that this group plotted the Panic of 1907, "to satisfy business, legislative and political grudges, and to advance their own selfish interests." He said, "Morgan was especially wroth with Morse, while Standard Oil had long awaited opportunity to wipe off old scores with Heinze." He named groups of banks associated with Standard Oil and J.P. Morgan which controlled the "financial interests of the country" through their membership on boards of directors. Finally, La Follette claimed that the Panic rescues were "done with due regard to stage effect and only when the spotlight was turned upon the Morgan-Standard Oil combination." He denounced those who termed either Morgan or the Standard Oil group "philanthropists or unselfish financiers."[2]

A Tendency Toward Consolidation

Activities of J. P. Morgan and New York financiers after 1907 strengthened allegations about a money trust. In December 1909, Morgan acquired control of the Equitable Life Assurance Society, one of the major insurance companies—and his firm held seats on the board of another leading insurer, New York Life, while Mutual Life (the third large New York insurance company) was controlled by Rockefeller associates.[3] The *Washington Post* worried that the takeover marked "a complete reversal of the old order under which the insurance companies controlled the destinies of the banks and trust companies."[4]

J. P. Morgan Jr. joined the board of National City Bank. In late 1909, Pierpont also engineered the merger of three New York trust companies—Morton, Fifth Avenue, and Guaranty—to produce a firm with $200 million in assets.[5] The *Chicago Daily Tribune* decried the "almost absolute control of the country's financial affairs . . . centralized in the hands of a few men who are acting in concert."[6]

Morgan's purchase of the Equitable brought with it control of the National Bank of Commerce,[7] the firm that had declined to clear for the Knickerbocker on October 20, 1907. Bank of Commerce had been a material player in the New York financial community and historically had been related to Morgan. But since at least 1907 it had not been so close to Morgan or the Rockefeller interests. Fearing that the bank would create other episodes of instability in the financial system, Morgan began acquiring more of the bank's shares.[8] In March 1911, a syndicate of J.P. Morgan & Company, City National Bank, and First National Bank gained complete control of the board.[9]

In all, by March 1911, the *Washington Post* observed that "there are only two-thirds as many national banks and large state banks in downtown New York as there were 20 years ago."[10] In hindsight, the Morgan-led consolidation wave in New York seems remarkably tone-deaf to the mounting public fears of a money trust.

Money Trust Investigation

On July 8, 1911, Representative Charles A. Lindbergh Sr., a progressive Republican from Minnesota (and father of the future famous aviator), declared that a "money trust" existed. Biographer Scott Berg described "Sr." as a distant father, poor businessman, and a progressive driven by strong principles.[11] He was in his third term as a representative. Lindbergh called for a Congressional investigation "to determine if there exists a combination of financiers in the United States operating in restraint of trade or violation of other laws."[12] Then and in other speeches that year he argued that the Aldrich–Vreeland bill would lead to another panic and "that the methods of the Money Trust, more than any other thing, are directly and indirectly responsible for the cost of living being several times higher than it should be."[13] Lindbergh's charge harnessed public ire about industrial trusts and shifted the spotlight onto the financial sector of the economy.

This was a logical consequence of the Panic of 1907. The lurid revelations about U.S. Steel's takeover of TC&I, reports of investor pools to manipulate stock prices, the Heinze–Morse ring, and the commanding ability of J. P. Morgan to marshal rescue funds were catnip to conspiracy theorists. By December, the Democratic majority in the House chartered an investigation by a subcommittee of the House Committee on Banking and Currency to be led by Arsène Pujo, a representative from Louisiana. The next month, the subcommittee hired Samuel J. Untermyer, a politically ambitious lawyer from New York, to serve as chief counsel. The committee began hearings on June 7, 1912 and concluded on January 15, 1913.

Before the hearings began, Untermyer had declared his belief in the existence of a money trust;[14] so did the House resolution that chartered the investigation:

> *. . . it has been charged, and there is reason to believe, that the management of the finances of many of the great industrial and railroad corporations of the country . . . is rapidly concentrating in the hands of a few groups of financiers . . . and that these groups by reason of their control over the funds of such corporations and the power to dictate the depositories of such funds, and by reason of their relations with the great life insurance companies . . . have secured domination over many of the leading national banks and other moneyed institutions . . . thus enabling them and their associates to direct the operations of the latter in the use of the money belong to their depositors.. . .*[15]

The hearings aimed to prove a belief by gathering targeted evidence, rather than to gather diverse evidence and form a belief. Launched shortly before the federal elections in November 1912, the hearings served to propel progressives toward the Democratic Party. Modern historians judged the hearings to be "extremely partial . . . exaggerated"[16] and consistent with a "paranoid style" in American politics that suspected a vast conspiracy to destroy American life.[17]

Called to Testify

The 2,198 pages of the subcommittee's report are a monument to prosecutorial investigation. Altogether 90 people testified at the money trust hearings. A few others were invited but declined due to ill health* or absence from the country. Was this a representative sample of the "financial rulers" that Senator Robert La Follette had charged in 1908 controlled the business of the nation?

* One invited witness, William Rockefeller, claimed illness. Perhaps sensing a ruse, Untermyer doggedly demanded medical opinions from two different doctors, who attested to Rockefeller's grave condition (apparently temporary, for he would live 10 more years). Even then, Untermyer and Pujo traveled to Rockefeller's residence intending to take sworn testimony from his bedside. The resulting interview lasted a few minutes with Untermyer concluding that "I should be unwilling to go further with the examination at this time, from what I have just heard and observed as to Mr. Rockefeller's condition." [*Money Trust Investigation,* 1913, pp. 2141–2142.]

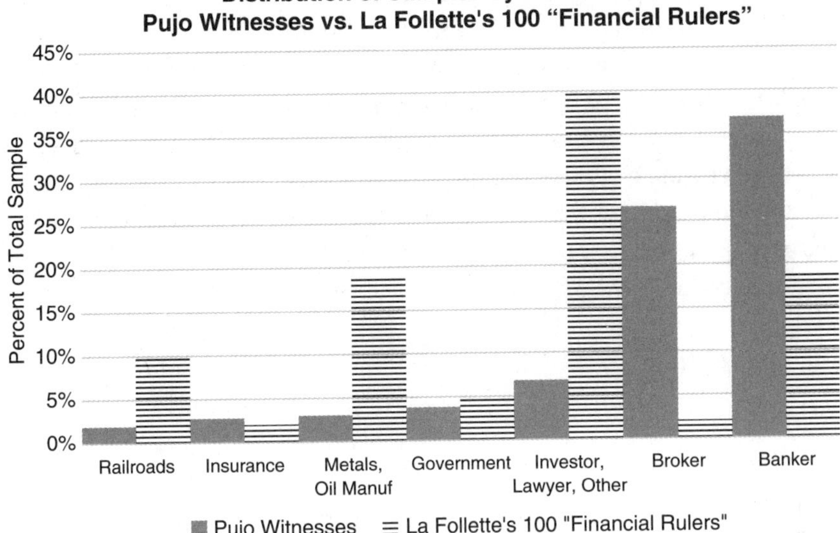

Figure 21.1 Percent of Total Hearings Accounted for by Witnesses from Various Fields

SOURCE: Authors' figure, prepared from data in "Financial Rulers Names by Senator La Follette," *Chicago Daily Tribune*, March 25, 1908, p. 4, and "Money Trust Investigation," U.S. Government Printing Office, 1913.

Analysis of the hearings shows that testimony from bankers and brokers accounted for almost two-thirds of the proceedings.* In comparison, La Follette's rogue's gallery was a more diverse lot, dominated by business executives and investors who inherited their wealth. Figure 21.1 compares the distribution of time under oath by witnesses in various fields to the distribution of La Follette's 100. The comparison suggests that the Pujo hearings were plowing different ground: more focus on the financial sector, less focus on the cross-section of business.

Only seven of the Money Trust witnesses had also appeared on La Follette's list of 100 "financial rulers." They were George F. Baker (First National Bank, who accounted for 11 percent of the total time under oath), James J. Hill (Great Northern Railroad and director in banks, 0.6

* We analyzed the distribution of Pujo witnesses based on the inches of text in the *Money Trust Investigation* that were devoted to dialogue between Untermyer and each of the witnesses. Percentages were calculated as the sum of inches for a witness, divided by the sum of inches across all witnesses. The distribution of the La Follette list of "financial rulers" reflects the number of each group as a percentage of the total sample.

percent), J. P. Morgan (6.7 percent), George W. Perkins (1.7 percent) Jacob Schiff (Kuhn, Loeb, 2.6 percent), Charles Steele (J. P. Morgan & Co., 0.2 percent), and Frank K. Sturgis (Strong, Sturgis & Co, NYSE, 3 percent)—these seven amounted to about a quarter of the accumulated testimony. The difference between the lists of La Follette and Pujo reveals a crucial point: the investigations were heavily focused on *finance,* not industry, and on Wall Street, not Main Street. Untermyer further sharpened the focus on Wall Street by inviting testimony from a few locales outside New York (such as Salt Lake City, Pittsburgh, and Boston). And even within the New York City financial community, Untermyer sought to distinguish the experience of trust companies and small banks apart from the members of the New York Clearing House.

The Proceedings

Untermyer was a tough interrogator: interrupting, asking leading questions, and in some cases badgering witnesses. Much of the testimony was banal, a recitation or confirmation of facts, some of which were widely known. And the thread of questioning frequently meandered into ancillary details raised by the witnesses. On occasion, the witnesses caught Untermyer off guard. He seemed to be playing to a jury of public opinion rather than the 11 representatives on the subcommittee. Much of the minutiae about business practices had little to no bearing on the conclusions the committee reached.

Yet it was not a fishing expedition. The investigator's questions revolved around a few themes: the control of corporate governance through interlocking directorships; control of securities underwriting by large New York firms; the power of the New York Clearing House; the concentration of bank reserves in the New York call money market; the exclusionary structure of underwriting syndicates, and so on. The breadth of these issues would eventually be knitted into an allegation of control of finance by a circle of individuals and firms located on Wall Street.

Untermyer's investigatory style was illustrated in his handling of the star witness, J. P. Morgan, who appeared on December 18–19, 1912. By then, Morgan was in his 75th year and in semi-retirement from his firm—he was suffering from a long illness and would die three months later.[18] Even-tempered and highly respectful of Untermyer, Morgan frequently asked his questioner to repeat a statement and was unable to recall details about his dealings, although he regularly offered to have the questions researched and answered later. Spectators did not expect what proved to be an assertive defense of the financial sector, Morgan's firm, and himself—this was Morgan's last hurrah.

The highlight of Morgan's testimony occurred when Untermyer sought to prove that banks only extended credit to wealthy persons. Untermyer asked whether Morgan would lend money to someone who had none.

Mr. Morgan: He might not have anything. I have known a man to come into my office, and I have given him a check for a million dollars when I knew he had not a cent in the world.

Mr. Untermyer: There are not many of them?

Mr. Morgan: Yes; a good many.

Mr. Untermyer: That is not business?

Mr. Morgan: Yes; unfortunately it is. I do not think it is good business, though.

Mr. Untermyer: Commercial credits are based upon the possession of money or property?

Mr. Morgan: What?

Mr. Untermyer: Commercial credits?

Mr. Morgan: Money or property or character.

Mr. Untermyer: Is not commercial credit based primarily upon money or property?

Mr. Morgan: No, sir; the first thing is character.

Mr. Untermyer: Before money or property?

Mr. Morgan: Before money or anything else. Money cannot buy it.

Mr. Untermyer: So that a man with character, without anything at all behind it, can get all the credit he wants, and a man with the property cannot get it?

Mr. Morgan: That is very often the case.

Mr. Untermyer: But that is the rule of business?

Mr. Morgan: That is the rule of business, sir.

Mr. Untermyer: If that is the rule of business, Mr. Morgan, why do the banks demand, the first thing they ask, a statement of what the man has got, before they extend him credit?

Mr. Morgan: That is what they go into; but the first thing they say is, "We want to see your record."

Mr. Untermyer: Yes; and if his record is a blank, the next thing is how much has he got?

Mr. Morgan: People do not care, then.

Mr. Untermyer: For instance, if he has got Government bonds or railroad bonds, and goes in to get credit, he gets it, and on the security of those bonds, does he not?

Mr. Morgan: Yes.

Mr. Untermyer: He does not get it on his face or his character, does he?

Mr. Morgan: Yes; he gets it on his character.

Mr. Untermyer: I see; then he might as well take the bonds home, had he not?

Mr. Morgan: Because a man I do not trust could not get money from me on all the bonds in Christendom.

Mr. Untermyer: That is the rule all over the world?

Mr. Morgan: I think that is the fundamental basis of business.[19]

Biographer Jean Strouse summed up Morgan's testimony: "He was as certain that he had been doing the country great service all his life as Untermyer was certain that the Money Trust was up to no good, and the gulf between their positions came out plainly on the subject of monopoly concentration. What to Untermyer represented an oligarchical "system, vicious and dangerous beyond conception" had for Morgan evolved as a practical solution to a range of economic problems."[20]

The Findings

The report of the subcommittee made three claims. First, the existence of underwriting syndicates of the same firms proved a high degree of coordination and alignment in the actions of a few banking firms. The report alleged that an inner group of three firms (J. P. Morgan & Co., National City Bank, and First National Bank) influenced seven other large institutions (Bankers Trust Co., Guaranty Trust Co., Astor Trust Co., National Bank of Commerce, Liberty National Bank, Chase National Bank, Farmers Loan & Trust Co.) to wield about $1.6 billion in resources.[21] In absolute terms, this was a material but not overwhelming portion of the nation's financial resources, equivalent for instance to about 10 percent of the U.S. money supply in 1913.[22]

Second, the hearings asserted that the money trust occupied an important position in bringing corporate securities to market, that it was the gatekeeper to the public capital markets. The source of its power was "other people's money," the access to cash that could be deployed into stock and bond offerings—or, into funding of the call loan market. Thus, it appeared that the money trust influenced the call loan market to promote the very securities that it underwrote.

Third, the subcommittee concluded that the money trust wielded influence through representation on many corporate boards. And by membership on the boards of competitors in the same industry, the money trust could promote a degree of coordination inconsistent with open competition. The evidence in support of this was a matrix of corporate directorships. The committee found that officers of the First National Bank were board directors in 49 corporations, with capital of $11.5 billion. For National City Bank, the figures were 41 corporations and $10.5 billion. J. P. Morgan & Co.'s officers were directors in 112 corporations with capital of $22.5 billion. In 1914, Louis Brandeis noted that in comparison the total capitalization of the NYSE was only $26.5 billion. Brandeis concluded:

> *The operations of so comprehensive a system of concentration necessarily developed in the bankers' overweening power. And the bankers' power grows by what it feeds on. Power begets wealth; and added wealth opens ever new opportunities for the acquisition of wealth and power. The operations of these bankers are so vast and numerous that even a very reasonable compensation for the service performed by the bankers, would, in the aggregate, produce for them incomes so large as to result in huge accumulations of capital. . . . We must break the Money Trust or the Money Trust will break us.*[23]

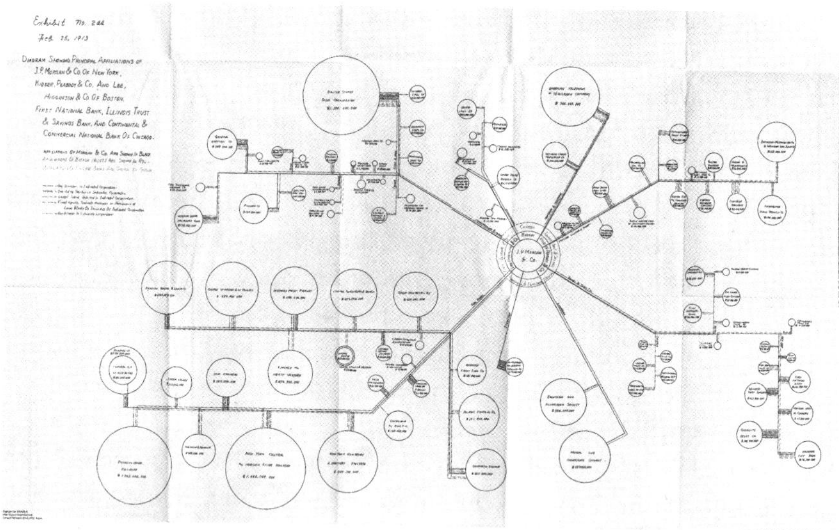

Figure 21.2 Structure of the Money Trust Presented by the Pujo Committee
Source: "Exhibit 244: Diagram Showing Principal Affiliations of J.P. Morgan & Co. of New York, Kidder, Peabody & Co. and Lee, Higginson & Co. of Boston, First National Bank, Illinois Trust & Savings Bank, and Continental & Commercial National Bank of Chicago," *Money Trust Investigation: Investigation of Financial and Monetary Conditions in the United States Under House Resolutions Nos. 429 and 504 Before a Subcommittee of the Committee on Banking and Currency*, U.S. House of Representatives (1912–1913), February 25, 1913. Downloaded from St. Louis Federal Reserve Bank, FRASER Archive,https://fraser.stlouisfed.org/title/money-trust-investigation-80/exhibit-244-diagram-showing-principal-affiliations-jp-morgan-co-new-york-kidder-peabody-co-lee-higginson-co-boston-first-national-bank-illinois-trust-savings-bank-continental-commercial-national-bank-chicago-23677.

The overarching idea of control of finance by a small group of Wall Street insiders proved to be both compelling and threatening. The octopus-like structure was depicted by the committee in drawings, such as given in Figure 21.2—though unreadable to anyone without a magnifying glass, the diagram showed the linkage of railroads (lower left), large manufacturing firms (upper left and upper right), and banks, trust companies, and insurance companies (lower right).

Proposals for Change

The majority report of the committee concluded its summation of findings with two proposals for new legislation. The first was an amendment of the original national banking laws to forbid actual or hypothetical practices that had been discussed in the hearings. These included discriminatory terms of loans, credits in support of the control of industry prices, terms of membership in clearinghouses, prohibition on bank directors borrowing from their own banks, forbidding banks to underwrite the offering of securities, and so on. The second proposed law involved the prevention of the use of the postal system, telegraph, or telephone to commit fraud on stock exchanges.

Notably absent from the suggested laws were regulations on the deployment of bank reserves. The immobility of bank reserves and gold currency was at the heart of the Panic of 1907. The absence reflected the division of labor within the House Committee on Banking and Currency: one subcommittee, led by Pujo, would investigate the thesis of industrial control by financial interests. Another subcommittee, led by Carter Glass, a representative from Virginia, took up Nelson Aldrich's proposal of a "National Reserve Association." Buoyed by the publicity and momentum from publication of the Pujo committee report, Untermyer lobbied behind the scenes to reopen and expand the hearings and to address central banking.

However, President Woodrow Wilson demurred. Inaugurated on March 4, 1913, he faced the task of installing a new administration and channeling a torrent of energy stimulated by his progressive agenda. Mexico, the next-door neighbor, had convulsed into revolution. Tariff reform, implementation of a progressive income tax, plans for a Federal Trade Commission, and reform of the financial system vied for his attention. Wilson decided that Carter Glass should carry forward the work on a central bank. Accordingly, the recommendations of the Pujo Committee faded, to be revisited later after these other initiatives had matured.

Reaction to the Report

Public reaction to the publication of the majority report flared and subsided quickly. Major newspapers covered the report and its critics. One Republican representative called the report "bunk, pure and simple."[24] J. P. Morgan & Co. responded with a vigorous defense in a memorandum to Pujo: it denied the "vestige of truth" in the idea of a money trust, attributed problems in the financial system to inappropriate regulation, and argued that meeting the capital needs of large corporations required cooperation among financial firms.[25] The committee's activities had been reported in detail previously and the substance of the final report had been anticipated.[26] In his inaugural address on March 4, Woodrow Wilson offered no direct comments on the Pujo findings. Thereafter, the establishment of the new administration occupied the headlines.

However, in the longer run, the "Money Trust" hearings proved to be enormously influential. They pioneered the quantitative analysis of the financial sector, setting a standard for many future investigations. They dominated newspaper headlines for months, as Wall Street leaders were called to testify before the committee. Of particular interest was the power of the New York Clearing House during the Panic of 1907 "to pronounce sentence of death upon every financial institution in [New York City]."[27] The findings of this investigation inflamed the public and seeped into the presidential election campaign of 1912. The Democratic Party candidate, Woodrow Wilson, said,

> *The great monopoly of this country is the monopoly of big credits. . . . A great industrial nation is controlled by its system of credit. Our system of credit is concentrated. The growth of the nation, therefore, and all our activities are in the hands of a few men who, even if their action be honest and intended for the public interest, are necessarily concentrated upon the great undertakings in which their own money is involved and who necessarily, by very reason of their own limitations, chill and check and destroy genuine economic freedom. This is the greatest question of all, and to this, statesmen must address themselves with an earnest determination to serve the long future and the true liberties of men.*[28]

Did the Investigation Prove What It Claimed?

Subsequent critical analysis has challenged the hearings' conclusions. Historian Vincent Carosso (1973) pointed out that the Pujo hearings operated with no particular definition of a money trust, a defect that led to rambling, expansive, and poorly tested assertions. Untermyer acknowledged in December 1911 that "money trust" was a "loose, elastic term" but that it meant to indicate "a close and well-defined 'community of interest' and understanding among the men who dominate the financial destinies of our country and who wield fabulous power over the fortunes of others through their control of corporate funds belonging to other people."[29] Carosso called Untermyer's definition "economic nonsense and demagoguery."[30]

Mary O'Sullivan (2016) noted big gaps in the data presented, a focus on only a few banking houses, and a failure to compare their impact to the entire size of the market. For instance, during the hearings, Jacob Schiff had argued that although the money trust banks held many board seats, they were too few on any single board to have decisive influence on the direction of a company. To test that assertion, O'Sullivan computed the percentage of board seats of all publicly listed corporations in 1913 that were held by J. P. Morgan & Co., City National Bank, and First National Bank, the core of the money trust. The percentages, displayed in Figure 21.3, support Schiff's point. The money trust banks enjoyed places at many board tables, but not the kind of voting muscle consistent with corporate dominance.

O'Sullivan concluded, "Overall, there is little evidence to support the Pujo report's claim that the money trust's numerous directorships

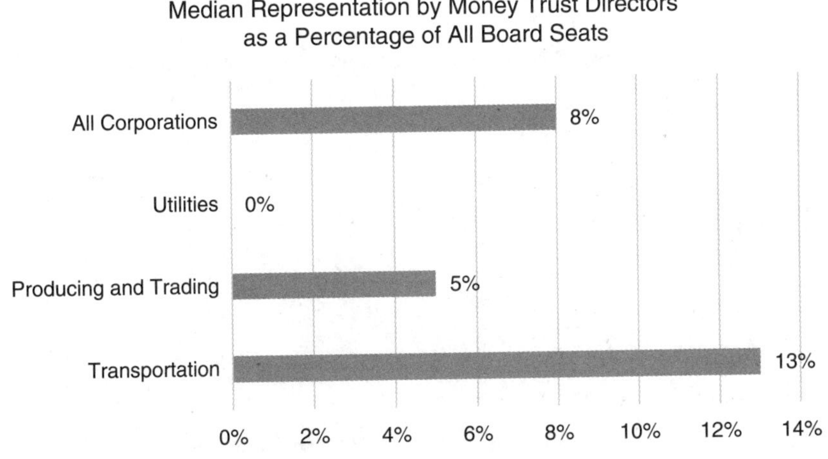

Figure 21.3 Money Trust Board Representation
SOURCE: Authors' figure, based on data given in O'Sullivan (2016), p. 302, based on Pujo Investigation Table of Interlocking Directorates, Exhibit 134-A, and Moody's Manual.

both enabled it, and motivated it, to 'throttle' competition. The investigation did not establish that the practice of putting bankers on boards was distinctive to the money trust nor that, as a general rule, bankers dominated the boards where they were represented."[31]

Similarly, O'Sullivan studied the total underwritings by money trust firms as a percentage of all U.S. corporate issues from 1908 to 1912. Figure 21.4 shows that the dollar proceeds amounted to about a third of all issues; and the number of issues was about 10 percent.

The disparity between dollar proceeds and the number of underwritings is explained presumably by underwriting fewer but larger securities offerings by the money trust firms.

The Pujo hearings' conclusions stumble on the vagueness of market control: What percentage share of market is too much? Earlier, Gary and Frick believed that U.S. Steel's acquisition of TCI avoided opposition by Roosevelt if it did not exceed a 60 percent share of market. The underwriting shares of the money trust of 10 percent to 35 percent pale in comparison. O'Sullivan concluded,

> *[T]he money trust did not dominate the underwriting and distribution of corporate securities to the extent that the Pujo report claimed. Its influence was greatest among giant railroad issues, but even there it was not as overwhelming as the Pujo report*

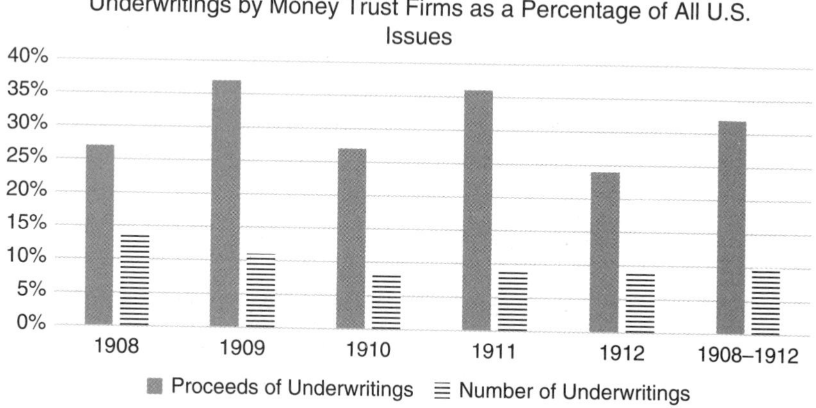

Figure 21.4 Money Trust Underwritings
SOURCE: Authors' figure, based on data given in O'Sullivan (2016), p. 285.

asserted. Moreover, the structural changes underway in the primary market—the shift from railroads to industrials and from larger to smaller issues—mean that it was evolving in ways that tended to diminish the money trust's dominance.[32]

Impact

The hearings generated huge media coverage. A computer search of newspaper articles containing the phrase "money trust" yielded 9,001 hits for 1911, 8,871 for 1912, and 7,989 for 1913.[33] As Figure 21.5 shows, the number of books mentioning the phrase spiked in tandem with the Panic, reaching a peak in 1913, then peaked again in the 1930s, and remained in the public's mind for decades.

Jurist Louis Brandeis quickly distilled the findings of the Money Trust Investigation into a series of articles, published in *Harper's Weekly*. The articles mobilized public sentiment in the spring of 1913 on behalf of financial reform. Brandeis collected the articles into a book, *Other People's Money*, published in 1914, that became one of the pillars of the Progressive Movement. Progressives feared that through the workings of a money trust, underwriting business would be directed to a few favored

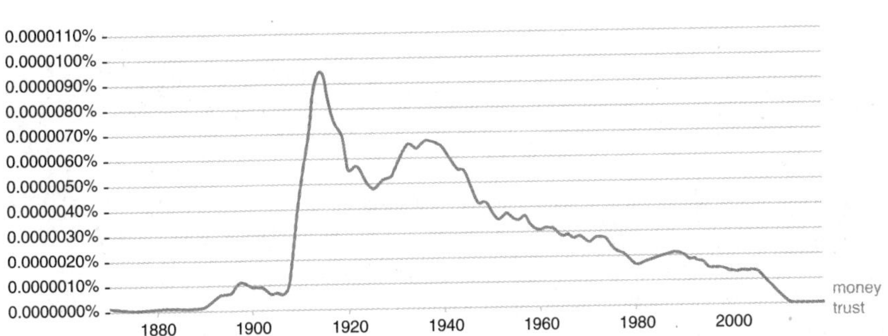

Figure 21.5 Frequency of Occurrence of the Phrase "Money Trust," 1800–2020

Note: This graph displays the frequency of occurrence of the phrase "money trust" found in a corpus of English language printed sources.

Source: Google Books Ngram viewer, downloaded June 21, 2022 from https://books.google.com/ngrams/graph?content=Money+trust&year_start=1800&year_end=2019&corpus=26&smoothing=3&direct_url=t1%3B%2CMoney%20trust%3B%2Cc0#t1%3B%2CMoney%20trust%3B%2Cc0.

firms, investment capital in the United States would be channeled to the advantage of a few powerful business leaders, and control of large corporations would go to the money trust. All of this was consistent with the thesis of William H. "Coin" Harvey in 1899.

The political reaction to the Panic of 1907 normalized the idea of the money trust and thrust it to center stage in the debates over stabilization of the financial system and the soundness of U.S. currency. For a century or more the idea underpinned public policy debates about the financial system and its regulation.

Chapter 22

A Central Bank

Really, we cannot go on in this way. Financial flurries and squeezes which are of such frequent occurrence at the great money centers of the country are the legitimate offspring of a bad financial system. These things do not occur in European countries where they have their banking system on a solid and enduring basis, under complete government control. Until we adopt a central bank of issue, or something like it, there can be no permanent relief.

—Senator Henry C. Hansbrough of North Dakota, November 23, 1907[1]

Through the tortuous process of financial crisis and civic reaction, public sentiment built inexorably toward acceptance of the idea of a central bank in the United States. By late November 1907, newspapers were declaring that the crisis had ended.[2] Yet already it was apparent that the Panic of 1907 had crystallized a change in attitude: as had been true for a century or more, the problem in a panic was the insufficiency of money and credit; the novelty of 1907 was to shift attention to the *structure* of the financial system.

However, what kind of bank would it be? Paul Warburg, an investment banker with Kuhn, Loeb, advocated a truly *centralized* bank such as existed in Britain, France, and Germany—one institution that could command the financial muscle to serve a growing economy and respond decisively in the event of a crisis. Populists, such as William Jennings Bryan, recoiled from the powers exercised by J. P. Morgan and George B. Cortelyou and sought the *decentralization* of bank reserves and money-making power. Populists said that decision makers on the Eastern Seaboard had neglected the needs and wants of the interior.

Governance of a central bank also proved contentious: bankers wanted a prominent role in running the institution; leaders in business and labor wanted to exclude the bankers in the belief that bankers would co-opt the central bank for their own benefit. The debate whipped up older antagonisms between Wall Street and Main Street. And then back to money: Whose obligation would paper money be? Populists and progressives sought the backing of the U.S. government. Conservatives, fearing inflation if the government backed the currency, favored a continuation of the same money system since the Civil War: banks would issue their own notes, backed by bonds placed on reserve with the government.

In short, what emerged after the elections of 1912 was a multidimensional multiparty negotiation over the design of a U.S. central bank.

Shift in Orthodox Thinking

The Panic of 1907 triggered immediate reflections on the potential role of government in managing bank reserves and stabilizing the financial system. Shortly after the panic, Republican Senator Henry Hansbrough of North Dakota mooted the establishment of a central bank for the United States—to be headquartered in Chicago "near the center of commerce and agriculture, as far away from the speculative atmosphere as possible."[3] Yet Senator Nelson Aldrich, chairman of the Senate Finance Committee, demurred, claiming "no disposition to hurry the consideration of so important a subject." Congress reflected a wide diversity[4] of opinion about a possible central bank and the approaching federal elections in 1908 discouraged the passage of important legislation.[5] Democrats in Congress offered legislation that proposed the establishment of a central bank, although Roosevelt considered it too inflationary; the Republican majority defeated the bill. Nevertheless, Roosevelt himself began to muse aloud about the benefits of establishing a central bank in the United States, as he wrote in November 1907:

> *I am inclined to think that from this side, a central bank would be a very good thing. Certainly I believe that at least a central bank, with branch banks, in each of the States . . . but I doubt whether our people would support either scheme at present, and there is this grave objection, at least to the first, that the inevitable popular distrust of big financial men might result very dangerously if it were concentrated upon the officials of one huge bank. Sooner or later there would be in that bank some insolent man whose head would be turned by his own power and ability, who would fail to realize other types of ability and the limitations upon his power, and would by his actions awaken the slumbering popular distrust and cause a storm in which he would be as helpless as a child, and which would overwhelm not only him but other men and other things of far more importance.*[6]

Necessary, But Insufficient

To stem political fury about the Panic and buy time for more thoughtful institutional design, Senator Nelson Aldrich mustered support for the Aldrich–Vreeland Act in May 1908, which chartered the National Monetary Commission. Under cover of the Commission, Aldrich embarked on a nearly three-year search for a feasible design. Gradually the staunch conservative accepted the need for a central bank, influenced particularly by visits to European institutions* and by the patient lobbying of Paul Warburg for reforms adopting their model.

* Overshadowing the debates about central banking in the United States were the examples of the central banks of Europe, all of which had been founded to serve the financial needs of monarchs and their imperial aspirations. The Bank of England (BoE) was the most prominent example, and the leading central bank in the world. The BoE had been privately owned since its founding in 1696, and operated under a special charter by the British government to act as its fiscal agent. The banknotes of the BoE became recognized as the British units of currency. Since 1866, the BoE served as the lender of last resort to ailing banks. A single institution without branches or subsidiaries, the BoE made no pretense toward representative engagement with regions or people beyond London's Threadneedle Street or the leadership of Britain's financial community.

Meanwhile, Populist anger about the Panic took shape in the advocacy of government guarantees of bank deposits. Eight states—mainly in the West and South—adopted such legislation from 1908 to 1917. And by the federal elections in 1908, national deposit guarantees were a leading plank in the platform of the Democratic presidential nominee, William Jennings Bryan.

In response, Taft, Roosevelt, and the Republican legislators promoted the idea of a postal savings bank system. This system would authorize local postmasters to accept deposits up to $500 to be guaranteed by the U.S. government. The system would reinvest the deposits in interest-bearing assets (mainly accounts at national banks) and retain one-half of a percent to cover the cost of administering the system.

This was hardly equal to a full-blown government guarantee of bank deposits. But its advocates hoped that it would win some support in the 1910 elections from farmers, immigrants, and small-balance savers. Taft signed the enabling act on June 25, 1910, although it proved insufficient to avert the Democratic Party victory in November 1910. Nevertheless, the Postal Savings Act proved to be a significant precedent toward broad government guarantee of deposits enacted in 1933. Subsequently, the opposition of bankers led to the termination of the postal savings system in 1971.

Jekyll Island

A pivotal event for Aldrich was a secret conference of financiers and politicians on Jekyll Island, Georgia, in November 1910. That meeting produced a design for a "National Reserve Association" that made its way into the final report of the National Monetary Commission. Senator Aldrich claimed the design was his, although it was strikingly like a plan advocated by Paul Warburg, partner in the firm, Kuhn, Loeb, earlier in the decade. Warburg was present at Jekyll Island, as was Frank A. Vanderlip, then president of National City Bank, who is credited with drafting the proposal to emerge from that conference. Others at the conference were A. Piatt Andrew (assistant secretary of the Treasury), Henry P. Davison (partner in J.P. Morgan & Company), Charles D. Norton (president of First National Bank of New York), and Benjamin Strong (vice-president of Bankers Trust). As progressives would later argue, these successors to J. P. Morgan, James Stillman, and George F. Baker imprinted the views of the "money trust" on the proposed National Reserve Bank. Yet in broad outline, the product of Jekyll Island bore several similarities to the central bank that President Woodrow Wilson, Treasury Secretary Carter Glass, and the Democrats would later claim credit for establishing.

Two months later, on January 16, 1911, Senator Aldrich formally submitted to the National Monetary Commission (and the public) a draft of legislation to establish a National Reserve Association. This draft was Aldrich's first step toward rallying political support, refining the text, and identifying opponents. A revised draft was included in the Commission's final report.

Report of the National Monetary Commission

The National Monetary Commission published its report on January 8, 1912, after a long gestation since founding in May 1908. The significance of the 24-volume report was its forthright criticism of the existing laws and institutions for banking and currency—the old orthodoxy. The report recommended starting afresh with the establishment of a "National Reserve Association" that would promote cooperation among banks.

The basis for the Commission's recommendations was a list of 17 "defects of the banking system, which were largely responsible for [the] disasters"[7] of the Panic of 1907. From the discussion in earlier chapters, many of these defects will be familiar to the reader and for brevity can be clustered into four general groups.

First, several defects dealt with issues regarding the concentration and immobility of bank reserves. The required reserves of banks were "pyramided" up to the big banks in New York City. And rescue capital was relatively immobile. Banks could not turn to a large reservoir of funds if they experienced a run. Laws restricted the use of bank reserves. And banks lacked the means to augment their reserves or expand loans to meet unexpected needs.

Second, the Commission noted the absence of a national coordinator who could view the entire country and even international conditions to deploy reserves more fairly and "enforce adoption of uniform standards with regard to capital, reserves, examinations, and the character and publicity of reports."[8] Without mentioning J. P. Morgan, the Commission clearly had in mind creating a powerful central force for intervention in the event of crises.

Third, the absence of a central bank with which to discount commercial paper led to episodes of credit illiquidity; and in buoyant times the absence motivated banks to place their surplus reserves into the call loan market in New York. The Commission grumbled about the lack of "equality in credit facilities between different sections of the country, reflected in less favored communities, in retarded development, and great disparity in rates of discount."[9]

Finally, the report criticized existing laws as inadequate to the needs of the current economy. Drawing particular attention were the National Banking Acts of the Civil War Era, and the Independent Treasury Act of 1840 that separated government from banking. The laws were restrictive and resulted in "discrimination and favoritism."[10]

To remedy these issues, the Commission recommended chartering a "National Reserve Association" to be sustained by a capital subscription of $100 million from all participating banks and by a contingent call for an equal amount in the event of a crisis. Membership in the association would be voluntary and open to all national banks, state banks, and trust companies. The National Reserve Association would consist of numerous local associations, chartered as branches of the national organization. Banks would elect the directors of the local associations. The United States would be divided into 15 districts, which would elect directors of the National Association. The Secretaries of Treasury, Agriculture, Commerce, and Labor, and the Comptroller of the Currency would be *ex officio* members of the National board—reflecting the need "to secure a proper recognition of the vital interest which the public has in the management of the association."[11] The Governor of the National Reserve Association would be appointed by the president of the United States for a term of 10 years.

The important functions of the local branches would be to discount commercial paper of their members, to clear checks among members, to facilitate domestic exchanges with different regions of the country, and to assure the redemption into gold of the banknotes of the members.

Even though the National Reserve Association would be a privately-owned corporation with stockholders, it would hold a special government charter to serve as the fiscal agent and financial depository of the U.S. government—this mirrored the status of the Bank of England (and the earlier Bank of the United States). The National Reserve Association would have the power to fix uniform rates of discount across the United States. Finally, all new currency would be issued by the National Reserve Association, against which it would hold gold reserves not less than 50 percent of the value of such currency.

In support of its recommendations, the Commission argued that the National Reserve Association would reduce expenses, respond more effectively to crises, and generally deal with the 17 defects it highlighted.

The Commission's report contained the draft of a 29-page bill that would enact its recommendations. The Commission's draft won the endorsement of the American Bankers Association and the National Citizens' League for the Promotion of a Sound Banking System. Aldrich introduced the bill in the Senate on January 9, 1912. The draft assumed the nature of a legacy for the venerable senator.

Unfortunately, the Aldrich draft proved to be dead on arrival, reflecting the rapidly changing political climate and the fact that Aldrich had recently retired owing to ill health. The Republican Party platform for 1912 gave scant attention to the proposal. And the Progressive Party platform openly opposed it, saying it ceded control to private hands rather than to the government.

Nevertheless, the publication of the National Monetary Commission's report and Aldrich's subsequent draft legislation marked a dramatic turn in the conversation about financial reform. The crises of the nineteenth century had focused reform discussion on the *currency* of the United States, whereas the new report focused reform on the *structure of the banking system* as the first step to achieving stable currency. Historian Richard McCulley attributed this sea change to Paul M. Warburg, a banker with Kuhn, Loeb who had been writing and debating reform for over a decade:

> *Warburg argued that the priority for financial reform was the development of a discount market to replace the call market as the principal outlet for the placement of banks' liquid funds in the United States. That could be accomplished, he*

explained, through the creation of a central bank with rediscounting powers that favored commercial bills and discriminated against call loans on stock exchange collateral. In Warburg's vision, therefore, the transformation of the nation's money market depended on the creation of a central bank; conversely, the effectiveness of the central bank depended on the creation of a discount market that would become the main vehicle for monetary policy to influence credit conditions in the United States . . . . [U]nder Warburg's influence, monetary reform came to be seen as inextricably linked to the structural reform of the US money market and its relationship to the banking system.[12]

New Political Landscape

The failure of Aldrich's draft reflected a political reality that dawned with the midterm elections of 1910: public support for the Republicans' coalition of conservatives and progressives was fading. Congress reflected a growing split between the two sides. For instance, in 1909, Congress passed the Payne–Aldrich Tariff, which raised duties on a range of imported goods and inflamed progressives and Democrats who saw the tariff as crony capitalism, a handout of import preferences to Nelson Aldrich's business friends. One progressive senator openly accused Aldrich of profiting from the tariff, which Aldrich vehemently denied.

The populist–progressive impulse following the Panic of 1907 assured a majority in opposition to Aldrich's proposed National Reserve Association. The Panic had polarized voters and their elected representatives, producing gridlock on financial reform. As things stood, banks would be prevented from branching or doing business across state lines, and there would be no central bank. Paul Warburg wrote that the polarization "led to an almost fanatic conviction that the only hope of keeping the country's credit system independent was to be sought in complete decentralization of banking.[13]

Also, the presidential administration changed. Theodore Roosevelt had pushed for priorities in conservation and favored regulation of trusts by means of negotiation rather than lawsuits. President Taft departed from the policies of his predecessor both in substance (he abandoned conservation and endorsed a Constitutional amendment to permit taxation of incomes) and style (by temperament, Taft recoiled from using the White House as a "bully pulpit" from which to mobilize supporters).

Into this breach came Woodrow Wilson. He was a progressive, favoring technocratic expertise to establish good public policies. But he also had to retain in his camp Populists led by William Jennings Bryan, and Southern legislators who were committed to Jim Crow discrimination against African Americans. Wilson's gift was an ability to broker compromises that would pass laws. Seeking to exploit the momentum of the election results, he marshaled party leaders in the House and Senate to accelerate progress on five progressive priorities: lower tariffs, a new income tax, direct election of U.S. senators, stronger antitrust laws, and reform of the financial system.

The cumulative effect of the Panic of 1907, the recession of 1910–1911, the restoration of Democratic Party power in the House, the Stanley Investigation, the Pujo Investigation, Aldrich's dilatory progress on financial reform, rising friction between progressives and conservatives, and the Republican Party's dramatic split in 1912 over the competing candidacies of Roosevelt and Taft swept the Democrats to control of both houses of Congress and the White House in 1912. It was a crushing denouement to what in 1906 seemed to be a durable political franchise for Republicans.

A Reserve System Emerges

Wilson's push for financial reform legislation stimulated a burst of lobbying and political wrangling by members of Congress. The first to take the initiative was Carter Glass, a representative from Lynchburg, Virginia who would assume the powerful role of chairman of the House Banking Committee. Glass met with Wilson on December 26, 1912 to sketch the outlines of a new central bank.

Carter Glass advocated a system of 15–20 regional reserve banks that would be relatively independent, but under the supervision of the federal government. Indeed, the degree of coordination among the regional reserve banks remained vague. The reserve banks would be owned by the banks in their district and would hold government deposits of gold with which to back notes (currency) that would replace the old national bank notes. The reserve bank would discount commercial paper, thus enabling banks to avoid the threat of illiquidity in a panic. Glass felt that private bankers should govern the reserve banks, owing to their expertise. And he posited that notes of the reserve banks should be obligations of the banks, not the U.S. government. "I pointed out the unscientific nature of [U.S. government obligations.]" Behind the Federal Reserve Note would be the liability of individual banks, the double liability of bank stockholders, the gold reserves, the reserves of discounted commercial notes, and the liability of member banks. "There is not, in truth, any government obligation!"[14]

Where Aldrich's plan called for a much more centralized reserve bank with up to 15 branches, Glass's plan emphasized decentralization into maybe 15 relatively autonomous banks. Glass wanted to prevent the aggregation of bank reserves in New York City. Instead, bank reserves would be held in the regional reserve banks. Glass believed that such decentralization harkened to Democratic Party values reaching back to Andrew Jackson and Thomas Jefferson.

When Wilson asked Glass who would oversee the regional reserve banks, Glass nominated the Comptroller of the Currency, who was already in charge of the National Banking System. However, Wilson wanted a *federal* governing structure of the system, in the form of a board to whom the regional banks would report. Glass was surprised, but after reflection began working on draft legislation to introduce upon Wilson's inauguration on March 4.

The draft that Glass circulated met stiff opposition from both bankers and populists. For instance, Benjamin Strong, president of Bankers' Trust, thought that it created too many reserve banks, gave too much power to political appointees and others who had no skill or experience in financial matters, would "return to the heresies of Greenbackism and fiat money," and ultimately would create moral hazard and political meddling.[15] As for the populists, William Jennings Bryan informed President Woodrow Wilson of his opposition to the bill on May 19, 1913, arguing that he couldn't support it because it permitted bankers onto the proposed Federal Reserve Board and enabled national banks to issue currency. "The government alone should issue money," he said.[16]

Competing Designs

Next came interventions from William Gibbs McAdoo, Wilson's new secretary of the Treasury. McAdoo had been a lawyer, securities dealer, president of the Hudson and Manhattan Railroad Company, and outspoken progressive before helping to lead Wilson's campaign for the presidency. McAdoo wanted Glass to add the secretary of agriculture as a member of the governing board of the system and wanted reserve banks placed no farther than a train trip from any point in the reserve district. And McAdoo urged that the regional institutions be titled *Federal* Reserve Banks—this pleased Wilson's vision of a federal structure. McAdoo's views continued to change, and by May amounted to Treasury Department control of a unitary central bank, with branches not unlike the venerable Subtreasury system that had been in use since the 1840s.

A third set of ideas came from Senator Robert Owen. He had been born in Lynchburg, Virginia into an affluent family as son of a railroad president. However, the Panic of 1873 followed by his father's death ruined the family. Owen departed for Oklahoma Territory to serve as a teacher, lawyer, journalist, and Federal Indian Agent (he was part Cherokee). When Oklahoma was admitted to the Union as a state in 1907, Owen was elected to serve as one of the state's two inaugural U.S. senators. Influenced by William Jennings Bryan, Owen brandished strong progressive views.

Senator Owen wanted the reserve banks to be distributed throughout the United States in districts independent of one another and controlled by the government. He argued that banknotes "should be the notes of the United States under the control of the Government and based on the taxing power, and that when these were loaned to the banks, they should be adequately secured by gold in fixed ratio and by United States bonds or commercial bills. . . . Some wished one bank, or as few as possible; others, from eight to twelve."[17]

Wilson Decides

The differences among the competing drafts modeled the ideological divides then wracking Congress. Wilson had ordered Congress to remain in session during what was proving to be a sweltering Washington, DC, summer in 1913. Now, the whole effort seemed threatened by intransigence among the three proponents.

Wilson broke the deadlock by a compromise on June 17. He threw his support strongly in favor of eliminating banker representation entirely from the Federal Reserve Board and by asserting that Federal Reserve Notes should be obligations of the federal government. Wilson said, "Control . . . must be public, not private, must be vested in the Government itself, so that the banks may be the instruments, not the masters, of business and of individual enterprise and initiative."[18] This satisfied Bryan, though it shocked Carter Glass. To mollify Glass, Wilson also decided that the reserve banks should hold gold reserves backing up the currency at no less than 33 percent. With that, Glass and Owen agreed to compromise.

The Federal Reserve Act was published on June 20 and introduced in the House and Senate on June 26, 1913. Figure 22.1 depicts the positions of Warburg, Aldrich, Bryan, Glass, Owen—and, ultimately, Wilson—on two dimensions: (1) the extent of public versus private control of the central bank, and (2) the extent of centralization or decentralization in the holding of reserves and making of monetary policy. As the figure suggests, Wilson's compromise divided the territory between Glass and Owen.

Glass began the final push in August with hearings in the House Banking Committee. There, three representatives from farm states stalled the bill with an amendment that would prohibit interlocking directorships among banks, a feature that Glass feared would make the bill unacceptable to a majority of the House. Therefore, Glass managed to move the bill to the Democratic Caucus, where a majority vote would bind all Democratic members to approve the bill. Privately, Bryan approached Glass to ask for an amendment that would allow the reserve banks to discount agricultural loans—Glass agreed and inserted some vague language to that effect. With that, Bryan expressed his support for the legislation and the opposition crumbled. The House approved the bill on September 18: 285 votes to 85.

In the Senate, Robert Owen encountered a range of amendments, including a government guarantee of deposits, a cut in reserve requirements, and permission for banks to trade securities and to discount

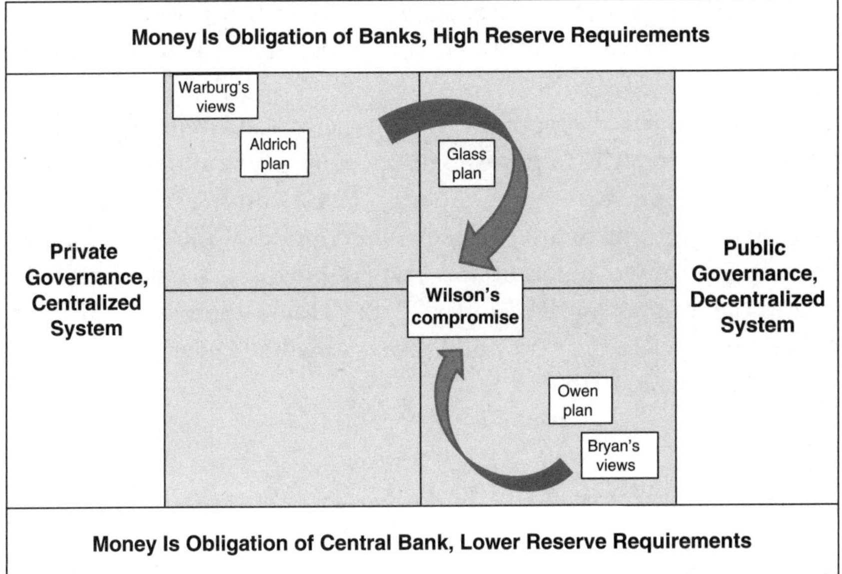

Figure 22.1 Wilson's Compromise among Competing Proposals to Establish the Federal Reserve System

NOTE: McAdoo's changing views are not easily depicted in this figure. In the final iteration, he favored public governance with a centralized system. Such a proposal was a nonstarter with Bryan, Glass, and Owen.

SOURCE: Authors' figure, inspired by a figure in Conti-Brown (2016), p. 23.

agricultural loans. Again, opposition seemed to mount. Bankers started to circulate an entirely different plan for a central bank. And the American Bankers Association officially announced its opposition to the Federal Reserve Act.

Resistance began to fade after Wilson signed the Revenue Act of 1913, which sharply cut tariffs and established a progressive income tax,* both initiatives that progressive legislators could celebrate to their supporters. Outside support came from endorsements by the U.S. Chamber of Commerce and the New York Merchants Association. In addition, Owen agreed to modifications to allow agricultural paper to be eligible for discount, to reduce the number of Reserve Banks from

*The act taxed annual incomes of $4,000 at 1 percent, which increased as income rose.

12 to 8, and to raise the gold reserve requirement for the Fed from 33 percent to 40 percent. On December 19, the Senate passed the bill by a vote of 54 to 34.

Wilson urged the conference of senators and representatives to align the terms of the respective bills speedily—he wanted to conclude the deliberations before the holiday recess, during which second thoughts might impede the subsequent adoption of the bill. The conference committee reported the revised bill back to the respective houses of Congress on December 22; the House approved it the same day and the Senate the next day. Wilson signed the Federal Reserve Act on December 23, 1913.

Perfecting the Fed's *Federal* Structure

Much of the tension among the progressives, populists, and Wall Street conservatives in Congress about the design of the new central bank focused on rule of the new institution. Conservatives wanted a centralized central bank close to the great money centers that would be run by people with expertise in money and banking—that is, bankers. Populists wanted a decentralized system of reserve banks whose reserve assets would be dispersed around the country and run by "Main Street" people. Progressives sought to distance the central bank from Wall Street, and wanted it controlled by the federal government's public servants with some expertise in money and banking. How did the competing visions work out in practice?

President Woodrow Wilson and Treasury Secretary William Gibbs McAdoo had their work cut out for them. Implementing the Federal Reserve Act began with setting the size and location of the Federal Reserve Districts. This took eight months and summoned appeals and protests that lasted a year. An organizing committee, chaired by McAdoo and Secretary of Agriculture David F. Houston, addressed the task of staffing and structuring the Federal Reserve System. They drew boundaries for 12 districts, each with a regional reserve bank. Only after confirming the districts could officials be appointed. The national oversight body, the Federal Reserve Board, was finally appointed in August 1914. Benjamin Strong, president of Bankers Trust, was appointed to be the first governor of the Federal Reserve Bank of New York. The 12 reserve banks opened on November 16, 1914.

Investment banker Paul Warburg was appointed to the first Federal Reserve Board in Washington, DC. He worried that ideologies and party politics would warp the technical operation of the new central bank.[19] Indeed, the Fed's governance* rendered it vulnerable to political considerations, a worry of Theodore Roosevelt and Nelson Aldrich. Anticorruption laws and sunshine provisions of the Progressive Era largely quelled fears of self-dealing and capture by the banking industry. Yet remaining was the risk that the Fed would lose its independence and become an instrument of a presidential administration. For instance, Theodore Roosevelt feared that a central bank might monetize the government's fiscal deficits or manage interest rates in ways to serve electoral benefits to the administration in power. As the following century revealed, such fears were foresightful.[20]

On the other hand, the Federal Reserve Act solved the problems outlined by the National Monetary Commission. It moved the setting of monetary policy and the lender of last resort function out of the private hands and into the public sector. The high cadence of banking panics that plagued the nineteenth century slowed sharply into the twentieth. When crises did arise, critics lamented the Fed's over- or underreaction. Over many years, the Fed seemed slow to adapt to the ever-changing and innovating financial sector. However, on balance the Fed served well the welfare of the nation.

Later, the Banking Act of 1935, which was a hallmark of New Deal monetary reforms, increased the central authority of the Federal Reserve Board and thus concentrated power over monetary policy. Where previously the 12 reserve banks could each set discount rates and conduct open-market operations, the new act gave authority over such powers to the national board. The Banking Act also revised the governance of the national board by lengthening the terms of board members from one

* As its governance was initially designed, members of the Federal Reserve Board served terms of only one year and were appointed by the president. The Secretary of the Treasury served as chairman of the board. The Comptroller of the Currency, an official who reported to the Treasury secretary, was also an ex officio member of the Board. Two factions formed within the board: (a) governors who were close to the Treasury Department, and (b) governors who reflected the concerns of the 12 reserve banks. The division within the board led to fraught policy making in the Fed's early years.

year to 14, thus mitigating the risk that a president might "pack" the board. Nonetheless, with the entry of the United States into World War II, the Fed again coordinated closely with the secretary of the Treasury, meaning that it lowered interest rates to help finance the government.

Not until 1951 did the Treasury Department and Federal Reserve Board agree to an "accord" that established the Fed's independence from intervention by elected officials (or their delegates) into Fed policy. Although not enacted by Congress (and thus vulnerable to possible future changes), Fed Chairman William McChesney Martin said that the Fed and Treasury "reached full accord with respect to debt management and monetary policies to be pursued in furthering their common purpose and to assure the successful financing of the government's requirements and, at the same time, to minimize monetization of the public debt."[21]

Chapter 23

The Changing Order

And slowly answer'd Arthur from the barge: "The old order changeth, yielding place to new."

—Alfred, Lord Tennyson, *Morte d'Arthur* (1842)

Tennyson's poem would have been familiar to Morgan, Roosevelt, and other participants in the Panic of 1907. It was a staple of assignments for high school and college students in the late nineteenth century. And its reference to a changing order must have haunted them as they dealt with the lingering effects of the panic. The old order was changing. How did the Knickerbocker emerge from its calamity—and what did this emergence presage for trust companies? Did the Progressive Movement sustain its momentum beyond the Federal Reserve Act and other achievements of President Wilson's first term? And what became of the leading protagonists in the Panic of 1907?

The Knickerbocker Trust Company

One of the sharpest points of contention in 1907 and since was the failure of the New York City financial community to assist the

Knickerbocker Trust Company. After its suspension on October 22, 1907, the Knickerbocker went into the hands of receivers. The New York State Superintendent of Banks oversaw a resolution process that hinged on two questions. First, was the trust company insolvent, or was it merely illiquid? Chapter 9 discusses the significance of this question. Second, if the trust company was solvent, what steps should be taken to resume operation?

To answer the first question, the Superintendent of Banks ordered an inventory and appraisal of the trust company's assets, which were completed on February 29, 1908. The appraisers determined that the market value of assets of $49.1 million had fallen 13 percent from the trust company's book value of assets of $56.5 million. These asset values compared to total deposits of about $47 million.[1] Superficially, the small positive difference between the appraised asset value and the claims of depositors would suggest that the Knickerbocker's problem was illiquidity, not insolvency. On that basis, a rescue might have been justified, an insight that probably motivated critics of the decisions of Mercantile National Bank, the NYCH, and J.P. Morgan not to assist the Knickerbocker on October 22.[2]

However, to judge the decision not to rescue the Knickerbocker requires better insights than those afforded by the appraisal. Essentially, one would want to know the quality* and appraised value of assets *on October 22*. Hannah's (1931) discussion suggests that the book value was measured somewhat before the onset of the Panic of 1907, and that the markdowns in appraised value reflected market conditions as of the appraisers' report of February 29, 1908. The four-month lapse poses very different capital market conditions. The extent of (in)solvency as of October 22, 1907 remains an important topic for future research.

As regards the second question, about recapitalization of the Knickerbocker, committees of depositors quickly formed to offer restructuring plans. One committee, representing large depositors, was advised by Louis Untermyer (the same person who led the Pujo Committee hearings five years later). A second committee of depositors, under the

* Bagehot's Rule, discussed in Chapter 10, suggested that in a crisis, the central bank should lend freely *against good collateral,* and at a penalty rate. Presumably, the markdowns of asset value by the appraisers reflected asset quality changes from when the assets were booked to mid-winter 1908. Instead, one would want to know the quality and market value of assets on October 22, 1907.

guidance of Herbert L. Satterlee (J. P. Morgan's son-in-law) represented a larger pool of depositors, of mainly medium- and small-dollar-value accounts. Satterlee's committee issued its proposal on November 29, prompting Untermyer's committee to criticize the proposal and offer its alternatives. Contentious issues were how fast the depositors could withdraw funds, whether they would be forced to accept illiquid securities in exchange for their deposits, and the composition of the new board of directors.

Slowly, most depositors swung to support Satterlee's proposal, while a few large depositors held out. Public endorsements of Satterlee's plan from celebrity depositors such as Mark Twain and former President Grover Cleveland helped to attract support. Finally, with 90 percent of depositors in accord, Satterlee petitioned the New York State Superintendent of Banks to approve the reorganization plan, which he did.

The Knickerbocker Trust Company reopened on March 26, 1908. About $1.5 million in net new deposits flooded in the first day, reflecting "a cheerful, almost holiday mood" among customers in the lobby, a large bouquet of flowers from Farmers Loan and Trust Company, and the arrival of numerous telegrams of congratulation. Satterlee said, "In all a fine example of what confidence will do. It was the depositors themselves who made the reopening possible, and to them belongs the credit. The hundreds who were at first worried over the outcome and at a loss to know what to do came to line when they found that most of their fellows had confidence in the bank's solvency."[3]

The Knickerbocker recovered and repaid its depositors ahead of schedule. In 1912, Columbia Trust Company acquired the assets of the Knickerbocker to form the Columbia-Knickerbocker Trust Company. In 1923, the company was acquired by Irving Trust Company. And in 1988, Irving Trust was acquired by Bank of New York, in a hostile takeover. In 2007, Bank of New York combined with Mellon Financial to form BNY Mellon, now the world's largest custodian bank and securities services company.

The Knickerbocker's descendants over the century after the Panic of 1907 illustrated the broader consolidation in the financial services industry: from 1907 to 2007, the number of depository institutions in the United States declined by about two-thirds,[4] along with growing concentration. By 2018, the four largest banks held 44 percent of all deposits.[5]

The High Tide of Progressivism

After 1913, the Progressive Movement began to wane as the country slipped into another recession. Fearing political gains by the Republicans, Wilson tempered his progressivism. Next, events in Europe distracted public opinion, prompting the New York Stock Exchange to close for more than four months with the onset of war in 1914.[6] War concerns diverted resources and attention from social issues to foreign policy.

Republicans regained control of Congress in the elections of 1918. The war ended on November 11, 1918, but not before Congress passed laws to limit espionage and seditious activities. Civil libertarians vehemently protested these laws. And anarchists reacted to these with civil unrest. On September 16, 1920, anarchists exploded a bomb outside the new offices of J. P. Morgan & Company at 23 Wall Street, killing 33 people and injuring 400.[7] The explosion closed the New York Stock Exchange for a day and left some scars on the side of the building that are visible a century later, but otherwise barely interrupted the work in the financial community. On the left wing of American politics, liberals recoiled from the resurgence of violence by radicals on the far left. With the deaths of Roosevelt in 1919 and Wilson in 1924, progressivism lost its most prominent champions.

The presidential election of 1920 displaced progressivism as the dominant impetus in American politics. From 1920 to 1932, Republicans occupied the White House, overseeing a retreat from progressive activism. But the Great Crash of October 1929 marked the onset of a scenario worse than 1907: panic, bank failures, economic contraction, and outcry for government intervention. President Herbert Hoover initially sought to mobilize volunteerism for relief efforts by the private sector. As the Depression deepened, Hoover turned to a program of fiscal stimulus by infrastructure spending. And he approved legislation to authorize the Fed to lend directly to businesses. However, these remedies failed to turn the tide by the end of Hoover's first term.

After the 1932 election of President Franklin D. Roosevelt and a new Congress, the political pendulum swung back to populist and progressive ideas. In 1933, Congress enacted regulations covering a raft of ills, not least those perceived of Wall Street in the first decade of the century. Motivated by hostility toward financial elites and market abuses that allegedly spawned the Great Crash, Congress passed the Glass–Steagall Act of 1933 separating commercial banking and investment banking. The same act established federal deposit insurance that would help to quell bank depositors' fears.

Financial institutions were no longer allowed to both take deposits and underwrite securities offerings. This proved to be a pivotal event in American financial markets that forced J. P. Morgan & Company to choose to limit its activities strictly to commercial banking. Morgan partner Henry S. Morgan (son of J. Pierpont Morgan, Jr.) led several J. P. Morgan & Company partners into forming the investment bank Morgan Stanley. The division of the financial services industry held until 1999, when Congress repealed the provisions of Glass–Steagall separating commercial and investment banking.

The Change Agents

The Panic of 1907 and its aftereffects turned the glare of public attention onto many individuals, either for what they did or did not do. Individually, the actions they took and views they espoused illustrated the significance of human agency as an influence on the Panic. Collectively, they represented the struggle for change from old to new orthodoxies in finance and public policy. What became of these change agents after their star turn in the crisis and its outcome?

Outsiders

F. Augustus Heinze met his downfall in the Panic of 1907. After his brother Otto's failed attempt to corner the stock of United Copper Company, Augustus was ousted from the Mercantile National Bank and took losses on falling stock prices in United Copper and other securities. His aspiration to enter the financial elite of New York lay in tatters.

In the wake of the panic, Heinze's firm was placed in the hands of a receiver. Heinze was indicted on 16 counts of financial malfeasance and various breaches of banking law. According to his brother Otto, Augustus maintained that he was blameless and that "the old line of bankers were bringing about a money panic in order to get rid of the new class of financiers and the new trust companies."[8] The government's case against Heinze drew headlines, though a journalist noted that he "maintained cool, unruffled, defiant, hedging behind constitutional rights."[9] Then in 1909 the court acquitted him.

Nonetheless, Heinze's reputation remained tarnished, the slump in copper prices had crushed his mining interests, his relationships with his brothers had dissolved, and his health suffered. Augustus again went West, where he purchased mining operations in Idaho and British Columbia, intending to turn them profitable. But a lawsuit by a creditor drew him back to New York in 1914. To finance his purchase of control in Mercantile National Bank in 1907, Heinze had given a note to the seller for $630,000, on which Heinze defaulted, following the Panic. Under cross-examination, Heinze testified that although he was president of the Mercantile, he never inspected its books, and instead left such tasks to a vice president of the bank.[10] The court awarded the seller $1.2 million in restitution and damages. In turn, Heinze sued Morse, who had defaulted on a pledge to finance the purchase with $500,000—however, Augustus died before the case could be heard.

Heinze's biographer, Sarah McNelis, wrote that "After the Panic of 1907, he was vastly older, disillusioned, almost distraught in appearance; although he was still quite young, his hair was almost white."[11] Only 44 years old, the garrulous *bon vivant* died alone on November 4, 1914, at his home in Saratoga, New York, from cirrhosis of the liver.[12] He left an estate estimated at $1.5 million[13] ($44 million in purchasing power in 2022).

Charles W. Morse, the confederate of F. Augustus Heinze, has been described as "physically ugly, amoral, rich beyond reason," rapacious, and shady.[14] In January 1910, Morse was convicted of misappropriating bank funds from the Bank of North America (a bank in which he had a controlling interest) and sentenced to 15 years in prison. He began his sentence at the federal penitentiary in Atlanta, where he met Charles Ponzi, who would later become famous for the eponymous pyramid scheme; Ponzi was serving a two-year sentence on a charge of sponsoring illegal immigrants.

Morse believed that he had done nothing wrong that did not occur daily in the financial community. Therefore, he launched a vigorous effort to spring himself, with the assistance of lawyers, lobbyists to the White House, and journalists such as Clarence W. Barron. Mysteriously, Morse grew ill; it was feared that he would die quickly. President Taft commuted Morse's sentence in January 1912 and released him from prison. Thereupon, Morse fled to Europe, after which it was revealed that Morse's "illness" was due to eating soap shortly before his medical exams.[15] In the fall of 1912, Morse returned to the United States and formed a new steamship company, having sold his Consolidated Lines to J. P. Morgan at a steep discount. With the advent of World War I, he bid on ship construction projects for his U.S. shipping company and won contracts for 36 vessels. In 1922, Morse was indicted for fraud and war profiteering but was acquitted.[16] He suffered strokes in the late 1920s and was judged incompetent to manage his own affairs. Morse died of pneumonia on January 12, 1933.

Charles T. Barney, president of the Knickerbocker, was forced out by the failure of the firm. He died from a self-inflicted gunshot wound on November 14, 1907, and was survived by his wife, Lily Whitney Barney, and their two sons. Lily Barney sold their home in Manhattan's Murray Hill district in 1912 and dropped from public view.

His demise might be regarded as indirect or collateral damage of the Panic. He had been affiliated with Charles Morse in some ventures but was not a participant in the attempted corner on United Copper. The Knickerbocker had extended a loan to Charles Morse, collateralized by securities of doubtful value. However, write-off of the loan ($200,000) was not enough to destabilize the Knickerbocker. The appraiser's report in February 1908 suggested solvency and seemed to affirm Barney's assertions in October that the trust company was solvent but suffered a problem of illiquidity.

John W. "Bet-a-Million" Gates was the organizer of the secret syndicate that aimed to build upon TC&I and other assets as a competitor to U.S. Steel. He reluctantly agreed to sell his shares in TC&I when he learned that other members of the syndicate had agreed to do so. He moved to Port Arthur, Texas, where he hoped to resume activities in banking, railroads, and other businesses. In 1911 he discovered a cancerous tumor in his throat, which nearly prevented his testimony at the Stanley Committee Hearings on U.S. Steel. Soon thereafter he traveled to Paris, where he hoped that a difficult operation would cure him. It did not. He died there on August 9, 1911, aged 56. The value of his estate was estimated at between $40 million and $50 million.[17] In a rather lurid biography, Lloyd Wendt and Herman Kogan wrote, "Gates played as fiercely as any, with a sort of barbaric splendor and freedom from scruples, yet sometimes with a peculiar courage and daring. He was without shame, without many moments of remorse."[18]

Grant Schley was the public face of the TC&I ownership syndicate. He sold his shares to U.S. Steel, enabling him to meet collateral calls and weather the Panic of 1907. Upon his death on November 22, 1917, the *New York Times* said that "he had been in failing health for several years and had not taken an active part in the direction of the affairs of his firm for the last ten years."[19] He had been a member of the NYSE and had served prominent clients in the Standard Oil circle.

Public Servants

Theodore Roosevelt acknowledged that he was "gravely harassed and concerned" over the Panic of 1907.[20] He was sensitive to the charges that his policies had triggered the panic and wrote, "I do not think that my policies had anything to do with producing the conditions which brought on the panic; but I do think that very possibly the assaults and exposures which I made, and which were more or less successfully imitated in the several States, have brought on the panic a year or two sooner than would otherwise have been the case. The panic would have been infinitely worse, however, had it been deferred."[21] His other sensitivity about the panic concerned his approval of the Tennessee Coal & Iron acquisition by U.S. Steel. His critics argued that the merger was unnecessary to stem the Panic and that it was a ruse to profit Morgan and his circle. Others complained that Roosevelt's political philosophy was rather empty. For instance, historian Elting E. Morison wrote, "The Square Deal rests upon no more substantial ground than the intuitive feelings of the executive; a broker who thinks of justice as a satisfactory working agreement."[22]

Still, six years later, Roosevelt wrote that his decision on the USS/TC&I deal "offered the only chance for arresting the panic and it did arrest the panic. . . . The panic was stopped, public confidence in the solvency of the threatened institution being at once restored."[23]

Roosevelt was an original item. No previous president offered the combination of massive energy, moral suasion, charisma, and belief in a very strong executive branch. He changed U.S. politics, although, unlike the other faces sculpted into the side of Mount Rushmore, he is remembered more for his style than his substance. Yet his words and policies resonated with the average American, as reflected in his landslide election in 1904 and his significant poll in the 1912 election, as a third-party candidate.

The biographer H. W. Brands wrote, "The frustrating fact for Roosevelt was that, as much as Americans loved him, they didn't particularly heed him."[24] After 1908, Roosevelt never regained the "bully pulpit" of powerful elected office. His political influence lay chiefly in the stream of speeches, articles, and books he produced in retirement. His proposal for progressive programs foreshadowed numerous initiatives of presidents later in the twentieth century. After his electoral defeat in 1912, he embarked on a dangerous exploration of the River of Doubt in Brazil that left him weakened from exertion and disease. An ardent advocate for the projection of U.S. power abroad, he reviled Wilson's policy of neutrality at the outbreak of World War I. When the United States did join the fight in 1917, his four sons volunteered. The youngest boy, Quentin, was killed in 1918, when his airplane was shot down. This plunged Roosevelt into a depression that muted, but did not totally suppress, his public voice. He died on January 6, 1919, in his sleep and was buried at his home, Sagamore Hill, on Oyster Bay, Long Island, New York.

John C. Spooner, who praised J. P. Morgan so lavishly in November 1907, had served in the U.S. Senate for 16 years. Seen by peers as the prominent constitutional authority of his day, he was one of the four powerful committee chairmen who ruled the Senate during the Gilded Age—along with Nelson Aldrich, William Allison, and Orville Pratt. Identified with the "old guard" conservative wing of the Republican Party, Spooner bitterly rejected the progressive impulses of his fellow senator from Wisconsin, Robert La Follette. Although he retired from the Senate in 1907, he remained a political force for years, even declining the offer of a cabinet post as secretary of state in the Taft Administration. Spooner's retirement from politics along with other powerful senators marked the profound shift in politics and orthodoxy during the 1906–1913 era. After leaving the Senate in 1907, Spooner practiced law in New York City and passed away on June 11, 1919.

Carter Glass, in 1913, succeeded Arsene Pujo as chair of the powerful House Banking and Currency Committee. Then, in 1918, Woodrow Wilson appointed Glass to be the secretary of the Treasury, in which post Glass oversaw the final Victory Loan bond issue after the Armistice. As Treasury secretary, he held a place on the Federal Reserve Board, where he pressured the Fed to maintain low interest rates until the completion of the bond flotation. The Fed's policies during Glass's tenure contributed to the wave of inflation after the end of World War I.

From 1920 until 1946, Glass served as U.S. senator from Virginia, ultimately rising to chair of the Senate Appropriations Committee and president pro tempore of the Senate. During the New Deal, Glass co-sponsored the Glass–Steagall Act of 1933 that divided commercial banks from investment banking and established federal deposit insurance. He also allied with the Southern bloc of legislators who supported states' rights and Jim Crow segregation. Glass opposed much of Franklin D. Roosevelt's New Deal agenda. He died on May 28, 1946.

In 1927 Glass published a memoir[25] of the development of the Federal Reserve Act. The book rebutted assertions about the paternity of the Fed, rejecting a professor's suggestion that Wilson's adviser, Colonel E. M. House, had designed the concept of the Federal Reserve System. And the book devoted a chapter to discounting Senator Aldrich's contributions. Glass acknowledged the contributions of Senator Owen, Secretary McAdoo, William Jennings Bryan, and President Wilson. However, the thrust of the book asserted the leading role he played in the design and passage of the Federal Reserve Act.

Nelson Aldrich served Rhode Island in the U.S. Senate from October 1881 until March 3, 1911, when he retired in declining health. He was committed to tariff protection and the gold standard, pillars of Republican orthodoxy during the Gilded Age. Progressives saw him as an ally of business interests and of the financial community. He died on April 16, 1915, aged 73.

His daughter, Abigail, married John D. Rockefeller, Jr.; their second son was Nelson A. Rockefeller, who served as governor of New York and vice president of the United States. Other descendants included David Rockefeller (chairman of Chase Bank), Richard Aldrich (U.S. representative), Jay Rockefeller (U.S. senator), and Winthrop Rockefeller (governor of Arkansas).

The economic historian Elmus Wicker (2000) argued that Nelson Aldrich had not been adequately recognized in histories of founding the Fed. He said that Aldrich was instrumental in shifting the focus of reform away from debates over asset-based currency and toward central banking. As a former defender of the old financial orthodoxy, his leadership for change was courageous and decisive. The Aldrich–Vreeland Act provided crucial liquidity during the financial crisis of 1914, a time when the new Fed was not entirely functional. And the Aldrich plan for a central bank offered several provisions that were eventually inserted into the Federal Reserve Act. Wicker wrote, "Carter Glass, the so-called 'father' of the Federal Reserve Act, and Parker Willis, his close associate, went out of their way to repudiate Aldrich's influence, but it is now becoming increasingly clear that Aldrich deserves equal, if not top billing with Glass as a cofounder of the Federal Reserve System."[26]

Robert M. La Follette served Wisconsin in the U.S. Senate from 1906 until the date of his death, June 18, 1925. A staunch progressive, he clashed with conservative Republicans and eventually helped to lead progressives out of the Republican Party. During World War I, he opposed American entry into the war. In 1924, he ran as a third-party candidate for the White House, advocating nationalization of railroads and electric utilities, affirmation of rights to unionize, income redistribution through taxation, opposition to child labor, and abundant credit provisions to farmers.

Augustus O. Stanley served in the House of Representatives until 1915, as governor of Kentucky from 1915 to 1919, and as U.S. senator from Kentucky until 1925. Stanley's politics reflected the rickety Democratic Party coalition of the early twentieth century: urban progressives, country populists, organized labor, and Southern segregationists. He fought official corruption, promoted workmen's compensation, railed against industrial concentration, opposed prohibition of alcohol, and advocated convict labor. However, he opposed bigotry and the Ku Klux Klan, which contributed to his defeat for reelection to the Senate in 1924. Thereafter, he practiced law, and served from 1930 to 1954 on the International Joint Commission that resolved boundary issues between the United States and Canada. He died in Washington, DC on August 12, 1958.

Charles A. Lindbergh, Sr. served five terms in the House of Representatives advocating progressive domestic policies and isolationist stances in foreign affairs. He ran unsuccessfully for the Senate in 1916 and for governor of Minnesota in 1918 and 1924. He died on May 24, 1924, three years before his son made the historic solo flight across the Atlantic.

Arsene Pujo represented Louisiana in the House of Representatives from 1903 until his retirement from politics in 1913. Returning to his hometown, Lake Charles, he practiced law. He died on December 31, 1939, aged 78.

Samuel L. Untermyer, after the conclusion of the Pujo Committee hearings, lobbied unsuccessfully to renew and broaden the investigation. Thereafter, he resumed the practice of law in New York, periodically engaging in federal and state-level appointments and in Democratic Party initiatives. An active Zionist, he also helped to found the Anti-Nazi League in 1933, which advocated a boycott of Germany. He died on March 16, 1940, aged 82.

William Gibbs McAdoo served as Secretary of the Treasury in the Wilson administration from 1913 to 1918. Among his boldest acts was to close the New York Stock Exchange at the outbreak of World War I to prevent panicked liquidation of U.S. securities by foreign investors, and generally to retain gold reserves in the United States. In 1914, he married Woodrow Wilson's daughter. During the war, he also served as director general of Railroads, essentially the leader of the nationalized railroad system. Though a serious candidate for U.S. president in 1920 and 1924, he failed to gain the Democratic Party nomination because of an unwillingness to denounce the Ku Klux Klan, among other reasons. He represented California in the U.S. Senate from 1933 to 1938 and died on February 1, 1941, aged 77.

Robert L. Owen joined the U.S. Senate in 1907, as one of the first two senators from Oklahoma and served until 1925. Active in many progressive causes, he promoted the candidacy of William Jennings Bryan for president, advocated reforms in Native American affairs, sought the reduction of import duties, and criticized the Federal Reserve for its deflationary policies in the 1920s and 1930s. In 1920, he sought unsuccessfully the Democratic Party nomination for president. He passed away on July 19, 1947, aged 91.

Woodrow Wilson's policies intervened in the private economy more extensively than any predecessor's—more so than Theodore Roosevelt and Taft, and subsequently eclipsed only by Franklin D. Roosevelt. Progressivism reached its zenith during Wilson's first term in the White House. He kindled or realized important initiatives in a variety of areas including financial-sector regulation, the income tax, direct election of senators, lowering the tariff, and strengthening antitrust regulation. During World War I, the executive branch nationalized major sectors of the economy, setting the precedent for extensive central planning during World War II.

Arguably, the Federal Reserve Act was the pinnacle of the Progressive Movement and of Wilson's first term. It aimed to displace market mechanisms with state direction, personal agency with institutional agency, opacity with transparency, rigid currency with "elastic" money, private oligopoly with government coordination, and concentration of reserves with broad distribution. Consistent with the progressives' belief in dispassionate research and expertise, oversight of the nation's money and banking would be placed in a committee of public-spirited national leaders and experts. What could go wrong? This transformation set a provocative example that would help to inspire the New Deal and Great Society administrations of Franklin D. Roosevelt and Lyndon B. Johnson, respectively.

Seeking to place America on the global stage, Wilson brokered the Versailles Treaty negotiations in 1919 (a plan that John Maynard Keynes famously savaged and that set the stage for global instability in the 1920s and 1930s). Unfortunately for Wilson's treaty, public sentiment in the United States swung from internationalism to isolationism. Undeterred, Wilson slogged on, ultimately resorting to a whistle-stop campaign across America to muster public support. During the trip in October 1919, Wilson suffered a debilitating stroke. Absent Wilson's advocacy, the Senate defeated the Treaty. For the next year, the First Lady and two presidential assistants virtually ran the Wilson administration, a development that eventually prompted adoption in 1967 of the 25th Amendment to the Constitution to provide for official succession in the event of presidential disability. Wilson died on February 3, 1924, at age 67.

Crisis Fighters

George F. Baker rose from president of First National Bank of New York to chairman of the board in 1909, in which role he served until 1926. He died May 2, 1931, at age 91, leaving an estate estimated as high as $500 million ($8.9 billion in 2022 purchasing power). His philanthropy supported 20 universities, 15 hospitals, and 17 New York institutions[27] and included a $5 million gift in 1924 to Harvard Business School for the construction of its campus. Upon the announcement of his death, contemporaries during the Panic of 1907 remembered Baker's leadership—George B. Cortelyou said that "he was always courageous, wise and far-seeing and therefore a great stabilizing force especially in times of stress and strain."[28]

He steadfastly resisted giving interviews to the press until late in life and was called the "Sphinx of Wall Street."[29] He told a reporter, "Business men of America should reduce their talk at least two-thirds. . . . Every one should reduce his talk. There is rarely ever a reason good enough for anybody to talk. Silence uses up much less energy. I don't talk because silence is the secret of success. There, I've broken my record. Tell the others they needn't come in. And get out."[30]

Henry P. Davison became a senior partner at J. P. Morgan & Company in 1909. In testimony at the Pujo hearings, Davison was one of the most articulate defenders of bankers as stewards of the public interest. Davison argued that the banker should be a director of corporations because of

> *. . . his moral responsibility as sponsor for the corporation's securities, to keep an eye upon its policies and to protect the interests of investors in the securities of that corporation . . . in general [bankers] enter only those boards which the opinion of the investing public requires them to enter, as evidence of good faith that they are willing to have their names publicly associated with the management.*[31]

In August 1914, Davison persuaded the governments of France and Britain to grant J. P. Morgan & Company a monopoly franchise on underwriting bonds issued by those governments in the United States. During World War I, he raised funds for the American Red Cross to supply ambulances to the American Army in France. He pressed for the formation of the International Red Cross, an association of the national Red Cross organizations, a goal that was achieved in 1919. Following two unsuccessful operations to excise a brain tumor, he died in 1922 at the age of 55.

George W. Perkins retired from J. P. Morgan & Company in 1910 at the age of 48. His early retirement was described by his family as a desire to "devote most of his time to public work."[32] He worked for Theodore Roosevelt's presidential campaign in 1912 and continued as a political adviser thereafter. During World War I, he worked to organize food supplies for the army and assisted the YMCA in raising money for relief work among soldiers. He also raised funds to create Palisades Park. Thereafter he subsided from public view, a remarkable change for one of the most creative and effective players in the New York financial community. Perkins had been a major architect of the combinations that created International Harvester and U.S. Steel, and had lifted New York Life Insurance Company to the top echelon of its industry by daringly eliminating intermediaries in the distribution of life insurance services in the United States.

Perkins died June 18, 1920, following a nervous breakdown in May. Papers reported that he contracted influenza in France and had not fully recovered when he resumed work. The *New York Tribune* said that he died from "acute inflammation of the brain, the result of complete nervous exhaustion due to intense and continuous overwork."[33]

James Stillman was president of National City Bank from 1891 to 1909 and chairman of the board from 1909 to 1919. A biographer described Stillman as a

> *carefully-dressed, smallish man, with the tall hat and the inevitable cigar, who didn't answer sometimes for twenty minutes, but fixed one with his clear, dark eyes and his air of immense dignity, presented a really fascinating enigma. His mental power*

> *was as great as his shyness and, like many shy people who inspire fear in others, he preferred those who were not afraid of him. . . . Throughout his day's work, there was manifest intensity visible in the concentration, in the careful calculation of each problem, in the dislike of hearing any details discussed, while yet expecting them to be carefully watched.*[34]

Stillman foresaw the massive economic changes in America and positioned the bank to serve them. He envisioned that National City Bank would provide "any service" that the modern large corporations would require. In February 1907, Stillman wrote:

> *I firmly believe . . . That the most successful banks will be the ones that can do something else than the mere receiving and loaning of money. That does not require a very high order of ability but devising methods of serving people and [of] attracting business without resorting to unconservative or unprofitable methods, that opens limited fields for study, ability and resourcefulness and few only will be found to do it.*[35]

Thereafter, National City Bank broadened its range of services, expanded its service to institutions and individuals, and reached to new locations. Stillman implemented a decentralized, multidivisional structure. Historians Harold Cleveland and Thomas Huertas have argued that by the start of the twentieth century, National City was a truly "modern" corporation, a leading firm in its industry. Stillman died, still chairman, in March 1918. In 1955, National City Bank merged with First National Bank of New York to form Citibank, forerunner of Citigroup, one of the largest American financial institutions in the early twenty-first century.

Benjamin Strong rose to president of Bankers Trust and served in that capacity until 1914, when he was appointed the first governor of the Federal Reserve Bank of New York. He served in that capacity until October 1928, when he died at age 55 of an intestinal abscess. He was the "prime mover . . . dominant figure" of the Federal Reserve System from its inception, said Milton Friedman and Anna Schwartz.[36] He had grasped the need for international coordination to assist Europe's recovery from World War I and was a leading proponent of "easy money" policies that drove the boom in the stock market in the 1920s and its eventual reckoning in 1929.[37]

In a note to another governor written shortly before his death, Strong advocated aggressive use of open market operations to flood the market with liquidity in the event of another financial crisis. Unfortunately, Strong's successors ignored the advice and for three years pursued deflationary policies with disastrous effect. Economists Friedman and Schwartz attributed the severity of the Great Depression to "the shift of power within the System and the lack of understanding and experience of the individuals to whom the power shifted."[38] The *Wall Street Journal* eulogized him: "His services were of the highest value and conditions today might have been different if his health had permitted undivided attention to his office for the past three months."[39]

Frank A. Vanderlip worked for National City Bank from 1904 until 1919. His most important contribution to the aftermath of the Panic of 1907 was to be the ghostwriter of the "Aldrich Plan," in which he drafted proposed legislation to establish the modern Federal Reserve System.[40] Vanderlip rose to president of National City Bank in 1909. His important innovation was the founding of the first foreign branch in Buenos Aires—this was the first foreign branch for *any* U.S. national bank. He also led the organizing of American International Corporation in November 1915, an investment trust intended to funnel American capital to foreign projects and companies. Vanderlip chafed under Stillman's voting control of National City Bank and sought from Stillman an option to buy his shares. Stillman refused. Poor in health, Stillman spent much of 1917 in Paris.

Vanderlip continued to promote the internationalization of the bank and made the unfortunate decision to open a branch in Moscow, just after the Russian Revolution. The branch's assets were soon nationalized, leaving National City Bank exposed to repay deposits in that branch from dollars in New York—an exposure equal to 40 percent of the bank's capital. Stillman returned to New York, placed Vanderlip on leave, and died soon thereafter. Control of the bank passed to Stillman's son. Vanderlip resigned in June 1919.[41] Stillman's son proved to be an incompetent executive and resigned in May 1921, turning management of the company over to a new cohort of professional executives who demanded, and were given, an equity interest in the bank. Frank Vanderlip died on June 29, 1927.

Thomas W. Lamont stayed with J. P. Morgan & Company for his entire career, becoming a partner in 1910 and rising to the position of chairman of the board in 1943. He was acting head of the firm on "Black Thursday," October 24, 1929, when he committed the company to large purchases of stocks in an effort to instill confidence in the market. He served on various semiofficial assignments for the U.S. government, including the 1919 Paris Peace Negotiations that led to the Treaty of Versailles. He died on February 2, 1948. His son, Corliss Lamont, was a philosophy professor at Columbia and a socialist. His other son, Thomas Stillwell Lamont, rose to vice chairman of Morgan Guaranty Trust Company. His grandson, Ned Lamont, was the antiwar candidate for U.S. Senate in Connecticut in 2006.

J. P. "Jack" Morgan Jr. arrived in Europe at the height of the Panic to assist his father with the attempt to arrange gold loans from the central bank of France to U.S. banks. The French, concerned about the deepening crisis, insisted on a guarantee of the loan from the U.S. government. Roosevelt refused on grounds that this would set the precedent for government guarantees of private deals. Eventually, Jack's negotiations led to gold imports from European sources. Jack was back in the United States by January 1908. He worked in the shadow of his famous father and the luminous financiers at J. P. Morgan & Company, such as George Perkins, Henry Davison, and Thomas Lamont. Jack's work at the firm proceeded quietly. In 1910, he was active in organizing the London affiliate, Morgan, Grenfell. Later that year, he sustained a partial nervous breakdown that removed him from business for some months. (Like his father, Jack suffered bouts of "the blues," as he called them.)

Jack followed the build-up to the Pujo hearings and then coached his father in preparing to testify. Upon Pierpont's death in 1913, Jack became the senior partner of the firm. The firm won the mandate as sole financier for French and British purchases in the United States during World War I. In 1915, a German sympathizer attempted to assassinate Jack, almost killing him with two shots in the abdomen. This generated popular sympathy for him. Upon his return to work, a crowd gathered to applaud. In the following years, he assisted the war effort, helped to reorganize General Motors, financed corporate growth in the 1920s, reorganized J. P. Morgan & Company in the 1930s, and rationalized his father's massive art collection. Though he was a senior partner of the firm, Jack relied increasingly upon Thomas W. Lamont as, in effect, chief executive. Jack died of a heart attack on March 13, 1943, at the age of 75. His biographer, John Forbes, said, "Morgan was a team player and submerged his own personality in the firm, where he managed with consummate skill to hold together a group of highly skilled and individualistic partners and make maximum use of their separate gifts to achieve very substantial results."[42]

Paul Warburg, after passage of the Federal Reserve Act in 1913, continued to advise on monetary matters, while working as an investment banker at Kuhn, Loeb. He accepted appointment to the first group of governors of the Federal Reserve, serving as a governor from 1914 to 1918. And then from 1916 to 1918, he served as vice chair of the Federal Reserve Board. He passed away on January 24, 1932, at the age of 63.

Arguably, Warburg was the intellectual locomotive of the movement toward a central bank. His early proposals for a central bank formed the core of the Jekyll Island plan and of Nelson Aldrich's proposal for a National Reserve Association. Even the Federal Reserve Act retained elements of his ideas. Certainly, his ceaseless advocacy before, during, and after the Panic of 1907 helped to drive the monumental shift in economic orthodoxy toward central banking. His two-volume memoir about the origin and growth of the Federal Reserve system, published in 1930, continued that advocacy, especially for centralization of the system and for control by experts who understood banking. The undercurrent of the memoir is a lament about the distortions of good ideas by ill-informed and inexpert politicians.

George B. Cortelyou remained as Secretary of the Treasury until the end of the Roosevelt administration in 1908. During the early jockeying of successors to Roosevelt, Cortelyou emerged as a potential candidate, only to be stopped when Roosevelt endorsed Taft. In January 1908, rumors circulated that Cortelyou was to be named president of the resurrected Knickerbocker Trust Company—until he disavowed his interest in the position. He threw his support behind the concept of a central bank for the United States, because, based on his experience, the Treasury did not have the power to maintain stability of the financial system during a crisis. Failing to win an appointment in the Taft administration, he left the public sector. On January 13, 1909, the *New York Times* reported that he would become the chief executive officer of Consolidated Gas Company, headquartered in New York City. He died on October 23, 1940, in New York.

The newspaper headlines, memoirs, and other accounts of the Panic of 1907 seem to relegate Cortelyou to subordinate status as a crisis fighter. This is unfortunate. Figure 23.1 shows that on short notice, Cortelyou deposited between $54 million and $64 million in cash into the national

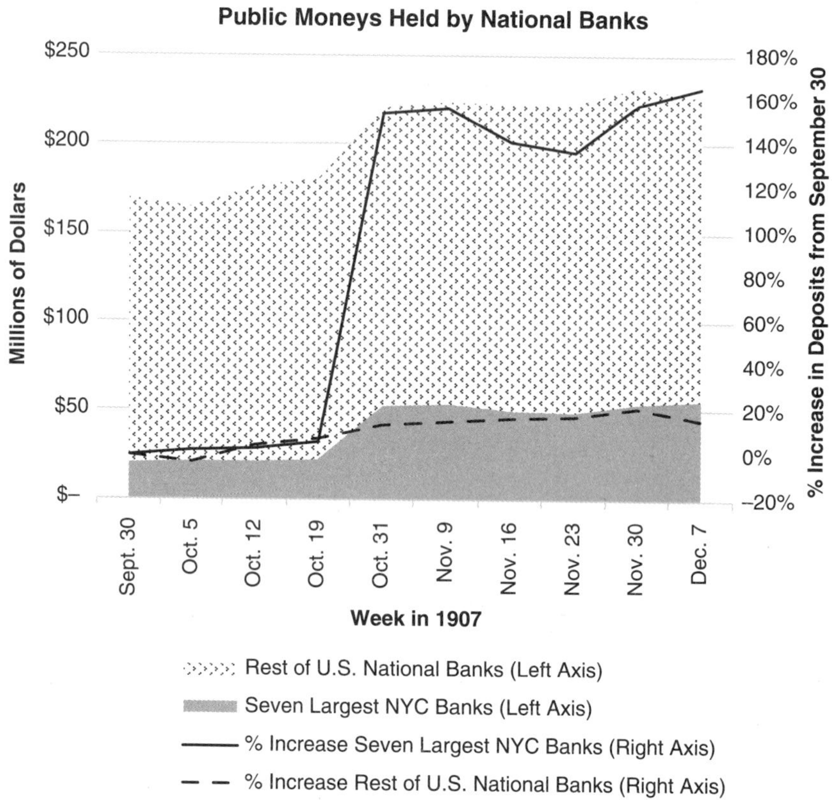

Figure 23.1 Time Series of the Stock of U.S. Treasury Deposits of Public Funds in National Banks During the Panic

NOTE: The lines in this figure indicate the cumulative percentage change in deposits from September 30 to the date indicated. The shaded areas indicate the balance of deposits at each date.

SOURCE: Authors' figure, based on data in *Response of the Secretary of the Treasury to Senate Resolution No. 33 of December 12, 1907*, January 29, 1908, Washington, DC: Government Printing Office, pp. 37–72.

banks across the nation, of which a maximum of $34 million went to seven large New York banks.[43] The asymmetry of how the deposits were distributed became a lightning rod of Congressional criticism for Cortelyou after the Panic.

The point is that Cortelyou mobilized such a large amount of money that it rendered him a major player during the crisis. Moen and Rodgers report that J. P. Morgan directed the deployment of about $96 million in facilities, to which his firm contributed as much as $50 million or as little as $1.5 million.[44] Research has yet to reveal whether and to what extent funds Morgan and his circle deployed were supplied by Cortelyou. But based on gross commitments, it appears that Cortelyou and Morgan deployed funds of a similar order of magnitude.

What may matter more than the size of rescue funds was the impact they achieved. Jon Moen and Mary Tone Rodgers note "[p]erhaps the timing of Morgan's facilities was more important than their sizes because they occurred near the beginning of the crisis, thus blunting contagion early on."[45] And as this narrative shows, the *focus* of Morgan's facilities was targeted toward particular rescues, serving as a lender of last resort on the spot at the center of the crisis.

In contrast, Cortelyou briefly visited New York City during the crisis and generally deployed funds from Washington, DC, to national banks across the country (but predominantly in New York), which he expected would reliquefy the financial system and direct funds to best use. And his proposed offering of Panama Canal bonds and 3 percent Notes in November enabled banks to expand the volume of banknotes in circulation, although in the final event this scheme had only marginal impact. Finally, Cortelyou's public expressions of confidence lent the weight of the federal government to the effort of redirecting public sentiment from fear to recovery. Cortelyou genuinely earned the praise he received as a crisis fighter.

In short, Cortelyou and Morgan played crucial but different roles in the Panic. Both deserved recognition for their significant efforts.

J. Pierpont Morgan emerged from the Panic of 1907 lauded by some and hated by others even more than before. Letters and cables of congratulations for his leadership poured in. He and his firm enjoyed a robust volume of corporate financing business buoyed by his reputation in the crisis. In 1910, Harvard granted him an honorary doctorate. By 1912, he was withdrawing seriously from daily business to focus on philanthropy and his beloved collection of books and art.

The panic had inflamed the longstanding belief among progressives that Morgan's success was due to anticompetitive behavior. Morgan, the organizer of large corporate combinations, was famous for combating "ruinous competition." Thus, the Pujo hearings, nominally covering the structure of corporate finance in America, was focused particularly on J. P. Morgan & Company, and its senior partner, Pierpont.

He left for Europe on January 7, 1913, shortly after giving testimony in the Pujo hearings. Touring through Egypt, he fell ill on February 13 with what his doctor said was "general physical and nervous exhaustion resulting from prolonged excessive strain in elderly subject."[46] Pierpont died in Rome on March 31, 1913, aged 75. Thomas Lamont wrote that the effect of the Pujo hearings "upon Mr. Morgan's physical powers was devastating."[47]

Without question, Morgan had promoted industrial consolidation throughout the Gilded Age, which earned the progressives' and populists' scorn for monopolization (or "Morganization," as some called it). His wealth, trips to Europe, and art collecting sharpened public concerns about economic inequality. His push for industrial consolidation was motivated by economic gain. Yet his words and deeds are also consistent with a desire to improve the performance of businesses whose securities he underwrote. He saw that technological innovation during the Second Industrial Revolution would yield new economies of scale and scope, if managed well. As the leading channel of foreign direct investment into the booming American economy, he stewarded the interests of foreign (and domestic) investors. It was a risky age for investors, before Generally Accepted Accounting Principles, public accounting, and federal regulations of markets, securities, corporations, and financial institutions. Displacing corrupt and incompetent management, shutting down inefficient operations, and rationalizing industries, Morgan disciplined the business economy to yield performance that investors—and society—needed.

In 1907, Morgan was not the only notable crisis fighter. Cortelyou and the New York Clearing House played important roles as well. But Morgan's signal contributions were to recognize threats to systemic stability before others and *quickly* to galvanize *collective action* among bankers in a *targeted* way. A study of lender-of-last-resort rescues by various actors during the Panic by Jon Moen and Mary Tone Rodgers found that Morgan's "individual LOLR efforts may have been distinguishable from institutional efforts by the Clearing House and the U.S. Treasury."[48] They ascribed Morgan's success to his reputation as an informed market agent, a source of valuable advice and rescue loans, and his experience in dealing with earlier crises. Morgan demonstrated an ability to mobilize his social and financial network in ways that others apparently could not. Quite simply, he *took action, persuaded others to do so, too, and had an effective impact.*

Morgan's leadership during the Panic of 1907 is of a piece with his values of stewardship and industrial stability. There is no question that throughout the Panic his firm earned interest on rescue loans (they were not gifts), that systemic stability aligned with his business interests, and that adversaries (Charles Barney and Charles Morse) suffered. But archives have yet to yield direct evidence that, as La Follette, Heinze, Lefèvre, and others claimed, Morgan and his associates engineered the panic for their own benefit with the intention of crushing adversaries—this claim warrants further research. So do the decisions by National Bank of Commerce, the NYCH, and Morgan not to support the Knickerbocker Trust Company. However, the preponderance of Morgan's leadership during the Panic is more consistent with stewardship for the public good than mere personal gain. To acknowledge that is less to elevate J. Pierpont Morgan to the status of a hero, and more to affirm the importance of human agency in business and economic affairs.

Chapter 24

Reflections and Lessons

History does not repeat itself.
But it rhymes.

—Mark Twain[1]

The recurrence of financial crises prompts analysts to scour history for precedents and solutions. This is right and useful. History matters. The thoughtful reader should draw insights from events such as the Panic of 1907. Yet caution is warranted: historical events rarely map perfectly onto the present day—they only *rhyme*. And history is easily abused, a fact that should prompt any reader to think critically of authors' attempts to draw large ideas from particular facts.[2] Nevertheless, narrating historical events without also discussing their implications is a classic error in the world of practical affairs. Therefore, with a sense of obligation tempered by humility we close this history by highlighting some lessons, questions, and avenues for future research:

- *The role of a boom before a crisis.* Not all booms spawn financial crises. So, what was it about 1897–1906 that should prompt one to scrutinize future booms as possible cradles for crises?

- *The attributes of a vulnerable financial system pre-crisis.* By general assent, the U.S. financial system was unprepared for the challenges of the Panic of 1907. To what aspects of unpreparedness should one give special attention?
- *Shocks.* Economic surprises happen all the time, yet major financial crises are less frequent. What was it about the San Francisco earthquake that should focus one's attention to those shocks worth worrying about?
- *Outbreak of crisis and contagion.* In a complex financial system, where do crises tend to begin? How and why might they spread quickly?
- *The crisis response.* The Panic of 1907 shows that speed, amount of resources, focus, leadership, and collective action have an impact. How and why do they matter?
- *The long tail.* We have argued that the entire *progression* of a crisis should include attention to spillovers into the economy, society, and polity—such ripples could extend for years.

These and other possible issues should summon the thoughtful reader to explore financial crises for what they can teach. Harvesting the teachable moment of the Panic of 1907 is the ultimate aim of this volume.

Boom Before a Crisis

If not all booms spawn financial crises, why did the boom of 1897–1906 end in one? How might one discern a crisis-prone boom from the rest?

The association of booms with financial crises is a staple of economic analyses. For instance, Austrian economists particularly point to excessive growth in credit. Keynesians assert that overinvestment in the private sector eventually leads to a realization that supply has outstripped demand and to layoffs and cutbacks in capital spending. A study by Robin Greenwood and colleagues found that rapid expansion of credit and asset price growth over a brief period such as three years is associated with a nearly 40 percent likelihood of entering a financial crisis in the next three years.[3]

"Irrational exuberance" and overshooting in asset prices are also standard attributes of the lore of stock market booms.[4] In the decade before 1907, a sentiment of optimism and confidence underpinned the boom. President Roosevelt's State of the Union addresses from 1901 to 1906 congratulated the nation on its prosperity.

The discussion in Chapter 1 profiled the decade before the Panic of 1907 as a time of rapid economic expansion, growth in credit that outpaced the growth in the economy, banks' declining cash reserves, vaulting optimism, and rising speculation in the stock market. Occurring independently, such factors may not be a concern. But in concert, they profile a boom that may be vulnerable to economic shocks.

A Vulnerable Financial System

The structure of a financial system can strengthen resilience against shocks or worsen a vulnerability to them. Chapter 1 gave evidence of the large number of financial institutions in the United States in 1907—21,986[5]—all without a central bank. The vast majority of these were small "unit" banks having no branches. The market for financial services was highly fractionalized and localized. Various institutions were linked through transactional and contractual (depositary) relationships. Also, many institutions served the same investors and depositors, deepening the interdependence among institutions. In short, what stands out about the U.S. financial sector in 1907 were the extensive linkages among institutions and high complexity of the system. Tight linkage and complexity set the stage of vulnerability.

Linkage arises from relationships among banks and from having many of the same borrowers, investors, and depositors. Bankers' reserves could be "pyramided," a practice that amplified the sensitive linkage among financial institutions, especially between interior and money center institutions. And the formation of bank clearing houses in selected cities in the nineteenth century ensured the linkage among banks in those cities. The difficulties of one financial intermediary could spread to others.

The complexity of a financial system means that it would be difficult for all participants in the financial system to be well informed. Inevitably, some people would know more than others—information asymmetry is the source of the problem of adverse selection (discussed in the Introduction and Chapter 7) that can trigger or worsen a financial crisis. Economists Charles Calomiris, Gary Gorton, and others[6] suggest that runs begin when some depositors observe negative information about the value of bank assets—shocking news of some kind—and withdraw their deposits. Unable to discriminate perfectly between sound and unsound banks and observing a wave of withdrawals, other depositors follow suit. A run begins. In a world of unequally distributed information, some depositors will find it costly to ascertain the solvency of their banks. Thus, runs might be a rational means of monitoring the performance of banks, a crude means of forcing the banks to reveal to depositors the adequacy of their assets and reserves.

Information asymmetry played a major role in the events of 1907. Viewed from a century later, one is struck by how little the average depositor—or even J. P. Morgan himself—could know about the condition of financial institutions. To resolve this asymmetry, Morgan privately chartered audits of the assets of various institutions and debtors. But he must have known that the more serious asymmetry lay not between him and the institutions, but between the public and the institutions—therefore, Morgan attempted to use the press, and even the pulpits, to shape public perceptions about the safety and soundness of the financial system.

To summarize, *linkages* mean that trouble can travel. *Complexity* makes it difficult to know the location and nature of the trouble. The architecture of the system sets the stage for crisis; complexity and linkage are always present in a financial system. What makes such a system prone to crisis is the lack of resilience owing, for instance, to the absence of or reduction in shock absorbers such as cash reserves (to maintain liquidity) and capital (to maintain solvency) in the face of shocks.

In a system, trouble spreads unless shock absorbers exist to stop it. In 1907, such shock absorbers took the form of the insurance companies, which paid claims on the San Francisco earthquake and fire damage; the Bank of England and the U.S. Treasury, which sought to promote a sufficient supply of currency; the required reserves of banks; and the pooling of risks in local clearing houses.

The difficulty facing banks and the financial system in 1907 was how to forestall the spread of the crisis throughout the country and abroad. Risk pooling and mutual assistance commitments through the formation of bank clearing houses were prominent lines of defense. The use of clearing house certificates was widespread in 1907—the dollar volume of certificates issued exceeded the volume of certificates issued in the previous great panic (1893) by a factor of between two and four times.[7] Some banks resorted to advertising the probity and connections of their directors, their financial record, and the size of their equity capital base.[8]

The whole question is whether the safety buffers in existence are adequate to prevent the spread of potential shocks. What matters is the resilience *relative* to the size of the available assets and the size of potential shocks, which the buffer is meant to absorb. Over time, the size and complexity of the economy will outgrow the sophistication of static financial safety buffers.

Economic Shocks

Shocks of some kind are all around us, yet the financial system wavers relatively infrequently. What was it about the San Francisco earthquake that should focus one's attention on the shocks worth worrying about?

Our narrative highlights several shocking events: the collapse of the copper corner and Otto Heinze & Company, the suspension of the Knickerbocker Trust Company, and the Bank of England's curtailment of the acceptance of American finance bills in London. Yet the catastrophe in San Francisco overshadows the other shocks in terms of four defining attributes of the word "shock":

1. *Real, not cosmetic.* A "real" event is one that affects economic fundamentals: a variation in agricultural harvest, the introduction of new technology or some other disruptive innovation, massive labor unrest, large demographic changes (such as due to war, immigration, or disease), the opening of new markets, deregulation or reregulation, or an earthquake.[9]
2. *Large and costly.* The trigger of a major financial crisis must be meaningful enough to shake the system. It must cause a material downward shift in outlook among most investors.

3. *Unambiguous.* A shock is a signal to investors. For it to cause a major shift in expectations among investors, the event must stand apart from the noise in the marketplace. And most investors must agree on its implications. Moreover, the signal must be authentic and impossible for a casual participant to send.
4. *Surprising.* For an event to qualify as a shock, it must be unanticipated. Indeed, it is the surprise that causes the sudden shift in expectations that triggers the crisis. Predicting shocks is an impossibility.[10]

From the perspective of these attributes, the trigger for the crisis in 1907 occurred well before the actual panic in the fall. The San Francisco earthquake commenced a process that, along with the Bank of England's restriction on finance bills and the financial strains from rapid economic growth, culminated in the Panic. Contrary to conventional accounts, the economic chain of causation in the Panic of 1907 began in April 1906 and not with the failure of the copper corner or the Knickerbocker Trust Company.

Outbreak of Crisis and Contagion

Not only are financial crises hard to foresee, but they are also hard to detect in their early stages. To what part of the financial system might one look for the outbreak of a crisis? And how and why do they spread quickly?

Origin in the periphery of the financial system. It is interesting that banks were relatively stable during the Panic of 1907.[11] Instead, a few New York City trust companies proved to be the source of greatest instability. Brokerage firms also featured prominently: the failure of Otto Heinze & Co. and the distress of Moore & Schley marked major turning points in the episode. The economists Ellis Tallman and Jon Moen (1990) found that the trust companies were a key source of instability leading up to the Panic of 1907. The unequal regulation of banks and trust companies led to a concentration of riskier assets in trust companies. The trusts took advantage of opportunities from which the banks were restricted. Moreover, the trusts were able to concentrate their portfolios more.

A chain is as strong as its most vulnerable link. Weak links in a financial system tend to be somewhat beyond the gaze of the guardians of prudence and stability—not only regulators, but also accountants, securities analysts, journalists, and even shareholders, few of whom were material influences on corporate governance in 1907. Hugh Rockoff argued that "it is always the shadow banks," unregulated or lightly regulated financial institutions, whose failure seems to herald crises.[12]

Contagion and sentiment. The events of 1907 suggest an emotional influence on the occurrence and severity of financial crises. Our history recounts suicides, manic or depressed markets, anxiety among depositors and bank executives, animated crowds in the streets of New York's financial district, use by financial leaders of public relations and the press in an attempt to build investor confidence—indeed, the very word *panic* suggests a suspension of rationality. In *The Psychology of the Stock Market*, published in 1912, G. C. Selden wrote:

> *Both the panic and the boom are eminently psychological phenomena. This is not saying that the fundamental conditions do not warrant sharp declines in prices and at other times equally sharp advances. But the panic, properly so-called, represents a decline greater than is warranted by conditions usually because of an excited state of the public mind accompanied by exhaustion of resources; while the term "boom" is used to mean an excessive and largely speculative advance. . . . It is really astonishing what a hold the fear of a possible panic has on the minds of many investors. The memory of the events of 1907 undoubtedly operated greatly to lessen the volume of speculative trade from that time to the present.*[13]

This echoes the perspective of a range of authors whose books' very titles argue the case: *Irrational Exuberance* (Robert Shiller); *Extraordinary Popular Delusions and the Madness of Crowds* (Charles Mackay); *The Crowd: A Study of the Popular Mind* (Gustave Le Bon); and *Manias, Panics, and Crashes* (Charles P. Kindleberger). In his classic text for investors, *Reminiscences of a Stock Operator*, Edwin Lefèvre wrote, "A speculator's deadly enemies are ignorance, greed, fear, and hope."[14] In his analytic exploration, *Why Markets Crash*, Didier Sornette has argued that the root of aberrant market trends is one of the best-documented findings: people tend to be overconfident. His analysis of crashes suggests that herding and imitative behavior by investors lead to self-reinforcing market trends that are ultimately sharply reversed.

Optimism or pessimism is defined *relative* to fundamental values.[15] The extent to which market prices depart from those dictated by economic fundamentals remains a topic of keen debate at the frontier of economics. A financial "panic" challenges assumptions about the rationality of economic decision makers. Rationality assumes that prices today reasonably reflect an expectation of prices tomorrow and that markets are efficient in impounding news into asset prices. On balance, large markets in standard assets appear to be rational on average and over time. But crashes and panics are the exceptions to such "average" assumptions. To suspend the assumption of rationality admits the possibility of a great deal of bizarre behavior.

The Crisis Response

We can map the ways in which leaders respond to financial crises along a range of dimensions, such as timeliness, amount of resources committed by crisis fighters, focus, commitment, rhetoric or exhortation, and collective action. How and why do they matter?

Timeliness. Professor Sprague criticized banks for their slow response to the rapidly worsening situation. Then and now observers judge that extending financial assistance to the Knickerbocker on October 22, 1907, would have forestalled the crisis. Economic historians Ellis Tallman and Jon Moen opined, "In retrospect, the decision to allow Knickerbocker Trust to fail appears to have been a mistake."[16] On the other hand, Morgan's timely loans in response to the distresses of the Trust Company of America and the NYSE proved adroit.[17]

Size. Secretary Cortelyou directed the deposit of up to $64 million into national banks for the purpose of meeting depositors' withdrawals reliquefying the financial system. Morgan's circle mobilized private funds of almost $100 million to provide targeted rescues. In 1907, such commitments were large and impressive—very early examples of "shock and awe" response.

Focus. Cortelyou disbursed money liberally into the national banks in the expectation that they would relend those funds to struggling trust companies, securities markets, and industrial and commercial firms. Morgan brought those rescue funds to bear at the sites of greatest need. The focus of Cortelyou's largesse on New York City was controversial. It fed populist assertions that the rescues were engineered to benefit the financial elites.

Commitment. Perhaps Morgan's most meaningful action to fight the panic was the commitment of his own firm's capital in support of threatened institutions. "Skin in the game" is a signal of commitment and certification. Modern research confirms the important role of experts to *certify* the veracity of conditions to a larger and less well-informed audience. The invention of the bank clearing house also helped to perform the certification function.

Leadership and human agency. In their monetary history of the United States, Milton Friedman and Anna Schwartz commented that key turning points in crises were affected by leadership or its absence:

> *The detailed story of every banking crisis in our history shows how much depends on the presence of one or more outstanding individuals willing to assume responsibility and leadership. It was a defect of the financial system that it was susceptible to crises resolvable only with such leadership. . . . In the absence of vigorous intellectual leadership . . . the tendencies of drift and indecision had full scope. Moreover, as time went on, their force cumulated. Each failure to act made another such failure more likely.*[18]

Human agency makes a difference; the path and outcome of crises are not simply the result of macro forces. The narrative here identifies at least seven instances in which the choices of decision makers affected the course of the story:

1. *Heinze's attempt to corner the stock of United Copper.* Otto Heinze faced puzzling (mis)information about the short interest in the shares of United Copper. Had he clarified or confirmed the data, he might have declined to commence the bear squeeze. There would have been no collapse of two brokerage firms and runs on institutions affiliated with Augustus Heinze and Charles Morse.
2. *Decisions by National Bank of Commerce, NYCH, and J. P. Morgan not to assist the Knickerbocker.* The archives shed little light on the deliberations of Morgan, Bank of Commerce, and NYCH. However,

Benjamin Strong's notes reveal that the effort to assess the solvency of the Knickerbocker was unfinished in the short time allotted. Yet the trust company's membership in the NYCH might have justified greater sympathy. Continued clearing by Bank of Commerce would have dampened a run on the Knickerbocker and the severity of the panic.

3. *Morgan's decision to rescue the Trust Company of America (and other trust companies).* J. P. Morgan's famous declaration on October 22 ("this is the place to stop the trouble then") finally commenced proactive intervention.
4. *Morgan's rescue loans to the New York Stock Exchange.* Perhaps better than others, Morgan could see that the depositors' withdrawals from trust companies and banks was forcing the liquidation of demand loans, and especially call loans. With the information that he aggregated from bankers in his circle he could see that flooding the NYSE with liquidity would have prevented a crash in stock prices, failures to meet collateral calls, loan loss write-offs, instability of financial institutions (especially trust companies), and failure to meet the demands of country banks for the return of their reserves. Morgan's quick decision and ability to organize a credit pool for the NYSE on October 25 was remarkable.
5. *New York Clearing House's suspension and issuance of loan certificates.* Professor Sprague criticized the NYCH for their slow response to the crisis. Earlier issuance of loan certificates and rationing of cash rather than complete suspension might have dampened the runs, systemic instability, and humanitarian distress much sooner.
6. *Roosevelt's decision to allow the acquisition of TC&I by U.S. Steel.* The record suggests that he had incomplete information about the condition of TC&I, U.S. Steel, and Moore & Schley. His approval relieved fears of a resumption of bank runs, although it laid the basis for more extensive ripples including the Stanley hearings, the Department of Justice antitrust lawsuit, and progressive alarmism.
7. *Trust companies' decision to support the Trust Company of America and Lincoln.* Inadequate reporting of their financial condition prevented trust company presidents from knowing the seriousness of the crisis among their peer firms. It took the trust companies nearly three

weeks to commit to collective action in support of ailing peers. Immediate commitment on October 22 would have helped to reassure trust company depositors and quell runs.

These examples illustrate the significant impact of choices by individual actors. Thus, incentives and constraints—along with temperament and cognitive biases—will affect those choices in good or bad ways.

Collective action. J.P. Morgan met with some or all trust company presidents virtually daily from when he returned to New York (October 20) to the memorable locked-door meeting in his library in the early morning of November 3. Why did it take so long to gain commitment among the trust companies to assist troubled peers? Chapter 14 discussed the dynamics of Morgan's collective action problem. Research on collective action underscores possible sources of Morgan's difficulty: the large size of the group, communication problems, diversity, distrust, strategic behavior, and adverse leadership among the trust companies.

In his classic study,[19] Mancur Olson argued that collective action is more costly and difficult to achieve as the number of players expands and as their interests diverge. The rapid growth of the number of trust companies after 1895 and the entry of insurgents such the Heinze–Morse group presaged division rather than alignment among them.

Game theory helps to illustrate how distrust, strategic behavior, communication problems, or adverse leadership might affect cooperation. Consider a hypothetical: two trust companies, A and B, have reserves of $1 million each. If they dissuade depositors from withdrawing their savings, they will do more business and each will have $1.1 million of reserves each at the end of the current period. However, there is a rumor that the trust companies have suffered loan losses that might threaten their stability. Depositors are fearful about the safety of their savings and begin to run on both trust companies. The trust companies contemplate a mutual assistance agreement to tell depositors that they have $2.0 million of (pooled) reserves as of the start of the period, which will quell the depositors' fears and stop the runs. Yet the pooling of reserves exposes each trust company to the possible losses of the other and to the risk that the other would renege on the promise of assistance. If they each decline to assist the other, the trust companies will experience full-scale runs and must liquidate assets rapidly to meet withdrawals, which will reduce each firm's reserves to $0.3 million. *But* if just one supports the other and the other doesn't reciprocate, the one who declines to support the other will sustain its own reserves at $1.0 million—and the one who pledges support but gets none in return will suffer a decline in reserves to zero. The outcomes in reserves look like this:

Reserves of Each Trust Company After Expected Depositor Runs	**Trust Company A Assists Trust Company B**	**Trust Company A Declines to Assist B**
Trust Company B Assists Trust Company A	A = $1.1 million B = $1.1 million Joint = $2.2 million	A = $1.0 million B = $0.0 million Joint = $1.0 million
Trust Company B Declines to Assist A	A = $0.0 million B = $1.0 million Joint = $1.0 million	A = $0.3 million B = $0.3 million Joint = $0.6 million

Each cell in the matrix contains the payoff, expressed as the ending reserves of the individual trust companies. The best outcome is the upper left-hand corner—there, mutual assistance pays off and both firms are better off. Total reserves between the two firms rise to $2.2 million. The worst outcome is in the lower right-hand corner: each player loses most of its reserves, compared to a starting reserve of $1 million. The tempting second-best outcomes are in the upper-right and lower-left corners, where one firm takes assistance but gives nothing to the other. The problem is that neither firm knows for sure whether the other firm will help. This uncertainty about the intentions and actions of the other firm might lead to the resistance to collective action that J. P. Morgan faced from the trust company presidents.

This is known as an "assurance" game: each trust company prefers to assist if it can have the *assurance* that the other will also assist, but if it fears that the other will decline to help, it will also decline. Coordination is needed to enable the participants to achieve the best outcome (Assist, Assist). In the absence of coordination, the game may end in the worst case (Decline, Decline). This is a classic failure of collective action, and amounts to a market failure: without coordination, the players arrive at an outcome that is suboptimal for all.[20]

Collective action might fail for several reasons. First, information about the condition of the counterparty might be inadequate—in 1907, financial statements of trust companies did not benefit from Generally Accepted Accounting Principles (GAAP), professional independent auditors, or government regulations of financial reporting. More generally, uncertainty owing to a lack of information is a reliable obstacle to collective action. Second, communications might break down or become corrupted by rumors and disinformation. Third, there may be a legacy of conflict or distrust among trust companies: uptown versus downtown, new versus old, aggressive versus conservative, and so forth. In 1907, the growing diversity of society may have nourished wariness of people and firms who did not conform to older norms. Fourth, coordination might dissolve because of strategic positioning: a desire to force the competing trust company out of the competitive field and take over its depositor base. And fifth, it may reflect a failure of leadership to motivate by persuasion, exhortation, and example. Sociologist Mark Granovetter[21] found that a relatively high cost of commitment and the absence of others committing themselves—particularly influencers—will depress one's own willingness to commit.* *Coordination is hard to achieve, even when it is the only path to survival.*

The Long Tail

We have argued that the entire cycle of a crisis should include attention to spillovers into the economy, society, and polity. Such ripples could extend for years.

This narrative shows that a financial crisis can amplify and accelerate a change in public sentiment with lasting consequences. Historian Robert Wiebe wrote: "The panic of 1907 acted as a catalyst in the [political] ferment. Most obviously, it convinced almost everyone, including the bankers, that financial reform was imperative . . . the panic released countless little pockets of pressure, turning concerned but comfortable citizens into active reformers and opening many more to the calls for

* For instance, Granovetter noted that the willingness of a person to join a riot is significantly influenced by the decision of an acquaintance to join or not join the riot.

change."[22] Indeed, with the end of the Panic, the political landscape had changed: new political coalitions gained traction and a change of leadership was in the public mind.

The impact of the Panic did not end when the long lines of depositors dispersed and financial stability returned. Chapter 19 discussed the lengthy social and economic spillovers within the United States and internationally. And Chapters 20, 21, and 22 described how the impacts of the Panic of 1907 preoccupied business and government leaders long after the visible panic subsided. Figure 24.1 displays the time sequences of various legislative and administrative actions discussed here.

The figure shows that civic reactions to the Panic continued for years afterward. And it shows that the ultimate consequence, the Federal Reserve Act, did not spring full-blown from the Panic of 1907. Rather, the design of a central bank advanced by stages in stopgap laws (Aldrich–Vreeland, Postal Savings Bank), research (National Monetary Commission), remedial actions (Stanley and Pujo hearings, Department of Justice antitrust lawsuit), and trial balloon proposals (Glass, McAdoo, Owen). The civic reaction to the Panic of 1907 was a *cascade* of events, rather than a momentary pivot, as suggested in some popular accounts.

The six-year saga of legislative and executive actions following the Panic of 1907 reveals how the aftershocks of institutional change echo

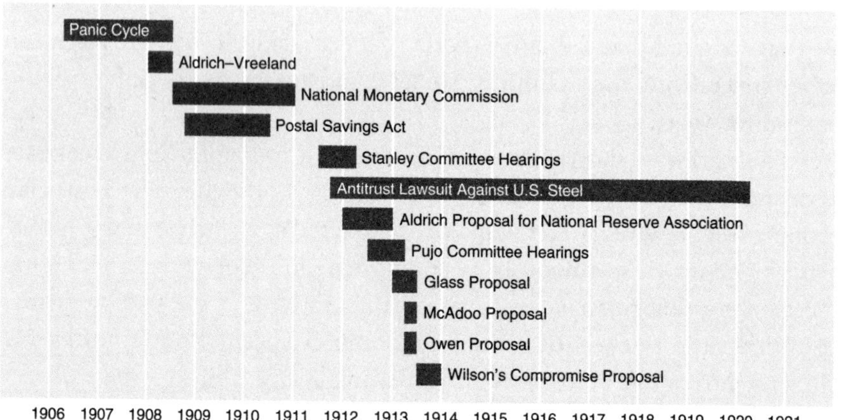

Figure 24.1 The Cascade of Civic Activity After the Panic of 1907
SOURCE: Authors' figure, based on the public record.

long after the immediate symptoms of crisis. Thus, a long perspective is useful in understanding financial crises.

Coda

The Panic of 1907 matters as a precursor to more than a century of economic turmoil—in Mark Twain's terms, the Panic has not repeated, but has rhymed over the decades. To understand that Panic is to inform one's understanding of other crises. It reminds us that the availability of information is crucial to anticipating human behavior in a financial crisis. It illustrates how incentives and expectations drive the dynamics of a crisis and how fear and cognitive biases can intervene in rational calculations. And it persuades us that crises exist not in a single *moment,* but in a cascade of events: crises have long antecedents and long tails. Such reminders are important because financial crises recur and can be phenomenally damaging. Considering such lessons, the cost of studying history is cheap, compared to the cost of ignorance.

Technical Appendix: Analysis of Trust Company Diversity and Deposit Runs

The diversity among trust companies in New York City is a recurrent issue in this narrative. It underpins the difficulty with which J. P. Morgan organized collective action among the trust companies to assist the most-distressed firms. The nature of this diversity informs the thesis that financial instability broke out *in the periphery* of the financial community—that is, by their absence from the New York Clearing House, the trust companies set themselves on the periphery of nationally and state-chartered banks. The narrative also suggests that there was even *a periphery within the periphery* (the Heinze–Morse affiliates), which was where the trouble really began. Finally, there was an aspect of this diversity among the trust companies that would later appear in the Money Trust hearings, namely, that the financial elites in

New York (the Morgan–Baker–Stillman circle) exploited the Panic for their own benefit. Recent studies on trust company performance during the Panic raise insights that highlight sources of diversity and invite future research.

Sources of Division: Business Model, Market Power, Exposure to Market Discipline

What can the movement of deposits during the Panic tell us about the relative significance of sources of division within the Manhattan trust company community? This appendix integrates and examines three perspectives as a supplement to the discussion of trust company diversity in previous chapters.

1. *Business model.* Hansen (2014) distinguishes recent entrants from long-term incumbents in the trust company field based on business model and location: "uptown" versus "downtown." He observed that the uptown trust companies tended to be smaller, younger, and more retail-oriented, with smaller average account sizes and larger numbers of deposit accounts. In contrast, downtown trust companies tended to have a wholesale orientation, treating commercial clients with larger accounts who may have been less prone to run in a financial crisis. The distinction reflected the clientele they served (commercial firms versus individuals), the value proposition they offered (e.g., convenient location for individuals living uptown), and service mix (e.g., investment management for families and a greater emphasis on checking accounts for individuals, even checking accounts for children). Despite smaller average deposit balances, the uptown firms could prosper nonetheless if they attracted more customers, which they were doing at the expense of commercial banks.
2. *Market power.* The Pujo Committee alleged the existence of an oligopoly—a "Money Trust"—that exploited market power at the expense of customers and conspired to restrain competition. Senator La Follette and others directly charged that the financial

elite used the Panic to discipline and suppress the aggressive growth of the trust companies in New York City. Given less attention in 1907 was the possibility that trust companies affiliated with the financial elite might have benefited from the Panic at the expense of unaffiliated trust companies. A study by Fohlin and Lu (2021) asked whether "opportunistic business adversaries took advantage of conditions that were ripe for a rumor-fed panic . . . those connections may have provided some business advantages and potentially a liquidity backstop to those connected trusts."[1] By studying the change in stock prices of trust companies (not the change in deposits) during the Panic, the authors found that "the connected trusts indeed benefited from their connections . . . the connected trusts rebounded much faster after the intervention by Morgan and the Treasury."[2]

3. *Exposure to market discipline.* Hansen (2014) pointed out that losses of deposits were concentrated at four trust companies: the Knickerbocker, Trust Company of America, Lincoln, and Fifth Avenue. Frydman, Hilt, and Zhou (2015) wrote, "The deposit losses . . . were strongly influenced by any observable connection to Charles Morse or the other speculators involved in the failed corner."[3] They found that the deposits of trust companies having an affiliation declined by 53 percent, as opposed to only 23 percent for those with no affiliation.[4] This is consistent with reports in contemporary newspapers and implies that the runs on those institutions were instances of depositors monitoring and disciplining bad actors by means of exercising the right to withdraw deposits. Therefore, perhaps the pattern of deposit losses had less to do with business model or market power, and more to do with the exercise by depositors of monitoring and market discipline. The thesis of market discipline has a long pedigree. For instance, Gorton and Mullineaux (1987) wrote,

> *A "bad" bank's failure or suspension, for example, would induce bank customers to monitor the quality of their own bank's liabilities. The cheapest way to monitor was to exercise the deposit contract [i.e., to withdraw deposits]. . . . A banking panic may be seen as an instance of customer monitoring. Exercising the deposit contract's*

> *option feature en masse represents a cheap way for bank customers to monitor the ability of their bank to perform, and in effect, to monitor the monitoring of the [clearing house].*[5]

These three explanations are not mutually exclusive. Nevertheless, integrating them in an examination of deposit changes in 1907 might help to illuminate the *relative* significance of any of the three explanations as a stimulus to future research. We offer the following analysis as a preliminary illustration of sources of diversity and of the challenges of interpreting those sources.

Data and Variables

We hand-collected data on trust company attributes from reports of the New York Superintendent of Banks[6] and focused on the 38 Manhattan-based trust companies described there.

Dependent variables. For robustness, we studied six dependent variables: the value and percentage change in the *number* of deposit accounts across 1907, the value and percentage change in the *dollar value* of deposits across 1907, and the value and percentage change in the *dollar value* of deposits from August 22 to December 19, 1907.

With respect to independent variables, three general factors motivated their selection and inclusion:

1. *Business model descriptors* included measures of each trust company as of January 1, 1907: the number of deposit accounts, average dollar size of the account, age of the firm, and location. Hansen's discussion suggests that retail-oriented trust companies were more vulnerable to depositor runs. Such firms tended to be younger, have a larger number of deposit accounts, smaller average deposit balances, and were located closer to their retail clientele, uptown. The age of the firm was estimated as the number of years since chartered by New York State. Regarding location, we used three variables. Two were dummy variables to indicate the location of the trust company headquarters as uptown or downtown—for a robustness check, one dummy variable assumed the dividing line

was 14th Street, and the other assumed Chambers Street.* As a third measure of location, we developed a continuous variable based on distance from Wall Street, estimated† as the shortest number of miles to walk to the headquarters of the trust company from the intersection of Broad and Wall Streets (the traditional heart of the financial district and the location of the New York Fed, the NYSE, and the headquarters of J.P. Morgan). If business model matters in explaining differences among the changes in deposits of trust companies, and if retail-oriented trust companies were more vulnerable to runs than wholesale firms, then variables associated with a retail model should be significant.

2. *Market power* measures included market share of deposits among the Manhattan trust companies. In the industrial organization literature, high-share firms are deemed to have more power to set prices and quantities (Bain, 1956). And consistent with the Money Trust theories, we included two dummy variables equaling 1 if the board contained familiar representatives or affiliates of J. P. Morgan, James Stillman, or George F. Baker, and zero if not, and the second to reflect whether the trust company maintained an affiliation with the NYCH (value of 1 if affiliated, and zero if not). Did a large market share and such affiliations serve to quell the loss of deposits? If so, the effects of market power should be significantly positive.
3. *Monitoring and discipline.* Did affiliation with Heinze and Morse overshadow other possible explanations for the change in deposits of trust companies? The list of affiliated trust companies given in note 28 in Chapter 7 was the basis for a dummy variable that took the value of 1 if the trust company were affiliated and zero if not. If

* The boundary that distinguishes "uptown" from "downtown" is a matter of judgment. In 1907, 14th Street separated less dense wealthier neighborhoods to the north (Gramercy Park, the Flatiron District, Murray Hill, and Lenox Hill) from denser neighborhoods to the south (Greenwich Village and the Ukrainian Village). As an alternative, Chambers Street approximately marked the northern boundary of the financial district in 1907.

† The distance was derived from Google Maps. Our comparison of the street grid in 1907 to that of 2022 suggested immaterial differences in walking distances for the purposes of this study.

the deposit changes are substantially a matter of monitoring and discipline, the association between the dummy variable and outcome measures should be negative and significant. A subset of the trust companies with an affiliation to Heinze and Morse experienced severe runs (Knickerbocker, Trust Company of America, and Lincoln).

Descriptive Statistics

Table A.1 gives a summary of the variables in this study. Several insights stand out. First, the Panic took a toll on the dollar value of deposits across the sample (lines 3–6). For the year 1907, the volume of deposits for the Manhattan trust companies declined on average nearly 21 percent (line 4); for the intense episode, deposits fell on average nearly 32 percent (line 6). However, the change in the *number* of deposits is more nuanced. We do not have data for the August–December period; but for the entire year, the percentage change in the number of deposit accounts was positive 6.8 percent on average, reflecting outsized percentage gains at a few of the smaller trust companies (line 2, and visible in Figure 16.2). But the absolute change in the number of deposit accounts was negative during the year (line 1). The minimum, maximum, and standard deviations of the deposit variables (lines 1–6) suggest great variation among the trust companies. This underscores the diversity among trust companies that frustrated J. P. Morgan.

Confirming the asymmetric size distribution of trust companies in Figure 16.1, lines 7 and 8 of Table A.1 reveal substantial variation in the number of deposit accounts and average dollar value of deposits. The measures of location (lines 9–11) show that about one-quarter of the trust companies was located uptown, consistent with the map in Figure 9.1. And the average age of the sample of trust companies, 21 years (line 12) underscores the notion that these financial institutions were somewhat more recent additions to the financial community than were national banks, the earliest of which were founded in 1863. The statistics about market share of deposits (line 13) suggest that the trust company industry

Table A.1 Descriptive Statistics

Line Number		*N*	Minimum	Maximum	Mean	Standard Deviation
	Dependent Variables					
1	Change in Number of Deposit Accounts, year 1907	33	–3,251	1,433	–199	862
2	% Change in Number of Deposit Accounts, year 1907	33	–49.9%	207.1%	6.8%	45.6%
3	Change in Value of Deposits, year 1907	34	–$25,384,000	$5,217,491	–$5,262,279	$6,139,396
4	% Change Value of Deposits, year 1907	34	–67.3%	98.3%	–20.8%	28.5%
5	Change in Value of Deposits, Aug. 22–Dec. 19, 1907	38	–$29,837,586	–$4	–$5,002,691	$5,471,515
6	% Change Value of Deposits, Aug. 22–Dec. 19, 1907	38	–70.7%	–0.8%	–31.8%	16.1%
	Independent Variables					
7	Number of Deposits, Jan. 1, 1907	34	241	10,714	2,446	2,450
8	Average Value of Deposits, Jan. 1, 1907	34	$1,529	$31,466	$11,011	$7,978
9	Distance from 23 Wall St. (Miles)	38	0.0	4.6	1.0	1.4
10	Uptown (North of 14th St. = 1)	38	0	1	0.24	0.431
11	Uptown (North of Chambers St. = 1)	38	0	1	0.29	0.46
12	Age of Trust Company (years)	38	0	85	21	21
13	Share of All Trust Co. Deposits	38	0.0%	10.0%	2.6%	2.4%
14	Affiliated with Heinze–Morse (yes = 1)	38	0	1	0.16	0.37
15	Affiliated with Financial Elite (yes = 1)	38	0	1	0.26	0.446
16	Member of NYCH (yes = 1)	38	0	1	0.08	0.273
17	Focus of Serious Runs (yes = 1)	38	0	1	0.08	0.273

Source: Authors' analysis.

was not very concentrated, with an average share of 2.6 percent and a maximum share of 10 percent.

Correlations

Table A.2 gives the bivariate correlations among variables in the study, transformed where appropriate.* Of greatest interest are the correlations of independent variables with dependent variables—the lower left quadrant (lines 7–17, columns A–F). In this quadrant, four independent variables stand out for their large and significant correlations with deposit changes.

First, the size and significance of the number of deposit accounts at the start of 1907 (line 7) is arresting: all the coefficients are negative and two are significant. Firms with a large number of deposit accounts suffered larger runs. Such firms would be the retail-oriented trust companies, suggesting that business model was indeed an important factor in the runs.

Second, affiliation with Heinze and Morse (line 14) is also uniformly negative, for which four of the six are significant. This is consistent with the monitoring and discipline hypothesis.

Third, market share (line 13) has two large and significantly negative coefficients. This contradicts the notion that market power (share of market) was strategically useful during the panic. Knickerbocker ($56 million in deposits) and Trust Company of America ($46 million) were, respectively, the second- and fifth-largest trust companies by dollar value of deposits at the start of 1907. The deposit losses of those two firms materially influenced the two large and significantly negative correlation coefficients. Thus, the results in line 13 may offer more support for the market discipline hypothesis than for the market power hypothesis.

Fourth, the "dog that did not bark" was the influence of financial elites, gauged either by board representation or by the trust's affiliation with the NYCH (lines 15 and 16). The absence of significant coefficient

* We took natural logs of the variables expressed in dollar values, miles, and age in years. Where those variables took negative values, we first transformed them to positive values by indexing them to a minimum value of 1.0.

Table A.2 Correlation Among Variables

Line	Column	LN index Change in Number of Deposits, 1907	% Change in Number of Deposits, 1907	LN index Change in Value of Deposits, 1907	% Change Value of Deposits 1907	LN index Change in Value of Deposits Aug. 22–Dec. 19, 1907	% Change Value of Deposits Aug. 22–Dec. 19 1907	LN Number of Deposits, Jan. 1, 1907	LN Average Value of Deposits, Jan. 1, 1907	LN Distance from 23 Wall St. (Miles)	Uptown (North of 14th St. = 1)	Uptown (North of Chambers St. = 1)	LN Age of Trust Company (years)	Share of All Trust Co. Dollar Deposits	Affiliated with Heinze-Morse	Affiliated with Financial Elite	Member of NYCH	Focus of Serious Runs
		Dependent Variables						**Independent Variables**										
		A	B	C	D	E	F	G	H	I	J	K	L	M	N	O	P	Q
	Dependent Variables																	
1	LN index Change in Number of Deposits, Year 1907	–																
2	% Change in Number of Deposits, 1907	0.298	–															
3	LN index Change in Value of Deposits, 1907	.978**	0.213	–														
4	% Change Value of Deposits 1907	0.273	0.193	0.259	–													
5	LN index Change in Value of Deposits Aug. 22–Dec. 19, 1907	.980**	0.209	.998**	0.230	–												
6	% Change Value of Deposits Aug. 22–Dec. 19 1907	.528**	0.093	.446**	.486**	.415**	–											
	Independent Variables																	
7	LN Number of Deposits, Jan. 1, 1907	–.407*	–.633**	–0.336	–0.333	–0.328	–0.090	–										
8	LN Average Value of Deposits, Jan. 1, 1907	0.154	0.073	0.035	–0.030	0.056	.441**	–0.192	–									
9	LN Distance from 23 Wall St. (Miles)	0.206	0.106	0.297	0.071	0.285	–0.234	–0.120	–.571**	–								
10	Uptown (North of 14th St. = 1)	–0.305	–0.110	0.118	0.111	0.075	–0.301	0.060	–.500**	.806**	–							
11	Uptown (North of Chambers St. = 1)	0.011	0.122	0.129	0.062	0.111	–.353*	–0.073	–.596**	.864**	.873**	–						
12	LN Age of Trust Company (years)	–0.035	–0.243	–0.121	–0.229	–0.117	0.106	.489**	.524**	–.586**	–.443**	–.507**	–					
13	Share of All Trust Co. Dollar Deposits	–0.290	–0.175	–.351*	–0.112	–.336*	0.058	.604**	.467**	–.349*	–0.138	–0.232	.671**	–				
14	Affiliated with Heinze-Morse	–.532**	–0.038	–.421*	–0.099	–.384*	–.434**	0.235	–0.299	0.118	0.268	0.201	–0.140	0.122	–			
15	Affiliated with Financial Elite	0.143	–0.027	0.080	0.130	0.080	0.275	0.193	0.324	–0.312	–0.192	–0.250	0.287	.360*	–0.259	–		
16	Member of NYCH	0.010	–0.098	0.067	0.164	0.051	0.162	0.306	–0.328	0.147	0.296	0.243	0.113	0.089	0.141	0.047	–	
17	Focus of Serious Runs	–0.117	–0.295	0.030	–0.204	0.028	–0.218	.419*	–0.222	.375*	.526**	.459**	0.009	0.222	.408*	–0.175	0.276	–

** Correlation is significant at the 0.01 level (2-tailed)--indicated in dark shading.
* Correlation is significant at the 0.05 level (2-tailed)--indicated in lighter shading.
Note: Highlighted cells indicate correlation coefficients significantly different from zero. Lighter-shaded cells indicate significance at 5 percent; darker-shaded cells indicate significance at 1 percent.
SOURCE: Authors' analysis.

coefficients with the dependent variables suggests less influence for the Money Trust hypothesis.

Finally, the lower right-hand quadrant (lines 7–17 and Columns G–Q) reveals collinearity among a number of the independent variables. Some of this is intuitively obvious: the measures of location would likely be related; the three most severe runs (Knickerbocker, Trust Company of America, and Lincoln) were located uptown, linking the variable of severe runs with uptown location; older trust companies tended to have larger average account sizes, either by virtue of their years in service or their focus on the wholesale model. These correlations underscore the challenge in attempting to isolate the sources of division among the trust companies in Manhattan. Multicollinearity renders statistical inferences about independent variables less reliable—it does not negate the ability to make *any* inferences. But it does caution the analyst to look actively for contingencies and interdependencies, to use econometric remedies where appropriate, and to vet quantitative estimates against other information where possible.

With caution, we find that the correlation coefficients are consistent with the notions that differences in business models were the dominant source of division and that affiliation with bad actors would expose a trust company to serious discipline. On the other hand, the correlation coefficients are not consistent with the thesis that market power (share of market, affiliation with the financial elite, or membership in the NYCH) would yield solid benefits in deposit changes during the Panic.

Regression Analysis

One approach to working with collinear data is to employ log-log stepwise regression analysis, suited to select independent variables both for their explanatory power and minimization of collinear effects.*

* To test the robustness of results presented here, we also studied untransformed regression estimates, also using stepwise analysis. For brevity, these other results are not presented here. The alternative estimates show some variance from the results in Tables A.2 and A.3, though qualitatively they tend to affirm the insights summarized here.

Table A.3 summarizes the results of stepwise regressions of the 11 independent variables against each of the six dependent variables. The collinearity statistics reveal low levels in the resulting models. The large and significant F-statistics show that five of the six models fit the data better than an intercept-only model (in Panel 4 the stepwise algorithm did not include any variables).

Of interest are five variables that stepwise regression selected. First is the dummy variable indicating an affiliation of the trust company with the Heinze–Morse circle (Panels 1, 3, 5, and 6). In all of these cases, the coefficients are negative and significant. This dummy variable is the most prevalent of the variables selected in the regressions.

The next two variables, the number of deposit accounts at the start of the year (Panels 1 and 2) and average value per deposit account at the start of the year (Panel 6), are indicators of the business model that the firm pursued. Large numbers of deposit accounts with relatively small account balances are consistent with the business model of retail-oriented trust companies. Consistent with this, the coefficient for number of deposit accounts is significantly negative—a greater number of deposit accounts is consistent with the retail business model, which suffers greater deposit loss during the Panic. And the coefficient for size of deposit balances is significantly positive—larger value per deposit account is consistent with a wholesale model, which suffers less deposit loss during the Panic.

The fourth variable of interest, distance from 23 Wall Street, appears in two estimates (Panels 3 and 5). The coefficients are positive and significant. After controlling for affiliation with Heinze and Morse, greater distance from the financial district is associated with *increases* in deposits. This result is consistent with Figure 16.2, which showed that three trust companies experienced large increases in the number of deposit accounts in 1907—together they averaged 2.9 miles to the north; and all three were small and young firms, averaging 1.6 years. Thus, the positive coefficients on distance from 23 Wall Street sustains Hansen's business model hypothesis in an unexpected way: the difference in business model from the downtown firms—perhaps proximity to their customers—seemed to yield an advantage in deposit changes during the panic.

Table A.3 Estimated Coefficients from Stepwise Regression

	Unstandardized Coefficients		Standardized Coefficients			Collinearity Statistic		Adjusted	
	B	Std. Error	Beta	*t*		Tolerance	VIF	*R*-Square	F
Panel 1: Dependent Variable: LN Index Change in Number of Deposit Accounts, Year 1907									
(Constant)	12.49	1.75		7.12	***			0.371	10.452***
Affiliated with Heinze–Morse	–2.14	0.61	–0.497	–3.53	***	0.99	1.01		
LN Number of Deposits, Jan. 1, 1907	–0.60	0.24	–0.359	–2.55	*	0.99	1.01		
Panel 2: Dependent Variable: % Change in Number of Deposit Accounts, 1907									
(Constant)	257.88	55.48		4.65	***			0.381	20.737***
LN Number of Deposits, Jan. 1, 1907	-34.06	7.48	-0.633	-4.55	***	1.00	1.00		
Panel 3: Dependent Variable: LN Index Change in Value of Deposits, 1907									
(Constant)	17.73	0.59		30.30	***			0.317	7.196**
Affiliated with Heinze–Morse	–3.91	1.21	–0.485	–3.22	***	0.97	1.03		
LN Distance from 23 Wall St. (Miles)	0.68	0.27	0.380	2.52	*	0.97	1.03		
Panel 4: Dependent Variable: % Change in Value of Deposits, 1907									
No variables were entered.								-	-

(Continued)

Table A.3 *(Continued)*

	Unstandardized Coefficients		Standardized Coefficients			Collinearity Statistic			
	B	Std. Error	Beta	*t*		Tolerance	VIF	Adjusted *R*-Square	F
Panel 5: Dependent Variable: LN Index Change in Value of Deposits, Aug. 22–Dec. 19, 1907									
(Constant)	17.95	0.59		30.33	★★★			0.315	7.138★★
Affiliated with Heinze–Morse	–3.96	1.23	–0.487	–3.23	★★★	0.97	1.03		
LN Distance from 23 Wall St. (Miles)	0.67	0.27	0.374	2.48	★	0.97	1.03		
Panel 6: Dependent Variable: % Change Value of Deposits, Aug. 22–Dec. 19 1907									
(Constant)	–116.94	26.47		–4.42	★★★			0.381	7.778★★★
LN Avg Value of Deposits, Jan. 1, 1907	9.26	2.87	0.484	3.22	★★★	0.83	1.20		
Member of NYCH	22.59	7.65	0.429	2.95	★★	0.89	1.13		
Affiliated with Heinze–Morse	–13.75	6.06	–0.326	–2.27	★	0.91	1.10		

★★★ Coefficient is significant at the 0.001 level (two-tailed).

★★ Coefficient is significant at the 0.01 level (two-tailed).

★ Coefficient is significant at the 0.05 level (two-tailed).

SOURCE: Authors' analysis.

The fifth variable, the dummy indicating affiliation with the NYCH, appears only in Panel 6 and shows a positive and significant coefficient. In this instance, it appeared that such affiliation yielded benefits. This is a surprising result, given the absence of significant correlation coefficients for this variable in Table A.2 (line 16).

Discussion

In general, these results build on previous studies and sustain at least four insights (with appropriate caution). First, differences in business models (wholesale versus retail) mattered significantly in the ability of trust companies to weather the Panic. The trust companies that followed a retail-oriented strategy suffered a relatively greater loss of deposits—except for three small and young trust companies noted earlier, which probably accounted for an apparent positive effect of distance from Wall Street. Location does matter as a material determinant of consumer behavior.[7] Thus, location warrants continued study as a proxy for attributes of the business model.

Second, depositors seemed to discriminate and discipline the bad managers, Heinze, Morse, and their associates. The deposit runs were concentrated especially on trust companies associated with Heinze and Morse whereas other trust companies experienced milder runs. The prevalence and significance of the Heinze–Morse effect *predominate* in the deposit changes for Manhattan trust companies.

Finally, the market power hypothesis gains weak support, at best. On one hand, Table A.2 shows that affiliations with the financial elite and with the NYCH yield insignificant correlations with deposit changes (rows 15–16, columns A–F). Affiliation with the financial elites appears in none of the stepwise regression results. Also, affiliation with the NYCH is absent from the regression results except for Panel 6 in Table A.3. This glimmer of association with deposit changes in Table A.3 offset by the absence of correlations for the NYCH dummy variable in Table A.2 yields no strong endorsement of the market power hypothesis.

An implication of these findings is that the resistance J. P. Morgan encountered as he tried to mobilize collective action among the trust companies sprang from differences in business strategy and from wariness about which firms were mired in the Heinze–Morse debacle. As the game theory model (discussed in Chapter 24) suggests, cooperation depends profoundly on trust; and trust among such diverse players must have been in short supply.

Further Research

This analysis has focused specifically on Manhattan-headquartered trust companies. Nearly 25 trust companies resided in the outer boroughs and could be studied for similar effects. In addition, state and national banks in New York City could be added to the sample.

Measures of liquidity and capital adequacy could help to distinguish among subgroups of the trust company community. Similarly, the fact that some trust companies *increased* their deposits during the Panic warrants explanation: Why did they gain?

Finally, the material (and sometimes significant) cross-correlations among independent variables cautions the interpretations of regression estimates and invites the application of other econometric techniques to strengthen the inferences about the independent variables.

Notes

Prologue

1. Contemporary accounts of the death of Charles Barney, which included numerous details of the shooting and the subsequent events of the day, appeared in a number of daily newspapers, including the *New York Times*, the *Washington Post*, the *Chicago Daily Tribune*, and the *Wall Street Journal*. The level of detail appears to have been reported for its relevance to the banking panic then underway, but also (of course) for its titillating value. Most of this particular reportage appeared in the aforementioned publications on November 15, 16, and 17, 1907.
2. *New York Times*, November 15, 1907, p. 1.
3. *Chicago Daily Tribune*, November 16, 1907, p. 2.
4. *Washington Post*, November 17, 1907, p. 3.
5. Higgins later recanted this statement, claiming he was misquoted. *Washington Post*, November 16, 1907, p. 1.
6. *New York Times*, November 15, 1907, p. 1.
7. Strouse (1999), p. 575.
8. *Washington Post*, October 22, 1907, p. 3.
9. *New York Times*, November 15, 1907, p. 1.

10. Ibid.
11. Ibid.
12. Ibid.
13. *Washington Post*, November 16, 1907, p. 1.

Introduction

1. William Faulkner, *Requiem for a Nun* (New York: Random House, 1951, reprinted 1994), p. 73.
2. Friedman and Schwartz (1963), pp. 156, 157.
3. Clews wrote, "The real causes of all the trouble can be summed up as follows: (1) the high finance manipulation in advancing stocks to a 3.5 to 4 percent basis, while the money was loaning at 6 percent and above, on six and twelve months, time on the best of collaterals; (2) capital all over the nation having gone largely into real estate and other fixed forms, thereby losing its liquid quality; (3) the making of injudicious loans by the Knickerbocker Trust Co., hence suspension; (4) the unloading by certain big operators of $800,000,000 of securities, following which were the immense sales of new securities by the railroads; (5) the California earthquake, with losses amounting to $350,000,000; (6) the investigation of the life insurance companies; (7) the Metropolitan Street Railroad investigation; (8) the absurd fine by Judge Landis of $29,400,000 against a corporation with a capital of $1,000,000; (9) the Interstate Commerce Commission's examination into the Chicago & Alton deal and the results thereof" (Clews 1973, p. 799).
4. Kindleberger (1990), p. 71.
5. Lowenstein (2004), pp. 218–219.
6. "Banks To Release Millions To-Day: Money Crisis Over," *New York Times*, November 25, 1907, p. 1; "Plan for Banks of Issue: Thinks Corner Has Been Turned," *Chicago Daily Tribune*, November 24, 1907, p. 1.

Chapter 1: A Buoyant Decade, a Fragile System, and Some Leaders at Its Apex

1. McCulley (2012 [1992]), p. 26.
2. "US Business Cycle Expansions and Contractions," National Bureau of Economic Research, downloaded August 21, 2022 from https://www.nber.org/research/data/us-business-cycle-expansions-and-contractions.

3. The analysis of growth rates draws on indices of U.S. industrial production drawn from "U.S. Industrial Production Index" of the National Bureau of Economic Research, downloaded from www.nber.org/data/industrial-production-index/.
4. Using the ProQuest Historical Newspapers search engine covering 10 major and regional newspapers, we searched for the number of articles containing the word "optimism." From 1897 to 1906, the trend rose from 124 to 336.
5. "The Chicago Market: Optimism Is General—Better Outlook for Investment Business—Numerous Active Stocks" *Wall Street Journal*, January 26, 1906, p. 8.
6. "Canadian Outlook Bright: Optimism General in Industrial and Financial Circles," *Wall Street Journal*, June 12, 1906, p. 8.
7. "Chicago's Building Boom: One Hundred Million in 1906 for New Building and Construction Work," *Wall Street Journal*, May 29, 1906, p. 3.
8. "Land Boom in Southwest: Railroads Carrying Out Great Trainloads of Homeseekers, Business Men Large Buyers," *Wall Street Journal*, September 5, 1906, p. 5.
9. "Building Boom in Atlanta: Nearly 100 Per Cent Increase Over Last October, and Bids Fair to Continue," *Wall Street Journal*, November 1, 1906, p. 8.
10. "Conditions in Chicago: All Industries There Working Under High Pressure. Railroad Traffic Continues to Break All Records. Big Movement of Grain Begins. Factories Maintain Record Output "Boom" in Real Estate Not Gaining Much Headway." *Wall Street Journal*, September 15, 1906, p. 8.
11. "Iron and Steel Notes: No Summer Let Up for Steel Workers, Owing to Great Boom," *New York Times*, June 24, 1906, p. 11.
12. See Noyes (1909a), p. 186.
13. In part, the financial houses these financiers built served as a certification of quality that the securities of U.S. firms being sold in Europe were attractive investment opportunities.
14. Other companies under the influence of Morgan also included Adams Express Co.; Atchison, Topeka, & Santa Fe Railroad; Baldwin Locomotive Co.; Chicago–Great Western Railroad; Erie Railroad; International Agricultural Co.; International Mercantile Marine Co.; Lehigh Valley Railroad; New York, New Haven, and Hartford Railroad; Northern

Pacific Railroad; New York Central Railroad; Pere Marquette Railroad; Philadelphia Rapid Transit Co.; Public Service Corporation of New Jersey; Pullman Co.; Reading Railroad; Southern Railroad; United States Steel Co; and Westinghouse Co.

15. Harbaugh (1963), pp. 157–158.
16. Allen (1952), p. 79.
17. Carosso (1987), p. 288.
18. V. I. Bovykin and Rondo Cameron (Eds.), *International Banking 1870–1914* (Oxford University Press, 1991), p. 67.
19. Logan (1981), p. 163.
20. Burr (1927).
21. Gold was typically imported through the sale of bonds or other promises to repay.
22. U.S. Bureau of the Census, "Financial Institutions and Markets," *Historical Statistics of the United States* (Washington, DC: Department of Commerce, 1975), Series X 410-419.
23. N. R. Lamoreaux, *The Great Merger Movement in American Business, 1895–1904* (Cambridge, UK: Cambridge University Press), p. 2.
24. De Long (1991), p. 3.
25. U.S. Bureau of the Census, *Historical Statistics of the United States, Colonial Times to 1970* (Washington, DC: Department of Commerce, 1975), Series X 580-587, p. 1019.
26. Sprague (1910), p. 239.
27. In 1894, the American Bankers Association proposed allowing national banks to expand their issuance of banknotes in a panic. That same year, the Secretary of the Treasury and the Comptroller of the Currency both proposed steps for alleviating a liquidity crunch.
28. Late in 1896 and early 1897, large gatherings of business leaders sought to mobilize a national movement for financial reform. The resulting conferences developed proposals in 1900 for the establishment of regional central banks, none of which attracted congressional support.
29. In 1901, the departing Secretary of the Treasury, Lyman Gage, proposed the creation of a central bank, to be structured as a *confederation* of regional banks, rather than a unitary bank such as the Bank of England. He envisioned the confederation of reserve banks funded by the banks themselves

and focused on concentrating and distributing "unemployed reserves from sections where such reserves were not needed, . . . as loans where most needed" (U.S. Department of the Treasury, "Annual Report of the Secretary of the Treasury on the State of the Finances for the Year 1901," 77, Federal Reserve Bank of St. Louis, https://fraser.stlouisfed.org/files/docs/publications/treasar/AR_TREASURY_1901.pdf).

30. In 1902, Gage's successor, Treasury Secretary Leslie Shaw, began a policy of monetary management to thwart the liquidity crunches that typically occurred during the crop-moving season. His aim was to make the money supply more elastic. Nevertheless, Shaw's experiments were criticized as "dangerous and indefensible" (A. Piatt Andrew, "The Treasury and the Banks Under Secretary Shaw," *Quarterly Journal of Economics,* August 1907, 566.)

31. In 1904, Senator Orville Pratt floated a trial balloon proposing the use of bank clearing houses to deal with bank crises. The novel suggestion was that clearing houses should issue their own asset-backed banknotes, and thus reflected the advantage of pooling bank reserves behind currency.

32. In 1906, the New York Chamber of Commerce chartered a committee to study the financial system. In November the committee recommended "centralization of financial responsibility . . . [and] creation of a central bank of issue under control of the government . . . [as] the best method of providing an elastic credit currency . . . [to be] privately owned or distributed among the banking institutions of the country" (quotation of NY Chamber of Commerce Committee report in McCulley (1992), 127.) This report was the first formal proposal to establish a central bank. Not to be outdone, the American Bankers Association prepared a detailed plan for banks to issue national currency.

33. President Theodore Roosevelt, State of the Union Address, December 3, 1906, accessed July 27, 2021 from https://www.infoplease.com/primary-sources/government/presidential-speeches/state-union-address-theodore-roosevelt-december-3-1906.

34. U.S. Department of the Treasury, "Annual Report of the Secretary of the Treasury on the State of the Finances for the Year 1906," 49, Federal Reserve Bank of St. Louis, https://fraser.stlouisfed.org/files/docs/publications/treasar/AR_TREASURY_1906.pdf.

35. *Commercial and Financial Chronicle,* January 4, 1907, p. 6.

36. Burr (1927), Volume 25.

Chapter 2: A Shock to the System

1. Just months before, a temblor of magnitude 8.8 hit the seabed off the coast of Ecuador, creating tsunamis that traveled as far as Japan. The largest previously recorded U.S. earthquake, of magnitude 7.7, hit Charleston, South Carolina, on August 31, 1886.
2. "1906 Earthquake," Berkeley Seismology Lab, downloaded April 30, 2022 from https://seismo.berkeley.edu/outreach/1906_quake.html.
3. The figure of $350 million was estimated by Albert Whitney, a professor at the University of California. Applying other methods yielded as much as $500 million. See Whitney (1907), p. 45. See also Douty (1977), p. 83.
4. U.S. Gross National Product in 1906 was $28.7 billion. U.S. Bureau of the Census, *Historical Statistics of the United States, 1789–1945:* a supplement to *Statistical Abstract of the United States* (Washington, DC: U.S. Department of Commerce), Series F 1-5, p. 224.
5. Our discussion of the economic impact of the San Francisco earthquake draws on research by Noyes (1909a, 1909b), Sprague (1910), McCulley (1992), and Odell and Weidenmier (2004).
6. The company later reorganized, offering its claimants a payment of half cash and half stock in the new company. For more discussion, see Thomas and Witts (1971), p. 188.
7. The facts about insurance companies are drawn from Odell and Weidenmier (2004), and from Thomas and Witts (1971).
8. Private cables, Morgan Grenfell Archives, Guildhall Library, London. Used with permission of Deutsche Bank.
9. To the queries from J. P. "Jack" Morgan Jr. about these rumors, Edward "Teddy" Grenfell, a partner in J. S. Morgan & Company in London, the British affiliate of J. P. Morgan & Company, denied any basis in fact.
10. Keynes (1930), vol. 2, pp. 306–307, quoted in Dam, (1982), p. 18.
11. Obstfeld, Shambaugh, and Taylor (2005), pp. 423–438.
12. Odell and Weidenmier (2004), p. 1012.
13. Ibid., p. 1014.
14. Quoted in Noyes (1909b), p. 355.
15. Sprague (1910), p. 239.
16. W. S. Burns to G. W. Perkins, October 20, 1906: "Cause of advance in Bank rate is to prevent withdrawals of gold, £2,000,000 out today, said for Egypt, and fear further requirements US of America." Private cables, Morgan

Grenfell Archives, Guildhall Library, London. Used with permission of Deutsche Bank.

17. Bank of England, historical statistics website, http://213.225.136.206/mfsd/iadb/Repo.asp?Travel=NIxIRx, accessed October 29, 2006.
18. The discussion of the Bank of England's actions in the fall of 1906 draws from Tallman and Moen (1995), Odell and Weidenmier (2002), and the *Commercial and Financial Chronicle.*
19. Sprague (1910), p. 241.
20. Series of telegrams from Private cables, Morgan Grenfell Archives, Guildhall Library, London. Used with permission of Deutsche Bank.
21. Letter from J. P. Morgan Jr. letterpress book (December 18, 1906). Quotation courtesy of the Morgan Library and Museum.
22. Letter from J. P. Morgan Jr. letterpress book (December 24, 1906). Quotation courtesy of the Morgan Library and Museum.
23. Letter from J. P. Morgan Jr. letterpress book (January 22, 1906). Quotation courtesy of the Morgan Library and Museum.
24. Clews (1973), p. 783.
25. Pierre Paul Leroy-Beaulieu, quoted in Noyes (1909a), p. 198–19.
26. James J. Hill, speech to Merchant's Club of Chicago, November 10, 1906, *Financial Chronicle,* November 17, 1906, p. 1198, quoted in Noyes (1909b), p. 359.
27. Noyes (1909a), p. 194.

Chapter 3: The "Silent" Crash

1. Letter from J. P. Morgan Jr. to Edward Grenfell, March 14, 1907, Morgan Library and Museum, Box 5, letterpress book 3, January 24, 1907–January 15, 1908. Used with permission.
2. *New York Times,* March 15, 1907, quoted in Silber (2007), p. 11.
3. The decline of 10.9 percent was calculated as the sum of monthly returns over the period. Source of data: National Bureau of Economic Research, "Average Prices of 40 Common Stocks for United States" [M11006USM315NNBR], retrieved from FRED, Federal Reserve Bank of St. Louis, https://fred.stlouisfed.org/series/M11006USM315NNBR, April 30, 2022. From February 1890 to August 1906, the mean monthly return on this index was 0.5 percent and the standard deviation was 0.052.

4. E. C. Grenfell to J. P. Morgan Jr., March 6, 1907. Used with permission of Deutsche Bank.
5. J. P. Morgan Jr. to E. C. Grenfell, March 6, 1907. Used with permission of Deutsche Bank.
6. Three telegrams between E. C. Grenfell and J. P. Morgan Jr., March 13, 1907. Used with permission of Deutsche Bank.
7. The loss of 8.29 percent was cited by Silber (2007), p. 33, second note and referring to an estimate by Jeremy Siegel, *Stocks for the Long Run* (New York: McGraw-Hill, 1998), p. 183.
8. *Commercial and Financial Chronicle*, March 9, 1907, p. 534.
9. Noyes (1909b), p. 359.
10. Sprague (1910), p. 239.
11. Ibid., p. 241.
12. J. P. Morgan Jr., March 14, 1907. Used with permission of Morgan Library and Museum.
13. J. S. Morgan & Company to J. P. Morgan Jr., March 22, 1907. Used with permission of Deutsche Bank.
14. J. P. Morgan Jr. to J. S. Morgan & Company, March 23, 1907. Used with permission of Deutsche Bank.
15. "Roosevelt 'Calls' Wall St. Bluff. President Unmoved by Stock Flurry, Suspected of Being Engineered to Alarm Him," *Chicago Daily Tribune*, March 14, 1907, p. 1.
16. "Treasury Aid to Check Panic: Cortelyou, After Conferring with Roosevelt Announces Relief Measures," *New York Times*, March 15, 1907, p. 3.
17. "Cortelyou Congratulated: Now the Administration Will Go to Killing Manipulative Panics," *New York Times*, March 16, 1907, p. 3.
18. "Schiff Praises President: Banker Declares Roosevelt Has Rendered Good Service to Corporations," *The Washington Post*, March 16, 1907, p.1.
19. *Commercial and Financial Chronicle*, March 23, 1907, p. 654.
20. "Cortelyou Calms Wall Street Anxiety: New York Financiers Ask Secretary's Aid in Quenching Fire They Started Themselves," *Chicago Daily Tribune*, March 26, 1907, p. 1.
21. "Aids Money Market: Cortelyou Places $16,900,000 More in Circulation," *The Washington Post*, March 27, 1907, p. 2.
22. "Bulls Force Rally: Active Stocks Move Upward and Bears Seek Cover," *The Washington Post*, March 27, 1907, p. 1.

23. "Power of the Treasury," *The Wall Street Journal*, April 25, 1907, p. 1.
24. J. P. Morgan Jr. to J. S. Morgan & Company, March 29, 1907. Used with permission of Morgan Library and Museum.
25. *Commercial and Financial Chronicle*, March 30, 1907, p. 716.
26. *Commercial and Financial Chronicle*, April 13, 1907, p. 832.
27. *Commercial and Financial Chronicle*, April 20, 1907, p. 851.
28. *Commercial and Financial Chronicle*, May 4, 1907, p. 1020.
29. Private cables, Morgan Grenfell Archives, Guildhall Library, London. Used with permission of Deutsche Bank.
30. A few of the most important works on this period are: McGerr (2003); Diner (1998); Wiebe (1967); D. Rodgers (1982); McCormick (1986), particularly Chapter 7, "Progressivism: A Contemporary Reassessment," and Chapter 8, "Prelude to Progressivism: The Transformation of New York State Politics, 1890–1910"; and Eisenach (1994).
31. Essay by E. E. Morison and J. M. Blum in Morison (1952), Vol. 5, p. xvi.
32. Cooper (1983), p. 83.
33. McGerr (2003), pp. 156–158.
34. Ibid., pp. 156–158.
35. *Commercial and Financial Chronicle*, June 1, 1907, p. 1270.
36. Ibid., p. 1276.
37. *Commercial and Financial Chronicle*, March 9, 1907, p. 534.
38. Morison, Blum, Chandler, and Rice (1952), Volume 5, p. 631.

Chapter 4: Credit Crunch

1. Private cables, Morgan Grenfell Archives, Guildhall Library, London. Used with permission of Deutsche Bank.
2. "Business Cycle Expansions and Contractions," Cambridge, MA: National Bureau of Economic Research, downloaded January 19, 2022 from https://www.nber.org/research/data/us-business-cycle-expansions-and-contractions.
3. *Commercial and Financial Chronicle*, May 24, 1907, p. 16.
4. Letter from J. P. Morgan Jr. to J. S. Morgan & Company, June 21, 1907. Used with permission of Morgan Library and Museum.
5. Odell and Weidenmier (2002), pp. 12, 14.
6. Sprague (1910), p. 241.

7. Tallman and Moen (1990), p. 4.
8. *Commercial and Financial Chronicle*, June 29, 1907, p. 1514.
9. Letter from J. P. Morgan Jr. to J. S. Morgan & Company, July 19, 1907. Used with permission of Morgan Library and Museum.
10. *Commercial and Financial Chronicle*, July 27, 1907, p. 184.
11. *Commercial and Financial Chronicle*, August 3, 1907, p. 248.
12. "Opens Cash Vaults: Cortelyou Adopts New Way to Help Money Market," *The Washington Post*, August 24, 1907, p. 1.
13. "Cortelyou Plan Wise: Money Distribution to Banks Indorsed [sic] by Ridgely," *Washington Post*, August 25, 1907, p. 14.
14. *Commercial and Financial Chronicle*, June 1, 1907, p. 1351.
15. Leroy-Beaulieu, quoted in Noyes (1909a), p. 199.
16. Clews (1973, p. 787) makes the point of the small book value of equity relative to the large fine imposed.
17. *Commercial and Financial Chronicle*, August 24, 1907, p. 28.
18. Ibid., p. 440.
19. Morison, Blum, Chandler, and Rice (1952), Volume 5, pp. 745–748.
20. *Commercial and Financial Chronicle*, September 7, 1907, p. 550.
21. Cable from J. S. Morgan & Co. to Jack Morgan, August 27, 1907 and from J.S. Morgan & Co. to J.P. Morgan Jr. Used with permission of Deutsche Bank.
22. *Commercial and Financial Chronicle*, September 21, 1907, p. 681.
23. "The Copper Situation: Further Concessions by Selling Agencies Likely This Week," *Wall Street Journal*, September 23, 1907, p. 7; and "The Copper Situation: Metal Sells at 15 and 15 ½ c. per pound," *Wall Street Journal*, September 24, 1907, p. 8.
24. "Amalgamated Copper Dividends: Returns to Stockholders of All Subsidiaries to Be Reduced Almost One-Half," *Wall Street Journal*, September 23, 1907, p. 7; and "Old Dominion Copper: Question of Continuing Dividends," *Wall Street Journal*, September 24, 1907, p. 5.
25. "Inter.-Met. Situation May Change with Ryan's Return: Question of Dividend on Metropolitan Stock Must Be Settled Soon by N.Y. City Railway," *Wall Street Journal*, September 23, 1907, p. 2.
26. "A Receiver for City Railway Only," *New York Times*, September 24, 1907, p. 5.
27. Sprague (1910), p. 246.

28. "Bank Suspension in Alexandria," *The Times of London*, June 22, 1907, p. 15.
29. See reports in *The Times of London* (June 8, 1907, p. 17; June 29, p. 15; July 11, p. 13; September 21, p. 13).
30. "Severe Depression," *The Times of London*, August 9, 1907, p. 11.
31. See Rodgers and Payne (2017); Franco Bonelli, *La crisi del 1907. Una tappa dello sviluppo industriale in Italia* (Torino: Fondazione Einaudi, 1971).
32. "Japan's Financial Crisis: Panic Checked by Banks—Great Losses in Prices of Securities," *New York Times*, July 29, 1907, p. 4, reprinting a report from Berliner Zeitung, July 28, 1907.
33. Odell and Weidenmier (2002), p. 14.

Chapter 5: Copper King

1. "A Review of the World," *Current Literature,* XLIV(1), January 1908.
2. McNelis (1968), p. 27.
3. Christopher P. Connolly, "The Fight of the Copper Kings," *McClure's Magazine*, May 1907.
4. Ibid.
5. McNelis (1968), p. 21.
6. "A Review of the World," *Current Literature*, XLIV(1), January 1908.
7. William R. Stewart, "Captains of Industry—Part XXI: F. Augustus Heinze," *Cosmopolitan*, XXXVI, January 1904.
8. Ibid.
9. "A Review of the World," *Current Literature*, XLIV(1), January 1908.
10. Ibid.
11. McNelis (1968), p. 209. However, reported estimates vary. Sobel (1968, p. 306) puts the payment to Heinze at $10.5 million, as does Glasscock (1935), p. 276.
12. "The Story of Morse," *Current Literature*, XLVIII, February 1910.
13. "C.W. Morse Quits the Banking Field," *New York Times*, October 20, 1907, p. 1.
14. "Ibid., and *Current Literature,* February 1910.
15. "Recent Lesson in Pyramidal Banking That Brought Crisis," *Wall Street Journal,* November 30, 1907, p. 6.
16. Tallman and Moen (1990), p. 5, and McNelis (1968), p. 153.

17. See Tallman and Moen (1990) and McNelis (1968).
18. McNelis (1968), p. 117.
19. Ibid., p. 156.
20. "Otto Heinze & Co.," *Wall Street Journal*, October 19, 1907, p. 1; "Features of the Market," *Wall Street Journal*, January 19, 1907; and "United Copper Co. Loaned to Heinzes," *New York Times*, April 13, 1907.
21. O'Sullivan (2016), p. 194.
22. Lawson (1906), pages excerpts from pages 26–31.
23. Sobel (1968), p. 308.

Chapter 6: The Corner and the Squeeze

1. Many of the details about the Heinzes' attempted corner of United Copper stock and the resultant fallout were gathered from contemporary accounts in the following publications: *The Arena*, the *Chicago Daily Tribune*, the *Commercial and Financial Chronicle*, *Cosmopolitan*, *Current Literature*, *Leslie's Monthly Magazine*, *McClure's Magazine*, the *New York Times*, the *Wall Street Journal*, and the *Washington Post*. Other contemporary references are cited below, in addition to a number of books that provide brief glimpses of and various perspectives on the events of October 1907, as well as the personal histories of Augustus Heinze and Charles W. Morse. The biography of Augustus Heinze by Sarah McNelis, who personally interviewed Otto Heinze, was especially helpful.
2. McNelis (1968) p. 156.
3. Tallman and Moen (1990), pp. 5–6.
4. "F.A. Heinze Shared in the Copper Pool: Government Shows that the Accused Operator Was Interested in the Stock Deals," *New York Times*, May 3, 1910, p. 20.
5. Rodgers and Payne (2017), p. 13.
6. McNelis (1968), p. 157.
7. Ibid.
8. *New York Times*, May 3, 1910, p. 20.
9. *Wall Street Journal*, October 17, 1907, p. 3.
10. Ibid.

11. *Chicago Daily Tribune*, October 15, 1907, p. 4; and *Wall Street Journal*, October 15, 1907, p. 8.
12. Ibid.
13. *New York Times*, October 15, 1907, p. 11; and *Wall Street Journal*, October 15, 1907, p. 8.
14. Rodgers and Payne (2017), p. 16.
15. McNelis (1968), p. 158.
16. "F.A. Heinze Shared in the Copper Pool: Government Shows that the Accused Operator Was Interested in the Stock Deals," *New York Times*, May 3, 1910, p. 20.
17. Ibid.
18. *Chicago Daily Tribune*, October 17, 1907, p. 2.
19. *New York Times*, October 17, 1907, p. 1.
20. *Chicago Daily Tribune*, October 17, 1907, p. 2.
21. *New York Times*, October 17, 1907, p. 1.
22. *Wall Street Journal*, October 17, 1907, p. 3; and *New York Times*, October 16, 1907, p. 13.
23. *Wall Street Journal*, October 16, 1907, p. 4.
24. *Wall Street Journal*, October 17, 1907, p. 3.
25. Ibid., pp. 3, 4.
26. Ibid., p. 3.
27. Ibid.
28. *New York Times*, October 17, 1907, p. 1.
29. Rodgers and Payne (2017), p. 10; they cite Woods (2011).
30. Sobel (1968), p. 309.
31. The National Bureau of Economic Research identifies May 1907 as a cyclical peak with a contraction in economic activity extending until the nadir in June 1908. See "U.S. Business Cycle Expansions and Contractions," https://www.nber.org/research/data/us-business-cycle-expansions-and-contractions, accessed February 22, 2022.
32. Rodgers and Payne (2017), p. 2.
33. O'Sullivan (2016), p. 206.

Chapter 7: Falling Dominoes

1. *New York Times*, October 17, 1907, p. 1.
2. *Washington Post*, October 18, 1907, p. 4.
3. *New York Times*, October 17, 1907, p. 1.
4. *Washington Post*, October 17, 1907, p. 3.
5. *Chicago Daily Tribune*, October 17, 1907, p. 2.
6. *Washington Post*, October 17, 1907, p. 3.
7. *New York Times*, October 17, 1907, p. 1.
8. *Chicago Daily Tribune*, October 17, 1907, p. 2.
9. *Wall Street Journal*, October 18, 1907, p. 7.
10. *New York Times*, October 17, 1907, p. 1.
11. Ibid.
12. *Washington Post*, October 18, 1907, p. 4.
13. Ibid., p. 11.
14. *Wall Street Journal*, October 19, 1907, p. 2.
15. *Washington Post*, October 18, 1907, p. 4.
16. *Wall Street Journal*, October 19, 1907, p. 2.
17. *Washington Post*, October 18, 1907, p. 11.
18. Ibid., p. 4.
19. *New York Times*, October 18, 1907, p. 1.
20. Ibid., p. 4; and *Washington Post*, October 17, 1907, p. 3.
21. *Washington Post*, October 18, 1907, p. 11.
22. *New York Times*, October 18, 1907, p. 1.
23. *New York Times*, October 17, 1907, p. 1.
24. Ibid., p. 1.
25. Ibid.
26. Ibid.
27. *New York Times*, October 18, 1907, p. 1.
28. Contemporary media and subsequent books give conflicting references to financial institutions affiliated with Augustus Heinze. It is not clear which of these references point to outright control versus mere interest or passive investment. Once the rumor mill of the Panic began working, such

distinctions probably fell by the wayside. This is a subject for future research. An unconfirmed comprehensive list drawn from the various sources refers to Heinze interests, affiliations, and investments as follows:

National banks: Mercantile National, Consolidated National, Northern National, Utah National, Merchants Exchange National, National Bank of North America, and National Bank of Salt Lake City.

State-chartered banks: newspaper references suggest up to 12 banks. We found specific references to four: Mechanics & Traders Bank, State Savings Bank of Montana, Bank of Discount, and Riverside Bank.

Trust companies: Carnegie, Empire, Hudson, Interboro, Knickerbocker, Lincoln, and Trust Company of America.

Insurance companies: Aetna Indemnity, Cosmopolitan Fire Insurance, Title & Guarantee of Rochester, and Provident Savings Life Assurance Society. Some observers suggested that Heinze had interests in six insurance companies. We were unable to identify the other two.

29. See, for instance, Charles Perrow, *Normal Accidents: Living with High-Risk Technologies* (Princeton, NJ: Princeton University Press, 1999) and Bruner (2005).

Chapter 8: Clearing House

1. Figures are for 1907 as given in *Historical Statistics of the United States,* Series X-634 and X-656 (Washington DC: Bureau of the Census, Department of Commerce). The number of non-nationally chartered banks would reach a peak of 22,926 in 1921, as compared with a peak of 8,024 national banks in 1922.
2. *Historical Statistics of the United States,* Series X-617 and 619 (Washington, DC: Bureau of the Census, Department of Commerce).
3. Data for mutual savings banks are given in *Historical Statistics of the United States: Colonial Times to the Present,* 1975, Part 2, Series X-683-688, p. 1031 (Washington DC: Bureau of the Census, Department of Commerce).
4. Data for private banks are given in *Historical Statistics of the United States: Colonial Times to the Present*, 1975, Part 2, Series X-683-688 (Washington DC: Bureau of the Census, Department of Commerce).
5. Larry Neal, "Trust Companies and Financial Innovation, 1897–1914," *The Business History Review* 45, no. 1 (Spring 1971): 38.
6. Source of information on trust companies: Moen and Tallman (1992).

7. *Historical Statics of the United States,* 1975, Part 2, Series X-668, X-671, X-646 and X-649 (Washington DC: Bureau of the Census, Department of Commerce).
8. See data in Sprague (1911), pp. 218–221.
9. The bank suspensions in 1906 included 34 state banks, 13 private banks, and 6 national banks. In 1907, there were 90 bank suspensions: 58 state banks, 12 national banks, and 20 private banks (most of these occurred in the fall, after the failure of the Knickerbocker Trust Company in October). In 1908, 153 bank suspensions were recorded: 83 state banks, 51 private banks, and 19 national banks. See U.S. Bureau of the Census (1949), chart Series N 135-140, Bank Suspensions-Number of Suspensions: 1864–1945, p. 273.
10. See New York Clearing House Association Records, 1853–2004, Columbia University Libraries, http://findingaids.cul.columbia.edu/ead/nnc-rb/ldpd_7094252/summary#history (accessed June 29, 2017).
11. For more discussion of the advent of clearing houses and their role in resolving information, accountability and other problems, see Gorton (1985b), Gorton and Mullineaux (1987), and Timberlake (1894).
12. For discussion of the monopolistic nature of clearing houses, see Donaldson (1993). Also see McAndrews and Roberds (1995)
13. Noyes (1909b), p. 369.
14. *New York Times*, October 18, 1907, p. 1.
15. *Wall Street Journal*, October 19, 1907, p. 1.
16. *New York Times*, October 18, 1907, p. 1.
17. Ibid.
18. *New York Times*, October 19, 1907, p. 1.
19. *Chicago Daily Tribune*, October 19, 1907, p. 4.
20. Ibid.
21. *New York Times*, October 20, 1907, p. 1.
22. Ibid.
23. Ibid.
24. *Chicago Daily Tribune*, October 19, 1907, p. 4.
25. *New York Times*, October 20, 1907, p. 1.
26. Ibid.
27. *Washington Post*, October 21, 1907, p. 1.

28. *Wall Street Journal*, October 22, 1907, p. 1; and *Washington Post*, October 22, 1907, p. 3.
29. *Washington Post*, October 22, 1907, p. 3.
30. *New York Times*, October 19, 1907, p. 1.
31. *New York Times*, October 22, 1907, p. 2.
32. Ibid.
33. *Wall Street Journal*, October 22, 1907, p. 1.

Chapter 9: Knickerbocker

1. Satterlee (1939), p. 455. Reprinted with the permission of Scribner, an imprint of Simon & Schuster Adult Publishing Group, from *J. Pierpont Morgan: An Intimate Portrait* by Herbert L. Satterlee. Copyright © 1939 by Herbert L. Satterlee; copyright renewed, © 1967 by Mabel Satterlee Ingalls. All rights reserved.
2. The descriptions of the Knickerbocker Trust Company and many of the details about the run on the Knickerbocker and its subsequent suspension appeared originally in various contemporary accounts in the following periodicals: the *Bankers' Magazine*, the *Chicago Daily Tribune*, the *Commercial and Financial Chronicle*, the *Independent*, the *New York Times*, the *Wall Street Journal*, and the *Washington Post*. The intervention of J. P. Morgan during this early phase of the crisis of 1907 has been ably told in several Morgan biographies, especially those by Chernow, Satterlee, and Strouse. The best details and primary source material of the actions of the bankers were the personal recollections of George W. Perkins and Benjamin Strong, which we accessed at the Morgan Library and Museum and the archives of the Federal Reserve Bank of New York, respectively.
3. This location would later become the site for the Empire State Building.
4. *Wall Street Journal*, November 2, 1903, p. 4.
5. Ibid., and *Bankers' Magazine*, November 1903, p. 719.
6. *Bankers' Magazine*, August 1907, p. 207.
7. Carosso (1970), pp. 98–99.
8. Moen and Tallman (1992), pp. 612–614.
9. Sprague (1910), p. 227.
10. Moen and Tallman (1992), p. 615.
11. Ibid., p. 613.

12. McCulley (1992), p. 205.
13. Hansen (2014), pp. 56. The three trust companies were Manhattan Trust, Van Norden Trust, and Knickerbocker Trust. The membership in NYCH of trust companies in the outer boroughs has not been established. However, if proximity was directly associated with membership in the NYCH, then the membership of those farther trust companies would have been less likely. Fohlin and Liu (2021) count 59 trust companies in New York City, implying that 21 trust companies were headquartered in the outer boroughs.
14. Generally, see La Follette (1908). See also the records of the Pujo Hearings of 1912–1913.
15. Hansen (2014), pp. 560–561.
16. Ibid., p. 555.
17. Sprague (1910), p. 228.
18. Sprague (1910), pp. 232–233, identified the six banks in order of significance: City, Bank of Commerce, First National, Park, Chase, and Hanover.
19. Sprague (1910), p. 234.
20. Satterlee (1939), pp. 464–465. Reprinted with the permission of Scribner, an imprint of Simon & Schuster Adult Publishing Group, from *J. Pierpont Morgan: An Intimate Portrait* by Herbert L. Satterlee. Copyright © 1939 by Herbert L. Satterlee; copyright renewed, © 1967 by Mabel Satterlee Ingalls. All rights reserved.
21. Ibid., pp. 464–465. Reprinted with the permission of Scribner, an imprint of Simon & Schuster Adult Publishing Group, from *J. Pierpont Morgan: An Intimate Portrait* by Herbert L. Satterlee. Copyright © 1939 by Herbert L. Satterlee; copyright renewed, © 1967 by Mabel Satterlee Ingalls. All rights reserved; and *Bankers' Magazine*, November 1903, p. 719.
22. "Charles Tracey Barney," *New York Times,* October 22, 1907, p. 2.
23. Satterlee (1939), p. 455. Reprinted with the permission of Scribner, an imprint of Simon & Schuster Adult Publishing Group, from *J. Pierpont Morgan: An Intimate Portrait* by Herbert L. Satterlee. Copyright © 1939 by Herbert L. Satterlee; copyright renewed, © 1967 by Mabel Satterlee Ingalls. All rights reserved.
24. Ibid., p. 455. Reprinted with the permission of Scribner, an imprint of Simon & Schuster Adult Publishing Group, from *J. Pierpont Morgan: An Intimate Portrait* by Herbert L. Satterlee. Copyright © 1939 by Herbert L.

Satterlee; copyright renewed, © 1967 by Mabel Satterlee Ingalls. All rights reserved.

25. *New York Times*, November 15, 1907, p. 1.
26. Satterlee (1939), p. 455. Reprinted with the permission of Scribner, an imprint of Simon & Schuster Adult Publishing Group, from *J. Pierpont Morgan: An Intimate Portrait* by Herbert L. Satterlee. Copyright © 1939 by Herbert L. Satterlee; copyright renewed, © 1967 by Mabel Satterlee Ingalls. All rights reserved.
27. Sprague (1908), p. 359.
28. Calomiris and Gorton (1991), p. 156.
29. "Clearing House Has Banking Situation Here Well in Hand," *Wall Street Journal*, October 22, 1907, p. 1.
30. "Knickerbocker Will Be Aided," *New York Times*, October 22, 1907, p. 1.

Chapter 10: A Vote of No Confidence

1. Satterlee (1939), pp. 464–465. Reprinted with the permission of Scribner, an imprint of Simon & Schuster Adult Publishing Group, from *J. Pierpont Morgan: An Intimate Portrait* by Herbert L. Satterlee. Copyright © 1939 by Herbert L. Satterlee; copyright renewed, © 1967 by Mabel Satterlee Ingalls. All rights reserved.
2. Quoted from "Statement by the Clearing House" as given in Hansen (2018), p. 257, and Wicker (2000), p. 89.
3. For a detailed discussion of this point and generally of the Knickerbocker receivership, see Hanna (1931), especially pp. 325 and 327–348.
4. *New York Times*, October 22, 1907, p. 1.
5. *Wall Street Journal*, October 23, 1907, p. 1.
6. *New York Times*, October 22, 1907, p. 1.
7. Ibid.
8. McCulley (1992), p. 179.
9. Sprague (1910), p.253.
10. *Chicago Daily Tribune*, October 22, 1907, p. 1.
11. Ibid.
12. Ibid.
13. Ibid.

14. Ibid.
15. *New York Times*, October 6, 1907, p. 12.
16. *Chicago Daily Tribune*, October 22, 1907, p. 1.
17. Strouse (1999), p. 575 (footnote).
18. Satterlee (1939), pp. 455–458. Reprinted with the permission of Scribner, an imprint of Simon & Schuster Adult Publishing Group, from *J. Pierpont Morgan: An Intimate Portrait* by Herbert L. Satterlee. Copyright © 1939 by Herbert L. Satterlee; copyright renewed, © 1967 by Mabel Satterlee Ingalls. All rights reserved.
19. See Moen and Rodgers (2022), p. 12, for a discussion of the failed Alaska salmon canning syndicate.
20. See, for general reference, Lefèvre, "(1908), and La Follette (1908).
21. Satterlee (1939), pp. 464–465. Reprinted with the permission of Scribner, an imprint of Simon & Schuster Adult Publishing Group, from *J. Pierpont Morgan: An Intimate Portrait* by Herbert L. Satterlee. Copyright © 1939 by Herbert L. Satterlee; copyright renewed, © 1967 by Mabel Satterlee Ingalls. All rights reserved.
22. *New York Times*, October 22, 1907, p. 1.
23. Woods (2011), p. 67.
24. Satterlee (1939), p. 456. Reprinted with the permission of Scribner, an imprint of Simon & Schuster Adult Publishing Group, from *J. Pierpont Morgan: An Intimate Portrait* by Herbert L. Satterlee. Copyright © 1939 by Herbert L. Satterlee; copyright renewed, © 1967 by Mabel Satterlee Ingalls. All rights reserved.
25. *Chicago Daily Tribune*, October 22, 1907, p. 1.
26. *Washington Post*, October 25, 1907, p. 2.
27. *New York Times*, October 23, 1907, p. 2.
28. Account by Perkins in Crowther (1933), unpublished manuscript.
29. Ibid.
30. This statement has been attributed to Frank Borman, a former astronaut who became CEO of Eastern Airlines, a company that ultimately went bankrupt. He allegedly added, "But it is hard to see any Good News in that" (J. Madeleine Nash, Bruce Van Voorst, and Alexander L. Taylor III, "The Growing Bankruptcy Brigade," *Time*, October 18, 1982).
31. Strouse (1999), p. 577.

32. These amounts are approximate, but not precise, as of October 21, 1907. They are drawn from *Annual Report of the Superintendent of Banks Relative to Savings Banks, Trust Companies, Safe Deposit Companies and Miscellaneous Corporations, for the Year 1907*, pp. 582–585, which reported Knickerbocker's condition as of January 1, 1907.

Chapter 11: A Classic Run

1. Diary of Marion Satterlee, pp. 13, 14.
2. *Washington Post*, October 23, 1907, p. 2.
3. Ibid.
4. *New York Times*, October 23, 1907, p. 2.
5. Ibid.
6. Ibid.
7. Ibid.
8. Ibid.
9. Ibid.
10. Ibid.
11. Ibid.
12. *Wall Street Journal*, October 23, 1907, p. 1.
13. *Washington Post*, October 23, 1907, p. 2; and *New York Times*, October 23, 1907, p. 2.
14. *New York Times*, October 23, 1907, p. 2.
15. Ibid.
16. Ibid.
17. Ibid.
18. Ibid.
19. Satterlee (1939), p. 466. Reprinted with the permission of Scribner, an imprint of Simon & Schuster Adult Publishing Group, from *J. Pierpont Morgan: An Intimate Portrait* by Herbert L. Satterlee. Copyright © 1939 by Herbert L. Satterlee; copyright renewed, © 1967 by Mabel Satterlee Ingalls. All rights reserved.
20. *New York Times*, October 23, 1907, p. 2.
21. Ibid.

22. *Washington Post*, October 23, 1907, p. 2.
23. *New York Times*, October 23, 1907, p. 2.
24. Ibid.
25. Gorton (1988), pp. 751–752.
26. For more, see Gorton and Mullineaux (1987), p. 601.
27. For more, see Gorton (1985), p. 178a.
28. Merton (1948), p. 195.
29. Diamond and Dybvig (1983).
30. The anecdote cannot be confirmed independently and may be apocryphal. We offer it for illustration only.
31. See, for instance, Shiller (2019).
32. See for instance, Behabib and Farmer (1995) and Gu (2022).

Chapter 12: Such Assistance as May Be Necessary

1. *Washington Post*, October 23, 1907, p. 2.
2. Ibid.; and *New York Times*, October 23, 1907, p. 2.
3. A memorandum report of Strong to Lamont in Benjamin Strong Papers, Federal Reserve Bank of New York archives, quoted in Carosso (1987), p. 538.
4. Starkman (2014), p. 57.
5. Tallman and Moen (2010a), p. 17.
6. Wicker (2000), p. 92.
7. Frydman, Hilt, and Zhou (2015), p. 936.
8. Hansen (2014), p. 556.
9. Strong (1924), 22-page letter to Thomas W. Lamont, Benjamin Strong Papers, Federal Reserve Bank of New York, New York.
10. *Washington Post*, October 23, 1907, p. 1.
11. Ibid., p. 2.
12. Ibid.
13. Ibid.
14. Ibid., p. 1.
15. *New York Times*, October 23, 1907, p. 1.
16. *Wall Street Journal*, October 23, 1907, p. 1.

17. Ibid.
18. Ibid.; and *Washington Post*, October 23, 1907, p. 1.
19. Satterlee (1939), p. 466.
20. Ibid.
21. Strong (1924), 22-page letter to Thomas W. Lamont, Benjamin Strong Papers, Federal Reserve Bank of New York, New York; and *Bankers' Magazine*, May 1905, p. 624.
22. *Wall Street Journal*, June 22, 1905, p. 8.
23. Strouse (1999), p. 577.
24. *Washington Post*, October 23, 1907, p. 1.
25. McCulley (1992), p. 147. Also *Response of the Secretary of the Treasury to Senate Resolution No. 33* (1908).
26. U.S. Department of the Treasury (1908), p. 14.
27. Noyes (1909b), pp. 374–375.
28. Account by Perkins in Crowther (1933), unpublished manuscript.
29. *New York Times*, October 23, 1907, p. 1.
30. See, for instance, U.S. House of Representatives (Stanley Committee), 1912, *Investigation of United States Steel Corporation Report* (Washington, DC: U.S. Government Printing Office, Report No. 1127), pp. 186–187.
31. Strong (1924), 22-page letter to Thomas W. Lamont, Benjamin Strong Papers, Federal Reserve Bank of New York, New York.
32. See *Annual Report of the Superintendent of Banks Relative to Savings Banks, Trust Companies, Safe Deposit Companies and Miscellaneous Corporations for the Year 1907*, March 16, 1908, Albany, NY: J.B. Lyon Company, State Printers. Pages 594-602.
33. Satterlee (1939), p. 467. Reprinted with the permission of Scribner, an imprint of Simon & Schuster Adult Publishing Group, from *J. Pierpont Morgan: An Intimate Portrait* by Herbert L. Satterlee. Copyright © 1939 by Herbert L. Satterlee; copyright renewed, © 1967 by Mabel Satterlee Ingalls. All rights reserved.
34. Ibid., p. 468. Reprinted with the permission of Scribner, an imprint of Simon & Schuster Adult Publishing Group, from *J. Pierpont Morgan: An Intimate Portrait* by Herbert L. Satterlee. Copyright © 1939 by Herbert L. Satterlee; copyright renewed, © 1967 by Mabel Satterlee Ingalls. All rights reserved.
35. Strong (1924), 22-page letter to Thomas W. Lamont, Benjamin Strong Papers, Federal Reserve Bank of New York, New York.

36. Ibid.
37. Ibid.
38. Bagehot (1873).

Chapter 13: Trust Company of America

1. Strong (1924), 22-page letter to Thomas W. Lamont, Benjamin Strong Papers, Federal Reserve Bank of New York, New York.
2. Data on Trust Company of America are drawn from its statement of condition at August 22, 1907, as reprinted in "Gov't and Private Capital Relieve Wall Street Strain," *New York Times,* October 24, 1907, p. 1.
3. Account by Perkins in Crowther (1933), unpublished manuscript.
4. *New York Times*, October 24, 1907, p. 10.
5. Satterlee (1939), p. 470. Reprinted with the permission of Scribner, an imprint of Simon & Schuster Adult Publishing Group, from *J. Pierpont Morgan: An Intimate Portrait* by Herbert L. Satterlee. Copyright © 1939 by Herbert L. Satterlee; copyright renewed, © 1967 by Mabel Satterlee Ingalls. All rights reserved.
6. Account by Perkins in Crowther (1933), unpublished manuscript. Italics were added to the original.
7. Sprague (1910), p. 279.
8. The figures are quoted in Sprague (1910), p. 262, as of October 26, approximately the nadir of the crisis.
9. Strong (1924), 22-page letter to Thomas W. Lamont, Benjamin Strong Papers, Federal Reserve Bank of New York, New York.
10. Ibid.
11. Ibid.

Chapter 14: Crisis on the Exchange

1. Recounted in Satterlee (1939), p. 477. Reprinted with the permission of Scribner, an imprint of Simon & Schuster Adult Publishing Group, from *J. Pierpont Morgan: An Intimate Portrait* by Herbert L. Satterlee. Copyright © 1939 by Herbert L. Satterlee; copyright renewed, © 1967 by Mabel Satterlee Ingalls. All rights reserved.
2. Ibid., p. 473. Reprinted with the permission of Scribner, an imprint of Simon & Schuster Adult Publishing Group, from *J. Pierpont Morgan: An*

Intimate Portrait by Herbert L. Satterlee. Copyright © 1939 by Herbert L. Satterlee; copyright renewed, © 1967 by Mabel Satterlee Ingalls. All rights reserved.

3. Ibid. Reprinted with the permission of Scribner, an imprint of Simon & Schuster Adult Publishing Group, from *J. Pierpont Morgan: An Intimate Portrait* by Herbert L. Satterlee. Copyright © 1939 by Herbert L. Satterlee; copyright renewed, © 1967 by Mabel Satterlee Ingalls. All rights reserved.
4. *Response of the Secretary of the Treasury to Senate Resolution No. 33* (January 1908), p. 227.
5. Quoted in the *New York Times*, October 25, 1907, p. 7.
6. In 1791, Treasury Secretary Alexander Hamilton deployed the resources of a bond sinking fund to stabilize the stock market in shares of the Bank of the United States after a corner attempt. Even that was a targeted intervention in one security. Cortelyou's intervention was the first *general* injection of liquidity into credit markets in U.S. history.
7. The estimates of $54 million and $64 million are derived from data in *Response of the Secretary of the Treasury to Senate Resolution No. 33* (January 1908), pp. 37–72.
8. An audit in 1902 showed that John D. Rockefeller Sr. was worth about $200 million; by comparison, at the time of his death in 1913, J. P. Morgan's estate was valued at approximately $80 million.
9. "Call Money Loans at 100%," *Wall Street Journal*, October 25, 1907, p. 8.
10. Account by Perkins in Crowther (1933), unpublished manuscript.
11. Rodgers and Payne (2014), p. 420.
12. Moen and Tallman (2003), pp. 10, 12.
13. Moen and Tallman (1992), p. 625.
14. Moen and Tallman (2000), p. 149.
15. Moen and Tallman (2014), p. 1.
16. Moen and Tallman (2003), p. 2.
17. The number of standard deviations is equivalent to a "Z-score," computed as $(X_t - \chi)/\sigma$, where X_t is the observed high–low spread for day t, χ is the average spread between daily high and low call money rate quotations from August 29 to September 29, 1907, and σ is the standard deviation of high–low spreads from August 29 to September 29. Over the hold-out period, χ was 1.76 percent and σ was 0.90 percent. Data were obtained from hand-collected quotations in the *Wall Street Journal* and *New York Times*.

18. Satterlee (1939), p. 474. Reprinted with the permission of Scribner, an imprint of Simon & Schuster Adult Publishing Group, from *J. Pierpont Morgan: An Intimate Portrait* by Herbert L. Satterlee. Copyright © 1939 by Herbert L. Satterlee; copyright renewed, © 1967 by Mabel Satterlee Ingalls. All rights reserved.
19. Account by Perkins in Crowther (1933), unpublished manuscript.
20. "Money: Loaning Power of Banks Reduced by Extending Aid to Others," *Wall Street Journal,* October 26, 1907, p. 1.
21. Account by Perkins in Crowther (1933), unpublished manuscript.
22. Ibid.
23. Satterlee (1939), p. 476. Reprinted with the permission of Scribner, an imprint of Simon & Schuster Adult Publishing Group, from *J. Pierpont Morgan: An Intimate Portrait* by Herbert L. Satterlee. Copyright © 1939 by Herbert L. Satterlee; copyright renewed, © 1967 by Mabel Satterlee Ingalls. All rights reserved.
24. Account by Perkins in Crowther (1933), unpublished manuscript.
25. Ibid.
26. Ibid.
27. "Call Money Rates," *Wall Street Journal,* October 26, 1907, p. 8.
28. Satterlee (1939), p. 479. Reprinted with the permission of Scribner, an imprint of Simon & Schuster Adult Publishing Group, from *J. Pierpont Morgan: An Intimate Portrait* by Herbert L. Satterlee. Copyright © 1939 by Herbert L. Satterlee; copyright renewed, © 1967 by Mabel Satterlee Ingalls. All rights reserved.
29. Account by Perkins in Crowther (1933), unpublished manuscript.

Chapter 15: A City in Trouble

1. *New York Times*, October 28, 1907, p. 1.
2. *New York Times*, October 23, 1907, p. 5.
3. Morison, Blum, Chandler, and Rice (1952), Volume 5, p. 823.
4. *New York Times*, October 26, 1907, p. 1.
5. *New York Times*, October 27, 1907, p. 5.
6. *New York Times*, October 26, 1907, p. 1.
7. *New York Times*, October 29, 1907, p. 2.
8. *New York Times*, October 27, 1907, p. 2.

9. *Response of the Secretary of the Treasury to Senate Resolution No. 33, of December 12, 1907* (U.S. Department of the Treasury, 1908), p. 14.
10. Ibid., pp. 23, 31.
11. Sprague (1908), p. 367.
12. The estimate of $200 million is from Maurice L. Muhleman, *Monetary and Banking Systems: A Comprehensive Account of the Systems in the United States* (New York: Monetary Publishing, 1908). The higher figure, $296 million, is from Noyes (1909a), p. 188.
13. The figure of 8 percent equals $233 million divided by $2,813 million, an estimate of currency in circulation given in *Historical Statistics of the United States* (1970) Series X420-423, Volume II, p. 993. The currency in circulation in 1907, $1.784 billion, is from Friedman and Schwartz (1963).
14. "Leaders'View of Situation," *Chicago Daily Tribune,* October 27, 1907, p. 2.
15. *Response of the Secretary of the Treasury to Senate Resolution No. 33, of December 12, 1907* (U.S. Department of the Treasury, 1908), p. 225.
16. For more information on the incentives and analytics around gold importation to the United States during the Panic of 1907, see Rodgers and Wilson (2011) and Rodgers and Payne (2014).
17. Wicker (2000), Chapter 5, "The Trust Company Panic of 1907."
18. Andrew (1908b), p. 507, estimates that $238 million in clearing house certificates were issued. Our total of $219 million derives from the *outstanding* certificates given in the report of the Comptroller of the Currency for 1907. Outstanding volumes would seem to give a better indication (than issuances) of the economic impact of the use of clearing house loan certificates.
19. Cannon (1910) identifies the use of clearing house loan certificates in the following cities: New York, New York; Augusta, Georgia; Baltimore, Maryland; Buffalo, New York; Canton, Ohio; Chicago, Illinois; Cincinnati, Ohio; Denver, Colorado; Des Moines, Iowa; Detroit, Michigan; Fargo, North Dakota; Fort Wayne, Indiana; Grand Rapids, Michigan; Harrisburg Pennsylvania; Kansas City, Missouri; Little Rock, Arkansas; Los Angeles, California; Omaha, Nebraska; Philadelphia, Pennsylvania; Portland, Oregon; St. Joseph, Missouri; St. Louis, Missouri; St. Paul, Minnesota; Salt Lake City, Utah; San Francisco, California; Savannah, Georgia; Seattle, Washington; Sioux City, Iowa; South Bend, Indiana; Spokane, Washington; Tacoma, Washington; Topeka, Kansas; Wichita, Kansas; and Wheeling, West Virginia. Casual review of newspapers and other publications that year suggests that this list is not exhaustive.

20. Andrew (1908b), p. 515.
21. The percentage estimate is calculated against all cash in the hands of the public, $1.784 billion, from Friedman and Schwartz (1963), p. 706.
22. *New York Times*, October 28, 1907, p. 1.
23. *New York Times*, October 29, 1907, p. 1.
24. Account by Perkins in Crowther (1933), unpublished manuscript.
25. Ibid.
26. Ibid.
27. Ibid.
28. Ibid.
29. *Response of the Secretary of the Treasury to Senate Resolution No. 33 of December 12, 1907, Calling for Certain Information in Regard to Treasury Operations, United States Depositaries, the Condition of National Banks, etc.* (U.S. Department of the Treasury, 1908), pp. 15, 16.

Chapter 16: Modern Medici

1. Strong (1924), 22-page letter to Thomas W. Lamont, Benjamin Strong Papers, Federal Reserve Bank of New York, New York.
2. Hansen (2014), p. 559.
3. Account by Perkins in Crowther (1933), unpublished manuscript.
4. Ibid.
5. Strong (1924), 22-page letter to Thomas W. Lamont, Benjamin Strong Papers, Federal Reserve Bank of New York, New York.
6. Satterlee (1939), p. 485. Reprinted with the permission of Scribner, an imprint of Simon & Schuster Adult Publishing Group, from *J. Pierpont Morgan: An Intimate Portrait* by Herbert L. Satterlee. Copyright © 1939 by Herbert L. Satterlee; copyright renewed, © 1967 by Mabel Satterlee Ingalls. All rights reserved.
7. Strong (1924), 22-page letter to Thomas W. Lamont, Benjamin Strong Papers, Federal Reserve Bank of New York, New York.
8. Ibid.
9. See, for instance, Olson (1965).
10. See, for instance, Ostrom (1990).

11. Hansen (2014), pp. 559–560. The report of the New York Superintendent of Banks for 1907 listed 38 trust companies in Manhattan, four of which started up in that year, thus reducing the data available to 34.
12. Fohlin and Liu (2021), p. 515.
13. On January 1, 1898, Manhattan, Brooklyn, Staten Island, Queens, and the Bronx consolidated into New York City.
14. The Herfindahl–Hirschman Index (HHI) measures industry concentration. The HHI for the Manhattan trust companies (based on distribution of deposits) was 495—this compares to modern U.S. antitrust standards, which deem an HHI below 1,500 to indicate a competitive marketplace. A second measure is the Gini Coefficient which measures the dispersion of an economic quantity among members of a group (today, commonly used to measure income or wealth inequality). This varies between zero (total equality) and 1.0 (total inequality). The Gini coefficient for the dispersion of deposits among the 38 Manhattan trust companies is 34 percent, which implies moderate concentration. These measures ignore deposits held in state and national banks in the New York City financial services market and are offered simply to illustrate the extent of concentration of deposits among New York trust companies.
15. Strong (1924), 22-page letter to Thomas W. Lamont, Benjamin Strong Papers, Federal Reserve Bank of New York, New York.
16. Lamont (1975), p. 81.
17. Strong (1924), 22-page letter to Thomas W. Lamont, Benjamin Strong Papers, Federal Reserve Bank of New York, New York.
18. Ibid.
19. Ibid.
20. Ibid.
21. Satterlee (1939), p. 485. Reprinted with the permission of Scribner, an imprint of Simon & Schuster Adult Publishing Group, from *J. Pierpont Morgan: An Intimate Portrait* by Herbert L. Satterlee. Copyright © 1939 by Herbert L. Satterlee; copyright renewed, © 1967 by Mabel Satterlee Ingalls. All rights reserved.
22. Lamont (1975), p. 81.
23. Ibid., p. 82.
24. Ibid.
25. Ibid.

Chapter 17: Instant and Far-Reaching Relief

1. *New York Times*, October 30, 1907, p. 3.
2. Wicker (2000), p. 96, quoting U.S. House of Representatives, Stanley Hearings, 1911, vol. 2, p. 936.
3. *New York Times*, October 30, 1907, p. 3.
4. *New York Times*, November 3, 1907, p. 3.
5. Cotter (1916), p. 71.
6. Tarbell (1933), p. 197.
7. Among the owners from whom TC&I was purchased was Oakleigh Thorne, the president of the struggling Trust Company of America; by 1907, in fact, the Trust Company held about $640,000 worth of TC&I stock.
8. Satterlee (1939), p. 486. Reprinted with the permission of Scribner, an imprint of Simon & Schuster Adult Publishing Group, from *J. Pierpont Morgan: An Intimate Portrait* by Herbert L. Satterlee. Copyright © 1939 by Herbert L. Satterlee, copyright renewed, © 1967 by Mabel Satterlee Ingalls. All rights reserved.
9. Account by Perkins in Crowther (1933), unpublished manuscript.
10. Satterlee (1939), p. 486. Reprinted with the permission of Scribner, an imprint of Simon & Schuster Adult Publishing Group, from *J. Pierpont Morgan: An Intimate Portrait* by Herbert L. Satterlee. Copyright © 1939 by Herbert L. Satterlee, copyright renewed, © 1967 by Mabel Satterlee Ingalls. All rights reserved.
11. Tarbell (1933), pp. 199–200.
12. Satterlee (1939), p. 487. Reprinted with the permission of Scribner, an imprint of Simon & Schuster Adult Publishing Group, from *J. Pierpont Morgan: An Intimate Portrait* by Herbert L. Satterlee. Copyright © 1939 by Herbert L. Satterlee; copyright renewed, © 1967 by Mabel Satterlee Ingalls. All rights reserved.
13. Ibid.
14. Gold bonds promised repayment in gold coin as opposed to silver coin or paper currency.
15. Account by Perkins in Crowther (1933), unpublished manuscript.
16. This entire exchange between Morgan and Gary was recounted in Tarbell (1933), p. 200.
17. Pringle (1931), pp. 441–442.

18. Tarbell (1933), p. 201.
19. Pringle (1931), p. 443, quoting U.S. House of Representatives, *Investigation of United States Steel Corporation* (1912), p. 1371.
20. Pringle (1931), p. 442.
21. Morison, Blum, Chandler, and Rice (1952), Volume 5: *The Big Stick, 1905–1907,* pp. 830–831.
22. *Commercial and Financial Chronicle*, November 9, 1907, p. 1176.
23. "Steel Trust Aid Not Opposed: No Likelihood of Invoking Anti-Trust Law," *New York Times*, p. 1.
24. *New York Times,* November 7, 1907, p. 13.

Chapter 18: Turning the Corner

1. Noyes (1909a), p. 211.
2. "Tennessee Coal & Iron: Possibility That Company Will Be Acquired," *Wall Street Journal*, November 5, 1907, p. 6. Also, "United Support For Trust Companies: Steel Corporation to Take Up Loans on Tennessee Coal and Iron Stock," *New York Times*, November 5, 1907, p. 2.
3. Account by Perkins in Crowther (1933), unpublished manuscript.
4. "Westinghouse Troubles Caused Purely by Money Stringency," *Manchester Guardian,* October 24, 1907, p. 14.
5. "Banks Leaving Trouble Behind," *New York Times,* October 27, 1907, p. 1.
6. "In Rush of Gold Helps Our Banks" *New York Times,* October 29, 1907, p. 1.
7. Noyes (1909a), p. 211.
8. Sprague (1908), p. 361.
9. *Commercial and Financial Chronicle*, November 9, 1907, p. 1177.
10. "American Stringency: Treasury Comes to the Relief," *The Manchester Guardian*, November 19, 1907, p. 7.
11. *New York Times*, November 9, 1907, p. 2.
12. Rodgers and Payne (2014), p. 427.
13. Rodgers and Wilson (2011), p. 173.
14. "President Roosevelt Gives Assurance: Tells People to Stop Hoarding—Not a Particle of Risk in Letting Business Take Its Course," *Washington Post*, p. 1.

15. *Response of the Secretary of the Treasury to Senate Resolution No. 33 of December 12, 1907* (U.S. Department of the Treasury, 1908), p. 17.
16. "Boston Thanks J.P. Morgan: Stock Exchange Expresses Gratitude for Action during Fight," *New York Times,* November 2, 1907, p. 2.
17. "John Pierpont Morgan A Bank in Human Form," *New York Times,* November 10, 1907, p. SM9.
18. *Literary Digest,* November 9, 1907, p. 676, cited in Goodwin (2013), p. 529.
19. Editorial, *The Seattle Star,* November 9, 1907, page 4.
20. William Jennings Bryan, ed. "Current Topics," *The Commoner* (Lincoln, NE), November 29, 1907, p. 8. Library of Congress: http://chroniclingamerica.loc.gov/lccn/46032385/1907-11-29/ed-1/.
21. "Votes Confidence in Banks: Chicago Labor Unions Follow President Gompers' Lead," *Washington Post,* November 5, 1907, p. 1.
22. "Digs at President: Spooner Sarcastic at New York Commerce Banquet," *Washington Post,* November 22, 1907, p. 1.
23. These figures are based on analysis of data in the *Annual Report of the Comptroller of the Currency*, 1908, pp. 65–66.
24. *Annual Report of the Comptroller of the Currency,* 1908 and 1907.

Chapter 19: Ripple Effects

1. "Banks in Good Shape: Perfect Stability Is Reported from Country at Large, New York Flurry Not Felt," *Washington Post*, October 23, 1907, p. 2.
2. "Western Banks on a Sound Basis: Chicago Loans Are on Tangible Assets, Not Stock Exchange Value. Flurry Not Felt Here," *Chicago Daily Tribune*, October 24, 1907, p. 2.
3. Ibid.
4. "A Sinister Feature: Strain Felt in Other Cities," *Manchester Guardian*, October 25, 1907, p. 9.
5. "Roosevelt Glad Panic Is Checked, President Congratulates Cortelyou and Financiers Who Aided Him in Crisis, Vote for Certificates, Clearing House Decides on Issue, Despite Opposition of Morgan Interests, Till the Crisis Passes, Other Cities Follow Suit," *Chicago Daily Tribune*, October 27, 1907, p. 1.
6. "Governor Keeps Banks Shut: Oklahoma Concerns Ordered to Take Precautionary Step," *Chicago Daily Tribune*, October 29, 1907, p. 2.

7. Cahill (1998).
8. "The West and the Money Crisis: Lessons of Essential Unity of the Country Is Being Taught," *Wall Street Journal*, November 13, 1907, 8.
9. "Times Decidedly Better," *Washington Post*, December 21, 1907, p. 6.
10. Ibid.
11. "Why the Panic Was Brief: The United States Too Prosperous to Be Frightened at This Time," *Washington Post* (from *Leslie's Weekly*), December 26, 1907, p. 6.
12. "Prosperity Wins Out," *Washington Post*, December 29, 1907, p. E4.
13. Calomiris and Gorton (1991), p. 161, date the end of suspension at January 4, 1908. Friedman and Schwartz (1963), p. 163, discuss that the U.S. Treasury resumed demanding payments in cash in December, but that some banks continued to restrict payments through January.
14. Francis B. Forbes, "Notes on the Financial Panic of 1907," *Publications of the American Statistical Association* 11, no. 18 (March 1908): 80–83.
15. James C. Bayles, "Unparalleled Year in Iron and Steel," *New York Times*, January 5, 1908, p. AFR30.
16. Noyes (1909a), p. 207.
17. Calomiris and Gorton (1991), p. 156.
18. Ibid. See also *Historical Statistics of the United States, Colonial Times to 1970* (U.S. Bureau of the Census, 1975), Part 2, Chapter V, series V 20–30, which shows a 34 percent spike in the number of business failures in 1908 over 1907, and a 12 percent increase in current liabilities in bankruptcies. This contests Sprague's assertion that "mercantile failures were not extraordinarily large in number or in amount of liabilities" (1910, p. 275).
19. Sprague (1908), pp. 368–371.
20. Noyes (1909a), p. 208.
21. Cahill (1998), p. 296.
22. Ibid.
23. J. P. Morgan Jr. Papers, ARC 1216, Box 5, letterpress book #4, January 16, 1908, to January 28, 1909, Morgan Library and Museum. Letter dated January 16, 1908.
24. Heckfeldt (2022).
25. Niles Carpenter Jr., "The Westinghouse Electric and Manufacturing Company, the General Electric Company, and the Panic of 1907: I," *Journal*

of Political Economy 24, no. 3 (March 1916): 230–253 and "The Westinghouse Electric and Manufacturing Company, the General Electric Company, and the Panic of 1907: II," *Journal of Political Economy* 24, no. 4 (April 1916): 382–399.

26. "Recent Financial Disturbances Viewed by Industrial Heads," *Wall Street Journal*, October 30, 1907, p. 5.
27. Bank of England, "A Millennium of Macroeconomic Data," downloaded August 30, 2022 from https://www.bankofengland.co.uk/statistics/research-datasets.
28. Both Alexander Noyes (1909a), pp. 202–206, and Charles Kindleberger (1977) mention that the Panic of 1907 occurred in a context of financial instability in foreign cities. The notion of contagion, or spread, of financial crises has been documented in the financial crises of the late twentieth century, but the global contagion in 1907 is not as fully documented. Flows of gold into and out of the United States in 1907 are well discussed in contemporary and recent writings on the Panic. It remains to be shown how these flows (or other mechanisms) actually transmitted the financial crisis globally in 1907.
29. Rodgers and Payne (2017), pp. 17–18.
30. Noyes (1909a), p. 206.
31. Cahill (1998), p. 795.
32. Ibid.
33. B. Eichengreen and R. Hausmann, "Exchange Rates and Financial Fragility," NBER Working Paper 7418 (Cambridge, MA: National Bureau of Economic Research, 1999).

Chapter 20: Reckoning and a Split

1. "Colonel Scored by La Follette," *Chicago Daily Tribune,* June 29, 1912, p. 7.
2. "La Follette Accuses the Insurance Companies: Charges Big Concerns Were in League with Morgan and Standard Oil Groups in Precipitating Panic," *New York Times,* March 20, 1908, p. 3.
3. William Jennings Bryan, *The Commoner,* November 22, 1907.
4. Chapter 2 of James Neal Primm, *A Foregone Conclusion: The Founding of the Federal Reserve Bank of St. Louis* (St. Louis: Federal Reserve Bank of St. Louis, 1989), gives a detailed and entertaining history of the legislative process that produced the Federal Reserve Act of 1913. See also Friedman

and Schwartz (1963), pp. 168–173, for a critical discussion of the banking reform efforts.

5. Letter from Roosevelt to George Otto Trevelyan, June 18, 1908, *Letters,* 17, n. 18.
6. Theodore Roosevelt, "State of the Union Address," December 2, 1902. Downloaded May 29, 2022 from https://www.gutenberg.org/files/5032/5032-h/5032-h.htm#dec1902.
7. John Oller, "George Wickersham: The Scourge of Wall Street," *Judicial Notice* 15 (2019).
8. McLaughlin (1971), p. 87. [Stanley used] "many extravagant and unsubstantiated allegations which were introduced as testimony during the hearings and later included in the Majority Report as facts, although neither the whole testimony or cross-examination supported the allegations."
9. For more discussion, see German (1972).
10. On the matter of TCI costs of production and transportation, see McLaughlin (1971), pp. 67–72.
11. John L. Moody, "The Steel Trust Consolidation," *The Commoner* 8, no. 4 (October 30, 1908). *Chronicling America: Historic American Newspapers.* Library of Congress, https://chroniclingamerica.loc.gov/lccn/46032385/1908-10-30/ed-1/seq-8/.
12. U.S. House of Representatives, *Investigation of United States Steel Corporation* (1912), p. 198. [Hereafter cited as *Investigation of United States Steel Corporation.*]
13. McLaughlin (1971), pp. 60–61.
14. *Investigation of United States Steel Corporation*, p. 190.
15. Ibid., p. 181.
16. Ibid., p. 192.
17. For brevity, this narrative omits subsidiary allegations in the Stanley Committee Majority Report. These include Gary's decision not to disclose the identity of Moore & Schley to Roosevelt, the probable open-market (unmanipulated) value of TCI shares, and so forth. See McLaughlin (1971) for more discussion of these and other points.
18. *Investigation of United States Steel Corporation*, p. 193.
19. Ibid., p. 196.
20. Ibid., p. 192.
21. Ibid., p. 206.

22. Ibid., p. 209.
23. "Steel Trust Is Attacked," *Fergus County Democrat*, October 31, 1911, p. 4, Image 4, downloaded June 30, 2022 from Fergus County Democrat. [volume] (Lewistown, Mont.) 1904-1919, October 31, 1911, Page 4, Image 4 « Chronicling America « Library of Congress (loc.gov).
24. "End of Steel Trust Sought in Big Suit," *Urbana Courier-Herald,* October 27, 1911, p. 2.
25. Letter of Roosevelt to Wheeler, October 30, 1911, Morison (1952), Vol. 7, pp. 429–430.
26. Letter of Roosevelt to James Garfield, October 31, 1911, Morison (1952), Vol. 7, pp. 430–431.
27. Theodore Roosevelt, *The Outlook,* XCVIII (August 19, 1911), pp. 849, 865–866.
28. Roosevelt (1913), p. 457.

Chapter 21: Money Trust

1. W. H. Harvey (1899), p. 130.
2. "100 Men Rule Nation, Says La Follette: In Standard Oil and Morgan Groups, and Plotted the Recent Panic, He Declares," *New York Times,* March 18, 1908, p. 1.
3. "Bought by Morgan: Banker Gets Control of Equitable Life Society," *Washington Post*, December 3, 1909," p. 1 and "Concerning New Money Power," *Wall Street Journal,* December 25, 1909, page 6.
4. "Bought by Morgan: Banker Gets Control of Equitable Life Society," *Washington Post*, December 3, 1909, p. 1.
5. "Money Institutions Combine," *Chicago Defender,* January 1, 1910, p. 1.
6. "Newest Combine in Money Trust," *Chicago Daily Tribune,* December 19, 1909, p. 5.
7. "Bought by Morgan," p. 1.
8. McCulley (1992), p. 179.
9. "Bank of Commerce to Morgan Group: Plans All Made," *New York Times*, p. 1.
10. "Great Banking Merger Planned," from the New York World. *Washington Post*, March 15, 1911, p. 6.
11. See A. Scott Berg, *Lindbergh* (New York: Putnam, 1998).

12. "Wants a Bank Inquiry: Republican Insurgent Sees Something Behind the Aldrich Plan," *New York Times,* July 9, 1911, p. 6.
13. "Big 'Money Trust" Attacked by Congressman from Minnesota," *Wall Street Journal,* December 16, 1911, p. 2.
14. "Untermyer to Lead Money Trust Inquiry . Has Expressed His Views," *New York Times,* January 5, 1912, p. 1.
15. "Money Trust Investigation," House of Representatives, Subcommittee of the Committee on Banking and Currency, Part 1, p. 4.
16. O'Sullivan (2015), p. 2.
17. Carosso (1973), p. 424, citing the argument of Richard Hofstadter, *The Paranoid Style in American Politics and Other Essays* (New York: Vintage, 1967), p. 29.
18. "Death of J.P. Morgan No Surprise to Wall Street: Long Illness Had Prepared Financial Community as Well as Friends for Inevitable End," *Wall Street Journal,* April 1, 1913, p. 1.
19. United States Congress. House. Committee on Banking and Currency, 1865–1974, Pujo, Arsène Paulin, 1861–1939 and Sixty-Second Congress, 1911–1913, "Part 15, Pages 1011–1101" in *Money Trust Investigation: Investigation of Financial and Monetary Conditions in the United States Under House Resolutions Nos. 429 and 504 Before a Subcommittee of the Committee on Banking and Currency, House of Representatives, (1912–1913)* (December 19, 1912), https://fraser.stlouisfed.org/title/80/item/23671.
20. Strouse (New York: Random House, 1999), p. 671.
21. O'Sullivan (2016), p. 291, summarizes the deposit funds and other resources on which the $1.6 billion estimate is based.
22. The M2 money supply estimate for 1913 of $15.73 billion is given in *U.S. Historical Statistics,* Bureau of the Census, U.S. Department of Commerce, 1975, Part 2, Series X 410-419, p. 992.
23. Brandeis, (1914), pp. 23 and 201.
24. "Untermyer Scored in House: Pujo Committee Counsel Denounced," *Chicago Daily Tribune*, February 28, 1913, p. 7.
25. "Morgan Defense in as Pujo Finishes," *New York Times,* February 28, 1913, p. 7.
26. "No Surprise Is Felt at Pujo Proposals," *New York Times,* March 1, 1913, p. 3.
27. Quotation of chief investigator Samuel Untermyer in McCulley (1992), p. 266.

28. This quotation of Woodrow Wilson corresponds to statements made in his campaign speeches and is reproduced in his book *The New Freedom: A Call for the Emancipation of the Generous Energies of a People* (New York and Garden City, NJ: Doubleday Page and Company, 1918), p. 185, https://books.google.com/books/about/The_New_Freedom.html?id=MW8SAAAAIAAJ.
29. Quoted in Carosso (1973), p. 423 from the *Commercial & Financial Chronicle,* XCIII (December 30, 1911), p. 1756.
30. Ibid., p. 437.
31. O'Sullivan (2016), p. 309.
32. Ibid., p. 290.
33. These numbers likely underestimate the volume of media attention to the phrase "money trust." We tallied the number of articles referencing "money trust" using the search engine for ProQuest Historical Newspapers. This source included only 10 publications: *New York Times, Wall Street Journal, Chicago Defender, Chicago Tribune, Norfolk Journal and Guide, Pittsburgh Courier, NY Amsterdam News, Baltimore Afro-American, Washington Post,* and *The Guardian & Observer.*

Chapter 22: A Central Bank

1. "Plan for Banks of Issue," *Chicago Daily Tribune,* November 24, 1907, p. 1.
2. "France Feels Sure Our Crisis Is Over," *New York Times*, November 24, 1907, p. C1. "Treasury to Allot $35,000,000 Threes; Crisis Considered Over," *New York Times*, November 29, 1907, p. 7.
3. "Plan for Banks of Issue: Senator Hansbrough Believes Central Bank Should Be in Chicago," *Chicago Daily Tribune*, November 24, 1907, p. 2.
4. "Congress for Currency Law: Poll of Members by the Times," *New York Times*, December 1, 1907, p. 1.
5. "Talk, Not Action, at This Congress: Imminence of Presidential Election Will Prevent Important Legislation at Washington," *Chicago Daily Tribune*, December 1, 1907, p. 1.
6. Letter from Theodore Roosevelt to Henry White, November 27, 1907, in Morison, Blum, Chandler, and Rice (1952), pp. 858–859.
7. *Report of the National Monetary Commission* (1912), p. 6. Hereafter "NMC Report (1912)."
8. NMC Report (1912), p. 9.

9. Ibid.
10. Ibid.
11. Ibid., p. 14.
12. McCulley (1992), p. 243.
13. Warburg (1930a), p. 12.
14. Details are from Glass (1927), pp. 124–126 and 173.
15. These points are summarized in Chandler (1958), pp. 34–40.
16. Bryan, quoted in Kazin (2006), p. 225.
17. Owen (1919), pp. 88–90.
18. As quoted from U.S. House of Representatives Committee on Banking and Currency, Subcommittee on Domestic Finance, 88th Congress, 2nd session, *A Primer on Money,* 1964 (Washington, DC: U.S. Government Printing Office), p. 79.
19. Warburg (1930a), p. 4.
20. Indeed, the Fed monetized federal government deficits during World War I, World War II, and the Vietnam War.
21. Quoted from the William McChesney Martin, Jr., Collection 1951 in Jessie Romero, "Treasury-Fed Accord," *Federal Reserve History*, https://www.federalreservehistory.org/essays/treasury_fed_accord (accessed September 29, 2018).

Chapter 23: Epilogue

1. The dollar value of deposits in the Knickerbocker Trust Company of $47 million was expressed in a statement by Herbert L. Satterlee in December 1907 and quoted in "Knickerbocker Trust Co.: Herbert L. Satterlee Speaks of Necessity of Cooperation by Depositors to Reopen Institution," *New York Times,* December 21, 1907, p. 8.
2. Sprague (1910, p. 251), Hansen (2014, pp. 556–557) and others have implied that the Knickerbocker was solvent but illiquid in arguments that Morgan used the crisis to discipline the trust companies.
3. "Joy at the Opening of Knickerbocker," *New York Times,* March 27, 1908, p. 6.
4. From 21,986 commercial and mutual savings banks, the number declined to 7,219 commercial banks at the end of 2007. See Federal Financial Institutions Examination Council (US) and Federal Reserve Bank of St. Louis, Commercial Banks in the U.S. (DISCONTINUED) [USNUM],

retrieved from FRED, Federal Reserve Bank of St. Louis; https://fred.stlouisfed.org/series/USNUM, July 8, 2022. Also see U.S. Bureau of the Census, *Historical Statistics of the United States: Colonial Times to 1970* (Washington, DC: Department of Commerce, 1975), Part 2, Series X580-587, p. 1019.

5. Dean Corbae and Pablo D'Erasmo, "Rising Bank Concentration," March 2020, Staff Report No. 594, Federal Reserve Bank of Minneapolis.
6. See Silber (2007) for details on the closing of the NYSE in 1914.
7. See Gage (2006) for details on the anarchist bombing at 23 Wall Street in 1920.
8. Manuscript of "The Life of F. Augustus Heinze," by Otto Heinze (1943), p. 62. Found among the papers of Sarah McNelis, Heinze's biographer.
9. New York Evening World, May 27, 1909, quoted in *Reveille*, May 28, 1909 and by McNelis (1968), p. 170.
10. McNelis (1968), p. 168.
11. Ibid., p. 183.
12. David Fettig (ed.), *F. Augustus Heinze of Montana and the Panic of 1907* (Federal Reserve of Minneapolis, 1989); also, *New York Times*, May 15, 1909, and November 5, 1914.
13. McNelis (1968), p. 184.
14. Zuckoff (2005), p. 49.
15. Details about Morse are drawn from Zuckoff (2005), pp. 49, 50.
16. Details about Morse after his return from Europe are drawn from Pringle (1939). Downloaded from www.doctorzebra.com/prez/z_x27morse_g.htm#zree16.
17. Wendt and Kogan (1948), p. 329.
18. Ibid., p. 331.
19. "Grant B. Schley, Financier, Dead: Head of Firm of Moore & Schley and Member of Stock Exchange for 36 Years; In Many Big Operations," *New York Times,* November 23, 1917, p. 11.
20. Letter to Douglas Robinson, November 16, 1907, excerpted in Hart and Ferleger (1941), p. 410.
21. Letter to Hamlin Garland, November 23, 1907, excerpted in Hart and Ferleger (1941), p. 411.
22. Elting E. Morison, "Introduction," in Morison, Blum, Chandler, and Rice (1952), Vol. 5, p. vii.

23. Quoted in Hart and Ferleger (1941), p. 607.
24. Brands (1997), p. 812.
25. Glass (1927).
26. Wicker (2005), p. 5.
27. Lopez (undated), "A Tarnished Legacy: George Fisher Baker, U.S. Steel, Convict Leasing and Columbia Athletics," Columbia University, downloaded August 17, 2022 from https://columbiaandslavery.columbia.edu/content/tarnished-legacy-george-fisher-baker-us-steel-convict-leasing-and-columbia-athletics.
28. "Leaders in Nation Eulogize Baker: Bankers Call Him 'Mentor' and Praise His Integrity and Unostentatious Charity," *New York Times,* May 3, 1931, p. 28.
29. "George F. Baker, 91, Dies Suddenly of Pneumonia; Dean of Nation's Bankers," *New York Times*, May 3, 1931, p. 1.
30. "Baker Was a Power in World Finance: With Elder Morgan and James A. Stillman, He Dominated Vast Network of Companies," *New York Times*, May 3, 1931, p. 28.
31. De Long (1991), p. 15, quoting Davison, Henry, (1913), *Letter from Messrs. J.P. Morgan and Co. in Response to the Invitation of the Sub-Committee (Hon. A.P. Pujo, Chairman) of the Committee on Banking and Currency of the House of Representatives,* New York [Harvard Graduate School of Business Baker Library, Thomas W. Lamont Papers, Box 210-26].
32. Quotation from George W. Perkins Collection, General File, Obituaries 1920. Box 18, Rare Books and Manuscripts, Butler Library, Columbia University.
33. *New York Tribune*, June 19, 1920, p. 4.
34. Burr (1927), p. 97.
35. Quotation of Stillman from Huertas (1985), pp. 147–148. Originally drawn from James Stillman, letter to Frank A. Vanderlip, February 12, 1907, Vanderlip MSS, Columbia University.
36. Friedman and Schwartz (1963), p. 411.
37. Roberts (2000), p. 13: "Strong's 'easy money' policies designed to assist Britain's return to the gold standard produced a speculative rise in stock prices on the New York Stock Exchange. But this picture hardly fits the Benjamin Strong who, in his support of the fateful decision in 1928 to raise interest rates and force a monetary contraction to bring down stock prices, was an economic nationalist. High interest rates in the United States

pulled capital out of Europe and forced monetary deflation there and elsewhere. The international gold standard that Strong had labored so hard to create became an engine of worldwide deflation."

38. Friedman and Schwartz (1963), p. 411.
39. Quotation of *Wall Street Journal* on Benjamin Strong given in *Time* magazine article, October 29, 1928. Downloaded from www.time.com/time/magazine/article/0,9171,928986,00.html.
40. Vanderlip's leadership in the design of the Federal Reserve System is discussed in chapter 2 of Primm (1989).
41. Details of Vanderlip's relations with Stillman are drawn from Huertas (1985).
42. Forbes (1981), p. x.
43. Cortelyou's *Response of the Secretary of the Treasury to Senate Resolution No. 33* (1908) does not simply state the total amount of funds he distributed. Indeed, the *Response* suggests various amounts. Figure 23.1 is derived from pages 37–72 of the *Response* that details public moneys deposited in national banks by week during the crisis. Other details in the *Response* suggest a range from $79.8 million (increase in public deposits, p. 14) to $103 million (the difference between all deposits in national banks on December 31, 1907 of $246 million (p. 31) and all deposits in national banks of $143 million on August 22 (p. 23)). Some of this variation is due to differences in the length of the measurement period.
44. Moen and Rodgers (2022), pp. 22–23.
45. Ibid., p. 23.
46. Quotation of Morgan's illness given in Forbes (1981), p. 72.
47. Quotation of Thomas Lamont given in Forbes (1981), p. 74. Source of quotation is a letter from T. W. Lamont to H. S. Commager, March 17, 1938, Partners file, J. P. Morgan Jr. Papers.
48. Moen and Rodgers (2022), p. 24.

Chapter 24: Reflections and Lessons

1. This oft-repeated statement is at best *attributed* to Mark Twain, reflecting the inability of researchers to find its specific source. Yet its instructional utility for recurrent events such as financial crises is invaluable. Quoted in Alex Ayres (ed.), *The Wit and Wisdom of Mark Twain* (New York: Harper & Row, 2005), p. 67.

2. Sins of omission and commission in history writing are legion. See, for instance, the excellent discussion in MacMillan (2009).
3. Greenwood Hanson, Shleifer, and Sorensen (2001). "Predictable Financial Crises," *Journal of Finance,* 77(2): 863-921.
4. See, for instance, Shiller (2001).
5. U.S. Bureau of the Census, *Historical Statistics of the United States, Colonial Times to 1970* (Washington, DC: Department of Commerce, 1975), Series X 580-587, p. 1019. The comparative figure for 2020 is 4,377—this is the number of national depository institutions reported by the St. Louis Fed, https://www.stlouisfed.org/on-the-economy/2021/december/steady-decline-number-us-banks.
6. See Gorton (1985a), Chari and Jagannathan (1988), Jacklin and Battacharya (1988), Calomiris and Schweikart (1991), and Calomiris and Gorton (1991).
7. Noyes (1909a), p. 188, found that "In 1907 NYC banks issued $101,060,000 clearing house loan certificates (vs. $41,490,000 in 1893). All US banks issued $238,053,175 in clearing house certificates versus $69,111,000 in 1893."
8. Horwitz (1990), p. 645, noted, "The difficulty facing the system then (and facing unregulated banks) is how to prevent localized runs from spreading to the whole system. One way banks tried to prevent contagion in 1907 was through advertising and use of their brand name capital. In addition to advertising the acceptability of the currency substitutes, banks advertised the soundness and trustworthiness of their institutions. Advertising trust and confidence was common practice in an era before federal deposit insurance programs. During the panic, banks immediately resorted to stronger and more innovative ways of advertising, especially through the use of their brand names. After the panic first began in New York, there was a marked increase in general advertising by banks. There were also changes in the kind of ads they ran. It became more common for banks to list their directors and owners in their advertising. They also offered such standard information as length of time in business and volume of business. In normal times, a bank might only rarely advertise its balance sheet. During the panic, however, various issues of the *New York Times* indicate that advertisements frequently included abbreviated balance sheets. In the October 25, 1907, issue at the height of the panic, there was a full page of bank ads (compared to the usual quarter or half page.). The ads included short versions of balance sheets and long, detailed lists of bank

personnel, including specific information on other business connections of the board members and management. The banks, like the public, were sensitive to concerns about interlocking directorates, and any connection with anyone questionable was bad for business."

9. Calomiris and Gorton (1991), Friedman and Schwartz (1963), and Sprague (1910) contend that "real disturbances" cause erosion of trust in the banking system and are the precursors to panics.
10. Sornette (2003), p. 321, attempted to identify telltale inflection points in security prices that might predict market crashes, but he concluded that such identification was exceptionally hard and not to be trusted.
11. In 1907, institutions suspending withdrawals were a very small percentage of the totals: 12 of 6,429 national banks, 58 of 14,959 state-chartered banks, 20 of 2,784 private banks, and 1 of 5,424 mutual savings banks. Source: *Historical Statistics of the United States, Colonial Times to 1970*, pp. 1038, 1031, and 1047, respectively.
12. Rockoff (2018), p. 77.
13. Selden (2005), p. 69 (originally published in 1912).
14. Lefèvre (1994), p. 286.
15. Harris (2003), p. 556, wrote: "Bubbles start when buyers become overly optimistic about fundamental values. The potential of new technologies and the potential growth of new markets can greatly excite some traders. Unfortunately, many of these traders cannot recognize when prices already reflect information about these potentials. They also may not adequately appreciate the risks associated with holding the securities that interest them. If enough of these enthusiastic traders try to buy at the same time, they may push prices up substantially. The resulting price increases may encourage momentum traders to buy, in the hope that past gains will continue . . . Order anticipators may buy in anticipation of new uninformed buyers. They will profit if they can get out before prices fall. The combined trading of these traders can cause a bubble in which prices exceed fundamental values . . . Value traders and arbitrageurs may recognize that prices exceed values, but they may be unable or unwilling to sell in sufficient volume to prevent the bubble from forming."
16. Tallman and Moen (2010b), p. 17.
17. Moen and Rodgers (2022), p. 23.
18. Friedman and Schwartz (1963), p. 418.

19. Mancur Olson, *The Logic of Collective Action: Public Goods and the Theory of Groups* (Cambridge, MA: Harvard University Press, 1965).
20. The authors gratefully acknowledge the benefit of correspondence with Professor Avinash Dixit regarding this example. For more discussion of assurance games, see Avinash K. Dixit and Barry J. Nalebuff, (*The Art of Strategy: A Game Theorist's Guide to Success in Business and Life* (New York: W.W. Norton, 2008).
21. Granovetter (1978).
22. Wiebe (1967), p. 201.

Technical Appendix: Analysis of Trust Company Diversity and Deposit Runs

1. Fohlin and Lu (2021), pp. 515, 516.
2. Ibid., pp. 517, 519.
3. Frydman, Hilt, and Zhou (2015), p. 909.
4. Ibid., p. 910.
5. Gorton and Mullineaux (1987), pp. 461, 463.
6. "Plan for Reorganization of Suspended Banks and Trust Companies," in *Trust Companies*, Vol. 6, January 1908, p. 13, and *Annual Report of the Superintendent of Banks 1907* (Albany, NY: J.B. Lyon Company, March 16, 1908); New York State, *Annual Report of the Superintendent of Banks Relative to Savings Banks, Trust Companies, Safe deposit Companies and Miscellaneous Corporations, for the Year 1905* (Albany, NY: Brandow Printing Company, State Legislative Printer, 1906); New York State, *Annual Report of the Superintendent of Banks Relative to Savings Banks, Trust Companies, Safe deposit Companies and Miscellaneous Corporations, for the Year 1907* (Albany, NY: J.B. Lyon Company, Printers, 1908).
7. "Since many trips to a store are, in part, quests for information, the location of retail stores can be profoundly affected by consumer efforts to acquire information." Philip Nelson, "Information and Consumer Behavior," *Journal of Political Economy* 78, no. 2 (1970): 311–329.

Bibliography

Archival Sources

Our research into the events of 1907 drew on diaries, letters, cables, memoranda, notes, newspaper clippings, and memoirs in the following archives:

- Benjamin Strong Papers, Federal Reserve Bank of New York, New York.
- George W. Perkins Papers, Rare Book and Manuscript Library, Columbia University, New York, New York.
- Herbert L. Satterlee Papers, Morgan Library and Museum, New York, New York.
- J. S. Morgan & Company Papers, Guildhall Library, London, United Kingdom.
- Morgan Grenfell & Company Papers, Guildhall Library, London, United Kingdom.
- Morgan Family Papers, Morgan Library and Museum, New York, New York.
- Thomas W. Lamont Papers, Baker Library, Harvard Graduate School of Business Administration, Boston, Massachusetts.

- Frank A. Vanderlip Papers, Butler Library, Columbia University, New York, New York.
- Otto C. Heinze Papers, Butte-Silver Bow Public Archives, Butte, Montana.

Contemporary Accounts

Five periodicals provided an excellent stream of contemporary reporting and opinion:

1. *Commercial and Financial Chronicle,* Volume 84, 1907
2. *New York Times*, 1897–1913
3. *Wall Street Journal*, 1897–1913
4. *Washington Post*, 1897–1913
5. *Chicago Daily Tribune*, 1897–1913

For a factual perspective on life in the first decade of the twentieth century, we consulted *Encyclopaedia Britannica*, 11th ed. (1910), Cambridge, UK: Cambridge University Press.

Contemporary accounts were supplemented by histories and biographical accounts written by contemporary observers of the events of 1907—see the works by Glass, Owen, Warburg, Satterlee, Clews, and Tarbell. The correspondence of Theodore Roosevelt was valuable concerning his thinking before, during, and after the Panic:

- Elting E. Morison, John Morton Blum, Alfred D. Chandler, Jr., and Sylvia Rice, eds., 1952. *The Letters of Theodore Roosevelt,* Volumes 5–6, Cambridge, MA: Harvard University Press.

Quantitative Data

We obtained quotations on financial assets from editions of the *Commercial and Financial Chronicle,* the *New York Times*, and the *Wall Street Journal* and economic data from these sources:

- National Bureau of Economic Research, Macrohistory Database, FRED Economic Data, Federal Reserve Bank of St. Louis.

- International Finance Center, Yale University School of Management, original databases on security prices.
- Jutta Bolt and Jan Luiten van Zanden. 2020. *Maddison Project Database*, version 2020, "Maddison style estimates of the evolution of the world economy. A new 2020 update."
- Bank of England Research Datasets.
- U.S. Department of Commerce, 1975. *Historical Statistics of the United States, Colonial Times to 1970.*

Government Reports, Addresses, and Documents

Materials published by the U.S. federal government and by the State of New York afforded a rich trove of data and insight into the evolution of views by elected and appointed government officials. Valuable resources related to the Panic of 1907 and the civic reaction are:

New York State. 1906. *Annual Report of the Superintendent of Banks Relative to Savings Banks, Trust Companies, Safe deposit Companies and Miscellaneous Corporations, for the Year 1905.* Albany: Brandow Printing Company, State Legislative Printer.

New York State. 1908. *Annual Report of the Superintendent of Banks Relative to Savings Banks, Trust Companies, Safe deposit Companies and Miscellaneous Corporations, for the Year 1907.* Albany: J.B. Lyon Company, Printers.

New York State. 1913. *Annual Report of the Superintendent of Banks Relative to Savings and Loan Associations For the Year 1912.* March 15, 1913. Albany: J.B. Lyon Company, Printers.

State of the Union Address, 1901. President Theodore Roosevelt, December 3, 1901.

State of the Union Address, 1902. President Theodore Roosevelt, December 2, 1902.

State of the Union Address, 1903. President Theodore Roosevelt, December 7, 1903.

State of the Union Address, 1904. President Theodore Roosevelt, December 6, 1904.

State of the Union Address, 1905. President Theodore Roosevelt, December 5, 1905.

State of the Union Address, 1906. President Theodore Roosevelt, December 3, 1906.

State of the Union Address, 1907. President Theodore Roosevelt, December 3, 1907.

State of the Union Address, 1908. President Theodore Roosevelt, December 8, 1908.

State of the Union Address, 1909. President William Howard Taft, December 7, 1909.

State of the Union Address, 1910. President William Howard Taft, December 6, 1910.

State of the Union Address, 1911. President William Howard Taft, December 5, 1911.

State of the Union Address, 1912. President William Howard Taft, December 3, 1912.

State of the Union Address, 1913. President Woodrow Wilson, December 2, 1913.

U.S. Bureau of the Census. 1975. *Historical Statistics of the United States: Colonial Times to 1970.* Washington, DC: U.S. Department of Commerce.

U.S. Department of the Treasury. 1908. *Response of the Secretary of the Treasury to Senate Resolution No. 33 of December 12, 1907, Calling for Certain Information in Regard to Treasury Operations, United States Depositaries, the Condition of National Banks, etc.* (January 29, 1908). Washington, DC: U.S. Government Printing Office, 60th Congress, 1st Session, Senate, Doc. 208.

U.S. Department of the Treasury. 1897. *Annual Report of the Secretary of the Treasury on the State of Finances for the Year 1896.* Washington, DC: U.S. Government Printing Office.

U.S. Department of the Treasury. 1898. *Annual Report of the Secretary of the Treasury on the State of Finances for the Year 1897.* Washington, DC: U.S. Government Printing Office.

U.S. Department of the Treasury. 1899. *Annual Report of the Secretary of the Treasury on the State of Finances for the Year 1898.* Washington, DC: U.S. Government Printing Office.

U.S. Department of the Treasury. 1900. *Annual Report of the Secretary of the Treasury on the State of Finances for the Year 1899.* Washington, DC: U.S. Government Printing Office.

U.S. Department of the Treasury. 1901. *Annual Report of the Secretary of the Treasury on the State of Finances for the Year 1900.* Washington, DC: U.S. Government Printing Office.

U.S. Department of the Treasury. 1901. *Annual Report of the Secretary of the Treasury on the State of Finances for the Year 1901.* Washington, DC: U.S. Government Printing Office.

U.S. Department of the Treasury. 1902. *Annual Report of the Secretary of the Treasury on the State of Finances for the Year 1902.* Washington, DC: U.S. Government Printing Office.

U.S. Department of the Treasury. 1903. *Annual Report of the Secretary of the Treasury on the State of Finances for the Year 1903.* Washington, DC: U.S. Government Printing Office.

U.S. Department of the Treasury. 1905. *Annual Report of the Secretary of the Treasury on the State of Finances for the Year 1904.* Washington, DC: U.S. Government Printing Office.

U.S. Department of the Treasury. 1906. *Annual Report of the Secretary of the Treasury on the State of Finances for the Year 1905.* Washington, DC: U.S. Government Printing Office.

U.S. Department of the Treasury. 1906. *Annual Report of the Secretary of the Treasury on the State of Finances for the Year 1906.* Washington, DC: U.S. Government Printing Office.

U.S. Department of the Treasury. 1907. *Annual Report of the Secretary of the Treasury on the State of Finances for the Year 1907.* Washington, DC: U.S. Government Printing Office.

U.S. Department of the Treasury. 1908. *Annual Report of the Secretary of the Treasury on the State of Finances for the Year 1908.* Washington, DC: U.S. Government Printing Office.

U.S. Department of the Treasury. 1909. *Annual Report of the Secretary of the Treasury on the State of Finances for the Year 1909.* Washington, DC: U.S. Government Printing Office.

U.S. Department of the Treasury. 1911. *Annual Report of the Secretary of the Treasury on the State of Finances for the Year 1910.* Washington, DC: U.S. Government Printing Office.

U.S. Department of the Treasury. 1912. *Annual Report of the Secretary of the Treasury on the State of Finances for the Year 1911.* Washington, DC: U.S. Government Printing Office.

U.S. Department of the Treasury. 1913. *Annual Report of the Secretary of the Treasury on the State of Finances for the Year 1912.* Washington, DC: U.S. Government Printing Office.

U.S. Department of the Treasury. 1913. *Annual Report of the Secretary of the Treasury on the State of Finances for the Year 1913.* Washington, DC: U.S. Government Printing Office.

U.S. Department of the Treasury. 1915. *Annual Report of the Secretary of the Treasury on the State of Finances for the Year 1914.* Washington, DC: U.S. Government Printing Office.

U.S. Department of the Treasury. 1896. *Annual Report of the Comptroller of the Currency.* Washington, DC: U.S. Government Printing Office.

U.S. Department of the Treasury. 1897. *Annual Report of the Comptroller of the Currency.* Washington, DC: U.S. Government Printing Office.

U.S. Department of the Treasury. 1898. *Annual Report of the Comptroller of the Currency.* Washington, DC: U.S. Government Printing Office.

U.S. Department of the Treasury. 1899. *Annual Report of the Comptroller of the Currency.* Washington, DC: U.S. Government Printing Office.

U.S. Department of the Treasury. 1900. *Annual Report of the Comptroller of the Currency.* Washington, DC: U.S. Government Printing Office.

U.S. Department of the Treasury. 1901. *Annual Report of the Comptroller of the Currency.* Washington, DC: U.S. Government Printing Office.

U.S. Department of the Treasury. 1902. *Annual Report of the Comptroller of the Currency.* Washington, DC: U.S. Government Printing Office.

U.S. Department of the Treasury. 1903. *Annual Report of the Comptroller of the Currency.* Washington, DC: U.S. Government Printing Office.

U.S. Department of the Treasury. 1904. *Annual Report of the Comptroller of the Currency.* Washington, DC: U.S. Government Printing Office.

U.S. Department of the Treasury. 1905. *Annual Report of the Comptroller of the Currency.* Washington, DC: U.S. Government Printing Office.

U.S. Department of the Treasury. 1906. *Annual Report of the Comptroller of the Currency.* Washington, DC: U.S. Government Printing Office.

U.S. Department of the Treasury. 1907. *Annual Report of the Comptroller of the Currency.* Washington, DC: U.S. Government Printing Office.

U.S. Department of the Treasury. 1908. *Annual Report of the Comptroller of the Currency.* Washington, DC: U.S. Government Printing Office.

U.S. Department of the Treasury. 1909. *Annual Report of the Comptroller of the Currency.* Washington, DC: U.S. Government Printing Office.

U.S. Department of the Treasury. 1910. *Annual Report of the Comptroller of the Currency.* Washington, DC: U.S. Government Printing Office.

U.S. Department of the Treasury. 1912. *Annual Report of the Comptroller of the Currency [for 1911].* Washington, DC: U.S. Government Printing Office.

U.S. Department of the Treasury. 1913. *Annual Report of the Comptroller of the Currency [for 1912].* Washington, DC: U.S. Government Printing Office.

U.S. Department of the Treasury. 1914. *Annual Report of the Comptroller of the Currency [for 1913].* Washington, DC: U.S. Government Printing Office.

U.S. Department of the Treasury. 1915. *Annual Report of the Comptroller of the Currency [for 1914].* Washington, DC: U.S. Government Printing Office.

U.S. House of Representatives. 1912. *Investigation of United States Steel Corporation,* 62nd Congress, 2nd Session. Report No. 1127. Washington, DC: U.S. Government Printing Office.

U.S. House of Representatives, Subcommittee of the Committee on Banking and Currency. 1913. *Money Trust Investigation: Investigation of Financial and Monetary Conditions in the United States under House Resolutions No. 429 and 504.* Washington, DC: U.S. Government Printing Office.

U.S. House of Representatives. 1913. *Federal Reserve Act: Public Law 63–43, 63d Congress, H.R. 7837: An Act to Provide for the Establishment of Federal Reserve Banks, to Furnish an Elastic Currency, to Afford Means of Rediscounting Commercial Paper, to Establish a More Effective Supervision of Banking in the United States, and for Other Purposes.* 63rd Congress. Downloaded from Federal Reserve Bank of St. Louis: https://fraser.stlouisfed.org/title/federal-reserve-act-966.

U.S. National Monetary Commission. 1912. *Report of the National Monetary Commission.* Washington, DC: U.S. Government Printing Office.

U.S. Senate. 1911. *Suggested Plan for Monetary Legislation Submitted to the National Monetary Commission by Hon. Nelson W. Aldrich.* 61st Congress, 3rd Session. Document No. 784. Washington, DC: U.S. Government Printing Office.

Articles, Books, and Working Papers

Abreu, Dilip, and Markus K. Brunnermeier. 2003. "Bubbles and Crashes." *Econometrica* 71(1) (January): 173–204.

Akerlof, George. 1970. "The Market for Lemons: Qualitative Uncertainty and the Market Mechanism." *Quarterly Journal of Economics* 84: 488–500.

Alderson, William T. 1959. "Taft, Roosevelt, and the U.S. Steel Case: A Letter of Jacob McGavock Dickinson." *Tennessee Historical Quarterly* 18(3) (September): 266–272.

Allen, Frederick Lewis. 1935. *The Lords of Creation.* New York: Harper & Row.

——. 1949. *The Great Pierpont Morgan.* New York: Harper & Brothers Publishers.

——. 1952. *The Big Change: America Transforms Itself 1900–1950.* New York: Harper & Brothers.

Andrew, A. Piatt. 1908a. "Hoarding in the Panic of 1907." *Quarterly Journal of Economics* 22: 290–299.

——. 1908b. "Substitutes for Cash in the Panic of 1907." *Quarterly Journal of Economics* 22: 497–516.

——. 1910. *Statistics for the United States, 1867–1909. National Monetary Commission.* 61st Congress, 2nd Session, Senate, Doc. 570. Washington, DC: U.S. Government Printing Office.

Anonymous. 1906a. "San Francisco and Its Catastrophe." *Scientific American* 94(17) (April 28): 347.

Anonymous. 1906b. "San Francisco Notes." *Scientific American* 94(21) (May 26): 434–435.

Anonymous. 1908. *"Bonum Meritum." A War of Words between President Roosevelt and J. Pierpont Morgan Concerning Railroad, Tariff, and Trust Questions and the Panic of 1907 as Supposed by the Author.* Chicago: M. A. Donohue & Company.

Bagehot, Walter. (1873) 1920. *Lombard Street: A Description of the Money Market,* New York: E.P. Dutton [originally London: Henry S. King & Company].

Bain, Joseph. 1956. *Barriers to New Competition: Their Character and Consequences in Manufacturing Industries*. Boston: Harvard University Press.

Baker, Malcolm, Richard S. Ruback, and Jeffrey Wurgler. 2004. "Behavioral Corporate Finance: A Survey." In Espen Eckbo (ed.). 2006. *Handbook of Corporate Finance: Empirical Corporate Finance*. New York: Elsevier/North Holland.

Barry, John M. 2004. *The Great Influenza: The Epic Story of the Deadliest Plague in History*. New York: Viking.

Beard, Patricia. 2003. *After the Ball: Gilded Age Secrets, Boardroom Betrayals, and the Party That Ignited the Great Wall Street Scandal of 1905*. New York: HarperCollins.

Behabib, Jess, and Roger E. A. Farmer. 1995. "Indeterminacy and Sector-Specific Externalities." Working paper, April 7.

Beinhocker, Eric. 2006. *The Origin of Wealth: Evolution, Complexity, and the Radical Remaking of Economics*. Boston: Harvard Business School Press.

Berg, A. Scott. 2015. *Wilson*. New York: Penguin.

Bernanke, Benjamin. 2006. "Hedge Funds and Systemic Risk" speech. Downloaded from www.federalreserve.gov/newsevents/speech/bernanke20060516a.htm.

Bernstein, Asaf, Carola Frydman, and Eric Hilt. 2022. "Securities Ratings and Information Provision." Working paper. Presented at University of Virginia, April 20, 2022.

Bernstein, Asaf, Eric Hughson, and Marc D. Weidenmier. 2010. "Identifying the Effects of a Lender of Last Resort on Financial Markets: Lessons from the Founding of the Fed." *Journal of Financial Economics* 98: 40–53.

Bertogg, Martin, Andrew Castaldi, and Maria Giovanna Guatteri. 2005. "A Shake in Insurance History: The 1906 San Francisco Earthquake." Zurich: Swiss Reinsurance Company, Records Management/Company Archives, publications@swissre.com.

Bhattacharya, Sudipto, and Anjan V. Thakor. 1993. "Contemporary Banking Theory." *Journal of Financial Intermediation* 3: 2–50.

Blinder, Alan B. 1982. "Issues in the Coordination of Monetary and Fiscal Policy." Cambridge, MA: National Bureau of Economic Research, working paper 982, September.

Blum, John Morton. 1977. *The Republican Roosevelt*. Cambridge, MA: Harvard University Press.

Boinanovsky, Mauro. 2009. "Wicksell on the American Crisis of 1907." Working paper, Universidade de Brasilia. Downloaded December 20, 2021 from https://papers.ssrn.com/sol3/papers.cfm?abstract_id=1529642

Bookstaber, Richard. 2007. *A Demon of Our Own Design*. Hoboken, NJ: John Wiley & Sons.

Bordo, Michael D. 1985a. "The Impact and International Transmission of Financial Crises: Some Historical Evidence, 1870–1933." *Revista di storia economica*, 2nd ser., vol. 2: 41–78.

——. 1985b. "Some Historical Evidence 1870–1933 on the Impact and International Transmission of Financial Crises." Cambridge, MA: National Bureau of Economic Research, working paper 1606, April.

Bordo, M. D., and Antu Panini Murshid. 2000. "Are Financial Crises Becoming Increasingly Contagious? What Is the Historical Evidence on Contagion?" Cambridge, MA:

National Bureau of Economic Research, working paper 7900, September. http://www.nber.org/papers/w7900

Bordo, M. D., and R. MacDonald. 2005. "Interest Rate Interactions in the Classical Gold Standard 1880–1914: Was There Any Monetary Independence?" *Journal of Monetary Economics* 52: 307–327.

Bordo, Michael D., and Christopher M. Meissner. 2005. "Financial Crises, 1880–1913: The Role of Foreign Currency Debt." Cambridge, MA: National Bureau of Economic Research, working paper 11173.

Bork, Robert. 1978. *The Antitrust Paradox: A Policy at War with Itself.* New York: Basic Books.

Boyer, Brian H., Tomomi Kumagai, and Kathy Yuan. 2006. "How Do Crises Spread? Evidence from Accessible and Inaccessible Stock Indices." *Journal of Finance* 61: 957–1003.

Brandeis, Louis. 1914. *Other People's Money and How the Bankers Use It.* New York: Frederick A. Stokes. Downloaded from https://louisville.edu/law/library/special-collections/the-louis-d.-brandeis-collection/other-peoples-money-chapter-i.

Brands, H.W. 1997. *TR: The Last Romantic.* New York: Basic Books.

Brown, Clair, John Haltiwanger, and Julia Lane. 2006. *Economic Turbulence: Is a Volatile Economy Good for America?* Chicago: University of Chicago Press.

Brownlee, W. Elliot. 1979. *Dynamics of Ascent: A History of the American Economy*, 2nd ed. New York: Knopf.

Bruner, Robert F. 2005. *Deals from Hell: M&A Lessons That Rise Above the Ashes.* Hoboken, NJ: John Wiley & Co.

Bruner, Robert F., and Sean D. Carr. 2007. "Lessons from the Financial Crisis of 1907." *Journal of Applied Corporate Finance* 19(4): 25–34.

Bruner, Robert F., Sean D. Carr, and Asif Mehedi. 2016. "Financial Innovation and the Consequences of Complexity: Insights from Major U.S. Banking Crises." In *Complexity and Crisis in the Financial System: Critical Perspectives on American and British Banking*, edited by Matthew Hollow, Folarin Akinbami, and Ranald Michie. London: Edward Elgar Publishing.

Brunnermeier, Markus K. 2009. "Deciphering the Liquidity and Credit Crunch 2007–2008." *Journal of Economic Perspectives* 23(1) (Winter): 77–100.

Brunnermeier, Markus K., and Stefan Nagel. 2004. "Hedge Funds and the Technology Bubble." *Journal of Finance* 59(5) (October): 2013–2040.

Brunnermeier, Markus K., and Lasse Heje Pedersen. 2009. "Market Liquidity and Funding Liquidity." *Review of Financial Studies* 22(6) (June): 2201–2238.

Bryan, William Jennings. 1896. "Address to the National Democratic Convention, 9 July 1896." http://projects.vassar.edu/1896/crossofgold.html.

Bulmer, Martin, Kevin Bales, and Kathryn Kish Sklar (eds.). 1991. *The Social Survey in Historical Perspective, 1880–1940.* Cambridge, UK: Cambridge University Press.

Burr, Anna Robeson. 1927. *The Portrait of a Banker: James Stillman 1850–1918* (New York: Duffield & Company, copyright by University of California).

Cahill, Kevin J. 1998. "The U.S. Bank Panic of 1907 and the Mexican Depression of 1908–1909." *The Historian* 60: 795–785.

Calomiris, Charles W. 2000. *U.S. Bank Deregulation in Historical Perspective*. Cambridge, UK: Cambridge University Press.

Calomiris, Charles W., and Gary Gorton. 1991. "The Origins of Banking Panics: Models, Facts, and Bank Regulation." In *Financial Markets and Financial Crises*, edited by R. Glenn Hubbard. Chicago: University of Chicago Press. This was also published as a chapter by the same title in Charles W. Calomiris (ed.). 2000. *U.S. Bank Regulation in Historical Perspective*. Cambridge, UK: Cambridge University Press.

Calomiris, Charles W., and Stephen H. Haber. 2014. *Fragile by Design: The Political Origins of Banking Crises & Scarce Credit*. Princeton, NJ: Princeton University Press.

Calomiris, Charles W., and Larry Schweikart. 1991. "The Panic of 1857: Origins, Transmission, and Containment." *Journal of Economic History* 51(4): 807–834.

Calverley, John P. 2004. *Bubbles and How to Survive Them*. London: Nicholas Brealey Publishing.

Cannon, James G. 1910. "Clearing House Loan Certificates and Substitutes for Money Used During the Panic of 1907." Speech delivered before the Finance Forum, New York City, March 30, 1910. Baker Library, Harvard Business School.

Canova, Fabio. 1991. "The Sources of Financial Crisis: Pre- and Post-Fed Evidence." *International Economic Review* 32(3): 689–713.

Cantillo Simon, Miguel. 1998. "The Rise and Fall of Bank Control in the United States: 1890–1939." *American Economic Review* 88(5) (December): 1077–1093.

Capen, E. C., R.V. Clapp, and W. M. Campbell. 1971. "Competitive Bidding in High-Risk Situations." *Journal of Petroleum Technology* (June): 641–645.

Carlson, Mark. n.d. "Causes of Bank Suspensions in the Panic of 1893." Washington, DC: U.S. Federal Reserve Board, working paper.

Carosso, Vincent P. 1970. *Investment Banking in America*. Cambridge, MA: Harvard University Press.

——. 1973. "The Wall Street Money Trust from Pujo through Medina." *Business History Review* 47(4) (Winter): 421–437.

——. 1987. *The Morgans: Private International Bankers, 1854–1913*. Cambridge, MA: Harvard University Press.

Cecchetti, S. G. 1995. "Distinguishing Theories of the Monetary Transmission Mechanism." *Review–Federal Reserve Bank of Saint Louis* 77: 83–97.

Chambers, David, Sergei Sarkissian, and Michael J. Schill. 2018. "Market and Regional Segmentation and Risk Premia in the First Era of Financial Globalization." *Review of Financial Studies* 31(10) (October): 4063–4098.

Chan, Nicholas, Mila Getmansky, Shane Haas, and Andrew Lo. 2005. "Systemic Risk and Hedge Funds." 2007. in M. Carey and R. Stulz, eds., *The Risks of Financial Institutions and the Financial Sector*. Chicago: University of Chicago Press.

Chandler, Lester V. 1958. *Benjamin Strong: Central Banker*. Washington, DC: The Brookings Institution.

Chapin, Robert Coit. 1909. "The Standard of Living among Workingmen's Families in New York City." New York City Charities publication committee, Russell Sage Foundation.

Chari, V. V., and Ravi Jagannathan. 1988. "Banking Panics, Information, and Rational Expectations Equilibrium." Federal Reserve Bank of Minneapolis Research Department, working paper 320.

Chernow, Ron. 1990. *The House of Morgan: An American Banking Dynasty and the Rise of Modern Finance*. New York: Atlantic Monthly Press.

——. 1998. *Titan: The Life of John D. Rockefeller Sr.* New York: Random House.

Cleveland, Harold van B., and Thomas F. Huertas. 1985. *Citibank, 1812–1970*. Boston: Harvard University Press.

Clews, Henry. (1908) 1973. *Fifty Years in Wall Street*. New York: Arno Press.

Cohen, Lizabeth. 1990. *Making a New Deal, Industrial Workers in Chicago, 1919–1939*. Cambridge, UK: Cambridge University Press.

Conti-Brown, Peter. 2016. *The Power and Independence of the Federal Reserve*. Princeton, NJ: Princeton University Press.

Conti-Brown, Peter, and Michael Ohlrogge. 2022. "Financial Crises and Legislation." *Journal of Financial Crises* 4(3): 1–49.

Cooper, John Milton. 1983. *The Warrior and the Priest: Woodrow Wilson and Theodore Roosevelt*. Cambridge, MA: Belknap Press of Harvard University Press.

Corey, Lewis. 1930. *The House of Morgan: A Social Biography of the Masters of Money*. New York: G. Howard Watt.

Cotter, Arundel. 1916. *The Authentic History of the United States Steel Corporation*. New York: Brody Magazine and Book Company.

Cowan, Ruth Schwartz. 1983. *More Work for Mother: The Ironies of Household Technology from the Open Hearth to the Microwave*. New York: Basic Books.

Crocker, Ruth Hutchinson. 1992. *Social Work and Social Order: The Settlement Movement in Two Industrial Cities, 1889–1930*. Urbana and Chicago: University of Illinois Press.

Crowther, Samuel. 1933. *Life of George W. Perkins*. Unpublished biography found among the papers of J. P. Morgan, Jr., Box 107.

Curran, Thomas J. 1975. *Xenophobia and Immigration, 1820–1930*. Boston: Twayne Publishers, a division of G. K. Hall & Co.

Dam, Kenneth. 1982. *The Rules of the Game*. Chicago: University of Chicago Press.

Daniels, Roger. 2004. *Guarding the Golden Door: American Immigration Policy and Immigrants since 1882*. New York: Hill and Wang.

Dash, Michael. 1999. *Tulipomania*. New York: Three Rivers Press.

Davis, Allen F. 1967. *Spearheads for Reform: The Social Settlements and the Progressive Movement, 1890–1914*. New York: Oxford University Press.

Davis, Emory. 1913. *Important Issues of the Day*. New York: Author.

Davis, Joseph H. 2003. "A Quantity-Based Annual Index of U.S. Industrial Production, 1790–1915: An Empirical Appraisal of Historical Business-Cycle Fluctuations." *Journal of Economic History* 63(2) (June): 517–522.

——. 2004. "A Quantity-Based Annual Index of U.S. Industrial Production, 1790–1915." *Quarterly Journal of Economics* 119(4): 1177–1215.

——. 2006. "An Improved Annual Chronology of U.S. Business Cycles Since the 1790s." *Journal of Economic History* 66(1) (March): 103–121.

Davis, Joseph H., Christopher Hanes, and Paul W. Rhode. 2009. "Harvests and Business Cycles in Nineteenth-Century America." Cambridge, MA: National Bureau of Economic Research, working paper 14686.

Davis, Lance. 1965. "The Investment Market, 1870–1914: The Evolution of a National Market." *Journal of Economic History* 25: 355–399.

De Cecco, Marcello. 2009. "International Currency Dynamics: Lessons from the pre-1914 Experience." In *The Future of the Dollar,* edited by Eric Helleiner and Jonathan Kirshner. Ithaca, NY: Cornell University Press.

De Long, J. Bradford. 1991. "Did Morgan's Men Add Value? An Economist's Perspective on Financial Capitalism." In *Inside the Business Enterprise: Historical Perspectives on the Use of Information.* Chicago: University of Chicago Press.

Deutsch, Sarah. 2000. *Women and the City, Gender, Space, and Power in Boston, 1870–1940.* New York: Oxford University Press.

Diamond, Douglas W., and Philip H. Dybvig. 1983. "Bank Runs, Deposit Insurance, and Liquidity." *Journal of Political Economy* 91(June): 401–419.

——. 1986. "Banking Theory, Deposit Insurance, and Bank Regulation." *Journal of Business* 59(1) (January): 55–68.

Diamond, Douglas W., Yunzhi Hu, and Raghuram G. Rajan. 2022. "Liquidity, Pledgeability, and the Nature of Lending." *Journal of Financial Economics* 143: 1275–1294.

Diner, Stephen J. 1998. *A Very Different Age: Americans in the Progressive Era.* New York: Hill & Wang.

Dixit, Avinash K., and Robert S. Pindyck. 1994. *Investment Under Uncertainty.* Princeton, NJ: Princeton University Press.

Dodd, Donald B. 1993. *Historical Statistics of the States of the United States: Two Centuries of the Census, 1790–1990.* Westport, CT: Greenwood Press.

Donaldson, R. Glenn. 1992. "Sources of Panics: Evidence from the Weekly Data." *Journal of Monetary Economics* 31: 277–305.

——. 1993. "Financing Banking Crises: Lessons from the Panic of 1907." *Journal of Monetary Economics* 31: 69–95.

Douty, Christopher Morris. 1977. *The Economics of Localized Disasters: The 1906 San Francisco Earthquake.* New York: Arno Press.

Edwards, Adolph. 1907. *The Roosevelt Panic of 1907.* New York: Anitrock Publishing Company.

Eisenach, Eldon J. 1994. *The Lost Promise of Progressivism.* Lawrence: University of Kansas.

Ethington, Philip J. 1996. *The Public City: The Political Construction of Urban Life in San Francisco, 1850–1900.* Cambridge, UK: Cambridge University Press.

Ewen, Elizabeth. 1985. *Immigrant Women in the Land of Dollars: Life and Culture on the Lower East Side, 1890–1925.* New York: Monthly Review Press.

Fink, Leon (ed.). 2001. *Major Problems in the Gilded Age and the Progressive Era.* 2nd ed. New York: Houghton Mifflin.

Fitzgerald, Keith. 1996. *The Face of the Nation, Immigration, the State, and the National Identity.* Stanford, CA: Stanford University Press.

Fitzpatrick, Ellen. 1990. *Endless Crusade: Women Social Scientists and Progressive Reform.* Oxford, UK: Oxford University Press.

Flandreau, Marc, and Stefano Ugolini. 2013. "Where It all Began: Lending of Last Resort at the Bank of England Monitoring During the Overend-Gurney Panic of 1866." Chapter 3 in *The Origins, History, and Future of the Federal Reserve: A Return to Jekyll Island*, edited by Michael D. Bordo and William Roberds. Studies in Macroeconomic History. Cambridge, UK: Cambridge University Press.

Fohlin, C., T. Gehrig, and M. Haas. 2015. "Rumors and Runs in Opaque Markets: Evidence from the Panic of 1907." CEPR discussion paper 10497, London.

Fohlin, Caroline, and Zhikun Lu. 2021. "How Contagious Was the Panic of 1907? New Evidence from Trust Company Stocks." *AEA Papers and Proceedings* 111: 514–519.

Forbes, John Douglas. 1981. *J. P. Morgan, Jr. 1867–1943*. Charlottesville: University Press of Virginia.

Friedman, Milton, and Anna Schwartz. 1963. *A Monetary History of the United States, 1867–1960*. Princeton, NJ: Princeton University Press.

Frydman, Carola, and Eric Hilt. 2013. "Investment Banks as Corporate Monitors in the Early 20th Century United States." Cambridge, MA: National Bureau of Economic Research, working paper 20544, October.

Frydman, C., E. Hilt, and L.Y. Zhou. 2015. "Economic Effects of Runs on Early 'Shadow Banks': Trust Companies and the Impact of the Panic of 1907." *Journal of Political Economy* 123(4): 902–940.

Gage, Beverley. 2006. *The Day Wall Street Exploded*. Oxford, UK: Oxford University Press.

Garber, Peter M. 2001. *Famous First Bubbles: The Fundamentals of Early Manias*. Cambridge, MA: MIT Press.

Garraty, John A. 1957. *Right-Hand Man: The Life of George W. Perkins*. New York: Harper & Brothers.

Geisst, Charles R. 1997. *Wall Street: A History*. Oxford, UK: Oxford University Press.

German, James C., Jr. 1972. "Taft, Roosevelt, and United States Steel." *The Historian* 34(4) (August): 598–613.

Glass, Carter. 1927. *An Adventure in Constructive Finance*. New York: Doubleday, Page & Company.

Glasscock, C.B. (1935) 2002. *The War of the Copper Kings*. Helena, MT: Riverbend Publishing.

Goodhart, C. A. E. 1969. *The New York Money Market and the Finance of Trade, 1900–1913*. Cambridge, MA: Harvard University Press.

Goodwin, Doris Kearns. 2013. *The Bully Pulpit: Theodore Roosevelt, William Howard Taft, and the Golden Age of Journalism*. New York: Simon & Schuster.

Gordon, John Steele. 1999. *The Great Game: The Emergence of Wall Street as a World Power 1653–2000*. New York: Scribner.

Gordon, Linda. 1994. *Pitied but Not Entitled, Single Mothers and the History of Welfare*. Cambridge, MA: Harvard University Press.

Gordon, Thomas, and Max Morgan Witts. 1971. *The San Francisco Earthquake*. New York: Stein and Day.

Gorton, Gary. 1985a. "Bank Suspension of Convertibility." *Journal of Monetary Economics* 15: 177–193.

Gorton, Gary. 1985b. "Clearinghouses and the Origins of Central Banking in the United States." *Journal of Economic History* 45(June): 277–284.

Gorton, Gary. 1988. "Bank Panics and Business Cycles." *Oxford Economic Papers* 40(December): 751–781.

Gorton, Gary. 2008. "The Subprime Panic." Working paper, September 30. Downloaded from http://papers.ssrn.com/sol3/papers.cfm?abstract_id=1276047.

Gorton, Gary, and Lixim Huang. 2002. "Banking Panics and the Origin of Central Banking," Cambridge, MA: National Bureau of Economic Research, working paper 9137.

Gorton, Gary, and D. Mullineaux. 1987. "The Joint Production of Confidence: Endogenous Regulation and Nineteenth Century Commercial-Bank Clearinghouses." *Journal of Money, Credit and Banking* 19(4): 457–468.

Gorton, Gary, and Ellis W. Tallman. 2016. "How Did Pre-Fed Banking Panics End?" Cambridge, MA: National Bureau of Economic Research, working paper 22036.

Gould, Lewis L. 2001. *America in the Progressive Era 1890–1914*. London: Pearson Education Limited.

Graham, Otis L. 1971. *The Great Campaigns: Reform and War in America, 1900–1928*. Englewood Cliffs, NJ: Prentice Hall.

Granovetter, Mark. 1978. "Threshold Models of Collective Behavior." *American Journal of Sociology* 83(6): 1420–1443.

Greenspan, Alan. 2007. *The Age of Turbulence*. New York: Penguin.

Greenwald, Bruce C., and Jeremy C. Stein. 1990. "Transactional Risk Market Crashes, and the Role of Circuit Breakers." Alfred P. Sloan School of Management, Massachusetts Institute of Technology, working paper 32226-90-EPA.

Greenwood, Robin, Samuel G. Hanson, Andrei Shleifer, and Jakob Ahm Sorensen. 2022. "Predictable Financial Crises." *Journal of Finance* 77(2): 863–921.

Grodecka, Anna, Sean Kenny, and Anders Ogren. 2018. "Predictors of Bank Distress: The 1907 Crisis in Sweden." Stockholm: Sveriges Riksbank Working Paper Series, no. 358, October.

Gu, Chao. 2022. "Noisy Sunspots and Bank Runs." *Macroeconomic Dynamics* 15 (3) (June): 398–418.

Hanes, Christopher, and Paul W. Rhode. 2013. "Harvests and Financial Crises in Gold Standard America." *Journal of Economic History* 73(1): 201–245.

Hanna, J. 1931. "The Knickerbocker Trust Co.: A Study in Receivership." *Temple Law Quarterly* 5: 319–348.

Hansen, Bradley A. 2014. "A Failure of Regulation? Reinterpreting the Panic of 1907." *Business History Review* 88(3) (Autumn): 545–569.

Hansen, Bradley A. 2018. "Trust Company Failures and Institutional Change in New York, 1875–1925." *Enterprise & Society* 19(2): 241–271.

Harbaugh, William H. 1961. *Power and Responsibility: The Life and Times of Theodore Roosevelt*. Newtown, CT: American Political Biography Press.

——. 1963. *The Life and Times of Theodore Roosevelt*. New York: Collier Books.

Harris, Larry. 2003. *Trading & Exchanges: Market Microstructure for Practitioners*. Oxford, UK: Oxford University Press.

Hart, Albert B., and Herbert R. Ferleger. 1941. *Theodore Roosevelt Cyclopedia*. New York: Roosevelt Memorial Association.

Harvey, George. 1928. *Henry Clay Frick: The Man*. Washington, DC: BeardBooks.

Harvey, William H. 1899. *Coin on Money, Trusts, and Imperialism*. Chicago, IL: Coin Publishing Company, p. 130.

Hays, Samuel P. 1964. "The Politics of Reform in Municipal Government in the Progressive Era." *Pacific Northwest Quarterly* 55(4) (October): 157–169.

Heckfeldt, Christopher. 2022. "Understanding the Scarring Effect of Recessions." *American Economic Review* 112(4) (April): 1273–1310.

Hendricks, Francis. 1905. *Preliminary Report on the Investigation into the Management ofThe Equitable Life Assurance Society of the United States Made to the Governor of the State of New York by the Superintendent of Insurance as of June 21, 1905*. New York: The Spectator Company.

Horwitz, Steven. 1990. "Competitive Currencies, Legal Restrictions, and the Origins of the Fed: Some Evidence from the Panic of 1907." *Southern Economic Journal* 56: 639–649.

Hoyt, Edwin P. Jr. 1966. *The House of Morgan*. New York: Dodd, Mead & Company.

——. 1967. *The Guggenheims and the American Dream*. New York: Funk & Wagnalls.

Hu, Yuanyuan. 2020. "Comparative Analysis Between the Panic of 1907 and the Financial Crisis of 2007." Master's thesis, Department of Management, Technology and Economics, ETHZurich, May 20.

Hunter, William C., George G. Kaufman, and Michael Pomerleano (eds.). 2003. *Asset Price Bubbles: The Implications for Monetary, Regulatory, and International Policies*. Cambridge, MA: MIT Press.

Huston, James L. 1987. *The Panic of 1857 and the Coming of the Civil War*. Baton Rouge: Louisiana State University Press.

Issel, William. 1988. "'Citizens Outside the Government': Business and Urban Policy in San Francisco and Los Angeles, 1890–1932." *Pacific Historical Review* 57(2) (May): 117–145.

Jacklin, Charles J., and Sudipto Battacharya, 1988. "Distinguishing Panics and Information-Based Bank Runs: Welfare and Policy Implications." *Journal of Political Economy* 96(3): 568–592.

James, John, James McAndrews, and David F. Weiman. 2012. "Wall Street and Main Street: The Macroeconomic Consequences of New York Bank Suspensions, 1866–1914." *Cliometrica, Journal of Historical Economics and Economic History* 7 (2): 99–130.

——. 2014. "Banking Panics, the 'Derangement' of the Domestic Exchanges, and the Origins of Central Banking in the United States, 1893 to 1914." Working paper.

——. n.d. "Panics and the Disruption of Private Payments Networks: The United States in 1893 and 1907." Working paper.

Kaminski, Graciela, and Sergio Schmukler. 1999. "On Booms and Crashes: Stock Market Cycles and Financial Liberalization." George Washington University and The World Bank, working paper.

Kazin, Michael. 2006. *A Godly Hero: The Life of William Jennings Bryan*. New York: Anchor Books.

Kazuo, N. "The Ashio Riot of 1907." In *A Social History of Mining in Japan*, edited by A. Gordon. Durham, NC: Duke University Press.

Kemmerer, E. W. 1910. *Seasonal Variations in the Relative Demand for Money and Capital in the United States*. National Monetary Commission. 61st Cong. 2d Sess. Senate Doc. 588. Washington, DC: U.S. Government Printing Office.

——. 1911. "American Banks in Times of Crisis Under the National Banking System." *Proceedings of the Academy of Political Science* I: 233–253.

Keynes, John Maynard. 1909. "Recent Economic Events in India." *Economic Journal* 19 (March): 51–67.

——. 1930. *A Treatise on Money*. London: Macmillan.

——. 1936. *The General Theory of Employment, Interest and Money*. London: Macmillan.

Kindleberger, Charles. 1978. *Manias, Panics, and Crashes: A History of Financial Crises*. New York: Basic Books. This book has been revised and published to the most recent edition (7th) dated 2015 that lists Charles P. Kindleberger and Robert Z. Aliber as co-authors.

Kindleberger, Charles. 1990. "The Panic of 1873 and Financial Market Volatility and Panics before 1914." Chapter 3 in *Crashes and Panics: The Lessons from History*, edited by Eugene White, 69–84. Homewood, IL: Business One Irwin.

Kloppenberg, James T. 1986. *Uncertain Victory*. Oxford, UK: Oxford University Press.

Kolko, Gabriel. 1963. *The Triumph of Conservatism*. Chicago, IL: Quadrangle Books.

Kroszner, Randall S. 2000. "Lessons from Financial Crises: The Role of Clearinghouses." *Journal of Financial Services Research* 18(2/3): 157–171.

Krugman, Paul. 2008. *The Return of Depression Economics and the Crisis of 2008*. New York: Norton.

Lacey, Michael J., and Mary O. Furner (eds.). 1993. *The State and Social Investigation in Britain and the United States*. Cambridge, UK: International Center for Scholars and Cambridge University Press.

La Follette, Robert M. 1908. *Centralization and Community of Control in Industry, Franchise, Transportation and Finance: The Panic of October 1907 and Its Lessons*. Washington, DC: U.S. Government Printing Office.

Lamont, Thomas W. 1975. *Henry P. Davison: The Record of a Useful Life*. New York: Arno Press, a New York Times Company.

Lawson, Thomas William. 1906. *Frenzied Finance: The Crime of the Amalgamated*. London: William Heinemann.

Lefèvre, Edwin. 1908. "The Game Got them: How the Great Wall Street Gambling Syndicate Fell into Its Own Trap." *Everybody's Magazine* 18 (January– June): 3–14.

——. (1923) 1994. *Reminiscences of a Stock Operator*. New York: John Wiley & Sons.

Leiby, James. 1978. *A History of Social Welfare and Social Work in the United States*. New York: Columbia University Press.

Lissak, Rivka Shpak. 1989. *Pluralism & Progressives: Hull House and the New Immigrants, 1890–1919*. Chicago: University of Chicago Press.

Logan, Sheridan A. 1981. *George F. Baker and His Bank: 1840–1955*. [Privately published].

Lowenstein, Roger. 2004. *The Origins of the Crash: The Great Bubble and Its Undoing*. New York: Penguin Press.

——. 2015. *America's Bank: The Epic Struggle to Create the Federal Reserve*. New York: Penguin Press.

MacMillan, Margaret. 2009. *Dangerous Games: The Uses and Abuses of History*. New York: Modern Library.

Mandelbrot, Benoit. 2004. *The (Mis)Behavior of Markets: A Fractal View of Risk, Ruin, and Reward*. New York: Basic Books.

Marburg, Theodore. 1908. "The Panic and the Present Depression: Address Delivered Before the American Academy of Political and Social Science." *Proceedings of the Academy,* April 10.

Markman, Gideon D., and Theodore L. Waldron. 2014. "Small Entrants and Large Incumbents: A Framework of Micro Entry." *Academy of Management Perspectives* 28(2) (May): 179–197.

Mason, Alpheus T. 1975. "The Case of the Overworked Laundress." In *Quarrels that Have Shaped the Constitution*, edited by John A. Garraty. New York: Harper & Row.

Massachusetts State Department of Health. 1917. *The Food of Working Women in Boston.* Boston: Wright & Potter Printing Co.

McAndrews, James J., and William Roberds. 1995. "Banks, Payments, and Coordination." *Journal of Financial Intermediation* 4: 305–327.

McCormick, Richard L. 1981. *From Realignment to Reform: Political Change in New York State 1893–1910.* Ithaca, NY: Cornell University Press.

——. 1986. *The Party Period and Public Policy: American Politics from the Age of Jackson to the Progressive Era.* Oxford, UK: Oxford University Press.

McCulley, Richard T. 1992. *Banks and Politics During the Progressive Era: The Origins of the Federal Reserve System, 1897–1913.* London: Routledge.

McGerr, Michael. 2003. *A Fierce Discontent: The Rise and Fall of the Progressive Movement in America.* Oxford, UK: Oxford University Press.

McLaughlin, John W. 1971. "The Acquisition of the Tennessee Coal, Iron and Railroad Company by the United States Steel Corporation: A legend re-examined." Master's thesis, University of Nebraska, Omaha, March. https://digitalcommons.unomaha.edu/studentwork/1458.

McNelis, Sarah. 1968. *Copper King at War: The Biography of F. Augustus Heinze.* Missoula: University of Montana Press.

Merton, Robert K. 1948. "The Self-Fulfilling Prophecy." *Antioch Review* 48(2): 193–210.

Milburn, John G., and Walter F. Taylor. 1913. *Brief on behalf of the New York Stock Exchange, Money Trust Investigation,* U.S. House of Representatives, Subcommittee of the Committee on Banking and Currency. 1913. *Money Trust Investigation: Investigation of Financial and Monetary Conditions in the United States under House Resolutions No. 429 and 504.* Washington, DC: U.S. Government Printing Office.

Mills, A. L. 1908. "The Northwest in the Recent Financial Crisis." *Annals of the American Academy of Political and Social Science* 1(31): 113–119.

Miron, Jeffrey A. 1986. "Financial Panics, the Seasonality of the Nominal Interest Rate, and the Founding of the Fed." *American Economic Review* 76(1) (March): 125–140.

Miron, Jeffrey A., and Christina D. Romer. 1990. "A New Monthly Index of Industrial Production, 1884–1940." *Journal of Economic History* 50: 321–337.

Mishkin, Frederic S. 1990. "Asymmetric Information and Financial Crises: A Historical Perspective." Cambridge, MA: National Bureau of Economic Research, working paper 3400; and in R. Glenn Hubbard (ed.). 1991. *Financial Markets and Financial Crises.* Chicago: University of Chicago Press.

——. 1991. "Anatomy of a Financial Crisis." Cambridge, MA: National Bureau of Economic Research, working paper 3934, published under "Anatomy of a Financial Crisis." *Journal of Evolutionary Economics* 2(2): 115–130.

Mishkin, Frederic S., and Eugene N. White. 2003. "U.S. Stock Market Crashes and Their Aftermath: Implications for Monetary Policy." In *Asset Price Bubbles*, edited by William C. Hunter, George G. Kaufman, and Michael Pomerleano. Cambridge, MA: MIT Press.

Moen, Jon R., and Mary Tone Rodgers. 2022. "How J.P. Morgan Picked the Winners and Losers in the Panic of 1907: An Exploration of the Individual over the Institution as Lender of Last Resort." *Essays in Economic and Business History* (forthcoming).

Moen, Jon R., and Ellis W. Tallman. 1992. "The Bank Panic of 1907: The Role of Trust Companies." *Journal of Economic History* 52: 611–630.

Moen, Jon R., and Ellis W. Tallman. 1999. "Why Didn't the United States Establish a Central Bank until after the Panic of 1907?," Federal Reserve Bank of Atlanta, working paper 99-16, November.

Moen, Jon R., and Ellis W. Tallman. 2000. "Clearinghouse Membership and Deposit Contraction during the Panic of 1907." *Journal of Economic History* 60(1) (March): 145–163.

Moen, Jon R., and Ellis W. Tallman. 2003. "The Call Loan Market in the U.S. Financial System Prior to the Federal Reserve System." Federal Reserve Bank of Atlanta, working paper 2003-43, December.

Moen, Jon R., and Ellis W. Tallman. 2010. "Liquidity, Contagion, and the Founding of the Federal Reserve System: The Panic of 1907." Federal Reserve Bank of Cleveland, working paper 10:10, July.

Moen, Jon R., and Ellis W. Tallman. 2014. "Outside Lending in the NYC Call Loan Market." Federal Reserve Bank of Cleveland, working paper 14-08, August.

More, Louise Bolard. 1907. *Wage Earners' Budgets: A Study of Standards and Costs of Living in New York City*. New York: H. Holt.

Morison, Elting E., John M. Blum, Alfred D. Chandler Jr., and Sylvia Rice (eds.). 1952. *The Letters of Theodore Roosevelt*, Vols. 5–6. Cambridge, MA.: Harvard University Press.

Morris, Edmund. 2001. *Theodore Rex*. New York: Random House.

Muncy, Robyn. 1991. *Creating a Female Dominion in American Reform, 1890–1935*. Oxford, UK: Oxford University Press.

Neal, Larry. 1971. "Trust Companies and Financial Innovation, 1897–1914." *Business History Review* 45(1) (Spring): 35–51.

Neal, L. D., and Weidenmier, M.D. 2003. "Crises in the Global Economy from Tulips to Today: Contagion and Consequences." In *Globalization in Historical Perspective,* edited by M. D. Bordo, A. M. Taylor, and J. G. Williamson. Chicago, IL: University of Chicago Press, 413–514.

Newell, George Arthur. 1914. "The Panic of 1907 and Subsequent Currency Legislation in the United States." Thesis for the Degree of Bachelor of Arts, Champagne-Urbana, IL: University of Illinois.

Noyes, Alexander D. 1909a. "A Year after the Panic of 1907." *Quarterly Journal of Economics* 23: 185–212.

——. 1909b. *Forty Years of American Finance*. New York: G. P. Putnam's Sons, The Knickerbocker Press.

Noyes, Alexander D. 1913. "The Money Trust." *The Atlantic Monthly* 111 (May 5): 653–667.

Obstfeld, Maurice, Jay C. Shambaugh and Alan M. Taylor. 2005. "The Trilemma in History: Tradeoffs Among Exchange Rates, Monetary Policies, and Capital Mobility." *Review of Economics and Statistics* 87(3): 423–438.

Odell, Kerry A., and Marc D. Weidenmier. 2002. "Real Stock, Monetary Aftershock: The San Francisco Earthquake and the Panic of 1907." Cambridge, MA: National Bureau of Economic Research, working paper 9176.

O'Grada, Cormac, and Eugene N. White. 2002. "Who Panics during Panics? Evidence from a Nineteenth Century Savings Bank." Cambridge, MA: National Bureau of Economic Research, working paper 8856.

Olson, Mancur. (1965) 1995. *The Logic of Collective Action: Public Goods and The Theory of Groups*. Cambridge, MA: Harvard University Press.

Ostrom, Elinor. 1990. *Governing the Commons: The Evolution of Institutions for Collective Action*. Cambridge, UK: Cambridge University Press.

O'Sullivan, Mary A. 2015. "Too Much Ado about Morgan's Men: The U.S. Securities Markets, 1908–1914." Working paper, Paul Bairoch Institute of Economic History, March 7.

——. 2016. *Dividends of Development: Securities Markets in the History of US Capitalism, 1866–1922*. Oxford, UK: Oxford University Press.

O'Toole, Patricia. 2005. *When Trumpets Call: Theodore Roosevelt After the White House*. New York: Simon & Schuster.

Owen, Robert L. 1919. *The Federal Reserve Act*. New York: The Century Company.

Parthemos, James. 1988. "The Federal Reserve Act of 1913 in the Stream of U.S. Monetary History." *Economic Quarterly* 74 (July/August): 19–28.

Payne, Elizabeth Anne. 1988. *Reform, Labor, and Feminism: Margaret Dreier Robins and the Women's Trade Union League*. Urbana: University of Illinois Press.

Perine, Edward Ten Broeck. 1916. *The Story of the Trust Companies*. New York: The Knickerbocker Press.

Perkins, Dexter. 1956. *Charles Evans Hughes and American Democratic Statesmanship*. Boston: Little, Brown and Company.

Perkins, George W. 1908. "The Modern Corporation." Address at Columbia University, February 7, 1908, Columbia University Rare Book and Manuscript Library.

——. 1910. "Some Things to Think About." Address at the Graduate School of Business Administration, Harvard University, April 15, 1910, Columbia University Rare Book and Manuscript Library.

Phillips, Ronnie J. 2003. "Coping with Financial Catastrophe: The San Francisco Clearinghouse during the Earthquake of 1906." In *Research in Economic History*, Vol. 21, edited by Alexander J. Field, Gregory Clark, and William A. Sundstrom, 79–102. New York: JAI Elsevier Science.

Phillips, Ronnie J., and Harvey Cutler. 1998. "Domestic Exchange Rates and Regional Economic Growth in the United States, 1899–1908: Evidence from Cointegration Analysis." *Journal of Economic History* 58(4) (December): 1010–1026.

Primm, James Neal. 1989. "Banking Reform 1907–1913." Chapter 2 in *A Foregone Conclusion: The Founding of the Federal Reserve Bank of St. Louis*. http://stlouisfed.org/publications/foregone/chapter_two.htm

Pringle, Henry F. 1931. *Theodore Roosevelt: A Biography*. New York: Harcourt, Brace and Company.

——. 1939. *The Life and Times of William Howard Taft: A Biography*. New York: Farrar & Rinehart, Inc.

Raftery, Judith. 1994. "Los Angeles Clubwomen and Progressive Reform." In *California Progressivism Revisited*, edited by William Deverell and Tom Sitton. Berkeley and Los Angeles: University of California Press.

Ramirez, Carlos. 1995. "Did J. P. Morgan's Men Add Value? Corporate Investment, Cash Flow, and Financial Structure at the Turn of the Century." *Journal of Finance* 50: 661–678.

Ranciere, Romain, Aaron Tornell, and Frank Westermann. 2005. "Systemic Crises and Growth." CESifo working paper 1451. Downloaded from http://SSRN.com/abstract=708994.

Reinhart, Carmen N., and Kenneth S. Rogoff. 2008. "Is the 2007 U.S. Sub-prime Financial Crisis so Different? An International Historical Comparison." Cambridge, MA: National Bureau of Economic Research, working paper 13761, January.

Ridgely, W. Barret. 1908. "An Elastic Credit Currency as a Preventive of Panics." *The Annals of the American Academy of Political and Social Science* 31 (March): 326–334.

Rill, James F., and Stacy L. Turner. 2014. "Presidents Practicing Antitrust: Where to Draw the Line?" *Antitrust Law Journal* 79(2): 577–599.

Ripley, William Z. 1916. *Trusts, Pools, and Corporations*. Boston: Ginn and Company.

Roberts, Priscilla. 2000. "Benjamin Strong, the Federal Reserve, and the Limits to Interwar American Nationalism." *Economic Quarterly* (March 22).

Rockoff, Hugh. 2000. "Banking and Finance, 1789–1914." Chapter 14 in *The Cambridge Economic History of the United States*, vol. II, "The Long Nineteenth Century," edited by Stanley L. Engerman and Robert E. Gallman. Cambridge, UK: Cambridge University Press.

——. 2018. "It Is Always the Shadow Banks: The Regulatory Status of the Banks that Failed and Ignited America's Greatest Financial Panics," in *Coping with Financial Crises: Some Lessons from Economic History*, edited by Hugh Rockoff and Isao Suto. New York: Springer Nature.

Rodgers, Daniel T. 1982. "In Search of Progressivism." *Reviews in American History* 10(4): 113–132.

——. 1992. "Republicanism: The Career of a Concept." *Journal of American History* 79(1) (June): 11–38.

Rodgers, Mary Tone, and James E. Payne. 2014. "How the Bank of France Changed U.S. Equity Expectations and Ended the Panic of 1907." *Journal of Economic History* 74(2) (June): 420–448.

——. 2015. "Was the Panic of 1907 a Global Crisis? Testing the Noyes Hypothesis." Working paper, May.

——. 2017. "Monetary Policy and the Copper Price Bust: A Reassessment of the Causes of the Panic of 1907." Working paper, November.

——. 2020. "Post-financial Crisis Changes in Financial System Structure: An Examination of the J.P. Morgan & Co. Syndicates after the 1907 Panic." *Review of Financial Economics* 38(51) (March 17): 226–241.

Rodgers, Mary Tone, and Beryl K. Wilson. 2011. "Systemic Risk, Missing Gold Flows, and the Panic of 1907." *Quarterly Journal of Austrian Economics* 14(2): 158–187.

Roll, Richard. 1986. "The Hubris Hypothesis of Corporate Takeovers." *Journal of Business* 59(2): 197–216.

Roosevelt, Theodore. 1913. *An Autobiography*. New York: Charles Scribner and Sons.

Rousseau, Peter L. 2011. "The Market for Bank Stocks and the Rise of Deposit Banking in New York City, 1866–1897." *Journal of Economic History* 71(4) (December): 976–1005.

Sandel, Michael. 1996. *Democracy's Discontent: America in Search of a Public Philosophy*. Cambridge, MA: Belknap Press of Harvard University Press.

Satterlee, Herbert L. 1939. *J. Pierpont Morgan: An Intimate Portrait*. New York: MacMillan.

Schumpeter, Joseph A. (1942) 1976. *Capitalism, Socialism and Democracy*. New York: Harper & Row.

——. (1934) 2004. *The Theory of Economic Development*. New Brunswick, NJ: Transaction Publishers.

Schwartz, Anna J. 1985. "Real and Pseudo Financial Crises." In *Financial Crises and the World Banking System*, edited by F. Capie and G. Wood. London: Macmillan.

Scott, Anne Firor. 1991. *Natural Allies: Women's Associations in American History*. Urbana: University of Illinois Press.

Selden, G. C. (1912) 2005. *The Psychology of the Stock Market*. New York: Cosimo Inc., 69.

Shiller, Robert. 2001. *Irrational Exuberance,* Princeton, NJ: Princeton University Press.

——. 2019. *Narrative Economics*. Princeton, NJ: Princeton University Press.

Silber, William L. 2007. *When Washington Shut Down Wall Street: The Great Financial Crisis of 1914 and the Origins of America's Monetary Supremacy*. Princeton, NJ: Princeton University Press.

Sinclair, Upton. 1908. *The Moneychangers*. New York: B.W. Dodge & Company.

Sklar, Katheryn. 1993. "The Historical Foundations of Women's Power in the Creation of the American Welfare State, 1830–1930." In *Mothers of a New World: Maternalist Politics and the Origins of Welfare States*, edited by Seth Koven and Sonya Michel. New York: Routledge.

Skocpol, Theda. 1992. *Protecting Soldiers and Mothers: The Political Origins of Social Policy in the United States*. Cambridge, MA: Belknap Press of Harvard University Press.

Smith, Dennis. 2005. *San Francisco Is Burning: The Untold Story of the 1906 Earthquake and Fires*. New York: Viking Press.

Sobel, Robert. (1968) 1988. *Panic on Wall Street: A Classic History of America's Financial Disasters—with a New Explanation of the Crash of 1987*. New York: E. P. Dutton, Truman Talley Books.

Sornette, Didier. 2003. *Why Stock Markets Crash: Critical Events in Complex Financial Systems*. Princeton, NJ: Princeton University Press.

Sprague, O. M. W. 1908. "The American Crisis of 1907." *Economic Journal* (September): 353–372.

——. 1910. *A History of Crises under the National Banking System*. National Monetary Commission. Washington, DC: U.S. Government Printing Office.

Starkman, Dean. 2014. *The Watchdog that Didn't Bark: The Financial Crisis and the Disappearance of Investigative Journalism*. New York: Columbia University Press.

Stathis, Stephen W. 1983. "Former Presidents as Congressional Witnesses." *Presidential Studies Quarterly* 13(3) (Summer): 458–481.

Stiglitz, Joseph. 2003. *The Roaring Nineties*. New York: Norton.

Stilwell, Arthur Edward. 1912. *Cannibals of Finance: Fifteen Years' Contest with the Money Trust*. 6th ed. Chicago: The Farnum Publishing Co.

Strouse, Jean. 1999. *Morgan: American Financier*. New York: Random House.

Swiss Re. 2006. "A Shake in Insurance History: The 1906 San Francisco Earthquake." January.

Taft, William H. 1908. *Present Day Problems: A Collection of Addresses Delivered on Various Occasions*. New York: Dodd, Mead & Company.

Taleb, Nassim Nicholas. 2004. *Fooled by Randomness: The Hidden Role of Chance in Life and in the Markets*. New York: Random House.

Tallman, Ellis W., and Jon R. Moen. 1990. "Lessons from the Panic of 1907." *Economic Review* 75(May/June): 2–13.

——. 1992. "The Bank Panic of 1907: The Role of the Trust Companies." *Journal of Economic History* 52(3): 611–630.

——. 1995. "Private Sector Responses to the Panic of 1907: A Comparison of New York and Chicago." *Economic Review* 80(March): 1–9.

Tallman, Ellis W., and Jon R. Moen. 2010a. "Banking and Financial Crises in United States History: What Guidance Can History Offer Policymakers?" Cleveland, OH: Federal Reserve Bank of Cleveland working paper 1009. Downloaded from http://ssrn.com/abstract=1657178.

Tallman, Ellis W., and Jon R. Moen. 2010b. "Liquidity Creation without a Lender of Last Resort: Clearing House Loan Certificates in the Banking Panic of 1907." Cleveland, OH: Federal Reserve Bank of Cleveland working paper 10-10, July.

Tallman, Ellis W., and Jon R. Moen. 2014. "The Transmission of the Financial Crisis in 1907: An Empirical Investigation." Cleveland, OH: Federal Reserve Bank of Cleveland working paper 14-09.

Tarbell, Ida. 1933. *The Life of Elbert H. Gary: A Story of Steel*. New York: D. Appleton-Century Company, Inc.

Thomas, Gordon, and Max Morgan Witts. 1971. *The San Francisco Earthquake*. New York: Stein and Day.

Tichenor, Daniel J. 2002. *Dividing Lines: The Politics of Immigration Control in America*. Princeton, NJ: Princeton University Press.

Timberlake, Richard H. 1984. "The Central Banking Role of Clearinghouse Associations." *Journal of Money Credit and Banking* (February): 1–15.

Torpey, John. 2003. "Passports and the Development of Immigration Controls in the North Atlantic World During the Long Nineteenth Century." Chapter 5 in *Migration Control in the North Atlantic World: The Evolution of State Practices in Europe and the United States from the French Revolution to the Inter-War Period*, edited by Andreas Fahrmeir, Olivier Faron, and Patrick Weil. New York and Oxford: Berghahn Books.

Tusset, G. 2011. "Speculation by the Next-Door Neighbor: The 1907 Italian Financial Crisis." Padua University working paper.

Unger, Nancy C. 2000. *Fighting Bob La Follette: The Righteous Reformer.* Chapel Hill: University of North Carolina Press.

Vanderlip, Frank A. 1911. "The Aldrich Plan for Banking Legislation." Commercial Club of Chicago

——. 1914. "Recollection of some of the first steps that were taken in New York to meet the financial crisis that arose on the declaration of war." Confidential File, Columbia University Libraries, Special Collections, D-15, August 28.

Van Kleeck, Mary. 1906–1907. "Working Hours of Women in Factories." *Charities and Commons* 17: 13–21.

——. 1913. *Artificial Flower Makers.* New York: Survey Associates, Inc., Russell Sage Foundation.

Warburg, Paul M. 1930a. *The Federal Reserve System: Its Origin and Growth, Reflections and Recollections.* Vol. 1. New York: The Macmillan Company.

——. 1930b. *The Federal Reserve System: Its Origin and Growth, Reflections and Recollections.* Vol. 2, "Addresses and Essays." New York: The Macmillan Company.

Warsh, David. 2006. *Knowledge and the Wealth of Nations: A Story of Economic Discovery.* New York: Norton.

Wendt, Lloyd, and Herman Kogan. 1948. *Bet a Million! The Story of John W. Gates.* New York: Bobbs-Merrill Company.

Weston, N.A. 1922. "Studies of the National Monetary Commission." *Annals of the American Academy of Political and Social Science* (January): 17–26.

Wheeler, Harry A. 1922. "The National Citizens' League: A Movement for A Sound Banking System." *The Annals of the American Academy of Political and Social Science.* Vol. 99, *The Federal Reserve System—Its Purpose and Work* (January): 26–29.

Whitney, Albert W. 1907. "Report on Insurance Settlements." In San Francisco Chamber of Commerce, *Annual Report, 1906.* San Francisco: H. S. Crocker.

Wicker, Elmus. 2000. *Banking Panics of the Gilded Age.* New York: Cambridge University Press.

Wiebe, Robert H. 1959. "The House for Morgan and the Executive, 1905–1913." *American Historical Review* 65: 49–60.

——. 1967. *The Search for Order: 1877–1920.* New York: Hill & Wang.

——. 1995. *Self Rule: A Cultural History of American Democracy.* Chicago: University of Chicago Press.

Winerman, Marc. 2008. "Antitrust and the Crisis of '07." *The Antitrust Source,* December. www.amanet.org/antitrust/at-source/08/12/Dec08-Winerman.pdf.

Wister, Owen. 1930. *Roosevelt: The Story of a Friendship 1880–1919.* New York: MacMillan.

Woods, Charlie. 2011. *Bath, Maine's Charlie Morse: Ice King & Wall Street Scoundrel.* Charleston: History Press.

Wyman, Mark. 1993. *Round Trip to America: The Immigrants Return to Europe, 1880–1930.* Ithaca, NY: Cornell University Press.

Youngman, Anna. 1906. "The Growth of Financial Banking." *Journal of Political Economy* 14(7) (July): 435–443.

Yue, Lori Qingyuan. 2016. "The Great and the Small: The Impact of Collective Action on the Evolution of Board Interlocks after the Panic of 1907." *American Sociological Review* 81(2) (April): 374–395.

Yue, Lori Qingyuan, Jiao Luo, and Paul Ingram. 2013. "The Failure of Private Regulation: Elite Control and Market Crises in the Manhattan Banking Industry." *Administrative Science Quarterly* 58(1) (March): 37–68.

Zeidel, Robert F. 2004. *Immigrants, Progressives, and Exclusion Politics: The Dillingham Commission, 1900–1927.* DeKalb: Northern Illinois University Press.

Zuckoff, Mitchell. 2005. *Ponzi's Scheme: The True Story of a Financial Legend.* New York: Random House.

About the Authors

Robert F. Bruner is University Professor, Distinguished Professor, and dean emeritus at the University of Virginia's Darden Graduate School of Business Administration. He also serves as the Compton Visiting Professor in World Politics at University of Virginia's Miller Center of Public Affairs. He has published research in various areas, including corporate finance, mergers and acquisitions, investing in emerging markets, financial crises, leadership, and general management. He is the author or co-author of numerous books, articles, teaching case studies, and notes. The Commonwealth of Virginia and University of Virginia granted him their highest teaching awards. He has been on the faculty of the Darden School since 1982. From 2005 to 2015 he served as dean of the Darden School. He holds a BA degree from Yale University and MBA and DBA degrees from Harvard University. Copies of his papers and essays may be obtained from his website, http://faculty.darden.edu/brunerb/. He may be reached via e-mail at brunerr@virginia.edu.

Sean D. Carr is the executive director and CEO of the Global Innovation Exchange at the University of Washington. He also holds an appointment as affiliate associate professor at the University of

Washington's Foster School of Business. Previously, he served as executive director of the Batten Institute for entrepreneurship, innovation, and technology at the University of Virginia Darden School of Business, where he was an administrator and faculty member from 2013 to 2022. His applied research in new ventures and corporate finance has contributed to the development of award-winning case studies, digital media, and other teaching materials. Previously, he spent nearly 10 years as a journalist, having served as a producer for both CNN and for ABC's *World News Tonight with Peter Jennings.* As a writer and researcher, he contributed to numerous business-related books. He holds an MBA and PhD in management from the University of Virginia, an MS in journalism from Columbia University, and a BA in classics from Northwestern University. He may be reached via e-mail at sdcarr@uw.edu.

Index